CHILDREN'S ATLAS OF WORLD HISTORY

Simon Adams

KINGFISHER

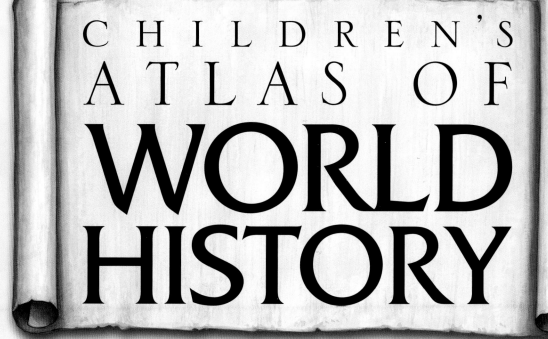

CHILDREN'S ATLAS OF WORLD HISTORY

CONTENTS

ANCIENT WORLD

Illustrated by Katherine Baxter

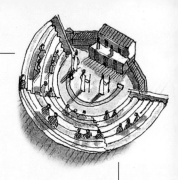

CONTENTS

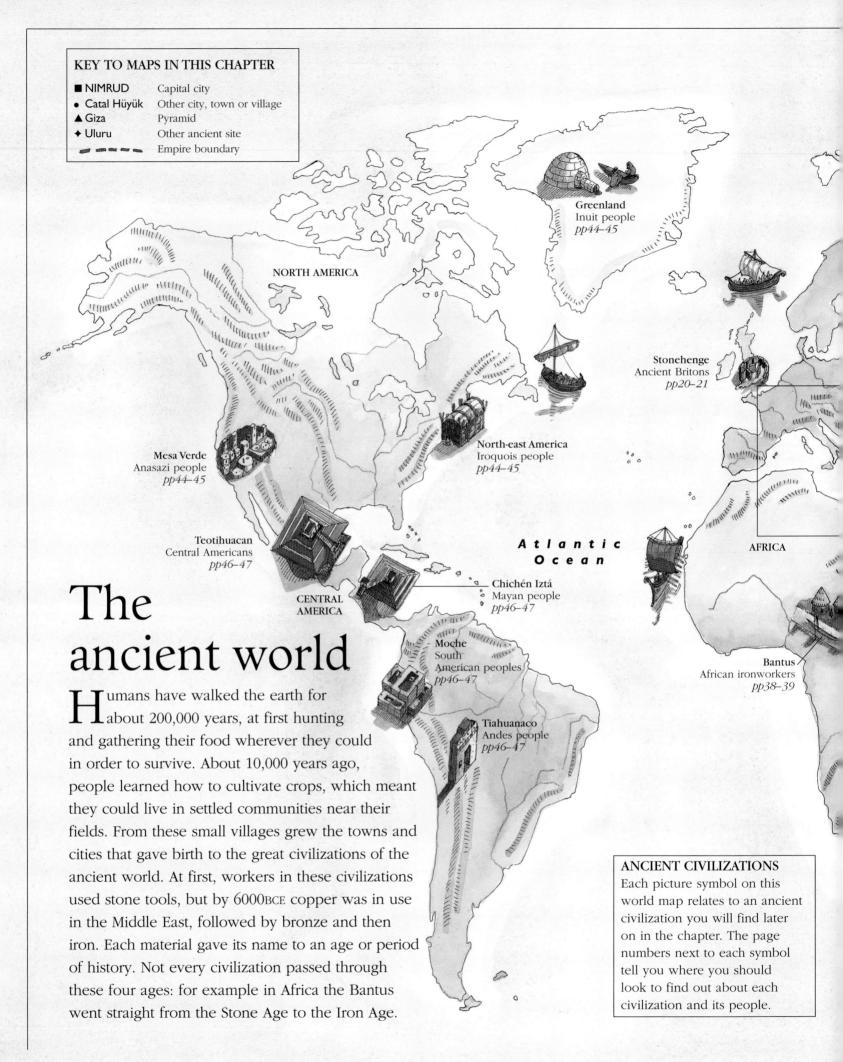

KEY TO MAPS IN THIS CHAPTER

- ■ NIMRUD   Capital city
- ● Catal Hüyük   Other city, town or village
- ▲ Giza   Pyramid
- ✦ Uluru   Other ancient site
- ━ ━ ━   Empire boundary

NORTH AMERICA

Greenland
Inuit people
pp44–45

Stonehenge
Ancient Britons
pp20–21

Mesa Verde
Anasazi people
pp44–45

North-east America
Iroquois people
pp44–45

Teotihuacan
Central Americans
pp46–47

CENTRAL
AMERICA

Chichén Iztá
Mayan people
pp46–47

*Atlantic
Ocean*

AFRICA

Moche
South
American peoples
pp46–47

Bantus
African ironworkers
pp38–39

Tiahuanaco
Andes people
pp46–47

The ancient world

Humans have walked the earth for about 200,000 years, at first hunting and gathering their food wherever they could in order to survive. About 10,000 years ago, people learned how to cultivate crops, which meant they could live in settled communities near their fields. From these small villages grew the towns and cities that gave birth to the great civilizations of the ancient world. At first, workers in these civilizations used stone tools, but by 6000BCE copper was in use in the Middle East, followed by bronze and then iron. Each material gave its name to an age or period of history. Not every civilization passed through these four ages: for example in Africa the Bantus went straight from the Stone Age to the Iron Age.

ANCIENT CIVILIZATIONS

Each picture symbol on this world map relates to an ancient civilization you will find later on in the chapter. The page numbers next to each symbol tell you where you should look to find out about each civilization and its people.

EUROPE

see inset

Italy
Etruscans
pp26–27

Rome
Romans
pp34–35

Athens
Ancient Greeks
pp30–31

Catal Hüyük
First town-dwellers
pp12–13

Nimrud
Assyrians
pp28–29

Mycenae
Myceneans
pp24–25

Knossos
Minoans
pp24–25

Babylon
Babylonians
pp28–29

Carthage
Phoenicians
pp26–27

Jerusalem
Hebrews
pp26–27

Giza
Ancient Egyptians
pp16–17

Ur
Sumerians
pp14–15

ASIA

Xianyang
Chinese
pp42–43

Mohenjo-Daro
Indus Valley
people
pp22–23

Persepolis
Persians
pp28–29

Sarnath
Mauryans
pp40–41

Axum
Ancient Africa
pp38–39

Meroë
Nubians
pp38–39

**I n d i a n
O c e a n**

AUSTRALIA

Uluru
Aboriginals
pp48–49

Pacific islands
Polynesians
pp48–49

DATING

In this book, we use the dating system
BCE (Before Common Era) and CE
(Common Era). We have used this system
because the common system that you
may find in other books – BC and
AD – is a Christian dating system and
so is misleading when dealing with
non-Christian cultures and civilizations.
The date 100BCE is the same as 100BC,
while 100CE is the same as AD100.

10000BCE–1000CE

10000BCE
10000 Hunter-gatherers roam many
parts of the earth

9000BCE
9000 Farmers keep herds
of sheep in mountains near
the Fertile Crescent

8000BCE
8000 First settled farming
communities in the Levant

7000BCE
7000 Settled farming communities
throughout Fertile Crescent
6700 Catal Hüyük is largest town
6500 Pottery in general use
throughout Fertile Crescent
6200 Copper smelting begins
in Anatolia

6000BCE
6000 Cattle first domesticated

5000BCE
5000 First towns and temples
built in Mesopotamia
4500 Copper Age begins in Balkans
(south-east Europe)
4300 Uruk in Mesopotamia is
world's first city

4000BCE
3400 Pictogram writing begins
in Mesopotamia
3300 First towns built in Egypt
3200 First wheeled vehicles
used in Sumer

3000BCE
3000 Megaliths built in Europe
2900 Cuneiform writing in Sumer
2630 First pyramid in Egypt
2600 Indus Valley civilization
2500 Bronze Age starts in Europe
2350 World's first law code written
in Mesopotamia

2000BCE
2000 Minoan civilization
in Crete
1800 Sumerian empire
1700 Babylonian empire
1450 Mycenean civilization
in Greece

1000BCE
1000 Iron Age begins in Europe
1000 Bantus in southern Africa
900 First Greek city-states
founded
510 Roman republic founded
500 Persian empire
350 Maya city-states emerge

0
100 Axum flourishes in Ethiopia
200 Hopewells build mounds in
North America

by **1000** Polynesians reach
New Zealand

1000CE

The ancient world:
How we know about the past

Although we cannot travel back in time to speak to people who lived in the ancient world, we can discover much about them from the objects they left behind. Buildings, aqueducts and roads, everyday objects such as pots, tools, coins and writing implements, and luxury items such as jewellery and gold ornaments, have all survived to tell their tale. Some buildings, like the Forum in Rome, are still partly standing, while other buildings and smaller objects were buried for centuries and have only recently been uncovered by archaeologists. All these remains tell us a great deal about the peoples of the ancient world and the lives they led. From them we can piece together a picture of what it was like to live in ancient Rome or China, to march with Alexander's army or sail the Pacific colonizing new islands.

Royal music
This silver lyre – a stringed musical instrument – was made in Ur, southern Iraq, about 4,500 years ago. It was found in the Royal Cemetery, a lavish burial site where the kings of Ur were buried with their servants. Its fabulous craftsmanship and its place of discovery suggest that it was played at the royal court, and was buried with the king so that he could continue to enjoy it in the afterlife.

The Forum
The Forum was the political, judicial and commercial centre of Rome and the vast Roman Empire. Here senators met to discuss the big issues of the day and judges tried legal cases. Much of the Forum is now in ruins, but enough of its fine buildings, arches and monuments survive for us to see just how impressive it must have been when Rome and its armies dominated the western world.

Cuneiform writing

Priests in the cities of Sumer developed the world's first writing around 3400BCE. It consisted of simple pictures, each representing a word or idea. By 2900BCE, this had developed into cuneiform, a writing system using wedge-shaped marks (*cuneus* is Latin for wedge) made by pressing a reed stylus into wet clay.

Hieroglyphics

In about 3300BCE the ancient Egyptians began to use a form of writing known as hieroglyphics. These were more complex than Sumerian picture writing, using about 700 different signs to represent different ideas, words and even individual letters. The hieroglyphs above date from the 1st century BCE.

Mayan writing

Zapotec scribes in the Americas developed their own, unique form of hieroglyphic picture writing in about 800BCE. Later, the Maya used these to develop their own advanced literary language with a glyph for every syllable. Many glyphs have only recently been translated.

Hands-on history

Archaeologists study the evidence left behind by previous generations. They examine a site or object, looking for clues that might tell them how old it is, who made it, and why it was found where it was. Even the tiniest scrap of evidence can provide a vital clue, and archaeology can be a lengthy process. Here, an archaeologist is examining a Roman mosaic uncovered during road construction in Israel.

Chinese coins

We use coins every day, but each coin is a piece of history with a story of its own to tell. They show rulers and important symbols, and we can tell a lot about trade from where they are found. The Chinese have been using coins since the 5th century BCE. These were made with a hole in the middle so that they could be kept on a string.

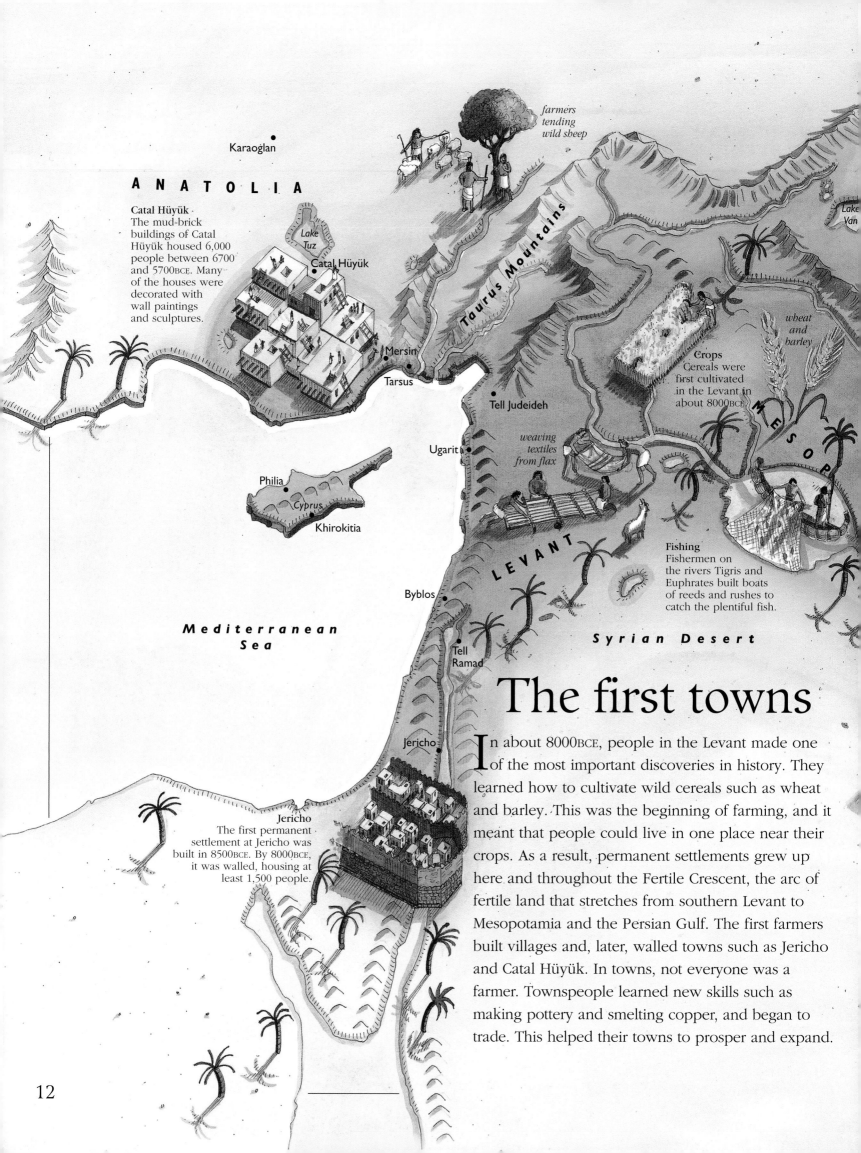

Karaoğlan

A N A T O L I A

Catal Hüyük
The mud-brick buildings of Catal Hüyük housed 6,000 people between 6700 and 5700BCE. Many of the houses were decorated with wall paintings and sculptures.

farmers tending wild sheep

Taurus Mountains

Lake Van

Lake Tuz

Catal Hüyük

Mersin

Tarsus

Tell Judeideh

Ugarit

weaving textiles from flax

Crops
Cereals were first cultivated in the Levant in about 8000BCE

wheat and barley

M E S O P

Philia

Cyprus

Khirokitia

L E V A N T

Fishing
Fishermen on the rivers Tigris and Euphrates built boats of reeds and rushes to catch the plentiful fish.

Byblos

S y r i a n   D e s e r t

*M e d i t e r r a n e a n
S e a*

Tell Ramad

The first towns

Jericho

Jericho
The first permanent settlement at Jericho was built in 8500BCE. By 8000BCE, it was walled, housing at least 1,500 people.

In about 8000BCE, people in the Levant made one of the most important discoveries in history. They learned how to cultivate wild cereals such as wheat and barley. This was the beginning of farming, and it meant that people could live in one place near their crops. As a result, permanent settlements grew up here and throughout the Fertile Crescent, the arc of fertile land that stretches from southern Levant to Mesopotamia and the Persian Gulf. The first farmers built villages and, later, walled towns such as Jericho and Catal Hüyük. In towns, not everyone was a farmer. Townspeople learned new skills such as making pottery and smelting copper, and began to trade. This helped their towns to prosper and expand.

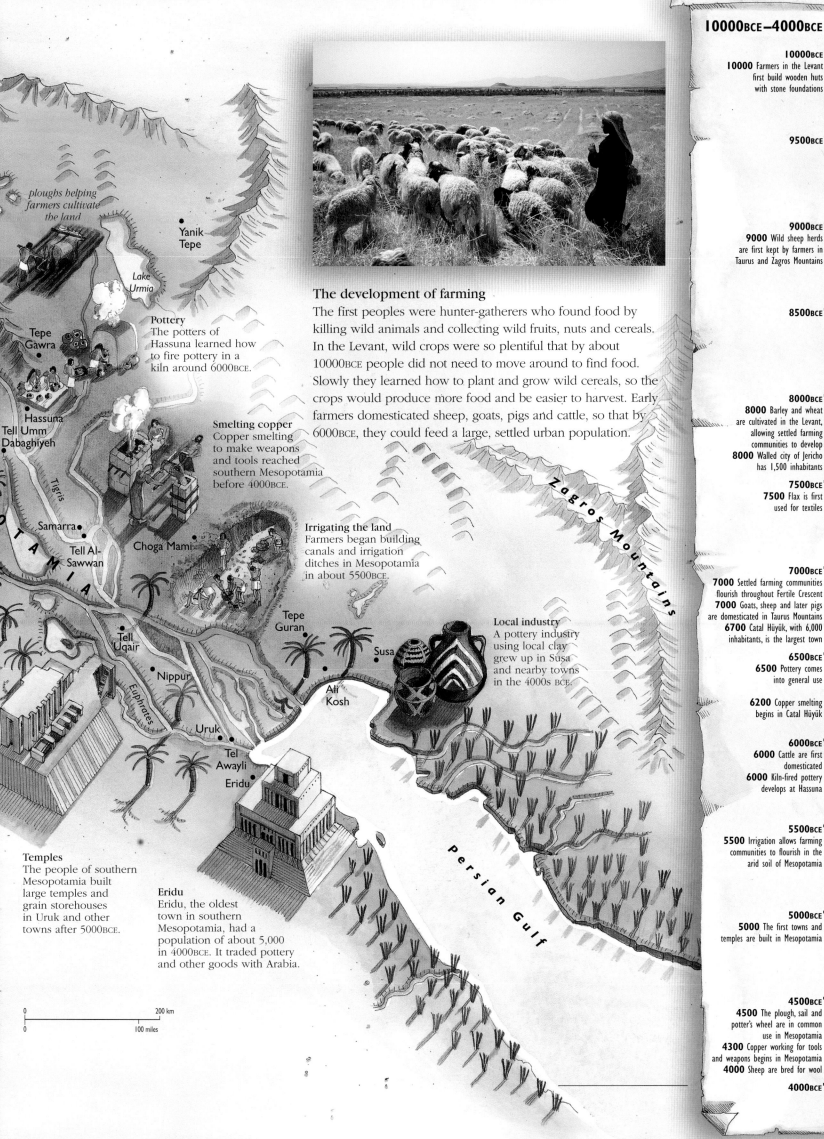

ploughs helping
farmers cultivate
the land

Yanik
Tepe

Lake
Urmia

Pottery
The potters of
Hassuna learned how
to fire pottery in a
kiln around 6000BCE.

Tepe
Gawra

Hassuna

Tell Umm
Dabaghiyeh

Tigris

Samarra

Tell Al-
Sawwan

Choga Mami

Smelting copper
Copper smelting
to make weapons
and tools reached
southern Mesopotamia
before 4000BCE.

Irrigating the land
Farmers began building
canals and irrigation
ditches in Mesopotamia
in about 5500BCE.

Tepe
Guran

Susa

Euphrates

Nippur

Ali
Kosh

Tell
Uqair

Uruk

Tel
Awayli

Eridu

Local industry
A pottery industry
using local clay
grew up in Susa
and nearby towns
in the 4000s BCE.

Zagros Mountains

Persian Gulf

The development of farming
The first peoples were hunter-gatherers who found food by
killing wild animals and collecting wild fruits, nuts and cereals.
In the Levant, wild crops were so plentiful that by about
10000BCE people did not need to move around to find food.
Slowly they learned how to plant and grow wild cereals, so the
crops would produce more food and be easier to harvest. Early
farmers domesticated sheep, goats, pigs and cattle, so that by
6000BCE, they could feed a large, settled urban population.

Temples
The people of southern
Mesopotamia built
large temples and
grain storehouses
in Uruk and other
towns after 5000BCE.

Eridu
Eridu, the oldest
town in southern
Mesopotamia, had a
population of about 5,000
in 4000BCE. It traded pottery
and other goods with Arabia.

0		200 km
0		100 miles

10000BCE—4000BCE

10000BCE
10000 Farmers in the Levant
first build wooden huts
with stone foundations

9500BCE

9000BCE
9000 Wild sheep herds
are first kept by farmers in
Taurus and Zagros Mountains

8500BCE

8000BCE
8000 Barley and wheat
are cultivated in the Levant,
allowing settled farming
communities to develop
8000 Walled city of Jericho
has 1,500 inhabitants

7500BCE
7500 Flax is first
used for textiles

7000BCE
7000 Settled farming communities
flourish throughout Fertile Crescent
7000 Goats, sheep and later pigs
are domesticated in Taurus Mountains
6700 Catal Hüyük, with 6,000
inhabitants, is the largest town

6500BCE
6500 Pottery comes
into general use

6200 Copper smelting
begins in Catal Hüyük

6000BCE
6000 Cattle are first
domesticated
6000 Kiln-fired pottery
develops at Hassuna

5500BCE
5500 Irrigation allows farming
communities to flourish in the
arid soil of Mesopotamia

5000BCE
5000 The first towns and
temples are built in Mesopotamia

4500BCE
4500 The plough, sail and
potter's wheel are in common
use in Mesopotamia
4300 Copper working for tools
and weapons begins in Mesopotamia
4000 Sheep are bred for wool

4000BCE

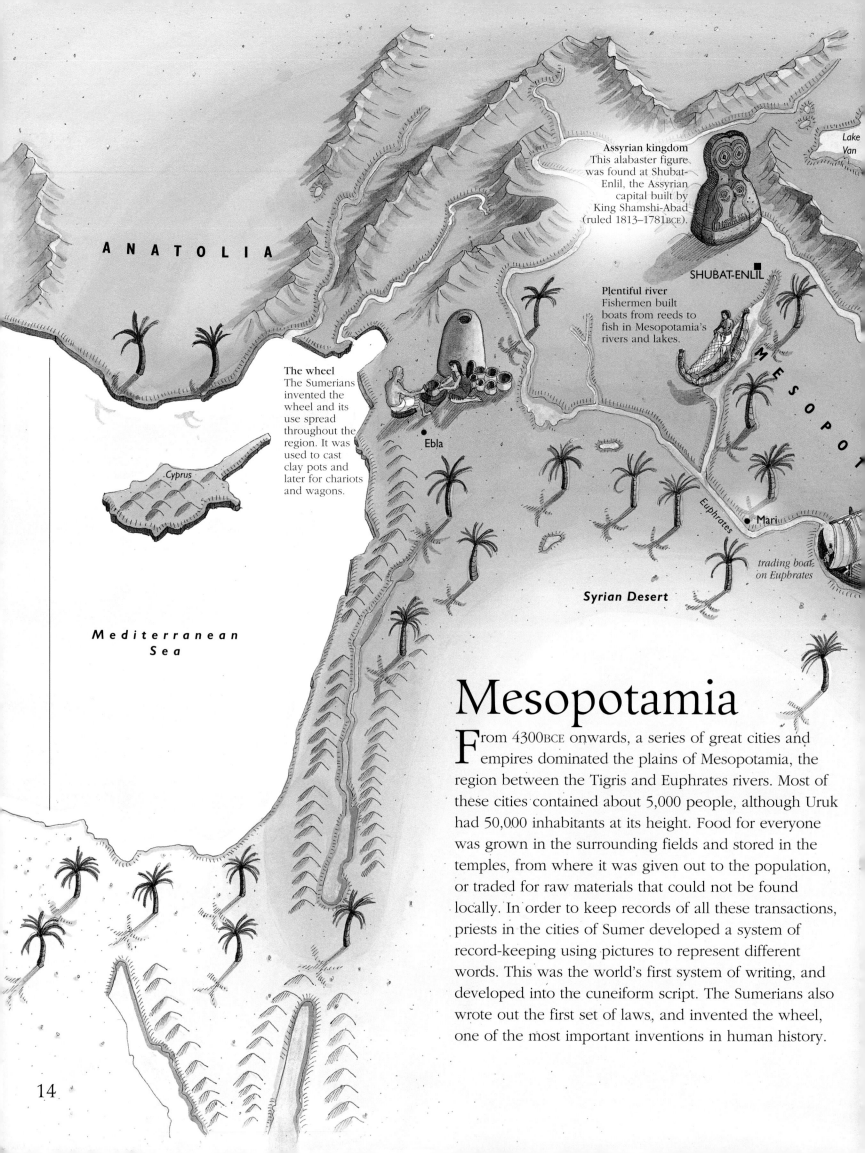

ANATOLIA

Assyrian kingdom
This alabaster figure was found at Shubat-Enlil, the Assyrian capital built by King Shamshi-Abad (ruled 1813–1781BCE).

Lake Van

SHUBAT-ENLIL

Plentiful river
Fishermen built boats from reeds to fish in Mesopotamia's rivers and lakes.

MESOPOT

The wheel
The Sumerians invented the wheel and its use spread throughout the region. It was used to cast clay pots and later for chariots and wagons.

Cyprus

• Ebla

Euphrates

• Mari

trading boat on Euphrates

Syrian Desert

Mediterranean Sea

Mesopotamia

From 4300BCE onwards, a series of great cities and empires dominated the plains of Mesopotamia, the region between the Tigris and Euphrates rivers. Most of these cities contained about 5,000 people, although Uruk had 50,000 inhabitants at its height. Food for everyone was grown in the surrounding fields and stored in the temples, from where it was given out to the population, or traded for raw materials that could not be found locally. In order to keep records of all these transactions, priests in the cities of Sumer developed a system of record-keeping using pictures to represent different words. This was the world's first system of writing, and developed into the cuneiform script. The Sumerians also wrote out the first set of laws, and invented the wheel, one of the most important inventions in human history.

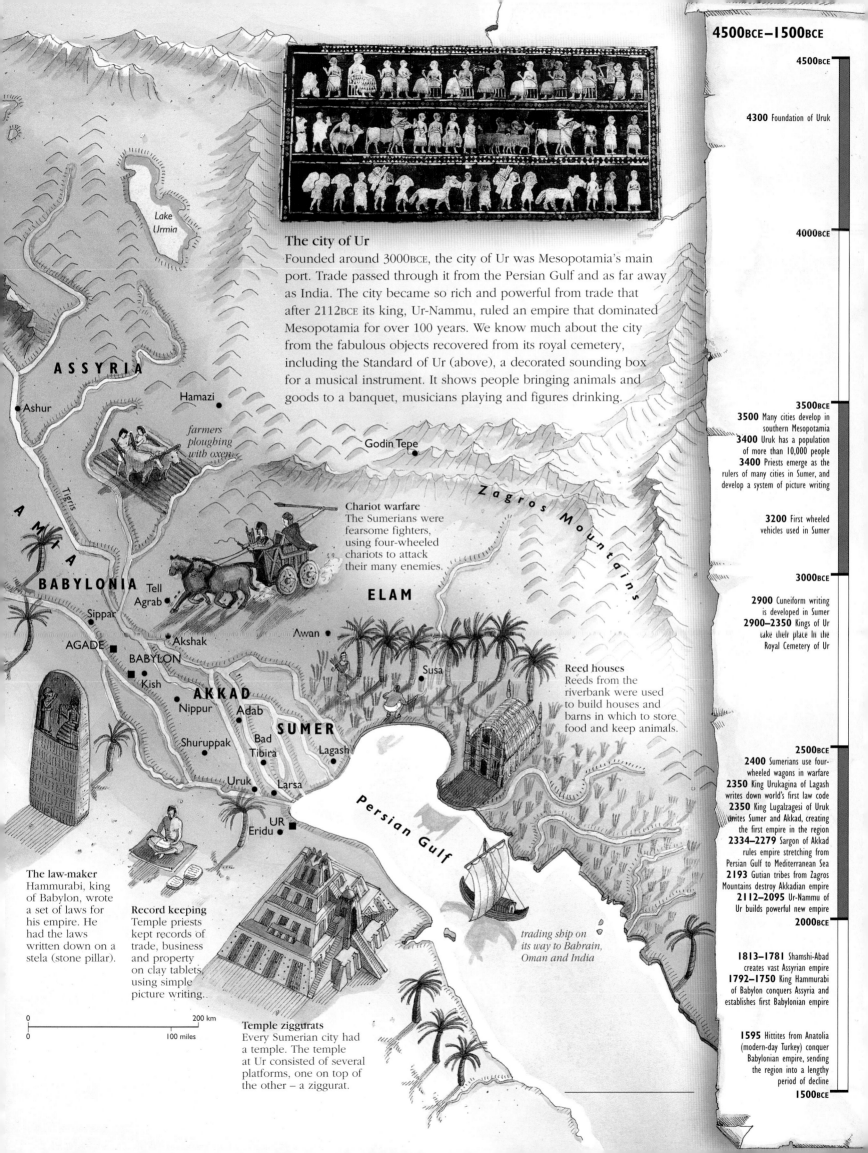

The city of Ur

Founded around 3000BCE, the city of Ur was Mesopotamia's main port. Trade passed through it from the Persian Gulf and as far away as India. The city became so rich and powerful from trade that after 2112BCE its king, Ur-Nammu, ruled an empire that dominated Mesopotamia for over 100 years. We know much about the city from the fabulous objects recovered from its royal cemetery, including the Standard of Ur (above), a decorated sounding box for a musical instrument. It shows people bringing animals and goods to a banquet, musicians playing and figures drinking.

ASSYRIA

Ashur

Hamazi

Lake Urmia

farmers ploughing with oxen

Godin Tepe

Tigris

A M M A

BABYLONIA

Tell Agrab

Zagros Mountains

Chariot warfare
The Sumerians were fearsome fighters, using four-wheeled chariots to attack their many enemies.

ELAM

Sippar

AGADE

Akshak

Awan

BABYLON

Kish

Susa

AKKAD

Nippur

Adab

SUMER

Shuruppak

Bad Tibira

Lagash

Reed houses
Reeds from the riverbank were used to build houses and barns in which to store food and keep animals.

Uruk

Larsa

UR

Eridu

Persian Gulf

The law-maker
Hammurabi, king of Babylon, wrote a set of laws for his empire. He had the laws written down on a stela (stone pillar).

Record keeping
Temple priests kept records of trade, business and property on clay tablets, using simple picture writing.

trading ship on its way to Bahrain, Oman and India

0 ———— 200 km
0 ———— 100 miles

Temple ziggurats
Every Sumerian city had a temple. The temple at Ur consisted of several platforms, one on top of the other – a ziggurat.

4500BCE

4300 Foundation of Uruk

4000BCE

3500BCE

3500 Many cities develop in southern Mesopotamia
3400 Uruk has a population of more than 10,000 people
3400 Priests emerge as the rulers of many cities in Sumer, and develop a system of picture writing

3200 First wheeled vehicles used in Sumer

3000BCE

2900 Cuneiform writing is developed in Sumer
2900–2350 Kings of Ur take their place in the Royal Cemetery of Ur

2500BCE

2400 Sumerians use four-wheeled wagons in warfare
2350 King Urukagina of Lagash writes down world's first law code
2350 King Lugalzagesi of Uruk unites Sumer and Akkad, creating the first empire in the region
2334–2279 Sargon of Akkad rules empire stretching from Persian Gulf to Mediterranean Sea
2193 Gutian tribes from Zagros Mountains destroy Akkadian empire
2112–2095 Ur-Nammu of Ur builds powerful new empire

2000BCE

1813–1781 Shamshi-Abad creates vast Assyrian empire
1792–1750 King Hammurabi of Babylon conquers Assyria and establishes first Babylonian empire

1595 Hittites from Anatolia (modern-day Turkey) conquer Babylonian empire, sending the region into a lengthy period of decline

1500BCE

Ancient Egypt

For more than 3,000 years, the Egyptians established a remarkable civilization along the banks of the river Nile. They were ruled by kings called pharaohs. The river was Egypt's main highway. People and goods travelled along it and it supplied fresh water for humans and animals and irrigated the crops. Surplus food, linen and papyrus were traded throughout the region in return for silver, copper, tin, timber, horses and human slaves, making Egypt a wealthy and powerful nation. The Egyptians were one of the first people to invent a system of picture writing, known as hieroglyphics. They were also skilled builders, constructing magnificent stone palaces, temples and pyramid-shaped tombs, many of which still survive today.

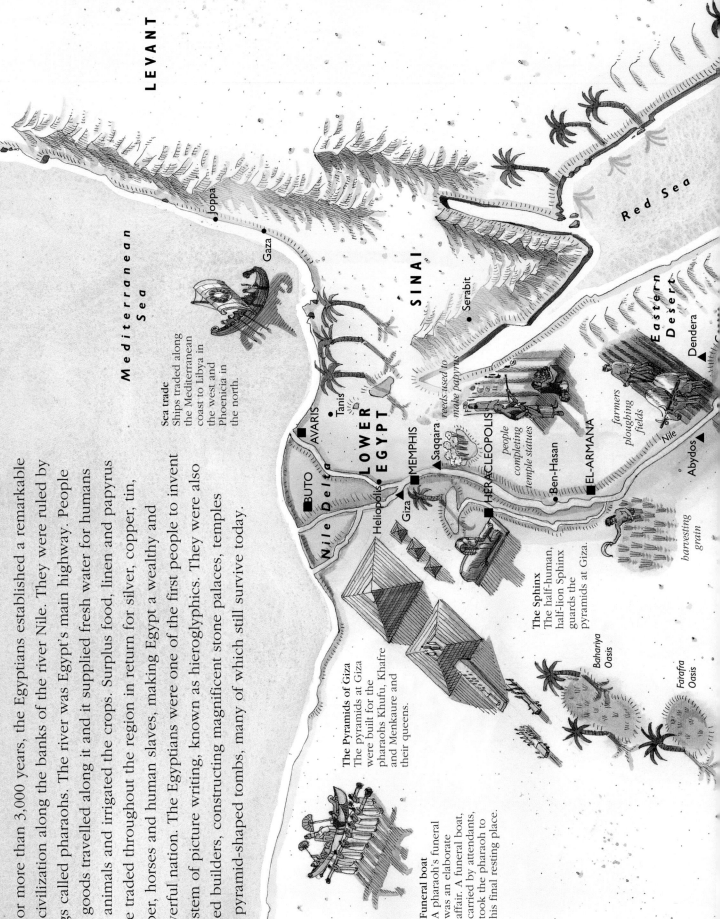

LEVANT

Mediterranean Sea

• Joppa

• Gaza

Red Sea

SINAI

• Serabit

Sea trade
Ships traded along the Mediterranean coast to Libya in the west and Phoenicia in the north.

• Tanis

■ AVARIS

■ BUTO

Nile Delta

LOWER EGYPT

■ MEMPHIS

Saqqara

▲ Heliopolis

▲ Giza

■ HERACLEOPOLIS

reeds used to make papyrus

people completing temple statues

• Ben-Hasan

■ EL-ARMANA

Eastern Desert

▲ Dendera

farmers ploughing fields

Nile

▲ Abydos

harvesting grain

Bahariya Oasis

Farafra Oasis

The Sphinx
The half-human, half-lion Sphinx guards the pyramids at Giza.

The Pyramids of Giza
The pyramids at Giza were built for the pharaohs Khufu, Khafre and Menkaure and their queens.

Funeral boat
A pharaoh's funeral was an elaborate affair. A funeral boat, carried by attendants, took the pharaoh to his final resting place.

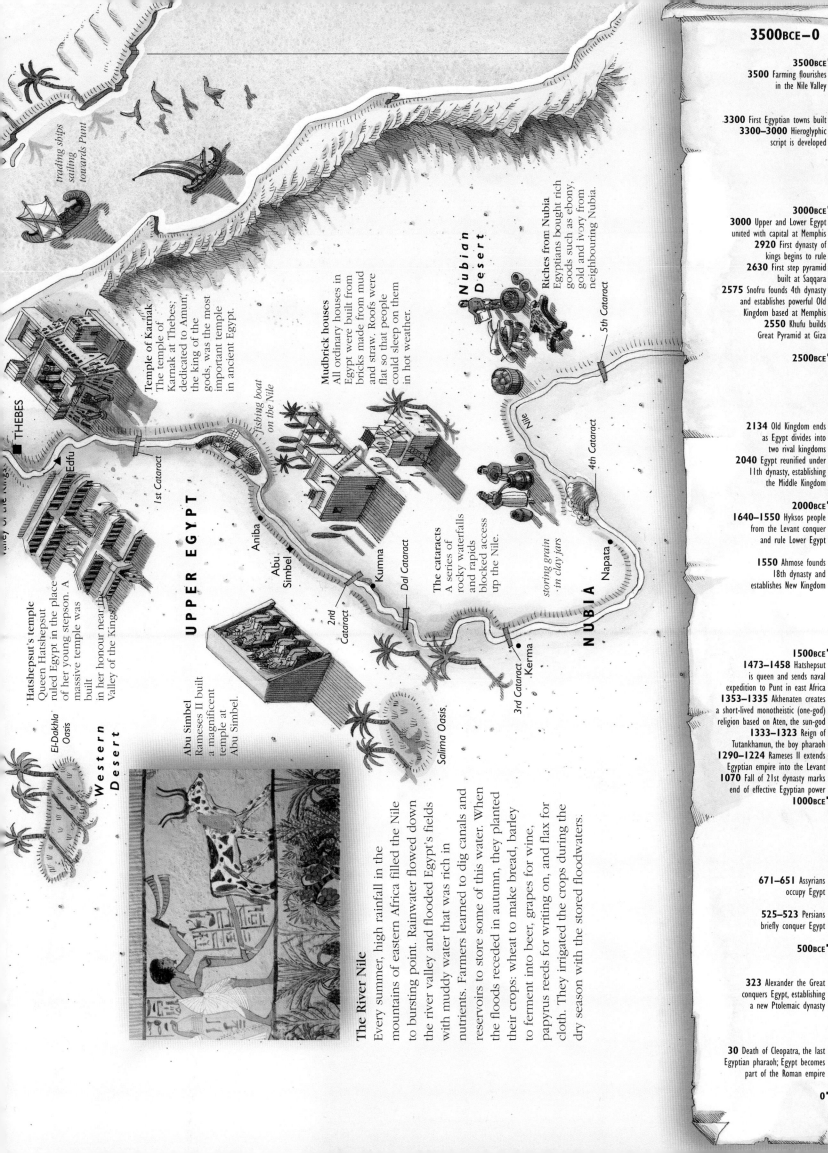

trading ships sailing towards Punt

THEBES

Edfu

Valley of the Kings

UPPER EGYPT

Western Desert

El-Dakhla Oasis

Hatshepsut's temple
Queen Hatshepsut ruled Egypt in the place of her young stepson. A massive temple was built in her honour near the Valley of the Kings.

Temple of Karnak
The temple of Karnak at Thebes, dedicated to Amun, the king of the gods, was the most important temple in ancient Egypt.

1st Cataract

Fishing boat on the Nile

Aniba

Abu Simbel

Abu Simbel
Rameses II built a magnificent temple at Abu Simbel.

2nd Cataract

Salima Oasis

Mudbrick houses
All ordinary houses in Egypt were built from bricks made from mud and straw. Roofs were flat so that people could sleep on them in hot weather.

Kumna

Dal Cataract

The cataracts
A series of rocky waterfalls and rapids blocked access up the Nile.

3rd Cataract

Kerma

N u b i a n   D e s e r t

Riches from Nubia
Egyptians bought rich goods such as ebony, gold and ivory from neighbouring Nubia.

5th Cataract

Nile

4th Cataract

storing grain in clay jars

NUBIA

Napata

The River Nile

Every summer, high rainfall in the mountains of eastern Africa filled the Nile to bursting point. Rainwater flowed down the river valley and flooded Egypt's fields with muddy water that was rich in nutrients. Farmers learned to dig canals and reservoirs to store some of this water. When the floods receded in autumn, they planted their crops: wheat to make bread, barley to ferment into beer, grapes for wine, papyrus reeds for writing on, and flax for cloth. They irrigated the crops during the dry season with the stored floodwaters.

3500BCE—0

3500BCE
3500 Farming flourishes in the Nile Valley

3300 First Egyptian towns built
3300–3000 Hieroglyphic script is developed

3000BCE
3000 Upper and Lower Egypt united with capital at Memphis
2920 First dynasty of kings begins to rule
2630 First step pyramid built at Saqqara
2575 Snofru founds 4th dynasty and establishes powerful Old Kingdom based at Memphis
2550 Khufu builds Great Pyramid at Giza

2500BCE

2134 Old Kingdom ends as Egypt divides into two rival kingdoms
2040 Egypt reunified under 11th dynasty, establishing the Middle Kingdom

2000BCE
1640–1550 Hyksos people from the Levant conquer and rule Lower Egypt

1550 Ahmose founds 18th dynasty and establishes New Kingdom

1500BCE
1473–1458 Hatshepsut is queen and sends naval expedition to Punt in east Africa
1353–1335 Akhenaten creates a short-lived monotheistic (one-god) religion based on Aten, the sun-god
1333–1323 Reign of Tutankhamun, the boy pharaoh
1290–1224 Rameses II extends Egyptian empire into the Levant
1070 Fall of 21st dynasty marks end of effective Egyptian power
1000BCE

671–651 Assyrians occupy Egypt

525–523 Persians briefly conquer Egypt

500BCE

323 Alexander the Great conquers Egypt, establishing a new Ptolemaic dynasty

30 Death of Cleopatra, the last Egyptian pharaoh; Egypt becomes part of the Roman empire

0

Ancient Egypt:
Preparing for the afterlife

The ancient Egyptians had a strong belief in the afterlife, as they dreaded the day their own world might come to an end. They developed an elaborate method of embalming and mummifying bodies so that they would last for ever. Important people, such as the pharaoh (king), were buried along with their belongings inside a great pyramid. Later, the pharaohs were buried in tombs in the Valley of the Kings. Although most of these pyramids and tombs have been robbed of their contents, a few have survived intact, giving us a good idea about the Egyptian way of life and death, 3,000 and more years ago.

Mummification

After death, the body was taken to a place known as the Beautiful House to be preserved. Embalmers removed the internal organs, leaving the heart so that it could be weighed in the afterlife. The body was then covered with crystals of a chemical called natron, to dry it out and prevent decay. After about 40 days, the body was ready for the next stage. It was stuffed with dry material such as sawdust or leaves and wrapped tightly in linen bandages. Lastly, it was put into a wood or stone coffin. Lowly people were buried in graveyards, but important people, such as the boy pharaoh Tutankhamun (right; ruled 1333–1323BCE) were placed in an elaborate container. This was made up of layers, each one beautifully decorated inside with gods of the underworld, and outside with hieroglyphs and magic symbols. Once safely in its coffin, the body was ready for the afterlife.

Weighing the heart

The Egyptians believed in an underworld called Duat, which contained lakes of fire and poisonous snakes. Spells to ward off these and other dangers were written on the coffin. The biggest danger was in the Hall of Two Truths, where a person's heart was weighed against past deeds (left). Here the dead person was asked about their life. If they told the truth, they were allowed to pass on into the afterlife.

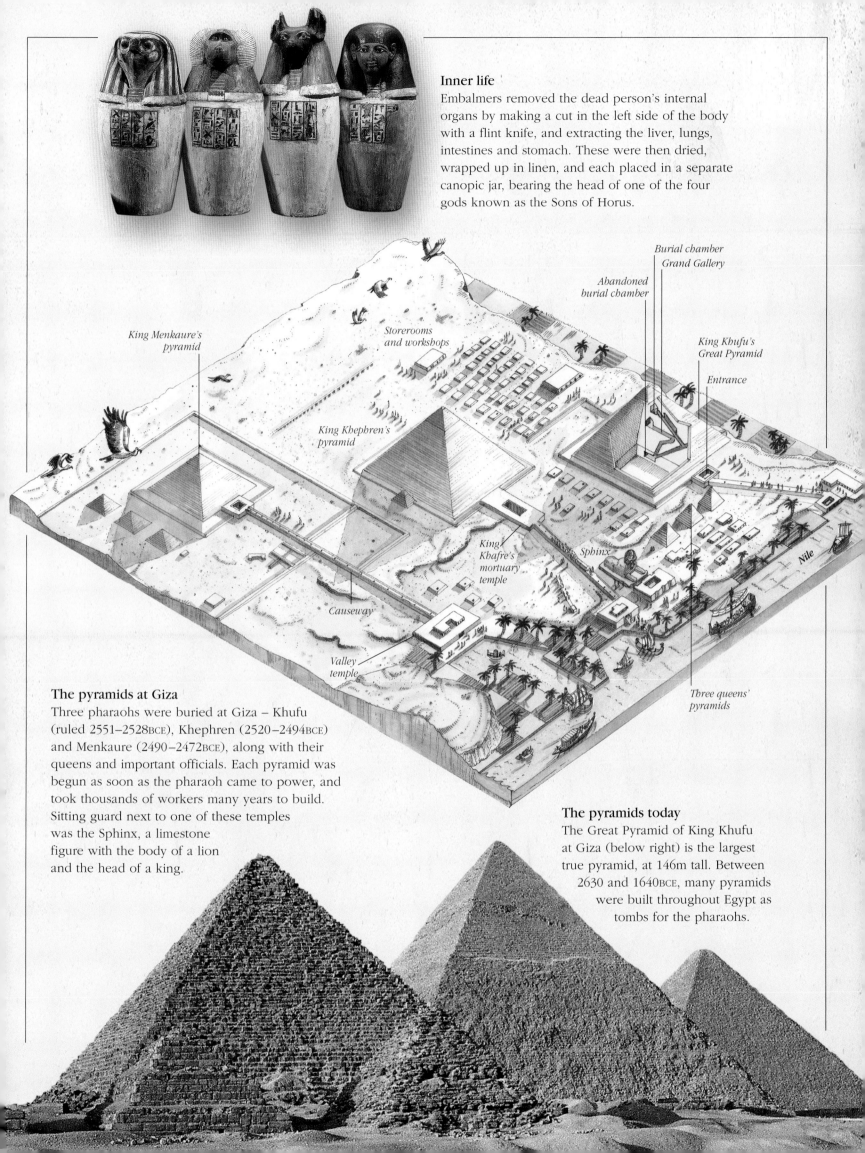

Inner life

Embalmers removed the dead person's internal organs by making a cut in the left side of the body with a flint knife, and extracting the liver, lungs, intestines and stomach. These were then dried, wrapped up in linen, and each placed in a separate canopic jar, bearing the head of one of the four gods known as the Sons of Horus.

King Menkaure's pyramid

Storerooms and workshops

Abandoned burial chamber

Burial chamber
Grand Gallery

King Khufu's Great Pyramid

Entrance

King Khephren's pyramid

King Khafre's mortuary temple

Sphinx

Causeway

Nile

Valley temple

Three queens' pyramids

The pyramids at Giza

Three pharaohs were buried at Giza – Khufu (ruled 2551–2528BCE), Khephren (2520–2494BCE) and Menkaure (2490–2472BCE), along with their queens and important officials. Each pyramid was begun as soon as the pharaoh came to power, and took thousands of workers many years to build. Sitting guard next to one of these temples was the Sphinx, a limestone figure with the body of a lion and the head of a king.

The pyramids today

The Great Pyramid of King Khufu at Giza (below right) is the largest true pyramid, at 146m tall. Between 2630 and 1640BCE, many pyramids were built throughout Egypt as tombs for the pharaohs.

Ancient Europe

Farming began in southeastern Europe during the Neolithic Age around 6000BCE, and slowly spread throughout Europe over the next 2,000 years. Farming allowed people to settle down and build houses and villages to live in, but the real advance came with the use of copper, bronze and then iron. These metals could be worked into tools and weapons, and items such as jewellery and other ornamental or ceremonial objects. In many places, chiefs and other important people were buried in megalithic (huge stone) tombs with beautiful offerings to the gods alongside them. People built vast circles and rows of standing stones and circular earth structures known as henges. Some of these line up with the sun and stars at certain times of the year, indicating a detailed knowledge of the calendar and astronomy.

Ancient sites
The key on page 4 tells you that places marked with a diamond are not cities, towns or villages but other kinds of ancient sites. On this map, these sites are stone circles, rows of standing stones or stone tombs. An example is ◆ Stonehenge.

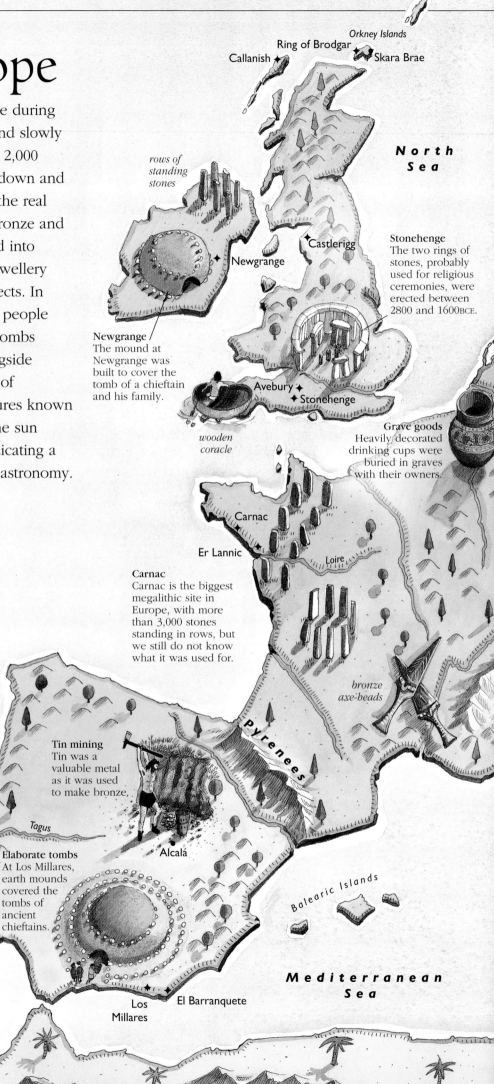

Orkney Islands

Ring of Brodgar

Callanish ◆

Skara Brae

rows of standing stones

North Sea

Castlerigg

Newgrange

Stonehenge
The two rings of stones, probably used for religious ceremonies, were erected between 2800 and 1600BCE.

Newgrange
The mound at Newgrange was built to cover the tomb of a chieftain and his family.

Avebury ◆

◆ Stonehenge

wooden coracle

Grave goods
Heavily decorated drinking cups were buried in graves with their owners.

Carnac

Er Lannic

Loire

Carnac
Carnac is the biggest megalithic site in Europe, with more than 3,000 stones standing in rows, but we still do not know what it was used for.

bronze axe-heads

Pyrenees

Tin mining
Tin was a valuable metal as it was used to make bronze.

Tagus

Alcalá

Elaborate tombs
At Los Millares, earth mounds covered the tombs of ancient chieftains.

Atlantic Ocean

Balearic Islands

Los Millares

El Barranquete

Mediterranean Sea

0	500	1000 km
0	250	500 miles

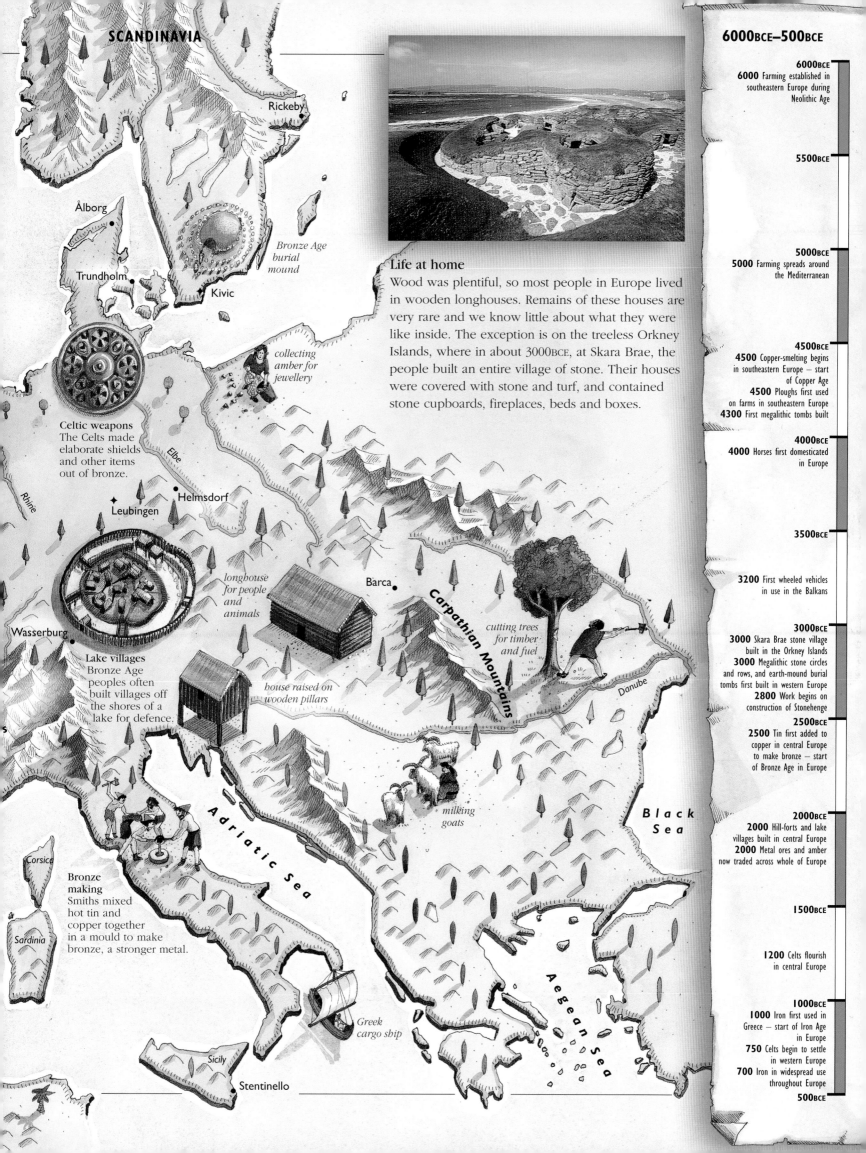

SCANDINAVIA

Rickeby

Ålborg

Trundholm

Kivic

*Bronze Age
burial
mound*

*collecting
amber for
jewellery*

Celtic weapons
The Celts made
elaborate shields
and other items
out of bronze.

Elbe

Rhine

Helmsdorf

Leubingen

Wasserburg

Lake villages
Bronze Age
peoples often
built villages off
the shores of a
lake for defence.

*longhouse
for people
and
animals*

*house raised on
wooden pillars*

Barca

*cutting trees
for timber
and fuel*

Carpathian Mountains

Danube

*milking
goats*

**B l a c k
S e a**

Corsica

Sardinia

**Bronze
making**
Smiths mixed
hot tin and
copper together
in a mould to make
bronze, a stronger metal.

A d r i a t i c   S e a

*Greek
cargo ship*

Sicily

Stentinello

Aegean Sea

Life at home

Wood was plentiful, so most people in Europe lived
in wooden longhouses. Remains of these houses are
very rare and we know little about what they were
like inside. The exception is on the treeless Orkney
Islands, where in about 3000BCE, at Skara Brae, the
people built an entire village of stone. Their houses
were covered with stone and turf, and contained
stone cupboards, fireplaces, beds and boxes.

6000BCE–500BCE

6000BCE
6000 Farming established in
southeastern Europe during
Neolithic Age

5500BCE

5000BCE
5000 Farming spreads around
the Mediterranean

4500BCE
4500 Copper-smelting begins
in southeastern Europe — start
of Copper Age
4500 Ploughs first used
on farms in southeastern Europe
4300 First megalithic tombs built

4000BCE
4000 Horses first domesticated
in Europe

3500BCE

3200 First wheeled vehicles
in use in the Balkans

3000BCE
3000 Skara Brae stone village
built in the Orkney Islands
3000 Megalithic stone circles
and rows, and earth-mound burial
tombs first built in western Europe
2800 Work begins on
construction of Stonehenge

2500BCE
2500 Tin first added to
copper in central Europe
to make bronze — start
of Bronze Age in Europe

2000BCE
2000 Hill-forts and lake
villages built in central Europe
2000 Metal ores and amber
now traded across whole of Europe

1500BCE

1200 Celts flourish
in central Europe

1000BCE
1000 Iron first used in
Greece — start of Iron Age
in Europe
750 Celts begin to settle
in western Europe
700 Iron in widespread use
throughout Europe

500BCE

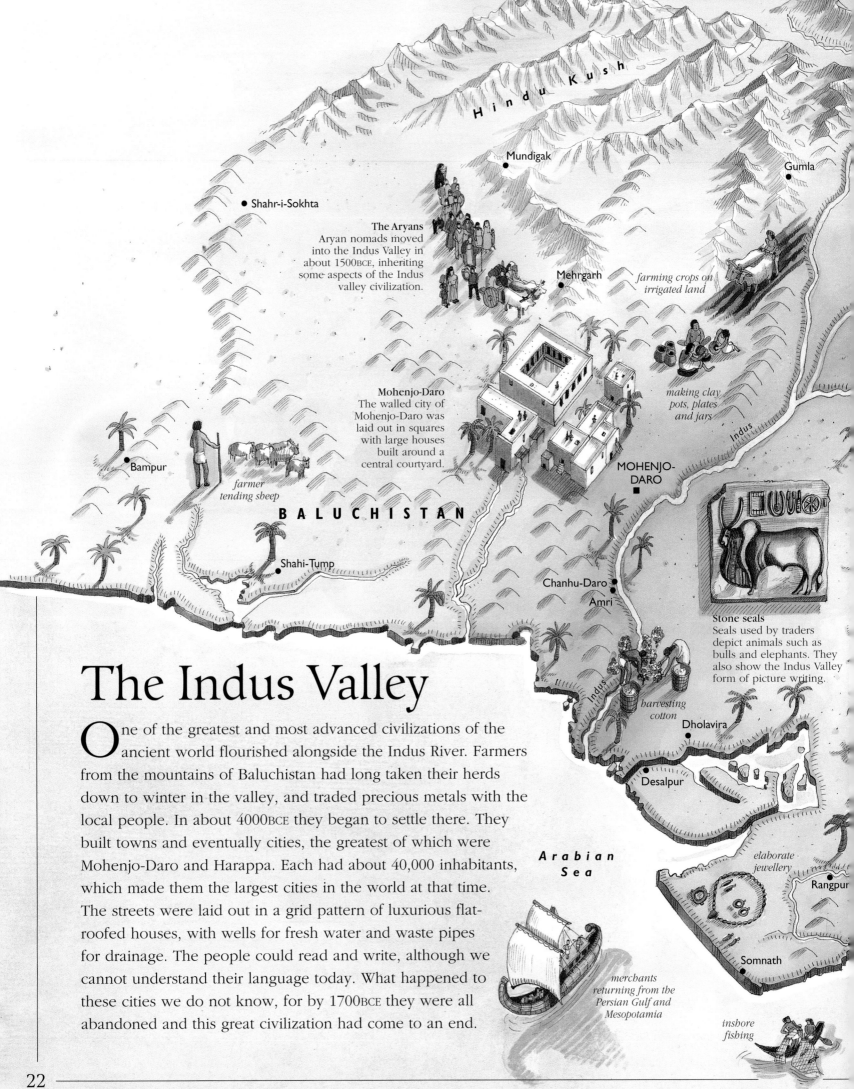

Hindu Kush

Mundigak

Gumla

Shahr-i-Sokhta

The Aryans
Aryan nomads moved into the Indus Valley in about 1500BCE, inheriting some aspects of the Indus valley civilization.

Mehrgarh

farming crops on irrigated land

making clay pots, plates and jars

Mohenjo-Daro
The walled city of Mohenjo-Daro was laid out in squares with large houses built around a central courtyard.

Indus

Bampur

MOHENJO-DARO

farmer tending sheep

B A L U C H I S T A N

Shahi-Tump

Chanhu-Daro

Amri

Stone seals
Seals used by traders depict animals such as bulls and elephants. They also show the Indus Valley form of picture writing.

Indus

harvesting cotton

Dholavira

Desalpur

The Indus Valley

One of the greatest and most advanced civilizations of the ancient world flourished alongside the Indus River. Farmers from the mountains of Baluchistan had long taken their herds down to winter in the valley, and traded precious metals with the local people. In about 4000BCE they began to settle there. They built towns and eventually cities, the greatest of which were Mohenjo-Daro and Harappa. Each had about 40,000 inhabitants, which made them the largest cities in the world at that time. The streets were laid out in a grid pattern of luxurious flat-roofed houses, with wells for fresh water and waste pipes for drainage. The people could read and write, although we cannot understand their language today. What happened to these cities we do not know, for by 1700BCE they were all abandoned and this great civilization had come to an end.

*A r a b i a n
S e a*

elaborate jewellery

Rangpur

Somnath

merchants returning from the Persian Gulf and Mesopotamia

inshore fishing

Gulf of Khabhat

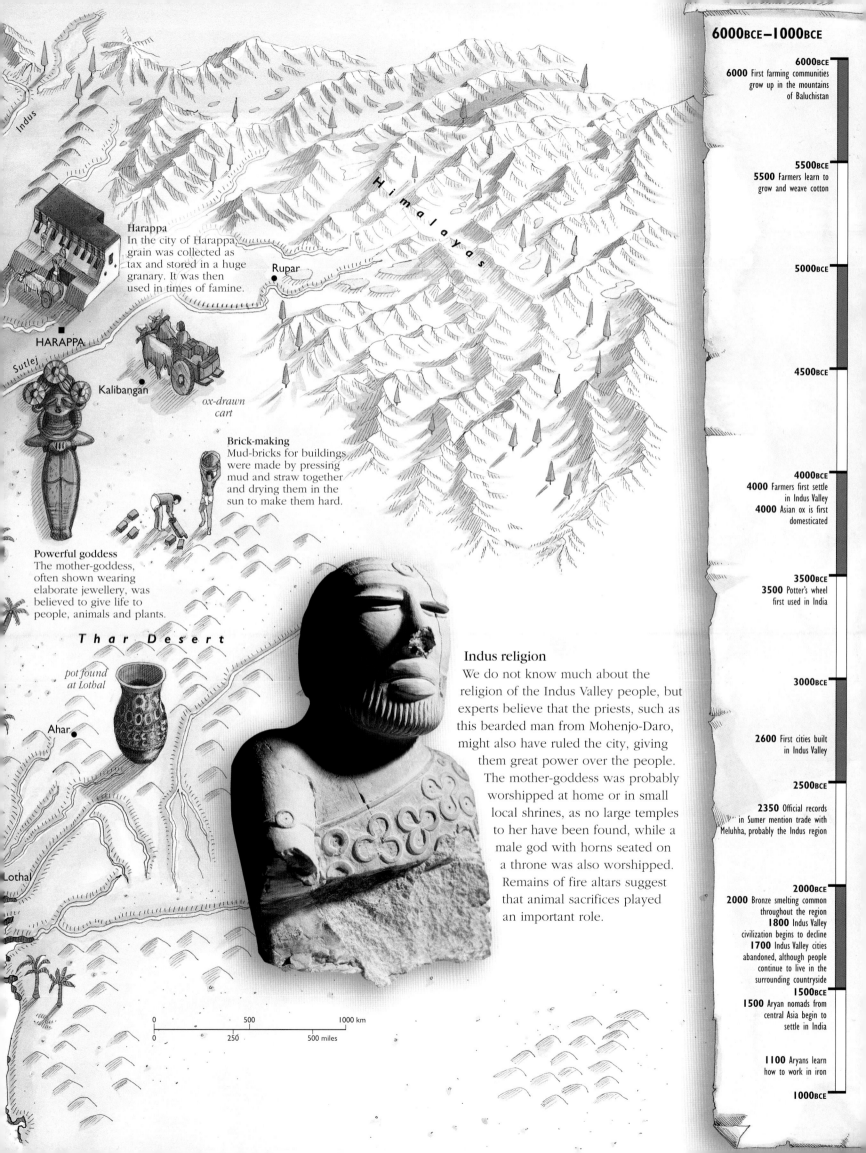

Harappa
In the city of Harappa, grain was collected as tax and stored in a huge granary. It was then used in times of famine.

HARAPPA

Indus

Sutlej

Rupar

Kalibangan

Himalayas

ox-drawn cart

Brick-making
Mud-bricks for buildings were made by pressing mud and straw together and drying them in the sun to make them hard.

Powerful goddess
The mother-goddess, often shown wearing elaborate jewellery, was believed to give life to people, animals and plants.

Thar Desert

pot found at Lothal

Ahar

Lothal

Indus religion

We do not know much about the religion of the Indus Valley people, but experts believe that the priests, such as this bearded man from Mohenjo-Daro, might also have ruled the city, giving them great power over the people. The mother-goddess was probably worshipped at home or in small local shrines, as no large temples to her have been found, while a male god with horns seated on a throne was also worshipped. Remains of fire altars suggest that animal sacrifices played an important role.

0   500   1000 km
0   250   500 miles

6000BCE–1000BCE

6000BCE

6000 First farming communities grow up in the mountains of Baluchistan

5500BCE

5500 Farmers learn to grow and weave cotton

5000BCE

4500BCE

4000BCE

4000 Farmers first settle in Indus Valley
4000 Asian ox is first domesticated

3500BCE

3500 Potter's wheel first used in India

3000BCE

2600 First cities built in Indus Valley

2500BCE

2350 Official records in Sumer mention trade with Meluhha, probably the Indus region

2000BCE

2000 Bronze smelting common throughout the region
1800 Indus Valley civilization begins to decline
1700 Indus Valley cities abandoned, although people continue to live in the surrounding countryside

1500BCE

1500 Aryan nomads from central Asia begin to settle in India

1100 Aryans learn how to work in iron

1000BCE

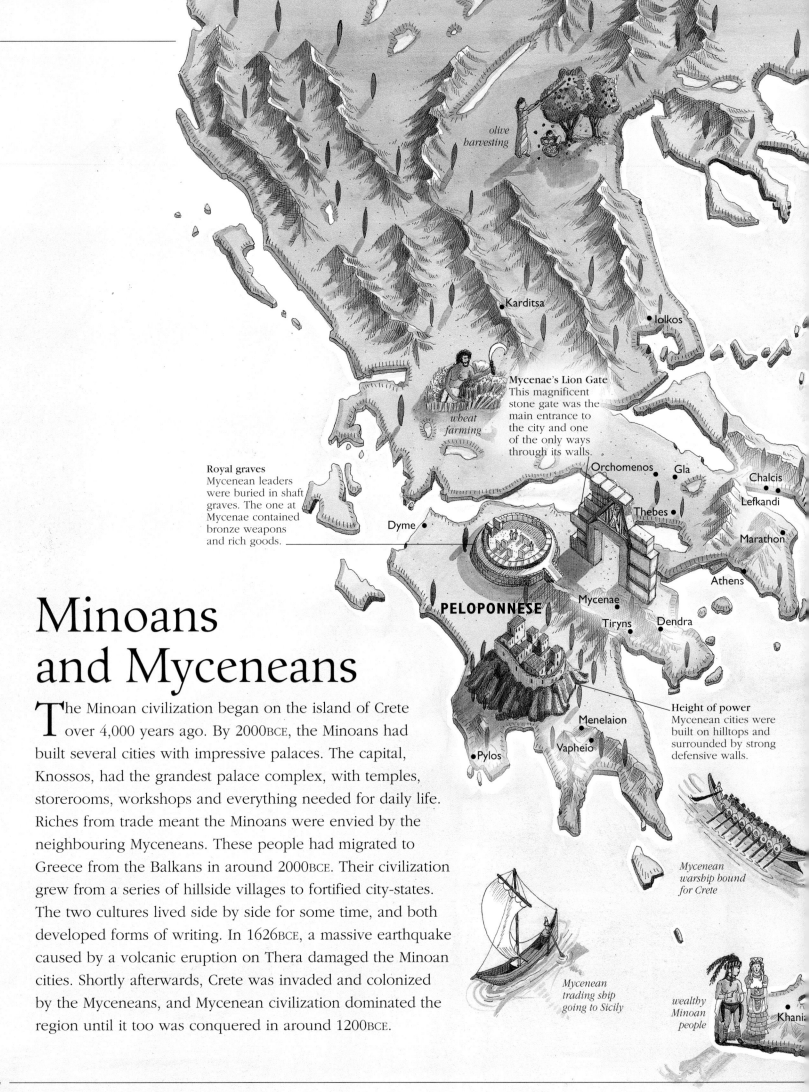

olive harvesting

Karditsa

Iolkos

Mycenae's Lion Gate
This magnificent stone gate was the main entrance to the city and one of the only ways through its walls.

wheat farming

Orchomenos Gla

Chalcis

Lefkandi

Thebes

Royal graves
Mycenean leaders were buried in shaft graves. The one at Mycenae contained bronze weapons and rich goods.

Marathon

Dyme

Athens

PELOPONNESE

Mycenae

Tiryns Dendra

Height of power
Mycenean cities were built on hilltops and surrounded by strong defensive walls.

Menelaion

Pylos

Vapheio

Minoans and Myceneans

The Minoan civilization began on the island of Crete over 4,000 years ago. By 2000BCE, the Minoans had built several cities with impressive palaces. The capital, Knossos, had the grandest palace complex, with temples, storerooms, workshops and everything needed for daily life. Riches from trade meant the Minoans were envied by the neighbouring Myceneans. These people had migrated to Greece from the Balkans in around 2000BCE. Their civilization grew from a series of hillside villages to fortified city-states. The two cultures lived side by side for some time, and both developed forms of writing. In 1626BCE, a massive earthquake caused by a volcanic eruption on Thera damaged the Minoan cities. Shortly afterwards, Crete was invaded and colonized by the Myceneans, and Mycenean civilization dominated the region until it too was conquered in around 1200BCE.

Mycenean warship bound for Crete

Mycenean trading ship going to Sicily

wealthy Minoan people

Khania

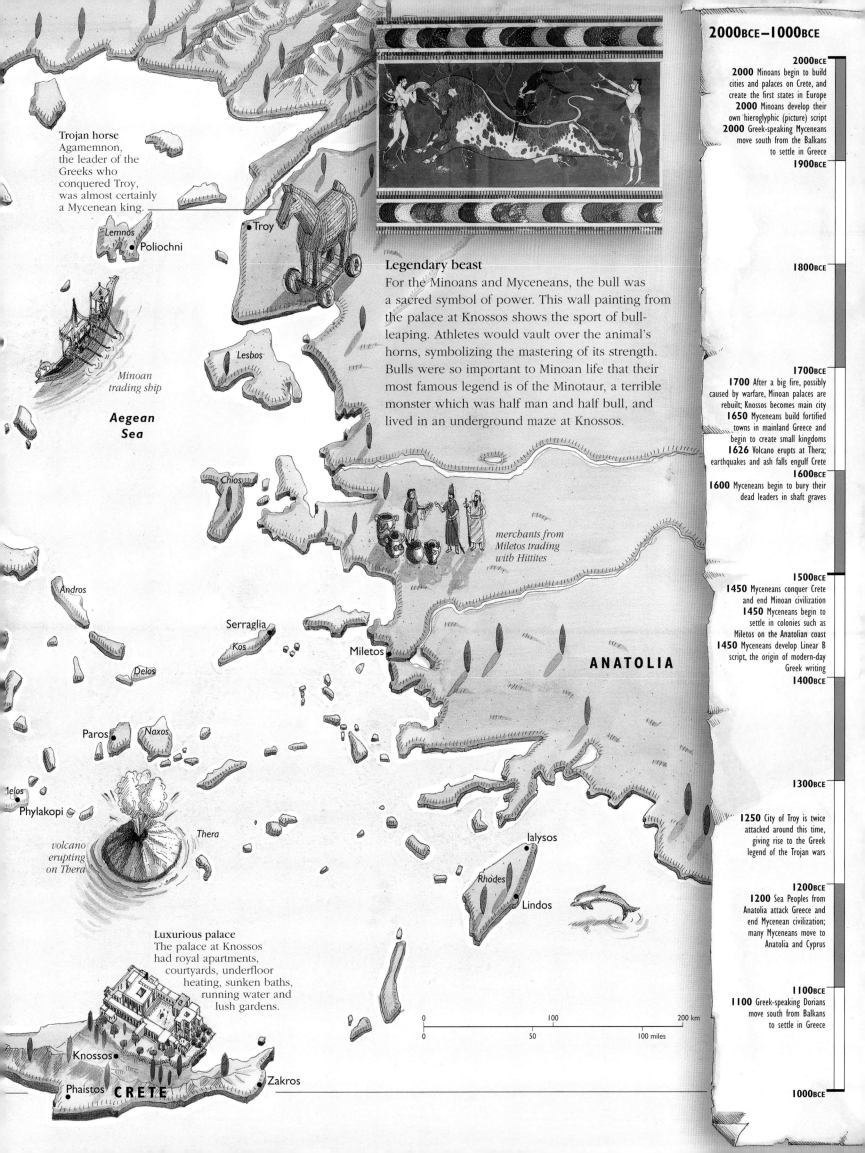

Trojan horse
Agamemnon, the leader of the Greeks who conquered Troy, was almost certainly a Mycenean king.

Minoan trading ship

Aegean Sea

Lemnos
Poliochni
Troy

Lesbos

Chios

merchants from Miletos trading with Hittites

ANATOLIA

Andros

Serraglia
Kos
Miletos

Delos

Paros
Naxos

Melos
Phylakopi

Thera

volcano erupting on Thera

Ialysos

Rhodes

Lindos

Legendary beast
For the Minoans and Myceneans, the bull was a sacred symbol of power. This wall painting from the palace at Knossos shows the sport of bull-leaping. Athletes would vault over the animal's horns, symbolizing the mastering of its strength. Bulls were so important to Minoan life that their most famous legend is of the Minotaur, a terrible monster which was half man and half bull, and lived in an underground maze at Knossos.

Luxurious palace
The palace at Knossos had royal apartments, courtyards, underfloor heating, sunken baths, running water and lush gardens.

Knossos
Phaistos **CRETE**
Zakros

| 0 | 100 | 200 km |
| 0 | 50 | 100 miles |

2000BCE

2000 Minoans begin to build cities and palaces on Crete, and create the first states in Europe
2000 Minoans develop their own 'hieroglyphic (picture) script
2000 Greek-speaking Myceneans move south from the Balkans to settle in Greece

1900BCE

1800BCE

1700BCE
1700 After a big fire, possibly caused by warfare, Minoan palaces are rebuilt; Knossos becomes main city
1650 Myceneans build fortified towns in mainland Greece and begin to create small kingdoms
1626 Volcano erupts at Thera; earthquakes and ash falls engulf Crete

1600BCE
1600 Myceneans begin to bury their dead leaders in shaft graves

1500BCE
1450 Myceneans conquer Crete and end Minoan civilization
1450 Myceneans begin to settle in colonies such as Miletos on the Anatolian coast
1450 Myceneans develop Linear B script, the origin of modern-day Greek writing

1400BCE

1300BCE

1250 City of Troy is twice attacked around this time, giving rise to the Greek legend of the Trojan wars

1200BCE
1200 Sea Peoples from Anatolia attack Greece and end Mycenean civilization; many Myceneans move to Anatolia and Cyprus

1100BCE
1100 Greek-speaking Dorians move south from Balkans to settle in Greece

1000BCE

BRITAIN

Phoenician ship sailing to Britain to get tin

FRANCE

Atlantic Ocean

Hannibal
In 218BCE the Carthaginian general Hannibal crossed the Alps to surprise his Roman enemies during the Second Punic War.

tin mining

A l p s

P y r e n e e s

ITALY

Massilia

Adriatic Sea

The Etruscans
The Etruscans – the major force in central Italy – ruled Rome before it became a republic in 509BCE.

Corsica

ROME

SPAIN

silver mining

Mediterranean Sea

Palma

Balearic Islands

Sardinia

Rome
Rome was originally a series of hilltop villages that gradually joined to become a single city.

Sulcis

Gades

Cartagena

Tingis (Tangier)

trading prized Phoenician cloth

Lixus

trading ship travelling along African coast

Cartenna

Sicily

CARTHAGE

Carthage harbour
The Phoenicians established the trading post of Carthage in 814BCE. It soon grew to become the most powerful nation in the Mediterranean.

Phoenician script
The Phoenicians had an alphabet of 22 consonants. The Greeks added vowels, making the alphabet we use today.

Peoples of the Mediterranean

For the people living near the Mediterranean, the sea presented either a barrier they could not cross or a wonderful opportunity to get rich through trade and conquest. The Greeks established trading colonies around the Mediterranean, while the Phoenicians were more adventurous and sent trading expeditions out into the Atlantic. The two peoples often fought. They were later joined by the Carthaginians in North Africa, the Etruscans from Italy and, eventually, the Romans, who dominated the Mediterranean Sea and much of its coastline by 100BCE.

Human sacrifice
The Carthaginians worshipped the sun and moon gods, offering human sacrifices in times of danger.

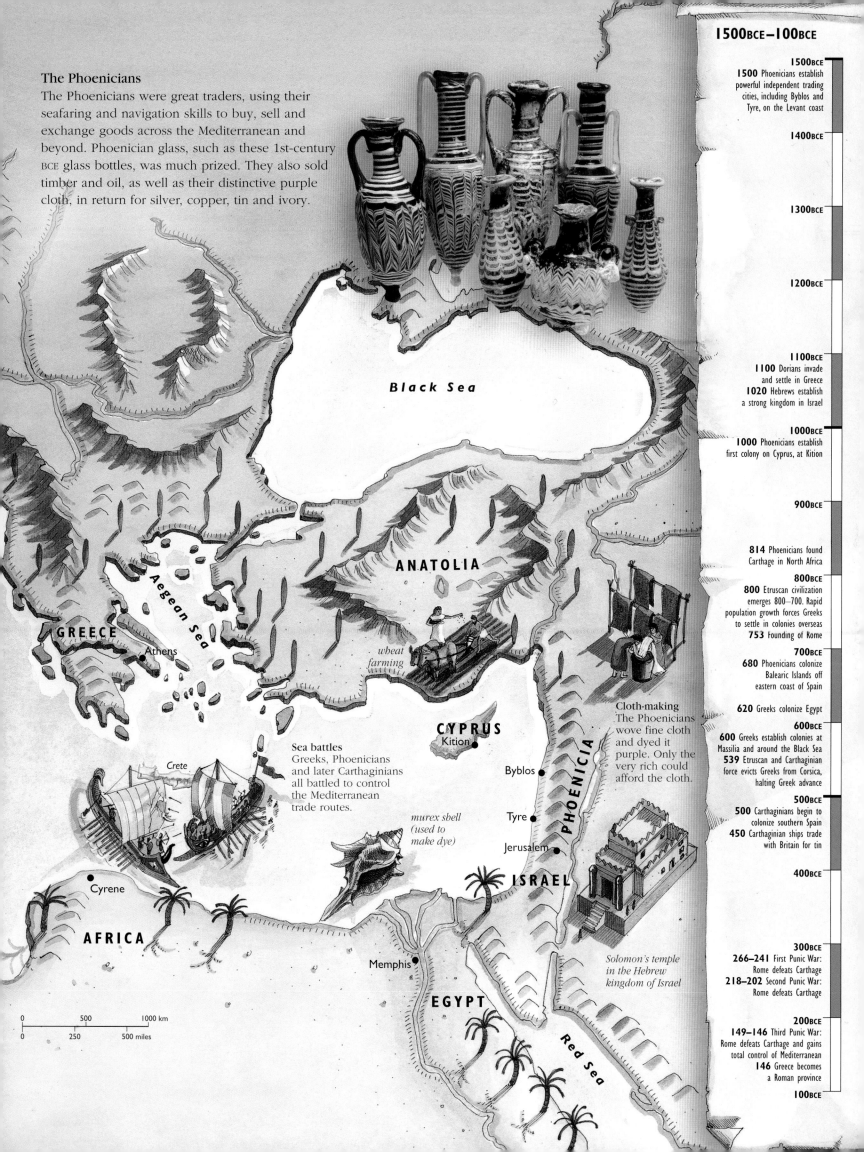

The Phoenicians

The Phoenicians were great traders, using their seafaring and navigation skills to buy, sell and exchange goods across the Mediterranean and beyond. Phoenician glass, such as these 1st-century BCE glass bottles, was much prized. They also sold timber and oil, as well as their distinctive purple cloth, in return for silver, copper, tin and ivory.

Black Sea

ANATOLIA

GREECE

Aegean Sea

Athens

wheat farming

Cloth-making
The Phoenicians wove fine cloth and dyed it purple. Only the very rich could afford the cloth.

CYPRUS
Kition

Sea battles
Greeks, Phoenicians and later Carthaginians all battled to control the Mediterranean trade routes.

Crete

murex shell (used to make dye)

Byblos

Tyre

Jerusalem

PHOENICIA

Cyrene

ISRAEL

Solomon's temple in the Hebrew kingdom of Israel

AFRICA

Memphis

EGYPT

Red Sea

| 0 | 500 | 1000 km |
| 0 | 250 | 500 miles |

1500BCE–100BCE

1500BCE

1500 Phoenicians establish powerful independent trading cities, including Byblos and Tyre, on the Levant coast

1400BCE

1300BCE

1200BCE

1100BCE
1100 Dorians invade and settle in Greece
1020 Hebrews establish a strong kingdom in Israel

1000BCE
1000 Phoenicians establish first colony on Cyprus, at Kition

900BCE

814 Phoenicians found Carthage in North Africa

800BCE
800 Etruscan civilization emerges 800–700. Rapid population growth forces Greeks to settle in colonies overseas
753 Founding of Rome

700BCE
680 Phoenicians colonize Balearic Islands off eastern coast of Spain

620 Greeks colonize Egypt

600BCE
600 Greeks establish colonies at Massilia and around the Black Sea
539 Etruscan and Carthaginian force evicts Greeks from Corsica, halting Greek advance

500BCE
500 Carthaginians begin to colonize southern Spain
450 Carthaginian ships trade with Britain for tin

400BCE

300BCE
266–241 First Punic War: Rome defeats Carthage
218–202 Second Punic War: Rome defeats Carthage

200BCE
149–146 Third Punic War: Rome defeats Carthage and gains total control of Mediterranean
146 Greece becomes a Roman province

100BCE

Black Sea

Scythian threat
Scythian archers were a constant threat to the Persian armies defending the empire's northern borders.

LYDIA

Pteria

The Royal Road
Riders carried messages for the Persian king along the 2,500-km Royal Road.

Royal Road

Sardis

Carchemish

SYRIA

Assyrian kings
Kings of Assyria, such as Ashurnasirpal II, had great religious and political power.

Aleppo

Lake Van

Van

Assyrian power
The throne room of the king's palace at Nimrud was guarded by two huge stone lions with wings and human faces.

Caspian Sea

Lake Urmia

MEDIA

The fatal blow
The Medes joined forces with Babylon to destroy the Assyrian empire in 612BCE.

Tigris

NINEVEH
Nimrud
Ashur

ASSYRIA

Hamadan (Ecbatana)

Cyprus

felling cedars for shipbuilding

Syrian Desert

beekeeping

M E S O P O T A M I A

keeping detailed records on clay tablets

Zagros Mountains

Sidon
Tyre

Damascus

Assyrian warfare
The Assyrians were fierce fighters, besieging cities until they surrendered.

Babylon
Nebuchadnezzar made Babylon the finest city in the world. He built a splendid temple with hanging gardens.

Euphrates

Sippar

BABYLON

BABYLONIA

SUSA

Nippur

Jerusalem

ISRAEL

Uruk

Ur

JUDAH

Babylonian exile
Nebuchadnezzar captured Jerusalem and took all the Jews to Babylon as slaves.

messenger keeping the king informed about events

Persian Gulf

The great empires

For more than 600 years, three great empires dominated the Middle East. The Assyrians were warlike and brutal, capturing or slaughtering their enemies. Their empire lasted for 300 years until the Babylonians, with the Medes, captured the Assyrian capital of Nineveh in 612BCE. The Babylonians turned Babylon into a fabulous city, but their power was short-lived. In 539BCE the Persians, under Cyrus the Great, seized Babylon and went on to conquer the greatest, most powerful empire the world had ever seen. The Persian kings built beautiful palaces and grew rich on trade and conquest, and their empire lasted for 200 years.

Red Sea

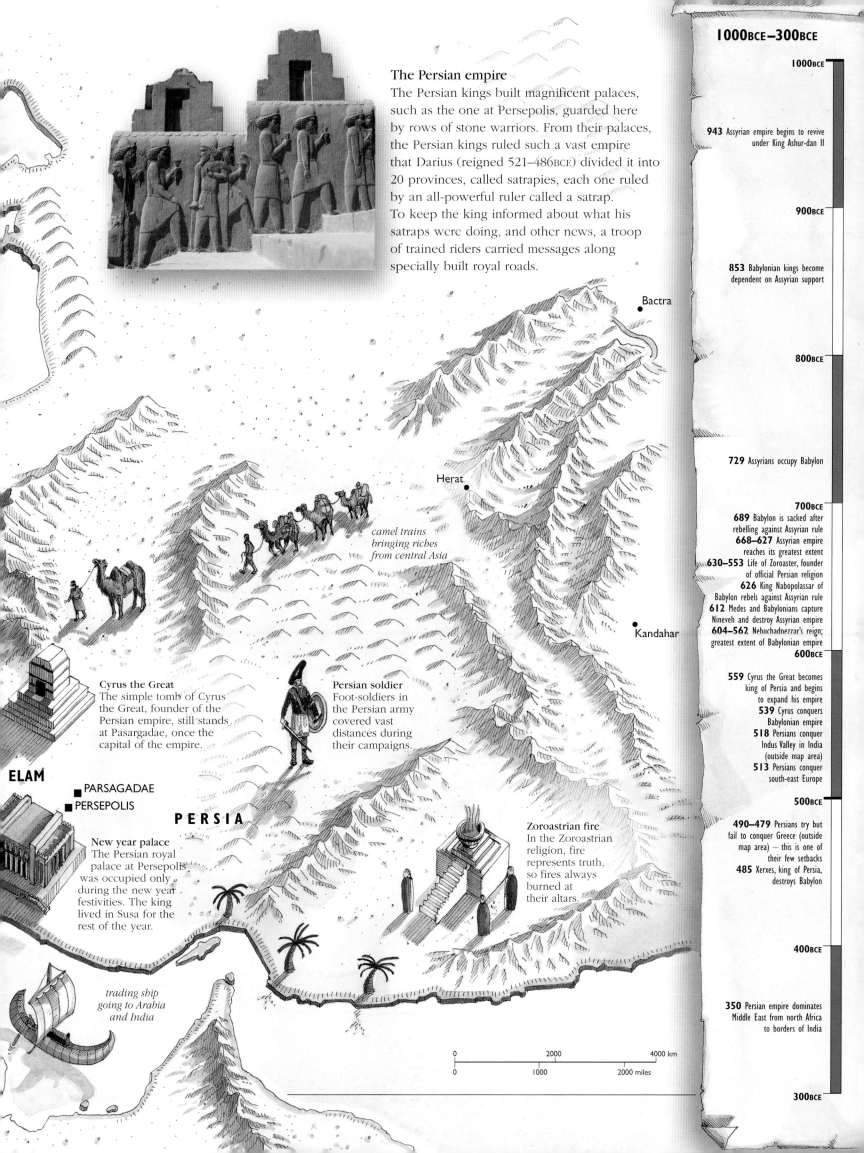

The Persian empire
The Persian kings built magnificent palaces, such as the one at Persepolis, guarded here by rows of stone warriors. From their palaces, the Persian kings ruled such a vast empire that Darius (reigned 521–486BCE) divided it into 20 provinces, called satrapies, each one ruled by an all-powerful ruler called a satrap. To keep the king informed about what his satraps were doing, and other news, a troop of trained riders carried messages along specially built royal roads.

Bactra

Herat

camel trains bringing riches from central Asia

Kandahar

Cyrus the Great
The simple tomb of Cyrus the Great, founder of the Persian empire, still stands at Pasargadae, once the capital of the empire.

Persian soldier
Foot-soldiers in the Persian army covered vast distances during their campaigns.

ELAM

■ PARSAGADAE
■ PERSEPOLIS

PERSIA

New year palace
The Persian royal palace at Persepolis was occupied only during the new year festivities. The king lived in Susa for the rest of the year.

Zoroastrian fire
In the Zoroastrian religion, fire represents truth, so fires always burned at their altars.

trading ship going to Arabia and India

| 0 | 2000 | 4000 km |
| 0 | 1000 | 2000 miles |

1000BCE–300BCE

1000BCE

943 Assyrian empire begins to revive under King Ashur-dan II

900BCE

853 Babylonian kings become dependent on Assyrian support

800BCE

729 Assyrians occupy Babylon

700BCE

689 Babylon is sacked after rebelling against Assyrian rule
668–627 Assyrian empire reaches its greatest extent
630–553 Life of Zoroaster, founder of official Persian religion
626 King Nabopolassar of Babylon rebels against Assyrian rule
612 Medes and Babylonians capture Nineveh and destroy Assyrian empire
604–562 Nebuchadnezzar's reign; greatest extent of Babylonian empire

600BCE

559 Cyrus the Great becomes king of Persia and begins to expand his empire
539 Cyrus conquers Babylonian empire
518 Persians conquer Indus Valley in India (outside map area)
513 Persians conquer south-east Europe

500BCE

490–479 Persians try but fail to conquer Greece (outside map area) — this is one of their few setbacks
485 Xerxes, king of Persia, destroys Babylon

400BCE

350 Persian empire dominates Middle East from north Africa to borders of India

300BCE

MACEDON

Mount Olympus
The Greeks believed that their gods and goddesses lived on top of this holy mountain.

Mount Olympus ◆

EPIRUS

Corcyra •

Painted pottery
Greek craftsmen produced decorated pots, showing the gods or scenes from their history.

Ambracia •

THESSALY

Public speaking
Greek city-states were the first democracies. Politicians spoke to large crowds of citizens.

horses were bred in Thessaly

Thermopylae •

AETOLIA

priestess consulting the Oracle at Delphi

BOEOTIA

Delphi •

Thebes •

Kephallenia

Olympic athletes
The ancient Olympic Games were held once every four years. Winners of each men-only event received a wreath of laurel leaves.

ATTICA
Marathon •
Athens •

Sykyon •
Megara •

ACHAEA
Corinth •

Argos •

Mantinea •

Olympia •

Tegea •

Acropolis
Originally a fort, the Acropolis at Athens was a great complex of shrines and temples dominating the city.

Ancient Greece

Ancient Greece was home to an impressive culture. It was the birthplace of democracy, and many Greek ideas and inventions in philosophy, theatre, architecture, mathematics and medicine still influence us today. Ancient Greece was made up of many independent city-states, which grew up from the 900s BCE. Each had its own laws and way of life. Each city had a market place at its heart, and a fort, or acropolis, built on high ground. City-states were competitive – they fought many wars and, although they formed alliances, they never united to become a country. Athens and Sparta were the most important city-states. Athens was a busy trading city and the first democracy. Sparta was a military state, where all male citizens had to be warriors. Throughout the Greek world, citizens built temples and theatres, where they held festivals involving plays, processions and games.

ARCADIA
Sparta •

Warrior state
The city-state of Sparta was known for its tough soldiers, called hoplites.

Mediterranean Sea

Kydonia •

CRETE

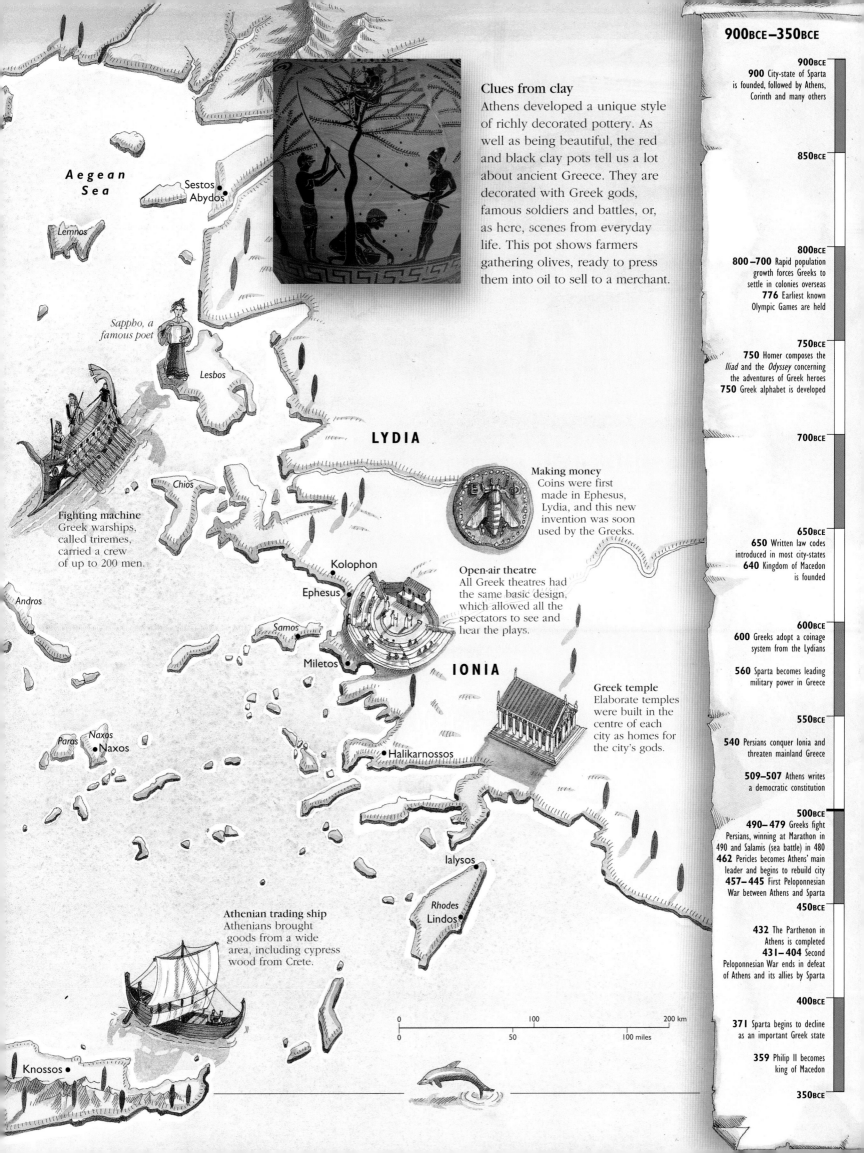

Clues from clay

Athens developed a unique style of richly decorated pottery. As well as being beautiful, the red and black clay pots tell us a lot about ancient Greece. They are decorated with Greek gods, famous soldiers and battles, or, as here, scenes from everyday life. This pot shows farmers gathering olives, ready to press them into oil to sell to a merchant.

Aegean Sea

Sestos
Abydos

Lemnos

Sappho, a famous poet

Lesbos

LYDIA

Chios

Fighting machine
Greek warships, called triremes, carried a crew of up to 200 men.

Making money
Coins were first made in Ephesus, Lydia, and this new invention was soon used by the Greeks.

Andros

Kolophon

Ephesus

Open-air theatre
All Greek theatres had the same basic design, which allowed all the spectators to see and hear the plays.

Samos

Miletos

IONIA

Greek temple
Elaborate temples were built in the centre of each city as homes for the city's gods.

Paros Naxos
       Naxos

Halikarnossos

Ialysos

Rhodes
Lindos

Athenian trading ship
Athenians brought goods from a wide area, including cypress wood from Crete.

0	100	200 km
0	50	100 miles

Knossos

900BCE
900 City-state of Sparta is founded, followed by Athens, Corinth and many others

850BCE

800BCE
800–700 Rapid population growth forces Greeks to settle in colonies overseas
776 Earliest known Olympic Games are held

750BCE
750 Homer composes the *Iliad* and the *Odyssey* concerning the adventures of Greek heroes
750 Greek alphabet is developed

700BCE

650BCE
650 Written law codes introduced in most city-states
640 Kingdom of Macedon is founded

600BCE
600 Greeks adopt a coinage system from the Lydians

560 Sparta becomes leading military power in Greece

550BCE
540 Persians conquer Ionia and threaten mainland Greece

509–507 Athens writes a democratic constitution

500BCE
490–479 Greeks fight Persians, winning at Marathon in 490 and Salamis (sea battle) in 480
462 Pericles becomes Athens' main leader and begins to rebuild city
457–445 First Peloponnesian War between Athens and Sparta

450BCE
432 The Parthenon in Athens is completed
431–404 Second Peloponnesian War ends in defeat of Athens and its allies by Sparta

400BCE
371 Sparta begins to decline as an important Greek state

359 Philip II becomes king of Macedon

350BCE

Ancient Greece:
The Greek world

From around 800BCE, the Greeks founded trading colonies around the shores of the Mediterranean and Black seas. Greece's population had been rising for some time but there was limited fertile land for growing crops to feed everyone. Spreading overseas solved this problem and made the Greeks richer at the same time. Some colonies were very successful, trading iron ore, tin, slaves and wheat in return for wine and other goods. They also spread Greek culture and language throughout a wide region. By the 300s, they had declined in importance as other states, especially Carthage, threatened their livelihood. Greece's fortunes changed, however, in 334, when Alexander the Great invaded the Persian Empire and made Greece the most important nation in the Middle East.

Greek culture

In their many colonies, the Greeks built amphitheatres, such as this one at Miletos in southwest Anatolia (modern-day Turkey), in which to stage plays and hold sporting events. The success of these colonies spread Greek language, literature, law, religion, philosophy, art and architecture far and wide throughout the Mediterranean world, particularly in Sicily and the Etruscan states of northern Italy, and brought great wealth back to Greece itself.

Alexander the Great

Alexander the Great was born in Macedon, northern Greece, in 356BCE. He became king after the death of his father, Philip, in 336, and after a series of epic marches and remarkable victories he conquered the Persian Empire. Although his empire fell apart after his death in 323, it left a lasting legacy of Greek cultural influence, known as Hellenism, that dominated the Mediterranean and the Middle East until the coming of Islam during the 7th century CE. This coin shows Alexander wearing an elephant-scalp headdress to commemorate his victories in India.

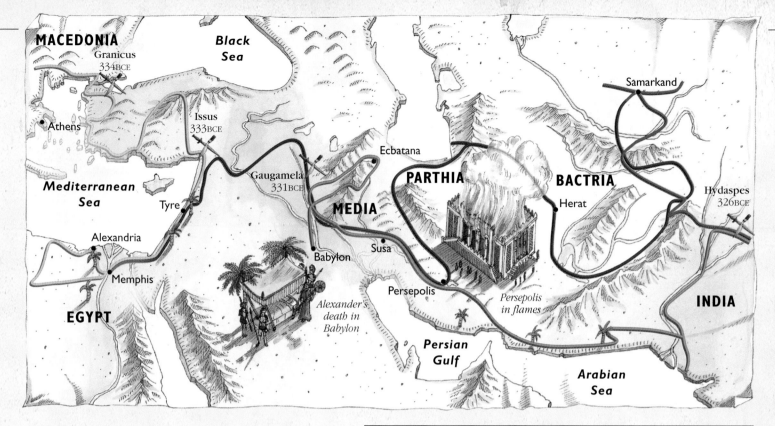

Black
Sea

Athens

Issus
333BCE

Ecbatana

Samarkand

PARTHIA

BACTRIA

Mediterranean
Sea

Tyre

Gaugamela
331BCE

MEDIA

Herat

Hydaspes
326BCE

Alexandria

Susa

Babylon

Memphis

Alexander's
death in
Babylon

Persepolis

EGYPT

*Persepolis
in flames*

INDIA

Persian
Gulf

Arabian
Sea

Conquering the world

Alexander and his army crossed into Asia in 334 and
defeated a Persian army by the River Granicus. He beat
an even larger Persian army at Issus in 333BCE. Having
conquered Egypt, he headed into the heart of the
Persian Empire, defeating the Persians for the third
time at Gaugamela. His march took him into central
Asia – destroying the Persian capital, Persepolis, along
the way – and on into India, where he achieved his
final victory. He died in Babylon in 323, aged only 32.

Alexander's legacy

Alexander left an immense legacy. His empire stretched
from Egypt to India and into central Asia, and at least 20
cities bore his name. Alexandria in Egypt soon became
one of the greatest cities in the ancient world. It boasted
a vast library said to contain all human knowledge
of the time. In 2003CE, a vast new library (right) opened
in Alexandria to commemorate the ancient library.

KEY TO MAP:	lines show four stages in Alexander's march
✕ Battle	334–331BCE 329–326BCE
	331–329BCE 326–323BCE

Alexander the Conqueror

Alexander was a superb military commander,
leading his Macedon troops into battle
often against overwhelming Persian
strength. At the Battle of Issus in
November 333, Alexander, seen
here on horseback on the left of
this mosaic, came face to face with
the Persian emperor Darius, riding
in a war chariot. After his army
was defeated, Darius was forced
to flee the battlefield, leaving
behind most of his family and
a vast amount of treasures.

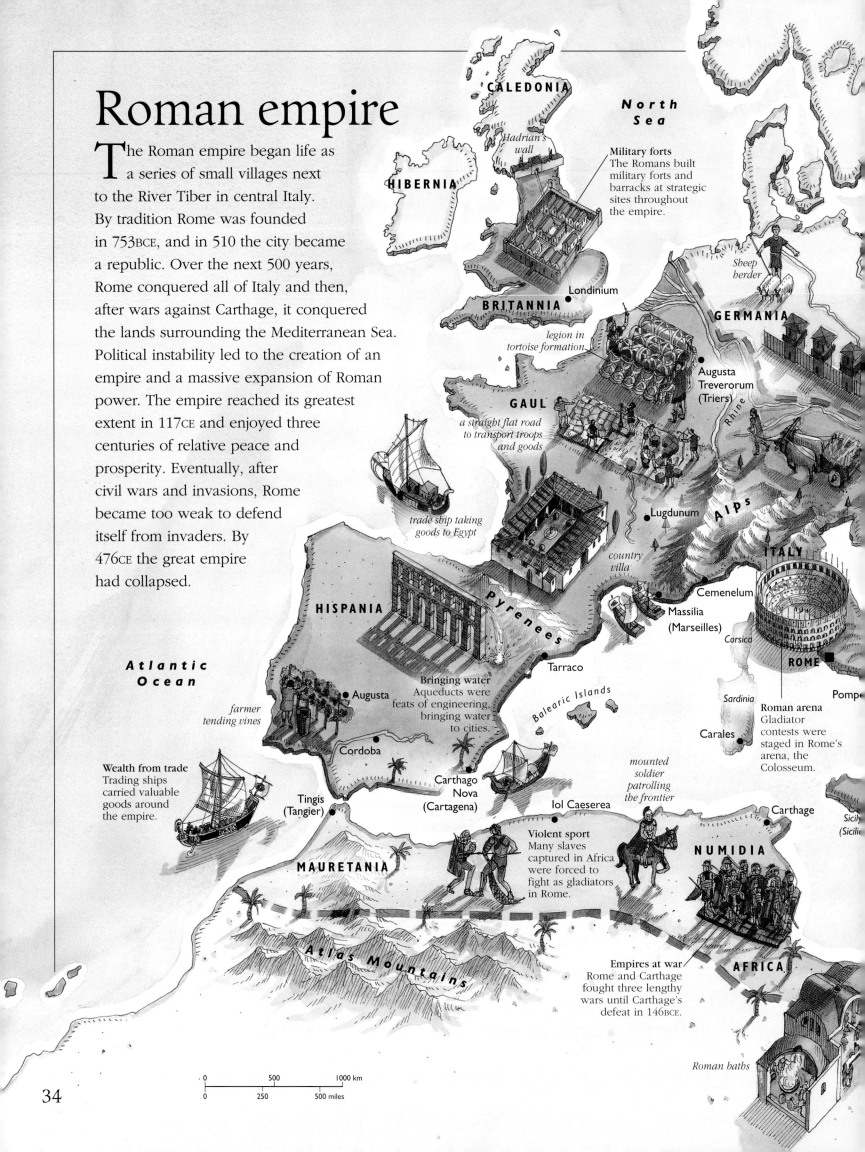

Roman empire

The Roman empire began life as a series of small villages next to the River Tiber in central Italy. By tradition Rome was founded in 753BCE, and in 510 the city became a republic. Over the next 500 years, Rome conquered all of Italy and then, after wars against Carthage, it conquered the lands surrounding the Mediterranean Sea. Political instability led to the creation of an empire and a massive expansion of Roman power. The empire reached its greatest extent in 117CE and enjoyed three centuries of relative peace and prosperity. Eventually, after civil wars and invasions, Rome became too weak to defend itself from invaders. By 476CE the great empire had collapsed.

CALEDONIA

North Sea

HIBERNIA

Hadrian's wall

Military forts
The Romans built military forts and barracks at strategic sites throughout the empire.

Sheep herder

Londinium

BRITANNIA

GERMANIA

legion in tortoise formation

Augusta Treverorum (Triers)

GAUL

a straight flat road to transport troops and goods

Rhine

trade ship taking goods to Egypt

Lugdunum

Alps

country villa

ITALY

Cemenelum

Massilia (Marseilles)

Corsica

ROME

HISPANIA

Pyrenees

Pomp

Atlantic Ocean

farmer tending vines

Augusta

Bringing water
Aqueducts were feats of engineering, bringing water to cities.

Tarraco

Balearic Islands

Sardinia

Roman arena
Gladiator contests were staged in Rome's arena, the Colosseum.

Carales

Cordoba

Wealth from trade
Trading ships carried valuable goods around the empire.

Tingis (Tangier)

Carthago Nova (Cartagena)

Iol Caeserea

mounted soldier patrolling the frontier

Carthage

Sicily (Sicili

MAURETANIA

Violent sport
Many slaves captured in Africa were forced to fight as gladiators in Rome.

NUMIDIA

Atlas Mountains

AFRICA

Empires at war
Rome and Carthage fought three lengthy wars until Carthage's defeat in 146BCE.

0	500	1000 km
0	250	500 miles

Roman baths

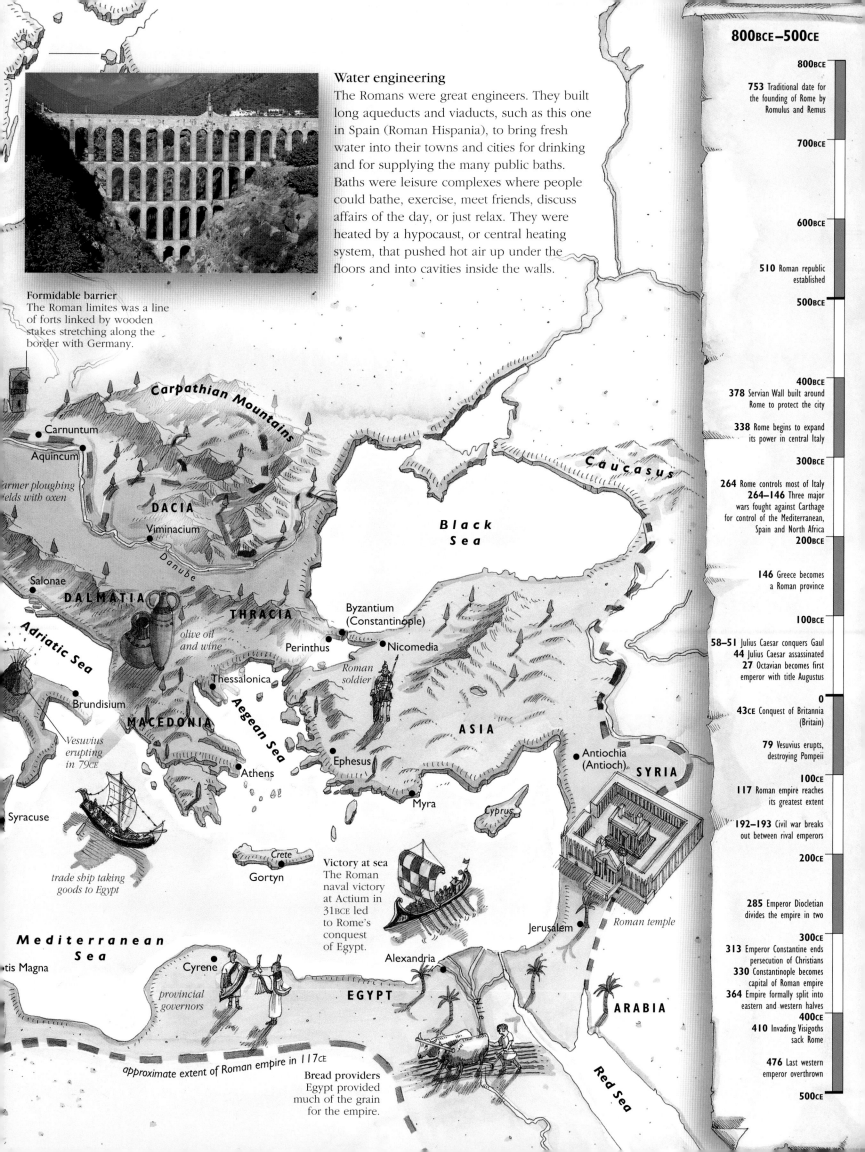

Water engineering

The Romans were great engineers. They built long aqueducts and viaducts, such as this one in Spain (Roman Hispania), to bring fresh water into their towns and cities for drinking and for supplying the many public baths. Baths were leisure complexes where people could bathe, exercise, meet friends, discuss affairs of the day, or just relax. They were heated by a hypocaust, or central heating system, that pushed hot air up under the floors and into cavities inside the walls.

Formidable barrier
The Roman limites was a line of forts linked by wooden stakes stretching along the border with Germany.

farmer ploughing fields with oxen

Carpathian Mountains

Carnuntum

Aquincum

DACIA

Viminacium

Danube

Salonae

DALMATIA

olive oil and wine

Adriatic Sea

Brundisium

Vesuvius erupting in 79CE

MACEDONIA

Thessalonica

THRACIA

Byzantium (Constantinople)

Perinthus

Nicomedia

Roman soldier

Aegean Sea

Athens

Ephesus

ASIA

Myra

Cyprus

Syracuse

trade ship taking goods to Egypt

Crete

Gortyn

Victory at sea
The Roman naval victory at Actium in 31BCE led to Rome's conquest of Egypt.

C a u c a s u s

Black Sea

Antiochia (Antioch)

SYRIA

Jerusalem

Roman temple

Alexandria

M e d i t e r r a n e a n S e a

tis Magna

Cyrene

provincial governors

EGYPT

ARABIA

Nile

Red Sea

approximate extent of Roman empire in 117CE

Bread providers
Egypt provided much of the grain for the empire.

800BCE–500CE

800BCE

753 Traditional date for the founding of Rome by Romulus and Remus

700BCE

600BCE

510 Roman republic established

500BCE

400BCE
378 Servian Wall built around Rome to protect the city

338 Rome begins to expand its power in central Italy

300BCE

264 Rome controls most of Italy
264–146 Three major wars fought against Carthage for control of the Mediterranean, Spain and North Africa

200BCE

146 Greece becomes a Roman province

100BCE

58–51 Julius Caesar conquers Gaul
44 Julius Caesar assassinated
27 Octavian becomes first emperor with title Augustus

0

43CE Conquest of Britannia (Britain)

79 Vesuvius erupts, destroying Pompeii

100CE

117 Roman empire reaches its greatest extent

192–193 Civil war breaks out between rival emperors

200CE

285 Emperor Diocletian divides the empire in two

300CE
313 Emperor Constantine ends persecution of Christians
330 Constantinople becomes capital of Roman empire
364 Empire formally split into eastern and western halves
400CE
410 Invading Visigoths sack Rome

476 Last western emperor overthrown

500CE

Roman empire:
The city of Rome

The imperial city of Rome, capital of the Roman empire, was by far the grandest and most important city in Europe. It was a vast but often shabby city. The first emperor, Augustus (ruled 27BCE–14CE), decided to make it beautiful, too, clearing away narrow streets and building public baths, theatres and temples. He set up a police and fire service to keep its citizens safe, and dredged and widened the River Tiber to prevent its frequent floods. By the end of the 1st century CE, Rome was a showcase for its empire, designed to impress visitors and enemies with the might of the Roman Empire.

Ruling the empire

From 27BCE to 476CE, Rome was governed by emperors. Some, such as Augustus, were outstanding, while others were brutal dictators or madmen. Beneath the emperor was the Senate, an unelected group of about 600 rich men called senators (below), who passed laws, controlled the treasury, and appointed governors to those Roman provinces not run by the emperor himself.

Street life

The streets of Rome were packed with shops selling every type of produce. Bread was made on shop premises (above), while traders brought in fresh food and other goods from outside the city on handcarts, and stocked up their shops each night ready for sale next day. Every street had its local bar, where wine and other drinks were sold, as well as many workshops, where everything from furniture and pots to fine clothes and jewellery were made. Although the main streets were swept clean, most of the smaller ones were very dirty, as people threw their rubbish out of their windows. At night, the city was pitch dark, for there was no street lighting.

Women were separated from men and watched events from their own terrace at the top of the building

City plan

At the centre of Rome was the Forum, the political, judicial and commercial heart of the city and the empire. Here the Senate met to pass laws, and magistrates judged important legal cases. As the empire grew, successive emperors added new buildings to enlarge the Forum. The city also contained public baths, fed by water brought from outside the city by aqueduct, and many public squares and open spaces. A massive stone wall surrounded the city to keep it safe from attack.

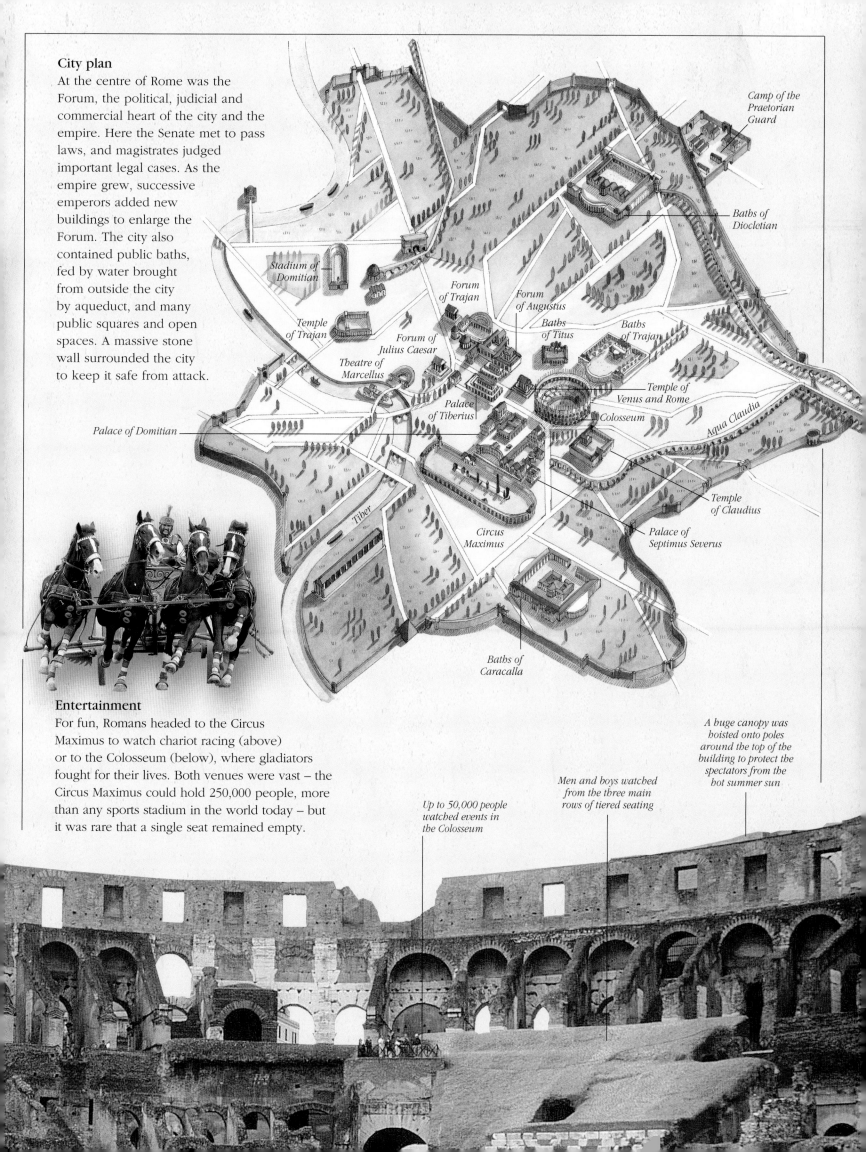

Camp of the Praetorian Guard

Baths of Diocletian

Stadium of Domitian

Forum of Trajan

Forum of Augustus

Temple of Trajan

Forum of Julius Caesar

Baths of Titus

Baths of Trajan

Theatre of Marcellus

Palace of Tiberius

Temple of Venus and Rome

Colosseum

Aqua Claudia

Palace of Domitian

Temple of Claudius

Circus Maximus

Palace of Septimus Severus

Tiber

Baths of Caracalla

Entertainment

For fun, Romans headed to the Circus Maximus to watch chariot racing (above) or to the Colosseum (below), where gladiators fought for their lives. Both venues were vast – the Circus Maximus could hold 250,000 people, more than any sports stadium in the world today – but it was rare that a single seat remained empty.

A huge canopy was hoisted onto poles around the top of the building to protect the spectators from the hot summer sun

Men and boys watched from the three main rows of tiered seating

Up to 50,000 people watched events in the Colosseum

Ancient Africa

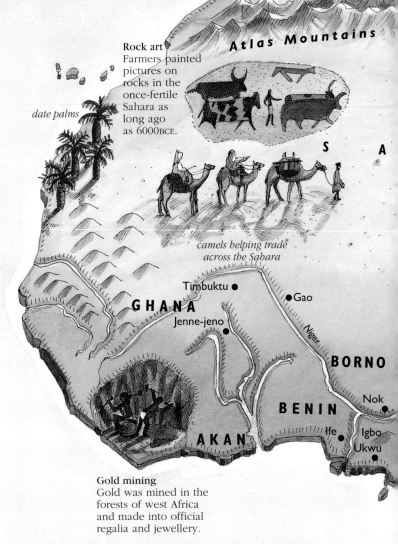

Rock art
Farmers painted pictures on rocks in the once-fertile Sahara as long ago as 6000BCE.

date palms

camels helping trade across the Sahara

About 5,500 years ago, the grassy plains of the Sahara began to dry out and turn to desert, cutting Africa in half. Until the introduction of the camel from Arabia in about 100BCE, there was little communication across this sandy desert. Many great civilizations flourished south of the Sahara. The oldest of these was in Nubia on the upper reaches of the Nile. At one time the Nubian kingdom was so powerful it ruled all of Egypt, but its successor Meroë was eventually conquered by the Christian kingdom of Axum, forerunner of modern-day Ethiopia. In the west, the people of Nok learned to work iron, and produced beautiful terracotta figures. The neighbouring Bantus were also skilled ironworkers, gradually spreading their language and technology east and south to all but the very southern tip of Africa. In many places, however, Africans remained in the Stone Age, hunting and gathering their food from the forests and plains around them.

Gold mining
Gold was mined in the forests of west Africa and made into official regalia and jewellery.

Atlantic Ocean

Nok culture

From about 500BCE, Nok craftworkers produced beautiful terracotta heads and figures, among the earliest surviving artworks from Africa south of the Sahara. They also learned to smelt iron ore to produce weapons and tools, a valuable skill when most of their enemies had only wooden spears and stones to use against them. Further up the Niger river valley, the city of Jenne-jeno, the earliest-known town in sub-Saharan Africa, became the hub of trade across the Sahara, where traders used camels to carry gold, silver, ivory and salt across the desert.

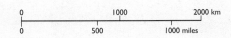

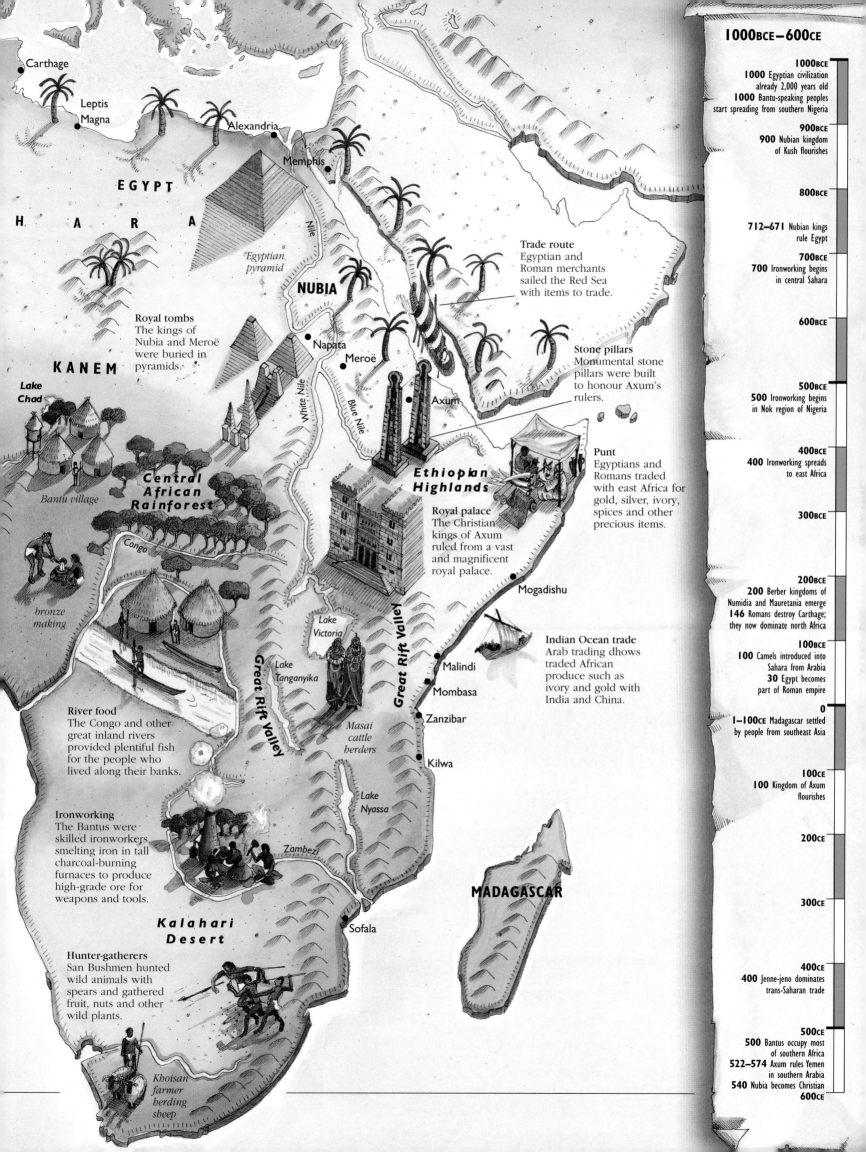

Carthage

Leptis
Magna

Alexandria

Memphis

EGYPT

S A H A R A

Egyptian pyramid

NUBIA

Nile

Royal tombs
The kings of
Nubia and Meroë
were buried in
pyramids.

KANEM

*Lake
Chad*

Napata

Meroë

White Nile

Blue Nile

Bantu village

**Central
African
Rainforest**

Congo

*bronze
making*

Axum

**Ethiopian
Highlands**

Royal palace
The Christian
kings of Axum
ruled from a vast
and magnificent
royal palace.

Trade route
Egyptian and
Roman merchants
sailed the Red Sea
with items to trade.

Stone pillars
Monumental stone
pillars were built
to honour Axum's
rulers.

Punt
Egyptians and
Romans traded
with east Africa for
gold, silver, ivory,
spices and other
precious items.

Mogadishu

River food
The Congo and other
great inland rivers
provided plentiful fish
for the people who
lived along their banks.

Ironworking
The Bantus were
skilled ironworkers,
smelting iron in tall
charcoal-burning
furnaces to produce
high-grade ore for
weapons and tools.

*Lake
Victoria*

*Lake
Tanganyika*

Great Rift Valley

Great Rift Valley

*Masai
cattle
herders*

Malindi

Mombasa

Zanzibar

Kilwa

*Lake
Nyassa*

Zambezi

Indian Ocean trade
Arab trading dhows
traded African
produce such as
ivory and gold with
India and China.

MADAGASCAR

**Kalahari
Desert**

Sofala

Hunter-gatherers
San Bushmen hunted
wild animals with
spears and gathered
fruit, nuts and other
wild plants.

*Khoisan
farmer herding
sheep*

1000BCE–600CE

1000BCE
1000 Egyptian civilization
already 2,000 years old
1000 Bantu-speaking peoples
start spreading from southern Nigeria

900BCE
900 Nubian kingdom
of Kush flourishes

800BCE

712–671 Nubian kings
rule Egypt

700BCE
700 Ironworking begins
in central Sahara

600BCE

500BCE
500 Ironworking begins
in Nok region of Nigeria

400BCE
400 Ironworking spreads
to east Africa

300BCE

200BCE
200 Berber kingdoms of
Numidia and Mauretania emerge
146 Romans destroy Carthage;
they now dominate north Africa

100BCE
100 Camels introduced into
Sahara from Arabia
30 Egypt becomes
part of Roman empire

0
1–100CE Madagascar settled
by people from southeast Asia

100CE
100 Kingdom of Axum
flourishes

200CE

300CE

400CE
400 Jenne-jeno dominates
trans-Saharan trade

500CE
500 Bantus occupy most
of southern Africa
522–574 Axum rules Yemen
in southern Arabia
540 Nubia becomes Christian

600CE

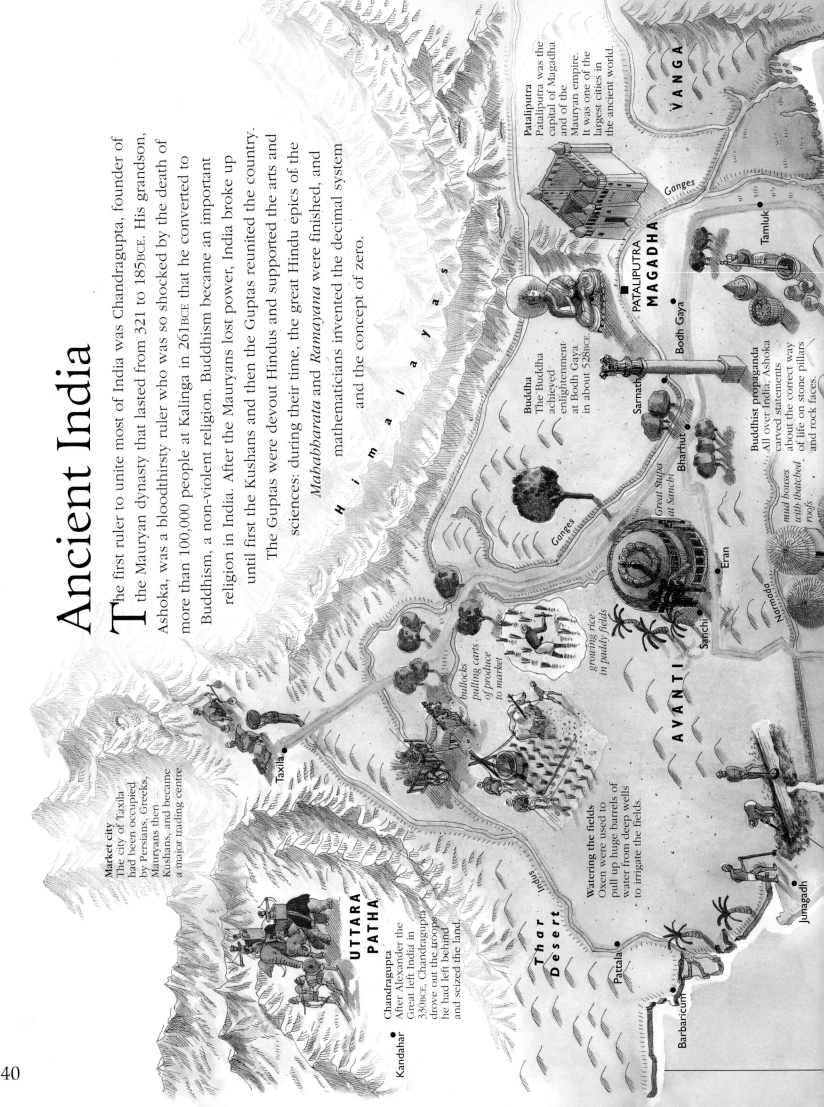

Ancient India

The first ruler to unite most of India was Chandragupta, founder of the Mauryan dynasty that lasted from 321 to 185BCE. His grandson, Ashoka, was a bloodthirsty ruler who was so shocked by the death of more than 100,000 people at Kalinga in 261BCE that he converted to Buddhism, a non-violent religion. Buddhism became an important religion in India. After the Mauryans lost power, India broke up until first the Kushans and then the Guptas reunited the country. The Guptas were devout Hindus and supported the arts and sciences: during their time, the great Hindu epics of the *Mahabharata* and *Ramayana* were finished, and mathematicians invented the decimal system and the concept of zero.

Market city
The city of Taxila had been occupied by Persians, Greeks, Mauryans then Kushans, and became a major trading centre.

● **Chandragupta**
After Alexander the Great left India in 330BCE, Chandragupta drove out the troops he had left behind and seized the land.

UTTARA PATHA

● Kandahar

bullocks pulling carts of produce to market

growing rice in paddy fields

Watering the fields.
Oxen were used to pull up huge barrels of water from deep wells to irrigate the fields.

Taxila ●

Thar Desert

Indus

Pattala ●

Barbaricum

Junagadh

AVANTI

Sanchi ●

Great Stupa at Sanchi

Eran ●

Narmada

Ganges

mud houses with thatched roofs

Buddhist propaganda
All over India, Ashoka carved statements about the correct way of life on stone pillars and rock faces.

Bharhut ●

Sarnath ●

Bodh Gaya ●

Buddha
The Buddha achieved enlightenment at Bodh Gaya in about 528BCE.

PATALIPUTRA
■ PATALIPUTRA
MAGADHA

Tamluk ●

Ganges

H i m a l a y a s

Pataliputra
Pataliputra was the capital of Magadha and of the Mauryan empire. It was one of the largest cities in the ancient world.

V A N G A

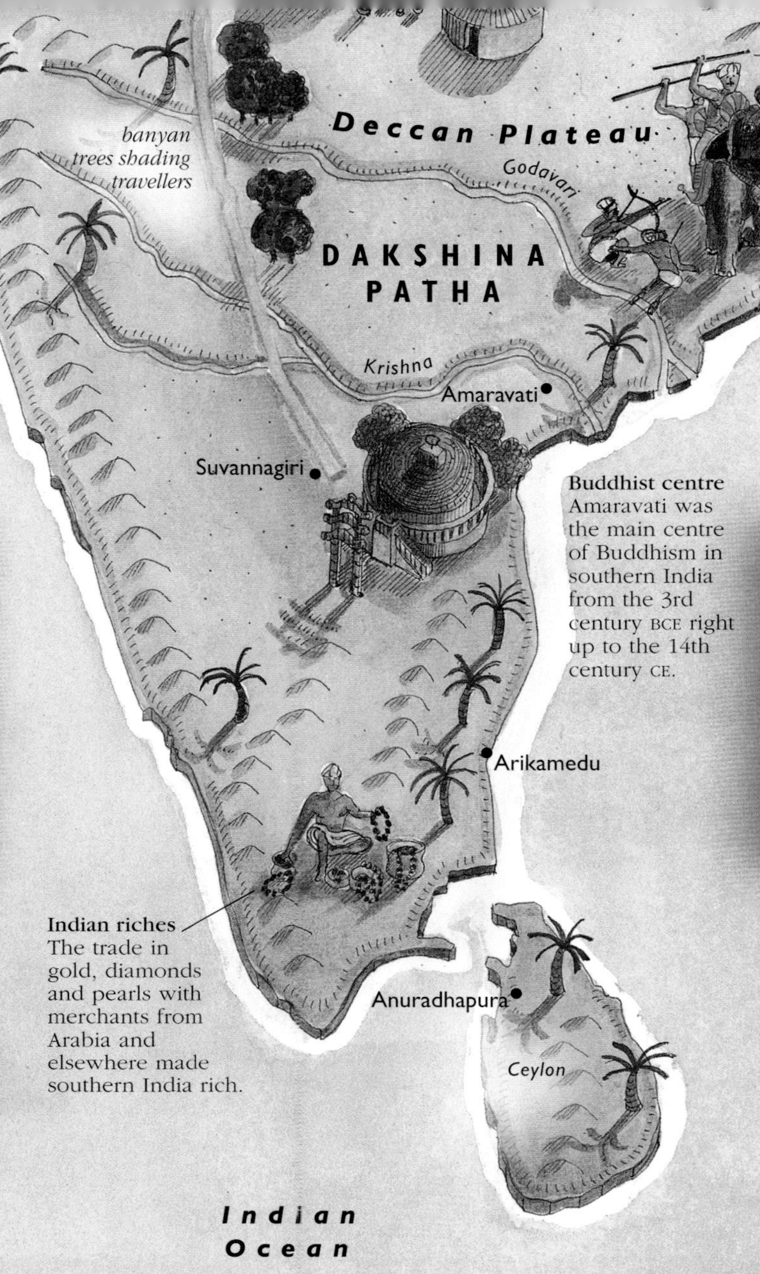

500BCE
500 Magadha is the main Hindu kingdom in northern India
500 The *Mahabharata* is first written down
483 Vijaya founds first kingdom in Ceylon
483 Death of Buddha

400BCE
364 Under the Nanda dynasty, Magadha dominates the Ganges Valley
327–325 Alexander the Great conquers Indus Valley
321 Chandragupta Maurya seizes power in Magadha

300BCE
300 The *Ramayana* is written down
293 Chandragupta Maurya abdicates in favour of Bindusara Maurya, who conquers southern India
268–233 Ashoka rules Mauryan empire

200BCE
185 Mauryan empire overthrown

100BCE

0

50CE Kushans conquer northwest India

100CE
130 Kushan empire at its peak

200CE
200 Hindu laws are first written down

300CE
320–335 Chandragupta I, founder of Mauryan dynasty, rules
335–380 Samudragupta conquers Kushan empire
380 Chandragupta II conquers western India

400CE

500CE
510 Gupta empire begins to decline, finally ending in 720
575 Indian mathematicians develop decimal system and concept of zero

600CE

Bay of Bengal

Battle of Kalinga
After the bloody and brutal conquest of Kalinga in 261BCE, Ashoka converted to Buddhism, which preaches non-violence.

Deccan Plateau

Godavari

DAKSHINA PATHA

Krishna

Amaravati

Buddhist centre
Amaravati was the main centre of Buddhism in southern India from the 3rd century BCE right up to the 14th century CE.

Suvannagiri

Arikamedu

Anuradhapura

Ceylon

Indian Ocean

State irrigation
The Mauryans built a massive dam, reservoir and irrigation project at Junagadh.

banyan trees shading travellers

Arabian Sea

Indian riches
The trade in gold, diamonds and pearls with merchants from Arabia and elsewhere made southern India rich.

800 km

400 miles

400

200

400

200

0

0

Hinduism

Hinduism is the world's oldest religion. The word Hindu comes from the Persian word *sindhu*, or 'river', for the religion began among the people who lived in the Indus Valley cities of Mohenjo-Daro and Harappa about 5,000 years ago. The Hindu scriptures were first written down in about 900BCE, by which time Hinduism was the major religion of India. There is no single belief in Hinduism, which has many gods. Their stories are written down in such epics as the Ramayana, a scene from which is shown above.

Buddhism

Siddhartha Gautama (c. 563–483BCE) was born a wealthy prince in northern India. He was distressed by the poverty he saw, and after his 'enlightenment' in about 528BCE he developed the Buddhist religion of non-violence and correct behaviour. At first, Buddhism was one of many religions in India, but when King Ashoka converted to it in 260, the religion spread. Ashoka built the Great Stupa at Sanchi (above) to house the remains of the Buddha's body.

Ancient China

In 221BCE, Zheng, ruler of Qin in central China, defeated his rivals and united China. He took the title Qin Shi Huangdi, or 'first sovereign Qin emperor'. Ever since 1122BCE, China had in theory been united under the Zhou kings, but real power lay with the many provincial leaders, who often had more power than the king himself. Shi Huangdi changed all this by setting up a strong state where all power rested with the emperor. He built the Great Wall to keep out invaders, as well as many roads and canals, but after his death a civil war broke out and the Han dynasty of rulers came to power in 202BCE. The Han expanded the empire south and east, but when they were overthrown in 220CE, China split into three kingdoms.

The Great Wall
The first emperor joined various state and city walls to form a single barrier 3,460km across the north of China. It was built of rammed earth reinforced with brushwood.

Dunhuang

The Silk Road
Merchants used camels to carry silk and other valuable goods along the Silk Road, which connected China to western Asia and Europe.

Huang He (Yellow River)

Qin Mountains

Silk Road

Qin

Buddhism
In about 100CE, Indian monks brought Buddhism to China.

Terracotta army
When Qin Shi Huangdi died, he was buried with 7,000 lifelike terracotta soldiers, to guard him in the afterlife.

tea growing in hilly areas

Jiaozhi

Buddhism
The Buddhist religion was introduced to China by monks from India – one of whom is shown here with Buddha himself – around 100CE. The peaceful teachings of Buddhism appealed to the Chinese during the troubled years after the fall of the Han dynasty in 220CE, and it soon became one of China's three major religions, alongside Confucianism and Daoism. The monks travelled into China along the Silk Road, a series of trade routes that connected the major cities of China with central Asia, the eastern Mediterranean and eventually Rome. Merchants travelled the road carrying silk, jade and, much later, fine porcelain.

MONGOLIA

Nomads
Warlike nomads living on the grassy steppes of central Asia often threatened China and sometimes invaded it. The Great Wall was built to keep them out.

traders bringing furs from Siberia

Loulang

teams of oxen ploughing the fields

Ji

Yinjang

person doing calligraphy

Huang He (Yellow River)

Linzi

coin with hole so it could be kept on a string

Qufu

Silk
The Chinese discovered how to make silk from the cocoon of the silkworm in about 500BCE. Only very important people were allowed to wear silk.

Xianyang

farmers using foot-driven irrigation machine

Chang'an

Luoyang

Gaixia

Nanjing

royal palace at Xianyang

Huai

Yellow Sea

Wu

Yangtze

Han

Boundary of Han Empire

Ying

The Han dynasty
At the battle of Gaixia in 202BCE, the Han ruler Gaozu established his supremacy over the whole of China.

Navigation
The Chinese invented the magnetic compass and used it to navigate successfully at sea.

rice planting in a paddy field

Keeping control
The first emperor burned the books of scholars who disagreed with him, and executed his opponents.

Lingling

Nanhai

Paper-making
Paper was made by pulping and then drying and pressing the fibres from silk rags, bamboo and mulberry bark.

South China Sea

Hainan

| 0 | 250 | 500 km |
| 0 | 125 | 250 miles |

600BCE–600CE

600BCE

551–479 Life of Confucius (a Chinese religious teacher)

500BCE

480–256 Warring States period as rival leaders fight for control of Zhou-led China

400BCE

361–338 Shang Yang turns Qin into strong, centralized state

315 Qin becomes the dominant state in China

300BCE

230–221 Zheng unites China
221 Zheng takes title Qin Shi Huangdi
209–202 Civil war leads to overthrow of Qin dynasty; Han dynasty set up

200BCE

150 Widespread use of iron weapons and tools

128–36 Xiongnu nomads in north pacified during long campaign

100BCE

100 Sima Qian writes first history of China

0

9–23CE Han dynasty briefly overthrown

100CE

100 Buddhism introduced into China
105 Paper first made in the imperial workshops
126 Major peasant revolt against landlords

200CE

220 Last Han emperor deposed; China splits into three kingdoms
280 China briefly reunited
291–308 'Rebellion of the eight princes' leads to break-up of northern China into many states

300CE

386–439 Toba nomads from Mongolia invade and conquer northern China

400CE

500CE

581 Yang Jian founds Sui dynasty in northern China
589 Yang Jian reunifies China under Sui dynasty

600CE

North American peoples

The first people arrived in North America from Siberia over the land bridge that existed about 17,000 years ago. They slowly moved southwards, spreading out over the vast plains, woodlands, deserts and mountains of the continent, living as hunter-gatherers as they went. From about 700BCE, the Adena people of the Ohio river valley began to cultivate wild plants for food, and built sacred earthworks and burial mounds. The later Hopewell people, who spread out from the Ohio into the Mississippi Valley, built towns, burial mounds, and a huge earthwork in the shape of a snake, although no one really knows why they did this. The people of the southwestern deserts began to settle down in farming communities by about 300CE, eventually building complex villages of adobe (dried mud) brick houses. In the far north of America, the Inuit learned how to live in the cold conditions, trapping wild animals for their fur, meat and bone.

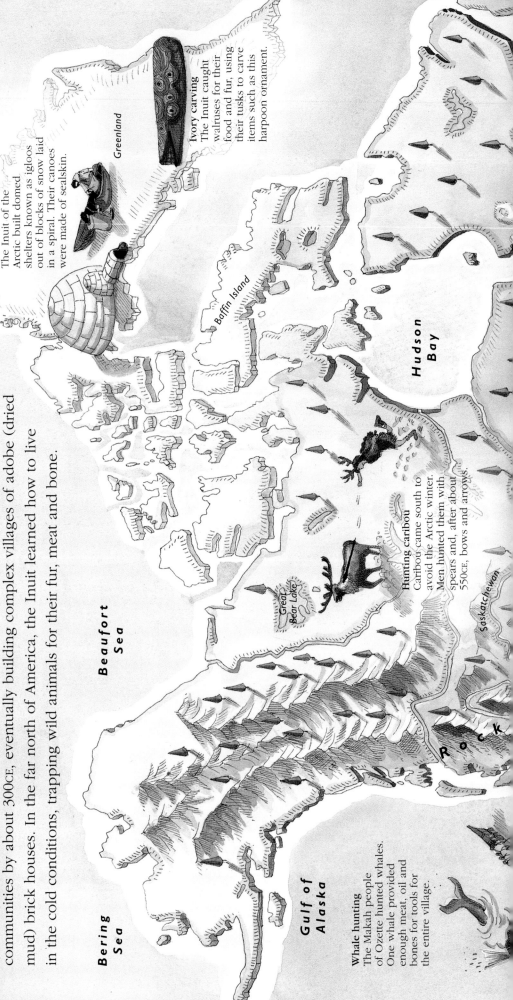

Greenland

The Inuit
The Inuit of the Arctic built domed shelters known as igloos out of blocks of snow laid in a spiral. Their canoes were made of sealskin.

Ivory carving
The Inuit caught walruses for their food and fur, using their tusks to carve items such as this harpoon ornament.

Greenland Sea

Baffin Island

Hudson Bay

Beaufort Sea

Hunting caribou
Caribou came south to avoid the Arctic winter. Men hunted them with spears and, after about 550CE, bows and arrows.

Great Bear Lake

Saskatchewan

R o c k

Bering Sea

Gulf of Alaska

Whale hunting
The Makah people of Ozette hunted whales. One whale provided enough meat, oil and bones for tools for the entire village.

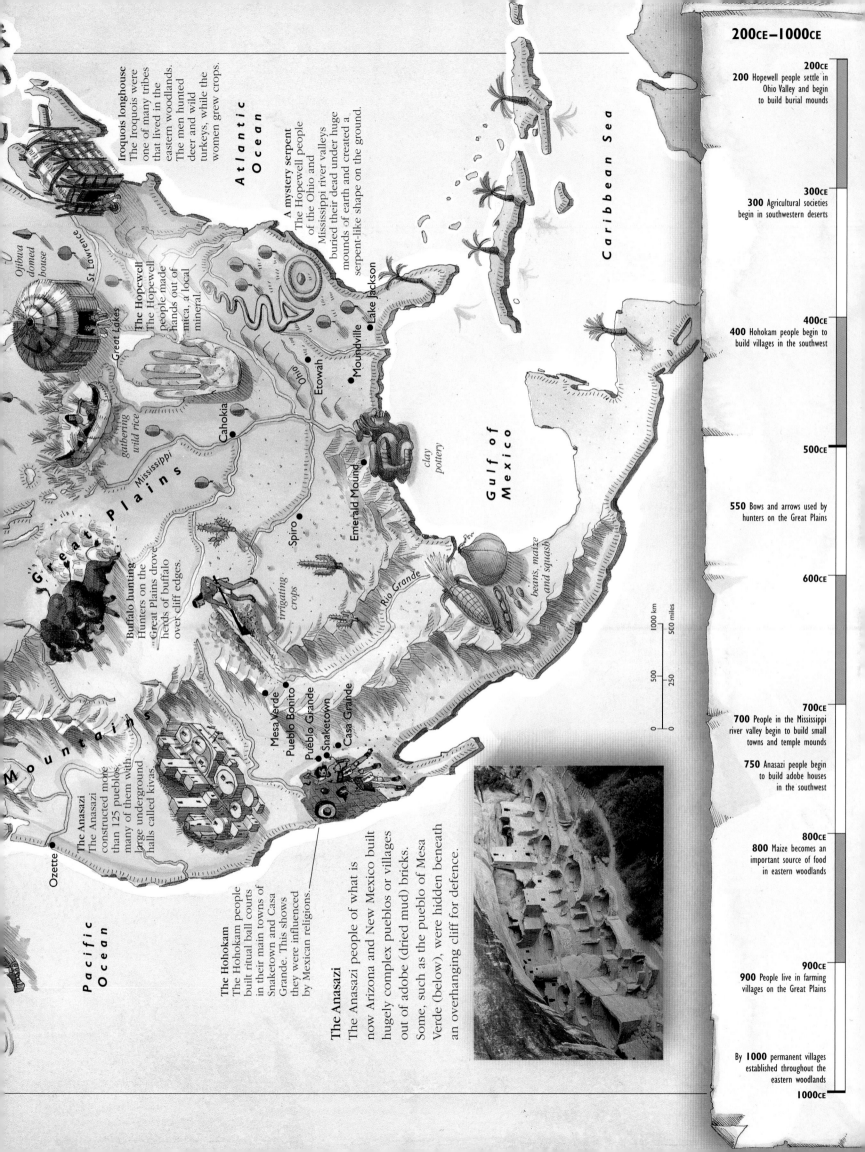

200CE–1000CE

200CE
200 Hopewell people settle in Ohio Valley and begin to build burial mounds

300CE
300 Agricultural societies begin in southwestern deserts

400CE
400 Hohokam people begin to build villages in the southwest

500CE
550 Bows and arrows used by hunters on the Great Plains

600CE

700CE
700 People in the Mississippi river valley begin to build small towns and temple mounds

750 Anasazi people begin to build adobe houses in the southwest

800CE
800 Maize becomes an important source of food in eastern woodlands

900CE
900 People live in farming villages on the Great Plains

By **1000** permanent villages established throughout the eastern woodlands

1000CE

Iroquois longhouse
The Iroquois were one of many tribes that lived in the eastern woodlands. The men hunted deer and wild turkeys, while the women grew crops.

Ojibwa domed house

The Hopewell
The Hopewell people made hands out of mica, a local mineral.

A mystery serpent
The Hopewell people of the Ohio and Mississippi river valleys buried their dead under huge mounds of earth and created a serpent-like shape on the ground.

Buffalo hunting
Hunters on the Great Plains drove herds of buffalo over cliff edges.

The Hohokam
The Hohokam people built ritual ball courts in their main towns of Snaketown and Casa Grande. This shows they were influenced by Mexican religions.

The Anasazi
The Anasazi constructed more than 125 pueblos, many of them with large underground halls called kivas.

The Anasazi
The Anasazi people of what is now Arizona and New Mexico built hugely complex pueblos or villages out of adobe (dried mud) bricks. Some, such as the pueblo of Mesa Verde (below), were hidden beneath an overhanging cliff for defence.

Atlantic Ocean

Caribbean Sea

Great Lakes

St Lawrence

Lake Jackson
Moundville
Etowah
Ohio
Cahokia
Mississippi

Great Plains

gathering wild rice

Spiro
Emerald Mound

Gulf of Mexico

clay pottery

Rio Grande

irrigating crops

beans, maize and squash

Mountains

Mesa Verde
Pueblo Bonito
Pueblo Grande
Snaketown
Casa Grande

Ozette

Pacific Ocean

1000 km
500 miles
500
250
0

Central and South America

A series of ancient civilizations, most based around a single city, rose and fell in Central and South America between 1000BCE and 1000CE. The Olmecs built ceremonial earth pyramid mounds and carved huge stone sculptures. To their north, the city of Teotihuacan grew larger than Rome and contained the biggest building in the ancient Americas: the Pyramid of the Sun. The major civilization in the region was the Maya, who built massive pyramid temple complexes and were skilled mathematicians and astronomers. In South America, Andean people built a huge stone temple mound with rooms filled with stone carvings of their gods. The Moche were skilled pottery makers, while the stonemasons of Tiahuanaco built vast temples and palaces.

Teotihuacan
The city of Teotihuacan started as a small village but grew by 500CE to cover 20km² and house perhaps 200,000 people. At its centre were the vast pyramids of the Sun and Moon.

nose pendant (worn by nobility)

Mayan temple
The Mayans built their temples on top of stepped pyramids. A new temple was dedicated to the gods by sacrificing prisoners captured during a war.

Mayan writing
The Maya wrote with hieroglyphic picture writing. Each glyph represented a syllable.

Pyramid at Copán
Copán was one of the most important cites in the Mayan empire and flourished during the 600s. The ruler of Copán was buried in this step pyramid which dominates the city.

Gulf of Mexico

Olmec stone sculpture

Mayan men playing ball game

Tres Zapotes

Teotihuacan

Monte Alban

San Lorenzo

Palenque

Yucatán Peninsula

Chichén Itzá

Tikal

Copán

jaguar

wild turkey kept for food

jade necklace from Teotihuacan

fishing from a reed boat

Caribbean sea

Pacific Ocean

weaving with alpaca and llama wool

Andes

Andes

gold panning in Andean streams

steep hillsides terraced and irrigated for farming

fishing on Lake Titicaca

Lake Titicaca

Tiahuanaco

Alto Rairez

San Pedro de Atacama

Tiahuanaco
The highest city in the Andes controlled a large empire. At its heart was a precinct of temples and palaces and the stone Gateway of the Sun.

Mocbe warrior graves

Moche
Cerro Vicus
Pampa Grande

Moche, capital of the Moche state, contained two huge adobe (mud-brick) platforms dedicated to the sun and moon and a vast royal burial site.

Viracocha

Moche

Pañamarca

maize grown in irrigated fields

Huarpa

Huari

Nazca

Pampa Ingenio

Nazca Lines
The Nazca people drew huge geometric shapes and outlines of animals, birds and insects in the desert sands.

The Maya

The Maya settled in central America from about 1000BCE. They began to build temple pyramids on which to worship their gods and by 350BCE were creating powerful city-states, such as Palenque, Tikal and Copán. The Mayans created the only complete picture writing system in the ancient Americas. It was a sophisticated system that could fully express their entire spoken language. They were also skilled mathematicians and studied the stars to draw up a detailed calendar that told them when eclipses of the sun and moon occurred.

Maya city-states dominated the region from 300 to 800CE, but then went into decline for reasons no one today fully understands. The exception was the northern city of Chichén Itzá, founded in about 850CE, which was dominated by the Castillo pyramid shown above. Eventually Chichén Itzá itself declined and was overrun by the Toltecs, which brought Mayan civilization to an end.

The Nazca

The Nazca people, like many others in South America, were skilled potters, creating this beautiful painted vase showing men hunting vicuna, a llama-like animal. The Nazca lived in the coastal plains of Peru, much of which was hot, dry desert. Here, they scratched into the sand vast outlines of figures, including a spider, a hummingbird and a monkey, and geometric shapes. These shapes are so big that they can only be seen properly from the sky. No one really knows why the Nazca created these shapes.

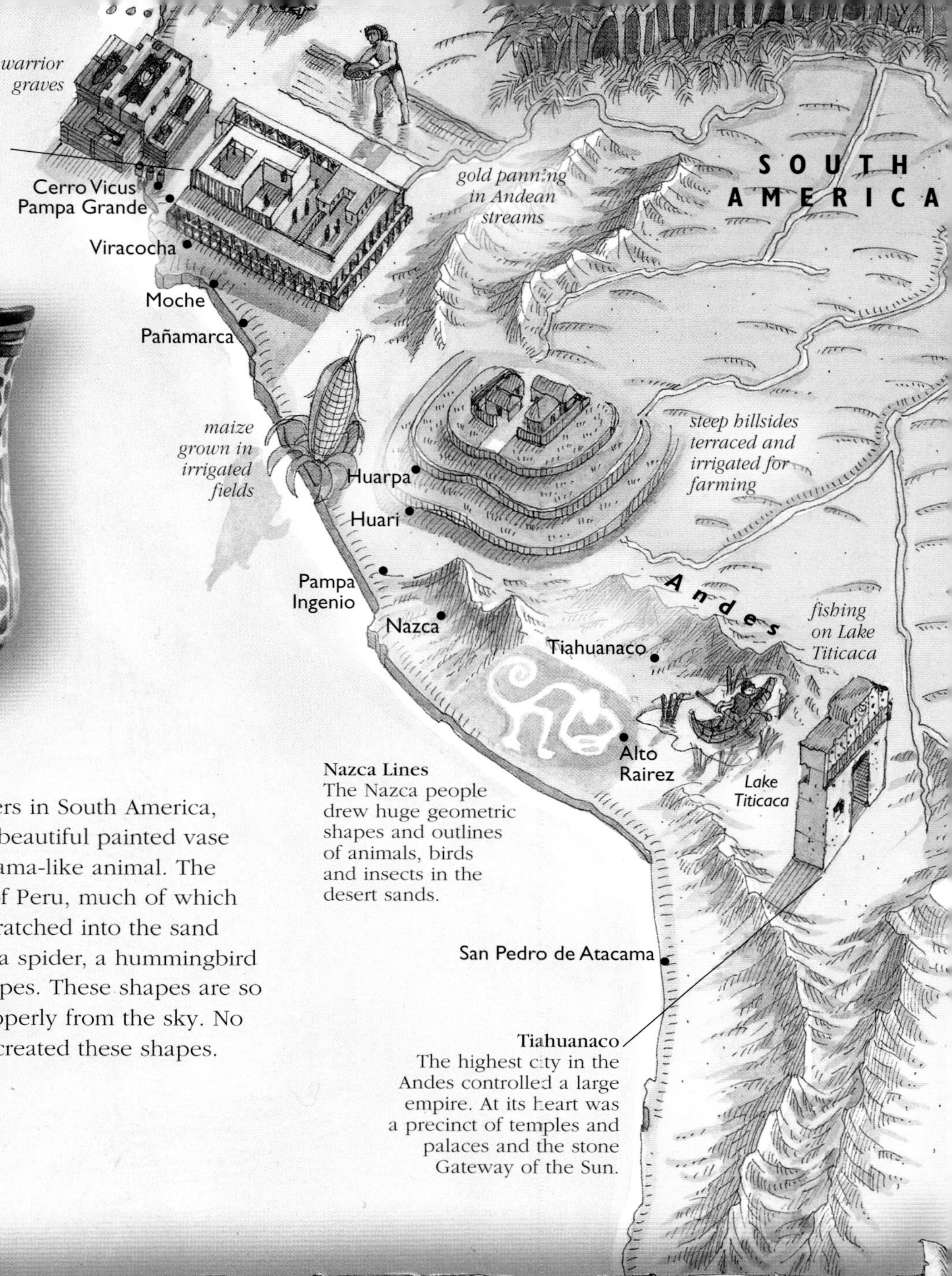

500BCE–1000CE

500BCE
500 Olmec civilization flourishes by the Gulf of Mexico
450 Monte Alban is centre of Zapotec culture

400BCE
400 Chavin de Huantar culture spreads throughout central Andes
350 First Maya city-state built in Yucatán Peninsula

300BCE
300 Olmec civilization declines

200BCE
200 City of Teotihuacan founded
200 Nazcas begin to draw lines in Peruvian desert
150 Maya first develop their picture writing around this time

100BCE
100 Moche state created in northern Peru

0

100CE
150 Pyramid of the Sun built in Teotihuacan

200CE
200 People in Huarpa begin to terrace and irrigate the Andes for agriculture

300CE
300 Moche state at its most powerful

400CE
450 Tikal is main Maya city-state

500CE
500 Huari state begins to create empire in central Andes

600CE
600 Tiahuanaco empire dominates southern Andes region

700CE
700 Huari empire overruns Moche
700 Teotihuacan sacked by armies from nearby rival city

800CE
800 Maya city-states begin to decline
850 Chichén Itzá, last major Maya city-state, founded

900CE
900 Centre of Mayan civilization moves north to Chichén Itzá
950 Toltecs migrate from Mexico and overrun remaining Maya city-states

1000CE

1000 km
500 miles

Australia and Polynesia

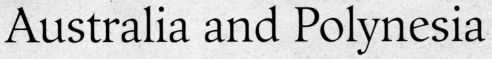

Some 40,000 years ago, nomadic people from southeast Asia arrived and settled in Australia. These Aboriginal people – the name we give to the original inhabitants of a country – were hunter-gatherers and, apart from in the far north of Australia, remained isolated from the rest of the world until the 18th century CE. The Polynesians gradually settled on the isolated islands of the Pacific Ocean in one of the most extraordinary feats of exploration in human history. With no navigational aids apart from the sun and stars, they sailed their canoes over vast expanses of ocean, observing wind and wave patterns, the formation of clouds, and the flight of birds to locate islands hidden over the horizon. By 1000CE they had reached their final destination – Aotearoa, the islands we call New Zealand.

Eating well
Polynesians kept chickens, dogs and pigs, grew bananas, breadfruit, sweet potatoes, yams and other crops.

North Pacific Ocean

Coral Sea

Gulf of Carpentaria

Living in the sky
People living on the swampy northern coastline built huts on raised platforms to guard against snakes.

people telling Dreamtime stories

Great Sandy Desert

grinding grass seeds between stones for food

Great Dividing Range

Uluru
This vast rock has always been a sacred place for Aboriginal people. Here and at other sacred sites, they would perform dances to the music of the didgeridoo.

◄Uluru

AUSTRALIA

hunting for turtles using outrigger canoes

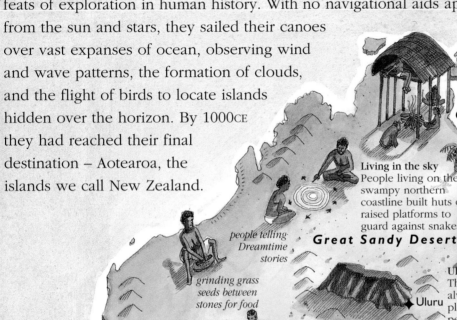

Kangaroo hunting
Aboriginal people hunted kangaroos for their meat with spears and boomerangs, curved sticks that returned when thrown.

searching for edible roots

digging a well for water

fishing with nets in eastern rivers

Darling

Lachlan

Murray

Great Australian Bight

Tasman Sea

collecting seashells to trade for other items

Tasmania

0   1000   2000 km
0   500   1000 miles

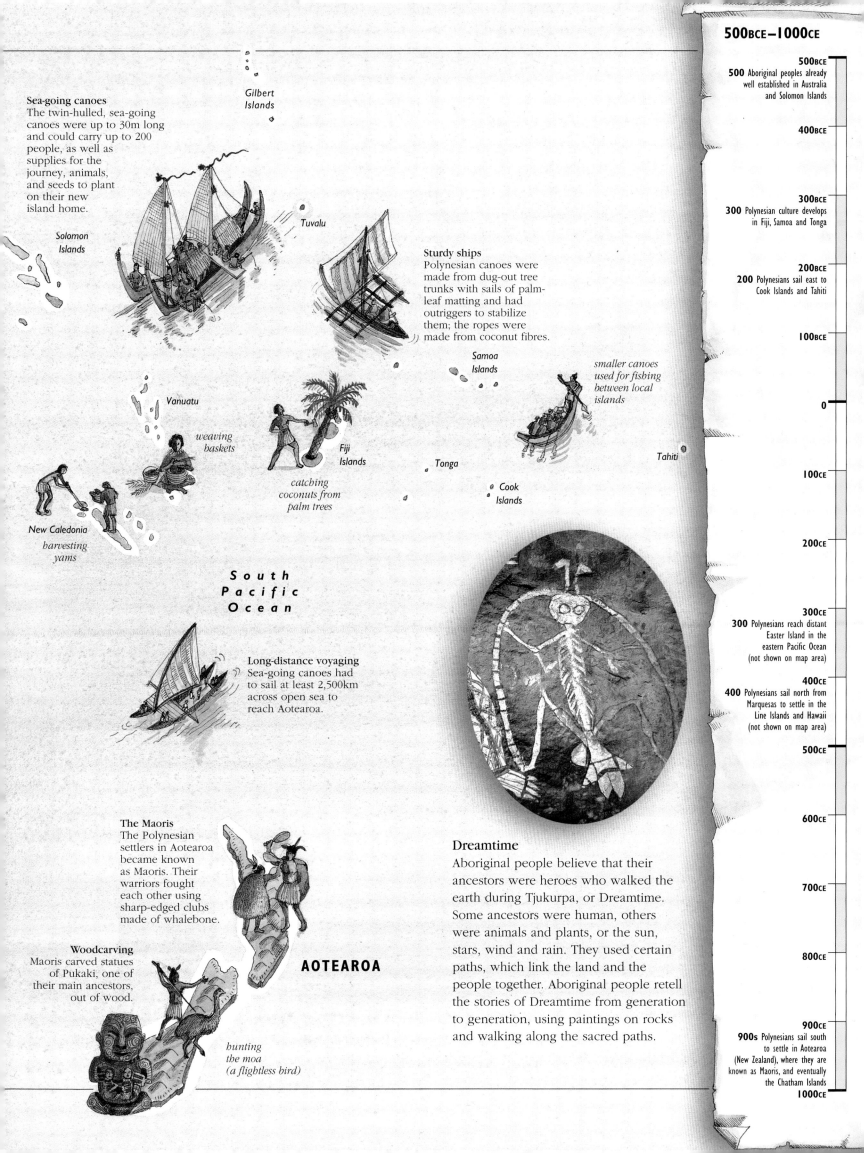

Sea-going canoes
The twin-hulled, sea-going canoes were up to 30m long and could carry up to 200 people, as well as supplies for the journey, animals, and seeds to plant on their new island home.

Gilbert Islands

Tuvalu

Solomon Islands

Sturdy ships
Polynesian canoes were made from dug-out tree trunks with sails of palm-leaf matting and had outriggers to stabilize them; the ropes were made from coconut fibres.

Samoa Islands

smaller canoes used for fishing between local islands

Vanuatu

weaving baskets

Fiji Islands

Tonga

Cook Islands

Tahiti

catching coconuts from palm trees

New Caledonia
harvesting yams

S o u t h
P a c i f i c
O c e a n

Long-distance voyaging
Sea-going canoes had to sail at least 2,500km across open sea to reach Aotearoa.

The Maoris
The Polynesian settlers in Aotearoa became known as Maoris. Their warriors fought each other using sharp-edged clubs made of whalebone.

Woodcarving
Maoris carved statues of Pukaki, one of their main ancestors, out of wood.

AOTEAROA

hunting the moa (a flightless bird)

Dreamtime

Aboriginal people believe that their ancestors were heroes who walked the earth during Tjukurpa, or Dreamtime. Some ancestors were human, others were animals and plants, or the sun, stars, wind and rain. They used certain paths, which link the land and the people together. Aboriginal people retell the stories of Dreamtime from generation to generation, using paintings on rocks and walking along the sacred paths.

500BCE
500 Aboriginal peoples already well established in Australia and Solomon Islands

400BCE

300BCE
300 Polynesian culture develops in Fiji, Samoa and Tonga

200BCE
200 Polynesians sail east to Cook Islands and Tahiti

100BCE

0

100CE

200CE

300CE
300 Polynesians reach distant Easter Island in the eastern Pacific Ocean (not shown on map area)

400CE
400 Polynesians sail north from Marquesas to settle in the Line Islands and Hawaii (not shown on map area)

500CE

600CE

700CE

800CE

900CE
900s Polynesians sail south to settle in Aotearoa (New Zealand), where they are known as Maoris, and eventually the Chatham Islands

1000CE

MEDIEVAL WORLD

Illustrated by Kevin Maddison

CONTENTS

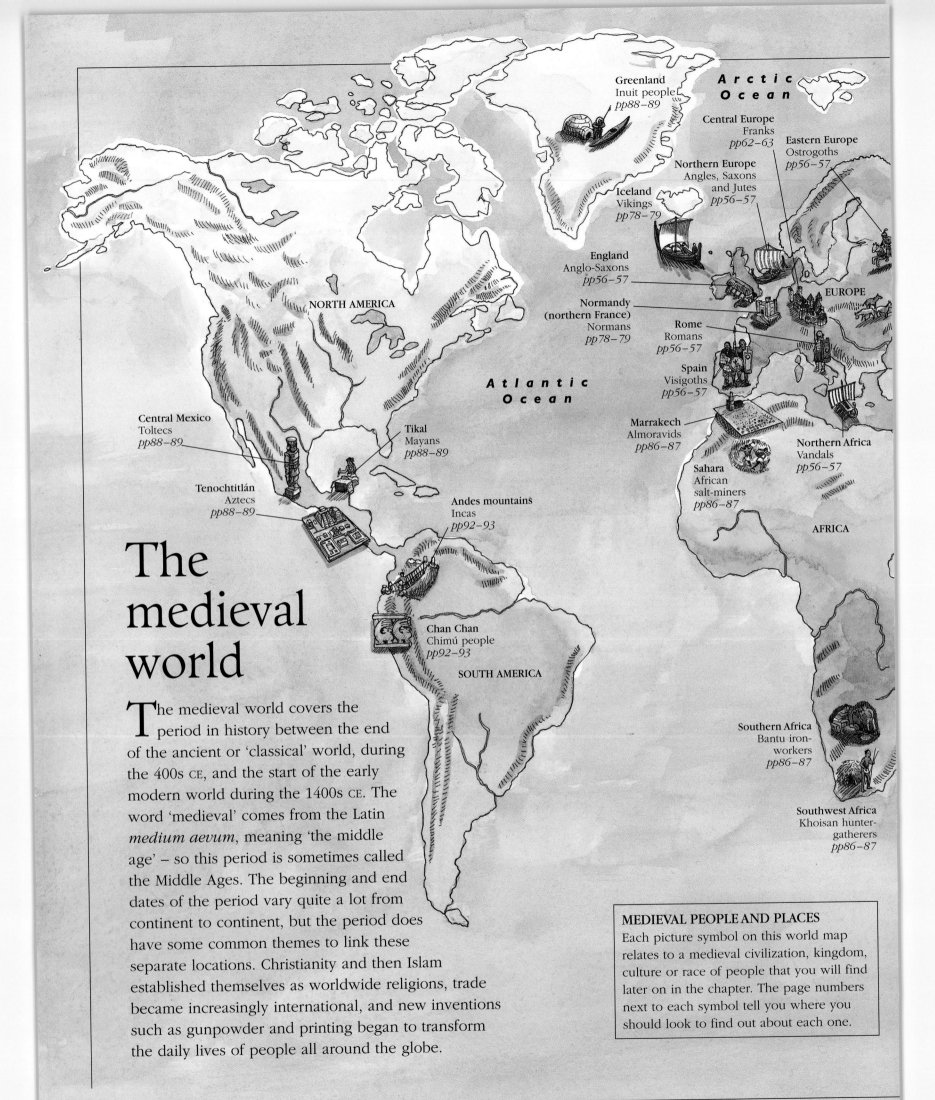

Greenland
Inuit people
pp88–89

Arctic Ocean

Central Europe
Franks
pp62–63

Eastern Europe
Ostrogoths
pp56–57

Northern Europe
Angles, Saxons
and Jutes
pp56–57

Iceland
Vikings
pp78–79

England
Anglo-Saxons
pp56–57

EUROPE

**Normandy
(northern France)**
Normans
pp78–79

Rome
Romans
pp56–57

Spain
Visigoths
pp56–57

NORTH AMERICA

Atlantic Ocean

Marrakech
Almoravids
pp86–87

Northern Africa
Vandals
pp56–57

Central Mexico
Toltecs
pp88–89

Tikal
Mayans
pp88–89

Sahara
African
salt-miners
pp86–87

AFRICA

Tenochtitlán
Aztecs
pp88–89

Andes mountains
Incas
pp92–93

The medieval world

Chan Chan
Chimú people
pp92–93

SOUTH AMERICA

The medieval world covers the period in history between the end of the ancient or 'classical' world, during the 400s CE, and the start of the early modern world during the 1400s CE. The word 'medieval' comes from the Latin *medium aevum*, meaning 'the middle age' – so this period is sometimes called the Middle Ages. The beginning and end dates of the period vary quite a lot from continent to continent, but the period does have some common themes to link these separate locations. Christianity and then Islam established themselves as worldwide religions, trade became increasingly international, and new inventions such as gunpowder and printing began to transform the daily lives of people all around the globe.

Southern Africa
Bantu iron-
workers
pp86–87

Southwest Africa
Khoisan hunter-
gatherers
pp86–87

MEDIEVAL PEOPLE AND PLACES
Each picture symbol on this world map relates to a medieval civilization, kingdom, culture or race of people that you will find later on in the chapter. The page numbers next to each symbol tell you where you should look to find out about each one.

Hungary
Magyar nomads
pp62–63

Anatolia
Seljuk Turks
pp58–59

ASIA

Mongol China
Mongols
pp84–85

Korea
Koreans
pp72–73

Middle East
Byzantines
pp58–59

China
Chinese
pp70–71

Japan
Japanese
pp72–73

Arabia
Arabs
pp58–59

Mecca
Muslims
pp64–65

India
Hindus
pp68–69

Southeast Asia
Khmer people
pp74–75

Pacific
Ocean

Indian
Ocean

AUSTRALIA

Tahiti
Polynesians
pp76–77

Aotearoa
(New Zealand)
Maoris
pp76–77

LOCATOR MAP

You will find a diagram like this along with every map in the chapter. This allows you to see exactly which part of the world the main map is showing you.

KEY TO MAPS IN THIS CHAPTER

CHINA	Main region or country
Anatolia	Other region
■ NARA	Capital city
• Tikal	City, town or village
Rhine	River or lake
Himalayas	Ocean, sea, desert or mountain range
– – – – –	Empire boundary

500CE

527 Emperor Justinian rules eastern Roman empire and regains territory lost to barbarian control
550 Slav peoples settle in eastern Europe
589 China reunited under Sui and Tang dynasties after long period of conflict

600CE

600 Frankish kingdom becomes the most powerful state in western Europe
610 Eastern Roman empire becomes the Byzantine empire
622 Muhammad flees from Mecca to Medina: the birth of Islam
632 Death of Muhammad: rapid expansion of Islam
680 Islam split between Sunni and Shi'a Muslims

700CE

711 Arabs invade Spain
732 Invading Arab army defeated by the Franks at Poitiers in France
750 Abbasids rule Muslim world from Baghdad
793 Vikings raid western Europe for the first time

800CE

800 Charlemagne crowned Emperor of the Romans by the pope in Rome
802 Creation of Khmer empire in Cambodia, Southeast Asia
850 Chinese first use gunpowder in warfare
850 Chimú empire founded in South America
868 World's first book printed in China

900CE

936 Korea emerges as a unified nation
962 Holy Roman empire created in Germany and Italy

1000CE

c. 1000 Polynesian navigators reach New Zealand
1000 Easter Islanders begin to carve stone statues
1000 Vikings settle in North America
1054 Final split between the Roman and Orthodox churches
1066 Norman conquest of England
1095 First Crusade to win back the Holy Land from Muslim control

1100CE

1171 England first rules Ireland
1175 Muslim conquest of northern India begins
1192 Military shogun government rules Japan

1200CE

c. 1200 Great Zimbabwe founded
1206 Genghis Khan begins Mongol conquests
1220 Inca empire founded
1241 Mongols invade eastern Europe
1250 Kingdom of Benin founded in west Africa
1279 Mongols conquer China
1280 Ottoman empire founded
1291 Muslims expel crusaders from Holy Land

1300CE

1325 Aztec empire founded
1337 England and France begin the Hundred Years' War
1347 Black Death starts to overwhelm Europe
1354 Ottomans begin conquest of the Balkans
1361 Timur creates new Mongol empire in central Asia
1368 Ming dynasty ends Mongol rule of China

1400CE

1415 Portuguese establish their first European colony in Africa
1432 Portuguese begin to explore west African coast

1500CE

The medieval world:
How we know about the past

The medieval world came to an end more than 500 years ago, but evidence from the period is all around us today. Medieval towns and castles, churches and cathedrals, temples and mosques, books and documents, ships and wagons, artefacts and jewellery, and much else besides still survive. These remains enable us to build up a good picture of what it was like to live and work all those years ago, while examining them can reveal how things were constructed in medieval times. We can also use documents from the period to re-enact festivals, battles and famous events.

Medieval towns
Many of the walled towns built during the medieval period still survive. Thanks to careful restoration in the 19th century, Carcassonne in France (shown below) is a perfect example. Its castle, walls, gatehouses and street plan are almost untouched since the town was fortified during the 13th century.

Town walls are 1,280m long and include three gatehouses and 21 towers

Documents
Medieval books and paper documents are rare. The Chinese had printing presses but European monks and scholars had to write each book out by hand, adding beautiful illustrations.

Reconstructions

Wooden artefacts can easily rot away. Luckily, this Viking ship from Oseberg in Norway was buried in boggy clay soil, which preserved most of its timbers. This allowed archaeologists to have the ship rebuilt to its original design.

Excavations

This medieval ship (above) was found buried in a muddy river in Newport, south Wales, UK. Every piece of timber and scrap of evidence was examined to build up an almost complete picture of how wooden trading ships were designed and built during this period.

Artefacts

This limestone figure from Central America is of Chicomecoatl, the Mayan goddess of maize. It also shows us the clothing and jewellery that an ordinary Mayan woman of the period might have worn.

Re-enactments

We cannot go back in time to fight a joust or win a battle, but we can re-enact them using medieval accounts as our guide. These jousters are taking part in a medieval fair staged in Sarasota, Florida, USA. Their costumes and weapons are modern recreations of the medieval originals.

55

After the Roman empire

The mighty Roman empire had dominated Europe for more than 500 years, but during the 5th century CE it slowly fell apart as waves of Germanic tribes from central Europe poured over its borders. The western half of the empire finally collapsed in 476CE, when the last western emperor, Augustulus, was overthrown. In its place came a series of tribal kingdoms that converted to Christianity and kept many of the old Roman institutions in place.

St Patrick
In 432 St Patrick arrived in Ireland to convert its people to Christianity.

Anglo-Saxons
Angles, Saxons and Jutes from northern Germany and Denmark crossed the North Sea to settle in eastern Britain after 450.

Barbarians
There were many 'barbarian' tribes in Germany, but most of them were helpful to the Romans.

Sutton Hoo
Anglo-Saxon lords were buried in their ships surrounded by treasures, such as this helmet from Sutton Hoo.

Theodoric
In 493 Theodoric, king of the Ostrogoths, conquered Rome and restored peace, keeping Roman civilization alive in Italy.

The Visigoths
The Visigoths came from the Balkans, and in 418 they settled in southwestern France as allies of Rome. They later conquered much of Spain.

Attacking Rome
In the 5th century, Rome was ransacked by the Visigoths in 410 and then by the Vandals in 455.

The Vandals
The Vandals from central Europe crossed over to North Africa and set up an independent kingdom in Carthage in 439.

Vandal pirates
Vandal pirates from North Africa attacked Roman ships in the Mediterranean, seizing valuable cargoes.

Ireland

Britain

North Sea

Saxon farmer

Gaul
wooden houses

Rhine

Germany

Alps

Atlantic Ocean

Suevic kingdom

Spain

ruined Roman villa

buildings in Ravenna

Ravenna

Kingdom of Odoacer

WESTERN ROMAN EMPIRE

ROME

Visigothic kingdom

Vandal kingdom

Carthage

North Africa

dotted line shows the extent of the Roman empire in the 5th century CE

The Slavs
No-one knows where the Slavs came from but during the 500s they settled across eastern Europe, later converting to Christianity.

The Ostrogoths
The Ostrogoths settled in the Balkans and eventually conquered Italy itself. They often helped Rome against its enemies.

Balkans

Danube

Constantinople
The eastern empire was governed from Constantinople. The city's massive walls kept it free from attack.

■ CONSTANTINOPLE

Black Sea

EASTERN ROMAN EMPIRE

Anatolia

Athens

0 — 500 km
0 — 250 miles

The legacy of Rome
The Roman empire left behind many achievements. The Romans introduced the calendar of 365 days – with an extra day every four years – devised by Julius Caesar in 45BCE. This system included the 12-month year, the seven-day week, and the names of our months. October is shown on this mosaic floor from the 3rd century CE. Other Roman legacies include the Catholic Church, the Latin language, a legal system and a system of republican government copied in modern France and the USA.

SASANIAN EMPIRE

Arabs
The eastern borders of the Roman empire were not threatened as often as those in the north, as the Arabs traded peacefully with the Romans. The Sasanian Persians, however, were a constant threat.

Mediterranean Sea

400CE
402 Capital of the western empire moves from Rome to the safer city of Ravenna
406 Vandals, Suevi and Alans invade Gaul (France) and later Spain
410 Visigoths sack Rome
418 Visigoths make peace with Rome and settle in Aquitaine (southwestern France)

429 Vandals cross from Spain to North Africa and conquer Carthage in 439
432 St Patrick begins to covert the Irish to Christianity

450CE
450 Anglo-Saxons from northern Germany begin to settle in Britain
455 Vandals sack Rome

476 Odoacer, a barbarian general, removes the last western Roman emperor, Augustulus, from power and rules Italy

486 Clovis founds the Frankish kingdom in Gaul

493–526 Theodoric rules Ostrogothic kingdom in Italy

500CE
507 Clovis drives the Visigoths out of Gaul into Spain

527–65 Justinian rules eastern Roman empire and reconquers much of the land lost to the barbarians

550CE
550 Slavs settle in eastern Europe and the Balkans

570s Visigoths dominate most of Spain

600CE
600 Frankish kingdom becomes the most powerful state in western Europe

626 Avar nomadic tribes threaten the eastern empire but fail to take Constantinople

639 After death of King Dagobert, a sequence of short-lived kings weakens the Frankish kingdom

650CE

679 Pepin II leads the Frankish kingdom and expands Frankish power into Germany

700CE

Byzantine architecture
The Byzantines developed a distinctive style of church architecture, using domes and mosaic walls. An example is the Basilica of St Mark in Venice.

Venice

Ravenna

Italy

Emperor Justinian
Justinian fought to regain Roman lands lost to the barbarians.

Rome

The Normans
In 1091 Norman knights from France conquered Byzantine lands in southern Italy and Sicily.

Sicily

Missionaries
In 863 Byzantine missionaries Saints Cyril and Methodius set out to convert the pagan Slavs of eastern Europe to Christianity.

craftsmen making a mosaic on a wall

Frontier forts
Justinian built a series of forts along the Danube to protect his frontier from attack by Slav raiders.

Danube

Byzantine priest

Bulgaria

Black Sea

Bari

Byzantine-style Christian church

Balathista

Adrianople

CONSTANTINOPLE

Thessalonica

Mount Athos

Mount Athos
Communities of religious men sprang up across the Byzantine empire, such as on Mount Athos.

dotted line shows the extent of the Byzantine empire in 1025

Constantinople
The Byzantine capital of Constantinople was founded in 324 by the Roman emperor Constantine.

Nicaea

Myriocephalum

farmer taking goat to market

Ephesus

Crete

BYZANTINE EMPIRE

The Byzantine empire

Despite the collapse of the western Roman empire in 476CE, the eastern empire continued to prosper. During the reign of Justinian (527–65), it even managed to regain land lost to the barbarians. But the empire was threatened by enemies all along its lengthy borders, so Heraclius (reigned 610–41) completely restructured the empire and changed its official language from Latin to Greek. He created a new 'Byzantine empire' – named after its capital city, Byzantium, the old Greek name for Constantinople. This new empire survived against its many enemies until 1453, when Constantinople finally fell to the Ottoman Turks.

Mediterranean Sea

Muslim rule
Arab armies swept out of Arabia in 632, bringing their new religion, Islam. Islam replaced Christianity throughout the eastern half of the empire.

newly-built mosque in Egypt

Egypt

0   500 km

0   250 miles

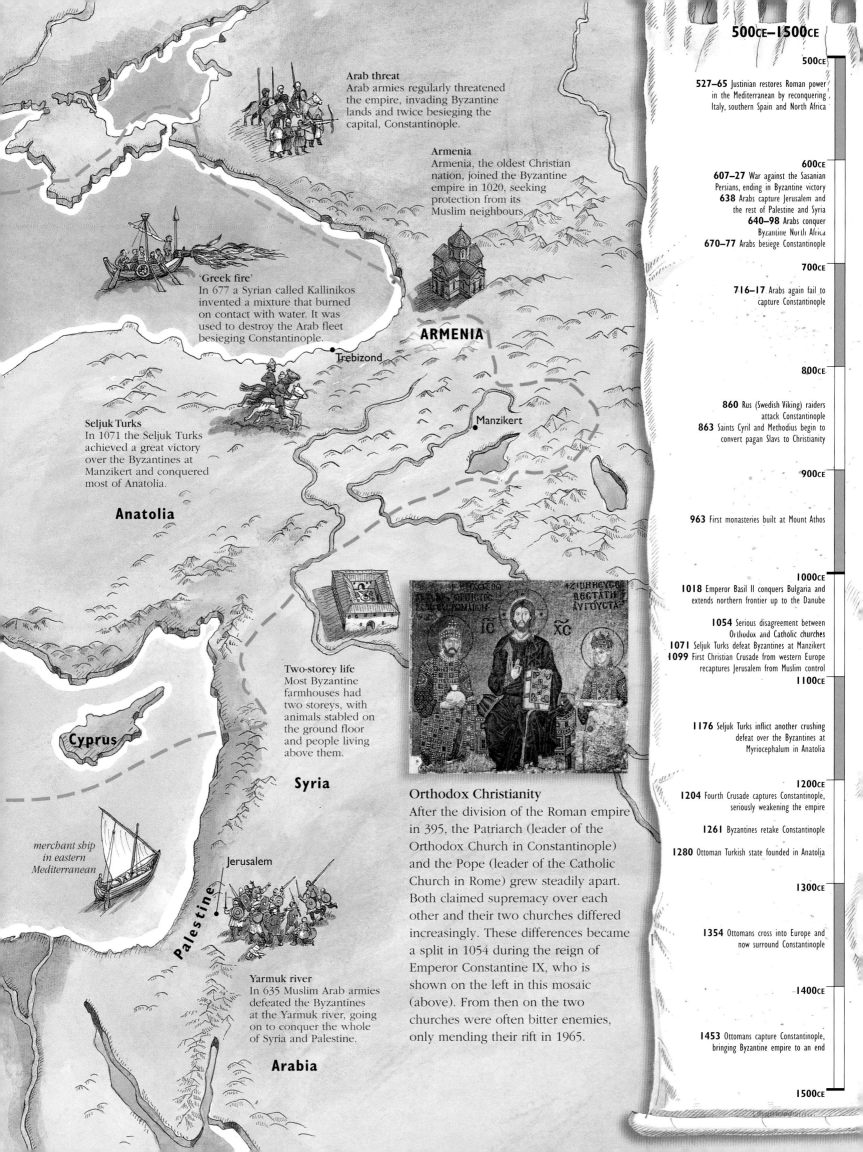

Arab threat
Arab armies regularly threatened the empire, invading Byzantine lands and twice besieging the capital, Constantinople.

Armenia
Armenia, the oldest Christian nation, joined the Byzantine empire in 1020, seeking protection from its Muslim neighbours.

'Greek fire'
In 677 a Syrian called Kallinikos invented a mixture that burned on contact with water. It was used to destroy the Arab fleet besieging Constantinople.

ARMENIA

Trebizond

Manzikert

Seljuk Turks
In 1071 the Seljuk Turks achieved a great victory over the Byzantines at Manzikert and conquered most of Anatolia.

Anatolia

Two-storey life
Most Byzantine farmhouses had two storeys, with animals stabled on the ground floor and people living above them.

Cyprus

Syria

merchant ship
in eastern
Mediterranean

Jerusalem

Palestine

Yarmuk river
In 635 Muslim Arab armies defeated the Byzantines at the Yarmuk river, going on to conquer the whole of Syria and Palestine.

Arabia

Orthodox Christianity

After the division of the Roman empire in 395, the Patriarch (leader of the Orthodox Church in Constantinople) and the Pope (leader of the Catholic Church in Rome) grew steadily apart. Both claimed supremacy over each other and their two churches differed increasingly. These differences became a split in 1054 during the reign of Emperor Constantine IX, who is shown on the left in this mosaic (above). From then on the two churches were often bitter enemies, only mending their rift in 1965.

500CE–1500CE

500CE

527–65 Justinian restores Roman power in the Mediterranean by reconquering Italy, southern Spain and North Africa

600CE

607–27 War against the Sasanian Persians, ending in Byzantine victory
638 Arabs capture Jerusalem and the rest of Palestine and Syria
640–98 Arabs conquer Byzantine North Africa
670–77 Arabs besiege Constantinople

700CE

716–17 Arabs again fail to capture Constantinople

800CE

860 Rus (Swedish Viking) raiders attack Constantinople
863 Saints Cyril and Methodius begin to convert pagan Slavs to Christianity

900CE

963 First monasteries built at Mount Athos

1000CE

1018 Emperor Basil II conquers Bulgaria and extends northern frontier up to the Danube

1054 Serious disagreement between Orthodox and Catholic churches
1071 Seljuk Turks defeat Byzantines at Manzikert
1099 First Christian Crusade from western Europe recaptures Jerusalem from Muslim control

1100CE

1176 Seljuk Turks inflict another crushing defeat over the Byzantines at Myriocephalum in Anatolia

1200CE

1204 Fourth Crusade captures Constantinople, seriously weakening the empire

1261 Byzantines retake Constantinople

1280 Ottoman Turkish state founded in Anatolia

1300CE

1354 Ottomans cross into Europe and now surround Constantinople

1400CE

1453 Ottomans capture Constantinople, bringing Byzantine empire to an end

1500CE

Pilgrimage
Pilgrimage was an important part of medieval Christianity. Rich and poor alike walked to shrines such as Canterbury in England, Santiago de Compostela in Spain, Rome and even Jerusalem in search of a miraculous cure or forgiveness for their sins. This stained-glass window from Canterbury cathedral shows pilgrims on their way to the shrine of St Thomas a Becket.

Monasteries
These are the remains of Fountains Abbey in Yorkshire, England, UK – once part of a large monastic estate founded by 13 Benedictine monks in 1132. Monasteries were major centres of learning and scholarship across Europe, running schools to provide education for boys.

Christian education
The Christian church played a major role in education across Europe, as priests and monks – such as those shown in this illuminated manuscript – were often the only people in the area who could read and write. Churches and cathedrals ran their own schools, and after the 11th century many cathedral schools set up universities to teach theology (the study of religious belief) and law.

Medieval Europe:
Christianity

Medieval Europe was entirely Christian, with the exception of southern Spain and, after the 14th century, the Balkans. In the west of Europe, the Catholic Church played a major role in society, providing schools and hospitals and encouraging people to make pilgrimages to holy places or shrines containing relics of saints. The Catholic Church also dominated politics and owned large expanses of land. The pope, based in Rome, was the head of the Catholic Church. He was often more powerful than most emperors and kings, although disputes between himself and these non-religious leaders often led to bitter arguments and even war.

Taller spire added in the early 16th century

West front survives from an earlier 11th-century cathedral, destroyed by fire in 1194

The Orthodox Church
Most people in eastern Europe were Orthodox Christians under the leadership of the Patriarch of Constantinople rather than the Catholic pope in Rome. In the 14th century – when this monastery was built in Kosovo, Serbia – most Orthodox Christians outside Russia and Georgia came under Ottoman Muslim rule, but they continued to practise their faith.

Stained-glass rose window showing religious scenes

Brightly painted interior

Flying buttress to support the walls and roof

Central part of cathedral, the nave, is 37m high

Sculptures on south porch depict New Testament scenes

Part of the front section is pulled away in this artwork to reveal the interior

Chartres cathedral
The largest building in any medieval European city was the cathedral, the seat of the local bishop. Constructing a cathedral employed hundreds of local stonemasons, carpenters, sculptors and glassmakers. The cathedral of Chartres, southwest of Paris, France, was begun in the early 1200s and took just 25 years to build. It has remained largely untouched since 1250, making it one of the finest surviving medieval cathedrals in existence.

ly.

or.

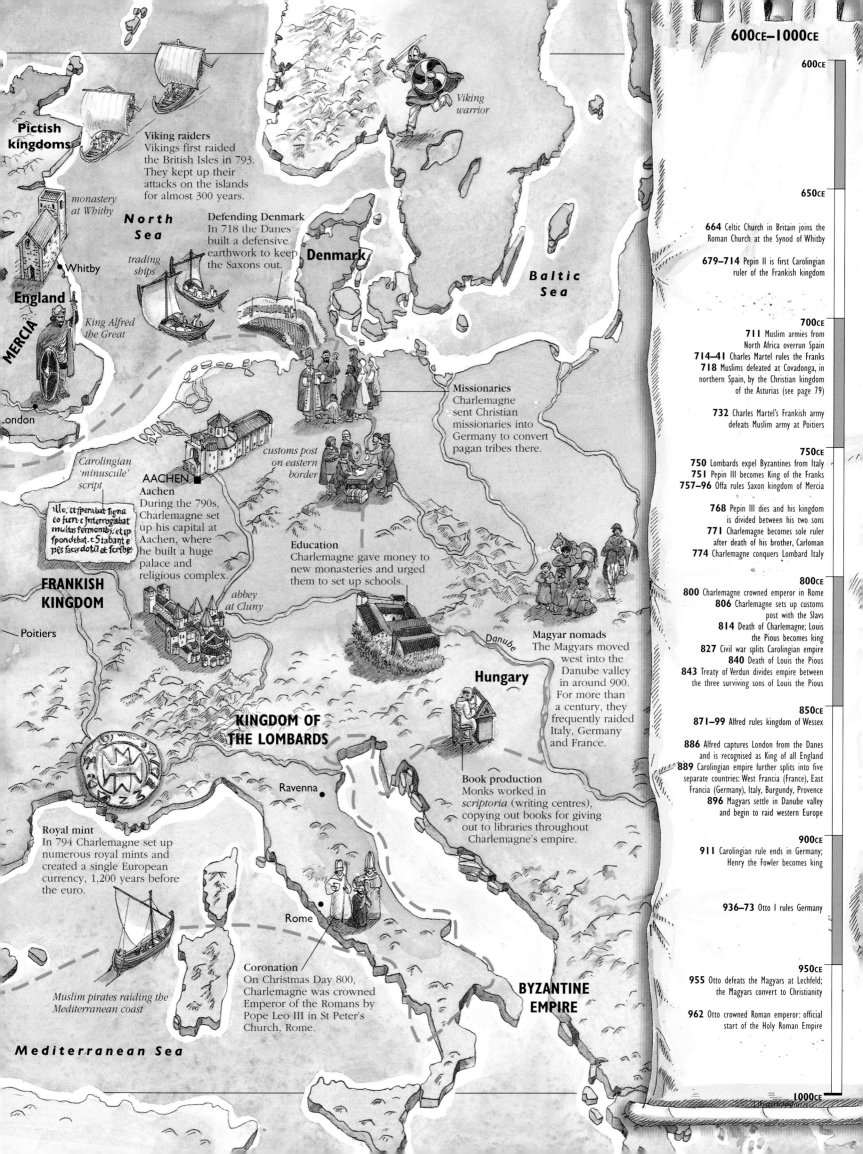

Pictish kingdoms

monastery at Whitby

Viking raiders
Vikings first raided the British Isles in 793. They kept up their attacks on the islands for almost 300 years.

Viking warrior

North Sea

Defending Denmark
In 718 the Danes built a defensive earthwork to keep the Saxons out.

Denmark

Baltic Sea

England

• Whitby

trading ships

MERCIA

King Alfred the Great

London

Missionaries
Charlemagne sent Christian missionaries into Germany to convert pagan tribes there.

Carolingian 'minuscule' script

customs post on eastern border

AACHEN ■

Aachen
During the 790s, Charlemagne set up his capital at Aachen, where he built a huge palace and religious complex.

Education
Charlemagne gave money to new monasteries and urged them to set up schools.

FRANKISH KINGDOM

abbey at Cluny

— Poitiers

KINGDOM OF THE LOMBARDS

Danube

Hungary

Magyar nomads
The Magyars moved west into the Danube valley in around 900. For more than a century, they frequently raided Italy, Germany and France.

Book production
Monks worked in *scriptoria* (writing centres), copying out books for giving out to libraries throughout Charlemagne's empire.

Ravenna •

Royal mint
In 794 Charlemagne set up numerous royal mints and created a single European currency, 1,200 years before the euro.

Rome •

Coronation
On Christmas Day 800, Charlemagne was crowned Emperor of the Romans by Pope Leo III in St Peter's Church, Rome.

Muslim pirates raiding the Mediterranean coast

BYZANTINE EMPIRE

Mediterranean Sea

600CE–1000CE

600CE

650CE

664 Celtic Church in Britain joins the Roman Church at the Synod of Whitby

679–714 Pepin II is first Carolingian ruler of the Frankish kingdom

700CE

711 Muslim armies from North Africa overrun Spain
714–41 Charles Martel rules the Franks
718 Muslims defeated at Covadonga, in northern Spain, by the Christian kingdom of the Asturias (see page 79)

732 Charles Martel's Frankish army defeats Muslim army at Poitiers

750CE

750 Lombards expel Byzantines from Italy
751 Pepin III becomes King of the Franks
757–96 Offa rules Saxon kingdom of Mercia

768 Pepin III dies and his kingdom is divided between his two sons
771 Charlemagne becomes sole ruler after death of his brother, Carloman
774 Charlemagne conquers Lombard Italy

800CE

800 Charlemagne crowned emperor in Rome
806 Charlemagne sets up customs post with the Slavs
814 Death of Charlemagne; Louis the Pious becomes king
827 Civil war splits Carolingian empire
840 Death of Louis the Pious
843 Treaty of Verdun divides empire between the three surviving sons of Louis the Pious

850CE

871–99 Alfred rules kingdom of Wessex

886 Alfred captures London from the Danes and is recognised as King of all England
889 Carolingian empire further splits into five separate countries: West Francia (France), East Francia (Germany), Italy, Burgundy, Provence
896 Magyars settle in Danube valley and begin to raid western Europe

900CE

911 Carolingian rule ends in Germany; Henry the Fowler becomes king

936–73 Otto I rules Germany

950CE

955 Otto defeats the Magyars at Lechfeld; the Magyars convert to Christianity

962 Otto crowned Roman emperor: official start of the Holy Roman Empire

1000CE

FRANKISH KINGDOM

armies invaded France, reaching as far north as Poitiers. Here, they were defeated by a large Frankish army.

Poitiers

successes, the Arabs twice failed to capture Constantinople, the capital of the Byzantine empire.

Constantinople

Anatolia

Taurus Mountains

Syria

DAMASCU

Palestin

Jerusaler

UMAYYAD CALIPHATE

Córdoba
From 756 to 1031 the Umayyads governed Spain from Córdoba, where they built a beautiful mosque. This mihrab from the mosque shows the direction of Mecca.

CÓRDOBA

Rome

BYZANTINE EMPIRE

Carthage

IDRISID CALIPHATE

AGHLABID CALIPHATE

Arabic
The Arab armies introduced a new language, Arabic, across their vast empire. Spoken Arabic varies from country to country, but written Arabic is the same everywhere.

Muslim raiders
Muslim pirates launched frequent raids across the Mediterranean, capturing Sicily, Sardinia and other islands.

Libya

Jerusalem
In 638 Arab armies captured Jerusalem and built the Dome of the Rock – the first major Islamic building outside Arabia.

North Africa

camel

Cairo
The Fatimid rulers of Egypt established a new city at Cairo in 969. It soon became one of the most important cities in the Arab world.

Cairo

Egypt

a Muslim praying towards Mecca

Nile

felucca on the Nile

The spread of Islam

In 610CE, Muhammad, a trader from Mecca in Arabia, began to experience divine revelations that were later written down in the Koran, the Islamic holy book. By the time of his death in 632, the new religion of Islam dominated the Arabian Peninsula. Arab armies then set out on a whirlwind campaign of conquest and conversion. They overwhelmed the Sasanian empire of Persia and took Islam from the borders of India across Asia and North Africa into Spain and southern Europe. Islam brought political and religious unity to a vast region, but divisions soon opened up. Weakened by these divisions, the Islamic world lost some of its territory to Christian forces in Europe.

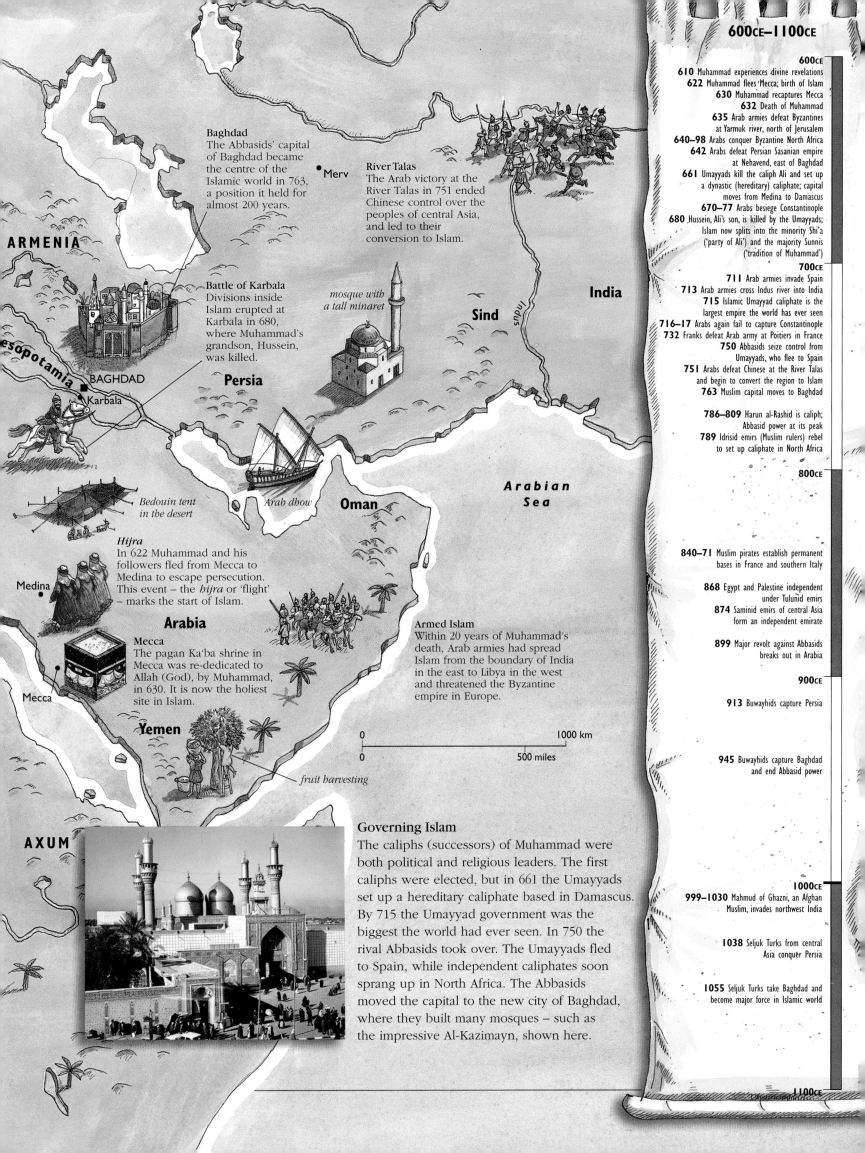

Baghdad
The Abbasids' capital of Baghdad became the centre of the Islamic world in 763, a position it held for almost 200 years.

● Merv

River Talas
The Arab victory at the River Talas in 751 ended Chinese control over the peoples of central Asia, and led to their conversion to Islam.

ARMENIA

India

Battle of Karbala
Divisions inside Islam erupted at Karbala in 680, where Muhammad's grandson, Hussein, was killed.

mosque with a tall minaret

Sind

esopotamia

BAGHDAD

Karbala

Persia

Indus

Arab dhow

Bedouin tent in the desert

Oman

Arabian Sea

Hijra
In 622 Muhammad and his followers fled from Mecca to Medina to escape persecution. This event – the *hijra* or 'flight' – marks the start of Islam.

Medina

Arabia

Armed Islam
Within 20 years of Muhammad's death, Arab armies had spread Islam from the boundary of India in the east to Libya in the west and threatened the Byzantine empire in Europe.

Mecca
The pagan Ka'ba shrine in Mecca was re-dedicated to Allah (God), by Muhammad, in 630. It is now the holiest site in Islam.

Mecca

Yemen

0 ————————————— 1000 km
0 ————————————— 500 miles

fruit harvesting

AXUM

Governing Islam
The caliphs (successors) of Muhammad were both political and religious leaders. The first caliphs were elected, but in 661 the Umayyads set up a hereditary caliphate based in Damascus. By 715 the Umayyad government was the biggest the world had ever seen. In 750 the rival Abbasids took over. The Umayyads fled to Spain, while independent caliphates soon sprang up in North Africa. The Abbasids moved the capital to the new city of Baghdad, where they built many mosques – such as the impressive Al-Kazimayn, shown here.

600CE–1100CE

600CE
610 Muhammad experiences divine revelations
622 Muhammad flees Mecca; birth of Islam
630 Muhammad recaptures Mecca
632 Death of Muhammad
635 Arab armies defeat Byzantines at Yarmuk river, north of Jerusalem
640–98 Arabs conquer Byzantine North Africa
642 Arabs defeat Persian Sasanian empire at Nehavend, east of Baghdad
661 Umayyads kill the caliph Ali and set up a dynastic (hereditary) caliphate; capital moves from Medina to Damascus
670–77 Arabs besiege Constantinople
680 Hussein, Ali's son, is killed by the Umayyads; Islam now splits into the minority Shi'a ('party of Ali') and the majority Sunnis ('tradition of Muhammad')

700CE
711 Arab armies invade Spain
713 Arab armies cross Indus river into India
715 Islamic Umayyad caliphate is the largest empire the world has ever seen
716–17 Arabs again fail to capture Constantinople
732 Franks defeat Arab army at Poitiers in France
750 Abbasids seize control from Umayyads, who flee to Spain
751 Arabs defeat Chinese at the River Talas and begin to convert the region to Islam
763 Muslim capital moves to Baghdad

786–809 Harun al-Rashid is caliph; Abbasid power at its peak
789 Idrisid emirs (Muslim rulers) rebel to set up caliphate in North Africa

800CE

840–71 Muslim pirates establish permanent bases in France and southern Italy

868 Egypt and Palestine independent under Tulunid emirs
874 Saminid emirs of central Asia form an independent emirate

899 Major revolt against Abbasids breaks out in Arabia

900CE

913 Buwayhids capture Persia

945 Buwayhids capture Baghdad and end Abbasid power

1000CE
999–1030 Mahmud of Ghazni, an Afghan Muslim, invades northwest India

1038 Seljuk Turks from central Asia conquer Persia

1055 Seljuk Turks take Baghdad and become major force in Islamic world

1100CE

The Arab world:
Islamic culture

In the centuries following the death of Muhammad and the Arab invasion of the Middle East, North Africa and Spain, Muslim scientists, scholars and engineers developed a culture unrivalled in the world at that time. They made huge advances in astronomy, medicine and mathematics – giving the world algebra, trigonometry and the decimal fraction – and translated many earlier Greek and Indian works into their own language, Arabic. They also developed a highly decorative architecture that made great use of garden design and calligraphy (decorative writing).

Art and calligraphy

The Islamic faith discourages the depiction of Allah (God) and Muhammad. If Muslim artists do show Muhammad, in books or paintings, they always cover his face with a veil. They also use beautiful calligraphy to write out and decorate the verses of the Koran, their holy book, as this 16th-century example shows.

Astronomy

Muslim scholars were world leaders in astronomy, and most major Muslim cities had at least one observatory. Muslim astronomers also developed the astrolabe (left). This is a device that was used by navigators to measure the height of the Sun at noon, so that they could work out their latitude – how far north or south they were.

Medicine

This Islamic painting shows a doctor visiting a patient. The most important Muslim physician was Ibn Sina (980–1037), a Persian scholar who wrote the 14-volume *Canon of Medicine*, which later formed the basis of European medicine until the 17th century. Muslims disapproved of surgery, but they did use it when necessary and were the first people to remove cataracts to restore sight.

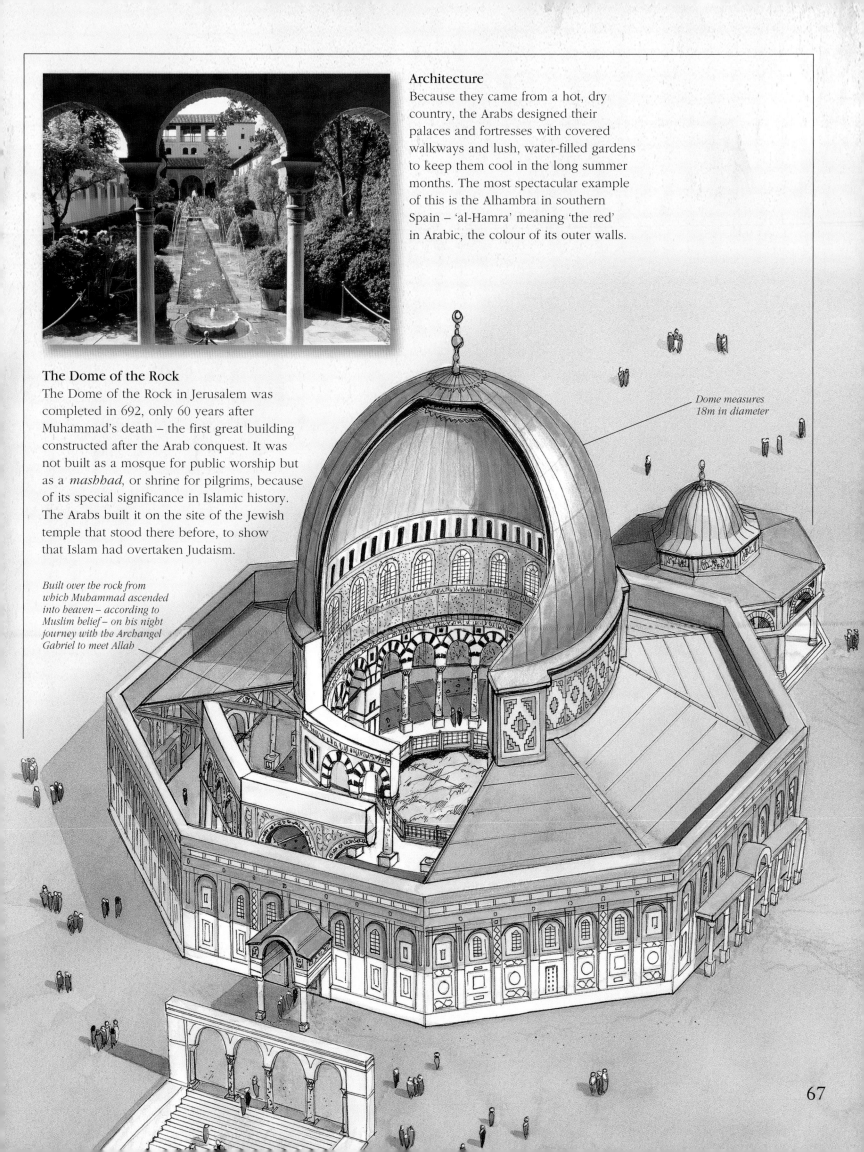

Architecture

Because they came from a hot, dry country, the Arabs designed their palaces and fortresses with covered walkways and lush, water-filled gardens to keep them cool in the long summer months. The most spectacular example of this is the Alhambra in southern Spain – 'al-Hamra' meaning 'the red' in Arabic, the colour of its outer walls.

The Dome of the Rock

The Dome of the Rock in Jerusalem was completed in 692, only 60 years after Muhammad's death – the first great building constructed after the Arab conquest. It was not built as a mosque for public worship but as a *mashhad*, or shrine for pilgrims, because of its special significance in Islamic history. The Arabs built it on the site of the Jewish temple that stood there before, to show that Islam had overtaken Judaism.

Built over the rock from which Muhammad ascended into heaven – according to Muslim belief – on his night journey with the Archangel Gabriel to meet Allah

Dome measures 18m in diameter

Medieval India

The Hindu and Buddhist dominance of India came to an end in 711CE, when Arab armies brought Islam across the Indus river into western India. From then on, Muslims (followers of Islam) and Hindus waged a constant battle to control the Indian subcontinent. In 1175, in what is now Afghanistan, Muhammad of Ghur and his army broke through into the Ganges river valley in the north. This paved the way for more than 600 years of Muslim domination in India. After Muhammad's death in 1206, one of his most trusted generals, Qutb-ud-Din, established the independent Sultanate of Delhi. This sultanate controlled all but the southern tip of the country by 1351.

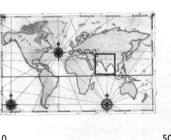

```
0              500 km
0         250 miles
```

Raiding party
The war-hungry Muslim ruler Mahmud of Ghazni launched 17 invasions of India after the year 999, raiding and destroying Hindu temples.

Ghur   Ghazni

Timur
In 1398 Timur the Lame, a Turkish nomad from central Asia, invaded India and ransacked Delhi.

Indus   **Multan**

Islam
Arab Muslims conquered Sind in 711, introducing Islam to the subcontinent. The new religion slowly spread eastwards and southwards across India.

Sind

making pots

Gujarat

inshore fishing

Arabian Sea

Hinduism

Although Muslims ruled much of India during this period, most people remained Hindu, with some keeping their Buddhist or Jain faith. Hindu kingdoms flourished in the south and east of the country, the Cholas of southern India even exporting Hinduism throughout southeast Asia. This picture shows the 11th-century Brahmeshwar Siva temple at Bhubaneshwar, in eastern India. Hindu temples of this kind were hugely wealthy, with large estates of land and donations from wealthy people anxious to please the gods.

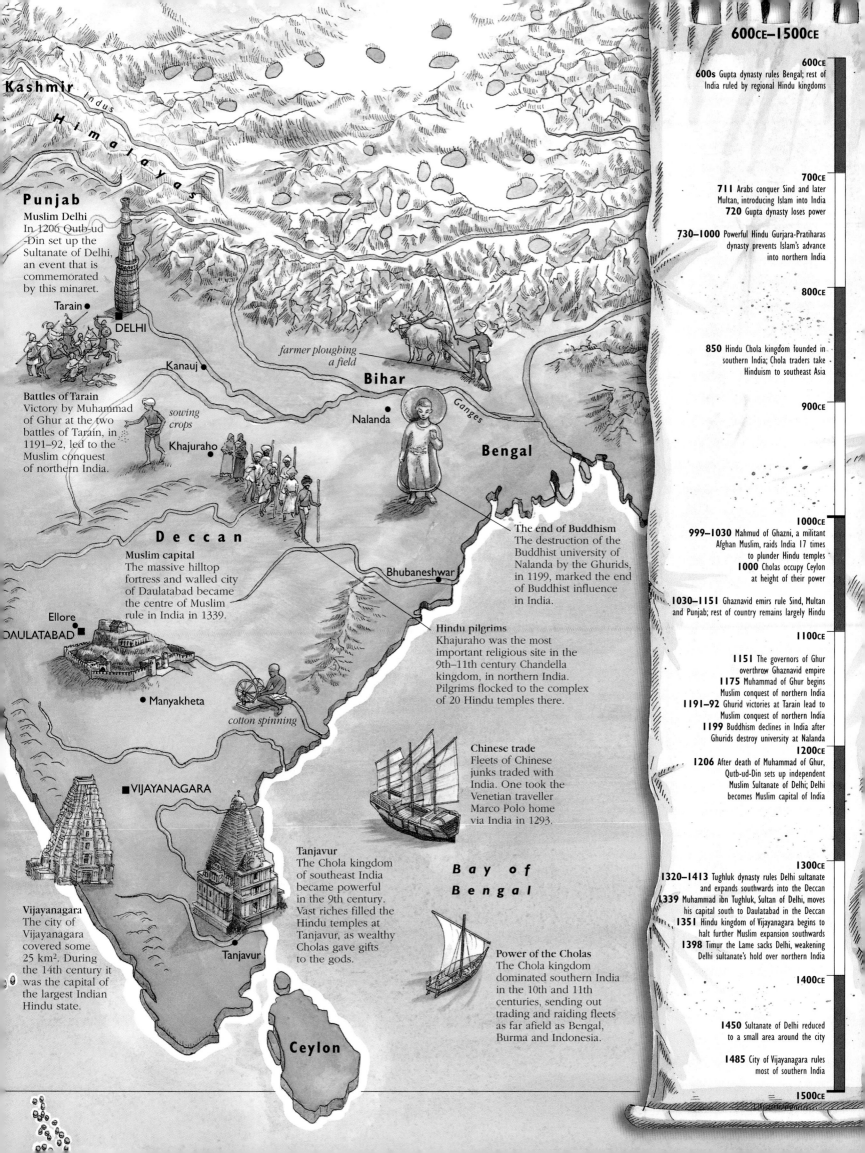

Kashmir

Indus

Himalayas

Punjab

Muslim Delhi
In 1206 Qutb-ud-Din set up the Sultanate of Delhi, an event that is commemorated by this minaret.

Tarain ●

● DELHI

Kanauj ●

farmer ploughing a field

Bihar

Ganges

Nalanda ●

Bengal

Battles of Tarain
Victory by Muhammad of Ghur at the two battles of Tarain, in 1191–92, led to the Muslim conquest of northern India.

sowing crops

Khajuraho ●

D e c c a n

Muslim capital
The massive hilltop fortress and walled city of Daulatabad became the centre of Muslim rule in India in 1339.

Ellore ●
■ DAULATABAD

● Manyakheta

cotton spinning

The end of Buddhism
The destruction of the Buddhist university of Nalanda by the Ghurids, in 1199, marked the end of Buddhist influence in India.

Bhubaneshwar ●

Hindu pilgrims
Khajuraho was the most important religious site in the 9th–11th century Chandella kingdom, in northern India. Pilgrims flocked to the complex of 20 Hindu temples there.

Chinese trade
Fleets of Chinese junks traded with India. One took the Venetian traveller Marco Polo home via India in 1293.

■ VIJAYANAGARA

Tanjavur
The Chola kingdom of southeast India became powerful in the 9th century. Vast riches filled the Hindu temples at Tanjavur, as wealthy Cholas gave gifts to the gods.

B a y o f B e n g a l

Vijayanagara
The city of Vijayanagara covered some 25 km². During the 14th century it was the capital of the largest Indian Hindu state.

Tanjavur ●

Power of the Cholas
The Chola kingdom dominated southern India in the 10th and 11th centuries, sending out trading and raiding fleets as far afield as Bengal, Burma and Indonesia.

Ceylon

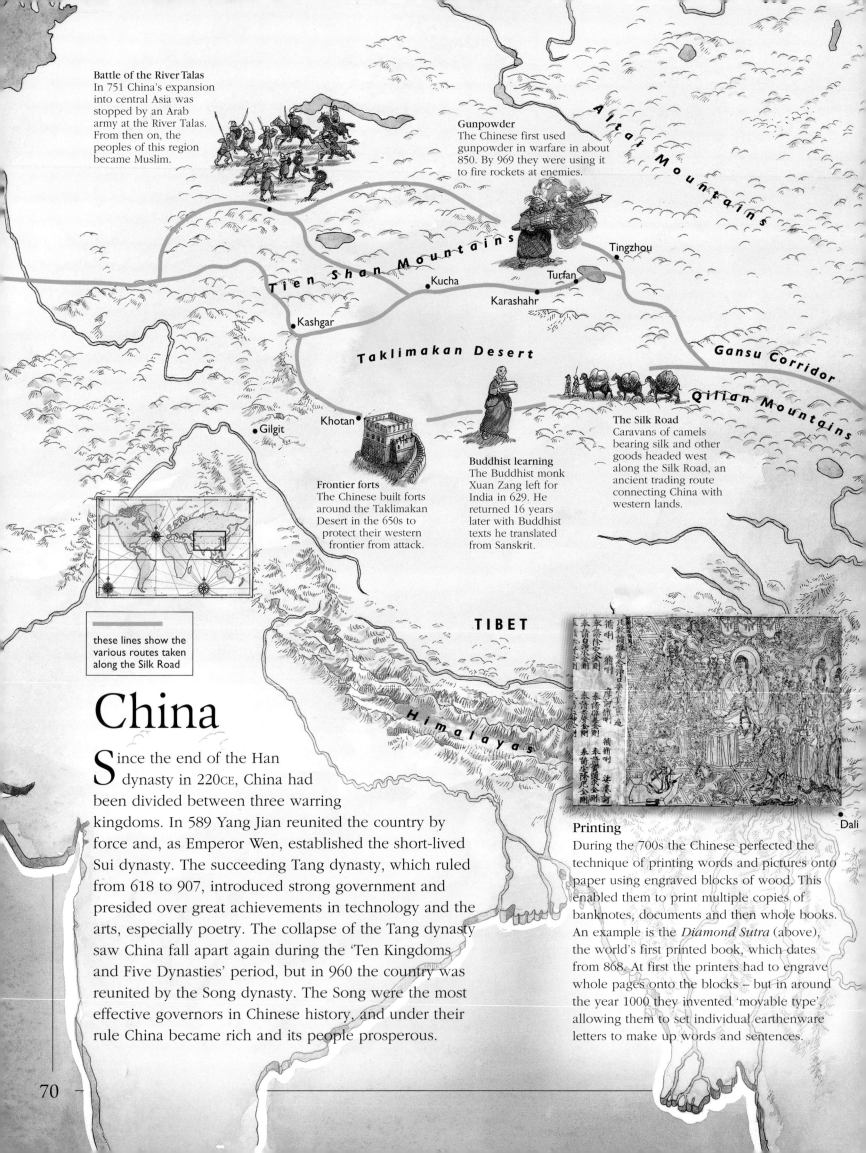

Battle of the River Talas
In 751 China's expansion into central Asia was stopped by an Arab army at the River Talas. From then on, the peoples of this region became Muslim.

Gunpowder
The Chinese first used gunpowder in warfare in about 850. By 969 they were using it to fire rockets at enemies.

Altai Mountains

Tingzhou

Tien Shan Mountains

Kucha

Turfan

Karashahr

Kashgar

Taklimakan Desert

Gansu Corridor

Qilian Mountains

Khotan

• Gilgit

The Silk Road
Caravans of camels bearing silk and other goods headed west along the Silk Road, an ancient trading route connecting China with western lands.

Frontier forts
The Chinese built forts around the Taklimakan Desert in the 650s to protect their western frontier from attack.

Buddhist learning
The Buddhist monk Xuan Zang left for India in 629. He returned 16 years later with Buddhist texts he translated from Sanskrit.

these lines show the various routes taken along the Silk Road

TIBET

Himalayas

Dali

China

Since the end of the Han dynasty in 220CE, China had been divided between three warring kingdoms. In 589 Yang Jian reunited the country by force and, as Emperor Wen, established the short-lived Sui dynasty. The succeeding Tang dynasty, which ruled from 618 to 907, introduced strong government and presided over great achievements in technology and the arts, especially poetry. The collapse of the Tang dynasty saw China fall apart again during the 'Ten Kingdoms and Five Dynasties' period, but in 960 the country was reunited by the Song dynasty. The Song were the most effective governors in Chinese history, and under their rule China became rich and its people prosperous.

Printing
During the 700s the Chinese perfected the technique of printing words and pictures onto paper using engraved blocks of wood. This enabled them to print multiple copies of banknotes, documents and then whole books. An example is the *Diamond Sutra* (above), the world's first printed book, which dates from 868. At first the printers had to engrave whole pages onto the blocks – but in around the year 1000 they invented 'movable type', allowing them to set individual earthenware letters to make up words and sentences.

Invasion from the north
In 1127 the Jurchen from Manchuria seized much of northern China, keeping control until the Mongols conquered their empire a century later.

The Great Wall
The Great Wall was regularly strengthened to keep out invaders from the north – but it did not always succeed in that purpose!

G o b i   D e s e r t

traders bringing furs from the north

● Beijing

fields being irrigated

KOREA

barges carrying grain and other products to Chang'an

The Grand Canal
In the early 600s the Chinese built a massive internal waterway, linking Yue to Beijing via Luoyang.

Yellow River
CHANG'AN   ● Kaifeng
                Luoyang ●

Chang'an
The Tang capital of Chang'an had more than one million inhabitants in 750. It was the world's biggest city at that time.

Granaries
Wen, the first Sui emperor, had granaries built to store grain – in case of a food shortage.

Yangtze

rice growing

oxen being used to plough fields

CHINA

Yue ●
Hangzhou ●

Government
Taizong, the second Tang emperor, created a strong, central administration, and introduced a tough entrance exam for new public servants.

Porcelain
The first true porcelain was made in eastern China during the Tang period. In the west, we call this pottery 'china'.

Tea
Buddhist monks brought tea bushes into China from the lower slopes of the Himalayas in India. Tea soon became a national drink.

Guangzhou ●

printing block for making books and documents

typical Chinese house

Death of an emperor
The last Song emperor drowned in a naval battle with the Mongols off the island of Yashan, near Guangzhou, in 1279.

0 ———— 600 km
0 ———— 300 miles

500CE–1300CE

500CE

589 General Yang Jian reunites China and, as emperor Wen, founds Sui dynasty

600CE

604–17 Wen's successor Yang tries to conquer Korea and fails; peasants revolt against him
606–09 Grand Canal is constructed
617 Li Yuan captures Sui capital of Luoyang
618 Li Yuan becomes first Tang emperor as Gaozu
626 Gaozu deposed (removed from power) by his son Taizong, one of China's most capable rulers

640–59 Chinese expand into central Asia

700CE

700s Block printing is invented

751 Arab victory over Chinese at Talas river ends Chinese control over central Asia

791 Tibetans seize western China after their military victory at Tingzhou

800CE

825 Chamber locks first installed on Chinese canals

c. 850 Gunpowder first used in warfare

859–84 Peasant revolts weaken Tang government

900CE

907 Tang empire collapses
907–60 China divided between the Five Dynasties state and the Ten Kingdoms
960 Song Taizu becomes emperor of the Five Dynasties and begins to reunite China
979 Song Taizu's brother Song Taizong reunites China and founds Song dynasty; start of Northern Song period

1000CE

c. 1000 Printing by movable type invented

1090 Water-driven mechanical clock constructed for Song court

1100CE

1117–24 Jurchen people of Manchuria conquer Liao state north of China and set up Jin empire
1127 Jin invade and capture Song capital of Kaifeng; Song retreat south and establish new capital at Hangzhou – start of Southern Song period

1150 Chinese navigators begin to use magnetic compass

1200CE

1200 Chinese build ships with watertight bulkheads to make them safer at sea
1200 Water-powered textile machinery first used
1226 Mongols overrun western China
1234 Mongols conquer northern China and begin to attack the Southern Song empire

1279 Mongols conquer Southern Song empire

1300CE

Japan and Korea

The histories of Korea and Japan are both entangled with that of their powerful neighbour, China. The Korean kingdom of Silla managed to throw the Chinese off the Korean Peninsula in 676CE and eventually unify the country under the ruling Koryo dynasty by 936. Both Korea and Japan tried to create strong, centralized states – as China had done – but in Japan powerful families undermined the authority of the emperor. One such family, the Fujiwaras, effectively became the rulers of the country in 858. However, as the emperor withdrew from public life, rival warlords and samurai (warrior knights) fought each other for control.

Mongol invasions
It took the Mongols almost 30 years to conquer mountainous Korea, which finally came under the control of Mongol China in 1258.

New borders
In the 15th century, the Yi dynasty expanded Korea to the northeast. They set up numerous border forts to protect their new frontier.

KOGURYO

The Long Wall
From 1033–44 the Koreans built a sturdy earth wall along their northern frontier to protect their country against invading armies from the north.

Buddhism
Monks first brought Buddhism to Korea from China in around 372, although Zen Buddhism did not establish itself until the 600s.

Korean Peninsula

Kaegyong

Seoul

Korean peasant growing rice

SILLA

Writing Korean
In 1444 King Sejong the Great introduced a new alphabetical script, known today as Hangul, to replace the difficult-to-use Chinese writing.

PAEKCHE

Medieval Japan
Powerful Japanese lords built castles – such as the 14th-century White Heron castle at Himeji, shown here – from which to dominate and often terrorize the surrounding countryside. These lords became the real power in the land after the emperor withdrew to his royal court in 794. They had huge private estates and employed private armies of samurai knights to protect their interests. During the 12th century the samurai took over in Japan, seizing control in 1192 and setting up a military dictatorship that lasted until 1868.

Yellow Sea

'Divine wind'
Mongol invasion fleets heading for Japan were twice scattered by typhoons. The Japanese named this wind *kamikaze*, or 'divine wind'.

| 0 | | 500 km |
| 0 | | 250 miles |

Independent islanders
Primitive hunter-gatherers, unrelated to the Japanese, lived on the northern island of Hokkaido, which did not become part of Japan until the 17th century.

Hokkaido

Trade links
Trade, cultural and religious links between China, Korea and Japan were common, but smugglers and pirates tried to evade customs fees and other restrictions.

Pacific Ocean

Sea of Japan

Wooden houses
Japanese houses were built of light wood so that they could easily be restored or rebuilt if damaged by an earthquake.

inshore fishing around Japan

rice growing in Japan

Honshu

Coming of spring
During the 8th century, the emperor decreed that people should celebrate the arrival of cherry blossom in the spring.

Tale of Genji
Lady Murasaki Shikibu wrote the epic *Tale of Genji*, one of the world's first novels, at the royal court in 1007.

End of the Taira
Samurai warriors from the Taira clan were defeated at the battle of Dannoura in 1185.

JAPAN

Mount Fuji
Mount Fuji, known locally as Fujisan, is the sacred mountain of Japan.

• Heian

• Himeji

■ NARA

Nara
In 710 the Japanese established their first capital at Nara, later an important centre for the Buddhist religion.

• Dannoura

Shikoku

• Hakata Bay

Kyushu

White Heron castle
Local warlords built large stone castles, such as the White Heron castle at Himeji. They commanded their estates from these castles.

Noh theatre
In the 14th century Kan'ami Kiyotsugo developed a formal style of drama known as Noh theatre, in which actors use expressive masks.

Whale hunting
Whales have always been an important source of food for the Japanese.

500CE

500s Koguryo, Silla and Paekche kingdoms emerge in Korea

552 Buddhism introduced into Japan from Korea
562 Japanese expelled from Korea after 200 years of occupation

600CE

604 Prince Shotoku introduces Chinese-style government, giving power to the Japanese emperor instead of to the nobility
646 New Taika reforms bring all Japanese land into imperial ownership
660–676 Chinese occupy most of Korea until driven out by Silla

700CE

700s Japanese Shinto religion merges with Buddhism
708 First official coins minted in Japan
710 Japanese capital set up at Nara
780 Struggle between king and powerful lords leads to break-up of Silla
794 Emperor Kammu moves Japanese royal court to Heian (modern-day Kyoto) and gives land to the nobility

800CE

858 Fujiwara Yorifusa becomes regent of Japan; his family now runs Japan

900CE

918–36 Koryo dynasty unifies Silla and unites Korea for the first time

1000CE

1007 Lady Murasaki Shikibu writes 'Tale of Genji' in the royal court at Heian

1033–44 Koreans build the Long Wall to protect their country from northern enemies

1100CE

1100s Fujiwaras lose power to armed samurai clans

1180–85 Gempei war in Japan between Taira and Minamoto samurai clans ends in Taira defeat
1192 Minamoto Yoritomo establishes military shogunate government in Japan

1200CE

1231–58 Mongols subdue Korea, which then falls under control of Mongol China

1274, 1281 Khubilai Khan's two attempts to invade Japan from Korea are both destroyed by 'kamikaze' ('divine wind') typhoons

1300CE

1333–36 Go-Daigo tries but fails to restore direct imperial rule in Japan
1356 End of Mongol rule in Korea

1392 Yi dynasty takes power in Korea (until 1910) and expands country to its borders of today

1400CE

1444 King Sejong the Great of Korea introduces the new alphabetical Hangul script

1467–77 Civil war between rival samurai clans in Japan

1500CE

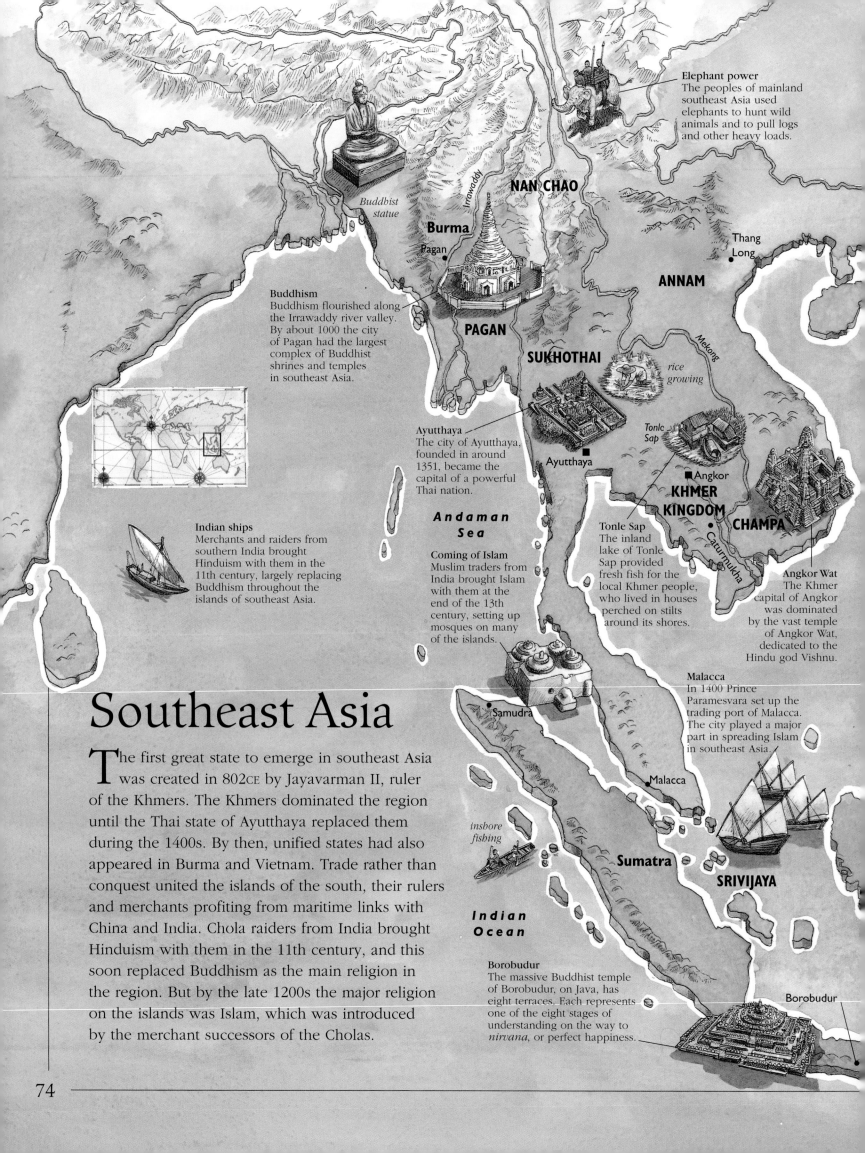

Elephant power
The peoples of mainland southeast Asia used elephants to hunt wild animals and to pull logs and other heavy loads.

Buddhist statue

NAN CHAO

Burma
Pagan

Irrawaddy

Thang Long

ANNAM

PAGAN

Buddhism
Buddhism flourished along the Irrawaddy river valley. By about 1000 the city of Pagan had the largest complex of Buddhist shrines and temples in southeast Asia.

SUKHOTHAI

Mekong

rice growing

Tonle Sap

Indian ships
Merchants and raiders from southern India brought Hinduism with them in the 11th century, largely replacing Buddhism throughout the islands of southeast Asia.

Ayutthaya
The city of Ayutthaya, founded in around 1351, became the capital of a powerful Thai nation.

Ayutthaya

Angkor

KHMER KINGDOM

CHAMPA

Andaman Sea

Coming of Islam
Muslim traders from India brought Islam with them at the end of the 13th century, setting up mosques on many of the islands.

Tonle Sap
The inland lake of Tonle Sap provided fresh fish for the local Khmer people, who lived in houses perched on stilts around its shores.

Caturmukha

Angkor Wat
The Khmer capital of Angkor was dominated by the vast temple of Angkor Wat, dedicated to the Hindu god Vishnu.

Malacca
In 1400 Prince Paramesvara set up the trading port of Malacca. The city played a major part in spreading Islam in southeast Asia.

Samudra

Malacca

Southeast Asia

The first great state to emerge in southeast Asia was created in 802CE by Jayavarman II, ruler of the Khmers. The Khmers dominated the region until the Thai state of Ayutthaya replaced them during the 1400s. By then, unified states had also appeared in Burma and Vietnam. Trade rather than conquest united the islands of the south, their rulers and merchants profiting from maritime links with China and India. Chola raiders from India brought Hinduism with them in the 11th century, and this soon replaced Buddhism as the main religion in the region. But by the late 1200s the major religion on the islands was Islam, which was introduced by the merchant successors of the Cholas.

inshore fishing

Indian Ocean

Sumatra

SRIVIJAYA

Borobudur
The massive Buddhist temple of Borobudur, on Java, has eight terraces. Each represents one of the eight stages of understanding on the way to *nirvana*, or perfect happiness.

Borobudur

74

CHINA

South China Sea

Mongol ships
During the 1200s the Mongols attacked the Burmese and Thai states, and even sent an invasion fleet south to Java in 1292–93.

Chinese trading junks
The Ming dynasty of China encouraged trade with southeast Asia. Fleets of junks carried spices and other precious goods.

Brunei

Borneo

native people

Java   **Bali**

The Khmers

The Khmer people lived in the Mekong river valley, establishing their first unified nation in around 400CE. In 802 Jayavarman II, a minor king, proclaimed himself *devaraja* ('god-king') and ruled all the Khmer peoples from his capital of Angkor. The Khmers had strong trading links with India, so they adopted the Hindu religion and Indian styles of architecture. In 1113 Suryavarman II began to build the massive temple complex of Angkor Wat (shown above) outside the capital.

0 ——— 1000 km
0 ——— 500 miles

600CE–1500CE

600CE
600 First Thai state of Nan Chao created in north of region

650 Buddhists establish first states in Burma

700CE
700 First Khmer state of Chen-La at its peak under King Jayavarman I, but soon declines

750 Srivijaya state dominates Sumatra and other islands

800CE
800 Work begins on the construction of Buddhist Borobudur temple on Java
802 Jayavarman II founds Khmer empire

850 Burmese establish state of Pagan

880 Khmers rule Mon and Thai people to their northwest

900CE
900 Indravarman I founds new Khmer capital at Angkor

939 Vietnamese set up first state of Dai Vet in Annam

1000CE
1000 Thais move south into Mon and Khmer kingdoms

1025 Cholas from southern India raid islands of southeast Asia and introduce Hinduism

1050 First unified Burmese state created by Pagan

1100CE
1113 Suryavarman II rules the Khmer people; work begins on his state temple complex at Angkor Wat

1150 Khmer empire at its height

1200CE
1250 Thais establish powerful Sukhothai state
1253 Mongols destroy Nan Chao

1287 Mongols sack Pagan
1290 Islam first introduced to Sumatra
1292–93 Mongol fleet threatens Java

1300CE
1300s Majapahit dynasty from Java dominates trade in the islands

1351 Thai state of Ayutthaya established

1378 Ayutthaya conquers Sukhothai and unites all Thai people

1400CE
1400 Trading port of Malacca is founded
1403–33 Chinese admiral Zheng He leads trading expeditions throughout region

1431 Khmers move capital south to Caturmukha to escape Thai pressure and abandon Angkor

1500 Khmers now a minor regional power

1500CE

The Pacific

For more than 1,000 years, intrepid Polynesian navigators from Tahiti, and elsewhere in the central Pacific Ocean, had sailed out to colonize the more remote islands. By about 1000CE they had reached Aotearoa, which we now call New Zealand. Its two large islands were far colder and wetter than their homelands further north, and they had to learn to cultivate new crops and build better shelters. They hunted the moa, a large flightless bird, for its meat and grew sweet potatoes and other crops. On many of the Pacific islands, the Polynesians built ceremonial platforms out of coral, called *marae*, where their priests conducted religious and social ceremonies.

Hawaii

Heiau
The *heiau* of Hawaii are very similar to the *marae* found on other Polynesian islands. They had raised platforms on which the priests stood to conduct religious ceremonies.

South Pacific Ocean

Line Islands

Basket weaving
Women wove baskets, bowls and other items from the leaves of the coconut palm.

Atoll fishing
Throughout the region, Polynesians caught fish by standing on the semi-submerged coral atolls and attacking fish with spears.

Tuvalu

Society Islands

Samoa

thatched home

Fiji

Cook Islands

Tonga

Fishing equipment
Fishermen carved pearl shells to make hooks. They twisted coconut fibres to create lines and nets.

Hillside terraces
On hilly islands, such as Hawaii and the Cook Islands, farmers built terraces on the steep hillsides in which to grow crops such as taro and other root vegetables.

musical instruments

Kermadec

Tasman Sea

Inshore fishing
Fishermen caught their catch of fish from a simple canoe stabilized by a special frame called an outrigger.

sails being made from palm leaves

Combat
Maori warriors fought each other with spears or clubs made of whalebone or greenstone, a type of jade.

Ocean-going canoe
The Polynesians travelled thousands of kilometres in twin-hulled canoes. These canoes could carry up to 200 people as well as all their supplies for the long voyage.

Maori tattoos
A Maori chief, or *rangatiri*, had his face tattooed as a mark of his importance. His clothes were made of flax and kiwi feathers.

Maori warrior hunting a moa

Aotearoa

Chatham Islands

500CE

by 500 Polynesians have reached the Hawaiian Islands, their most northerly settlement in the Pacific

600CE

600 Ceremonial 'marae', or platforms, common throughout the Pacific islands

700CE

700 Easter Islanders begin to build ceremonial 'ahu', or platforms

800CE

900CE

c. 900 Polynesians settle in remote Pitcairn Islands

1000CE

c. 1000 Polynesians begin to settle in Aotearoa (New Zealand)
1000 Easter Islanders begin to carve giant statues
1050 South American sweet potato grown on Cook Islands, suggesting contact between Polynesians and native Americans

1100CE

1100 Polynesians reach Chatham Islands, their last settlement in the Pacific

1200CE

1200 Tribal chiefdoms develop throughout Polynesia

1300CE

1300 Conflict between rival Maori tribes leads to construction of 'pas' (fortified settlements) in Aotearoa

1400CE

1500CE

Easter Island

Polynesian navigators reached the remote Easter Island, in the eastern Pacific, in around 300CE. In about 1000CE, the 7,000 or so inhabitants of the island began to carve huge stone statues in the island's three main quarries. They used hammers made of basalt rock because they had no iron. Once finished, the Polynesians hauled these massive statues across the island on wooden sledges, using palm trunks as levers and rollers to help them, and erected the statues on platforms in their ceremonial *ahu* – the equivalent of the *marae* platforms found elsewhere in the Pacific.

Leaf plates
Polynesians lived off seafood, yams and fruit, eating their food from plates made of leaves.

Marquesas Islands

Tahiti

Marae
A *marae* was used for religious and ceremonial purposes. It consisted of a flat court paved with coral and a series of raised platforms. Upright slabs marked where the priests and officials stood.

rope being made from coconut palm fibres

Pitcairn Islands

outrigger canoe

Island statues
Easter Islanders carved and erected more than 1,000 stone statues – probably to honour their ancestors. Some of these statues had inlaid eyes of white coral and red obsidian, a dark volcanic glass.

Easter Island

South Pacific Ocean

humpback whale

0	2000 km
0	1000 miles

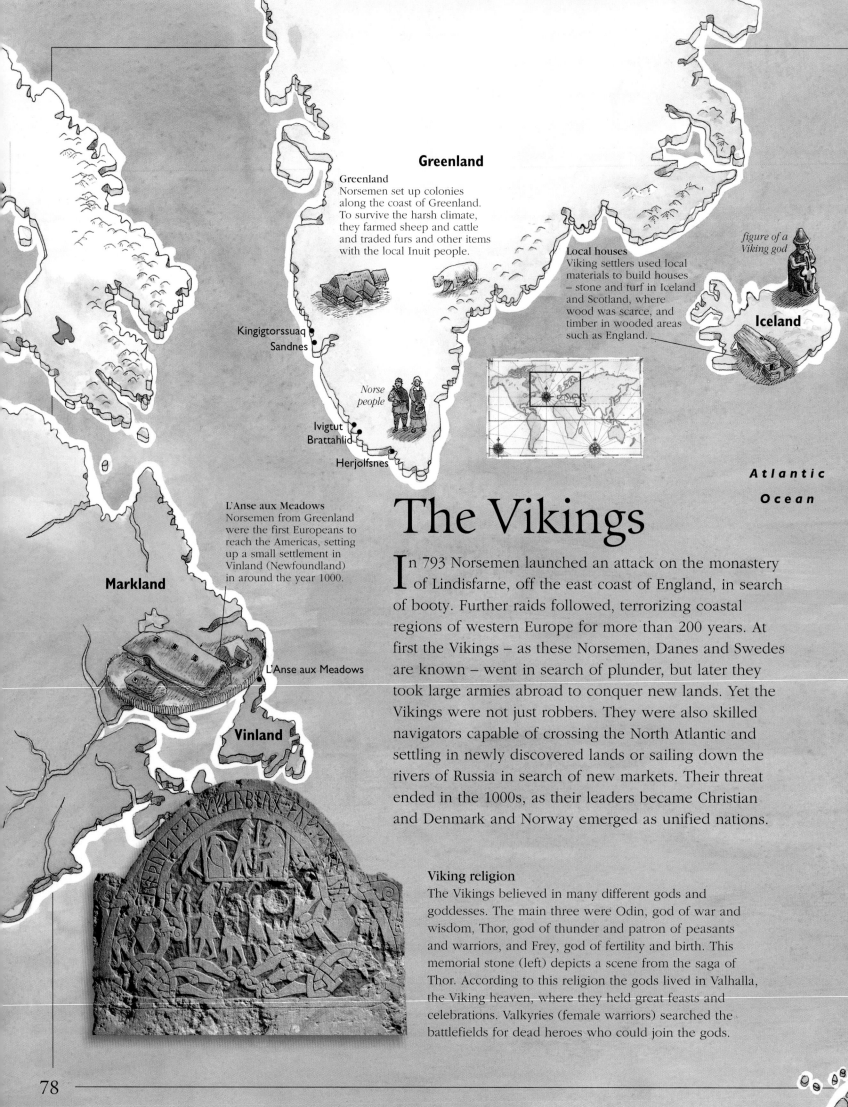

Greenland

Greenland
Norsemen set up colonies along the coast of Greenland. To survive the harsh climate, they farmed sheep and cattle and traded furs and other items with the local Inuit people.

Local houses
Viking settlers used local materials to build houses – stone and turf in Iceland and Scotland, where wood was scarce, and timber in wooded areas such as England.

figure of a Viking god

Iceland

Kingigtorssuaq
Sandnes

Norse people

Ivigtut
Brattahlid

Herjolfsnes

Atlantic Ocean

L'Anse aux Meadows
Norsemen from Greenland were the first Europeans to reach the Americas, setting up a small settlement in Vinland (Newfoundland) in around the year 1000.

Markland

L'Anse aux Meadows

Vinland

The Vikings

In 793 Norsemen launched an attack on the monastery of Lindisfarne, off the east coast of England, in search of booty. Further raids followed, terrorizing coastal regions of western Europe for more than 200 years. At first the Vikings – as these Norsemen, Danes and Swedes are known – went in search of plunder, but later they took large armies abroad to conquer new lands. Yet the Vikings were not just robbers. They were also skilled navigators capable of crossing the North Atlantic and settling in newly discovered lands or sailing down the rivers of Russia in search of new markets. Their threat ended in the 1000s, as their leaders became Christian and Denmark and Norway emerged as unified nations.

Viking religion

The Vikings believed in many different gods and goddesses. The main three were Odin, god of war and wisdom, Thor, god of thunder and patron of peasants and warriors, and Frey, god of fertility and birth. This memorial stone (left) depicts a scene from the saga of Thor. According to this religion the gods lived in Valhalla, the Viking heaven, where they held great feasts and celebrations. Valkyries (female warriors) searched the battlefields for dead heroes who could join the gods.

Runestones
The Vikings celebrated battles and heroes by erecting stones carved with pictures and words in their runic alphabet.

Funeral ships
Viking chieftains were buried in their ships with all they would need for the afterlife. Some ships were covered with mounds of earth while others were set alight.

Sailing to Iceland
Between 870 and 930, more than 10,000 Norsemen made the seven-day crossing of the North Atlantic to settle in Iceland.

Viking log wood home

longhorn cow

woolly sheep

Gotland
Paviken in Gotland was the major Viking commercial centre in the Baltic, trading amber and furs for silks, spices and silver from as far away as Constantinople and Baghdad.

Norway

Sweden

Gotland

Novgorod

silver brooch

Scotland

Lindisfarne monastery raided by Vikings

king port Dublin

Lindisfarne

York

Dublin

England

Ireland

Danelaw

Wessex

North Sea

Baltic Sea

Smolensk

Rus traders
Swedish traders sailed down the Dnieper and Volga rivers to the Black and Caspian seas. The locals called these Vikings 'Rus'.

Denmark

Hamburg

Viking forts
During the 980s King Harald Bluetooth built four huge circular forts in Denmark.

Rhine

Louvain

CAROLINGIAN EMPIRE

Viking trade
Vikings erected runestones along their trade routes, which covered a wide area. Arab silver coins have been found in Sweden.

Kiev

Normans
In 911 the French king allowed Danes to settle around Rouen in France.

Rouen

Nantes

Loire

Viking warriors

Arles

Pisa

Black Sea

Viking sword

Santiago de Compostela

KINGDOM OF THE ASTURIAS AND LEÓN

Narbonne

UMAYYAD EMIRATE

Lisbon

Seville

Algarve

IDRISID CALIPHATE

North Africa

Constantinople

BYZANTINE EMPIRE

Plunder
Vikings raided Mediterranean ports for booty, sailing up the rivers to attack inland towns.

Mediterranean Sea

0 — 1000 km
0 — 500 miles

700CE

750CE

793 Norse raiders attack Lindisfarne monastery on coast of England, the first of many raids against the British Isles
799 First Norse raids on Frankish coast; Charlemagne sets up coastal defences to protect his empire

800CE

830s Start of large-scale raids against British Isles and Carolingian empire

841 Norsemen establish a trading base at Dublin
845 The Franks buy off the raiders by paying them Danegeld (protection money)

850CE

859–62 Viking raiders attack Mediterranean ports
862 Rus create first Russian state around Novgorod
865 Danish Great Army invades England
870 Norsemen settle in Iceland

878 Alfred, King of Wessex, defeats Danes and restricts them to the eastern Danelaw region of Britain

900CE

911 Charles the Simple of France allows Danes to settle around Rouen, leading to the creation of Normandy

950CE

954 Viking kingdom of York falls to English king

965 Harald Bluetooth of Denmark is first Viking king to be baptised a Christian

980 Danes renew their raids on England
986 Erik the Red founds Norse settlements in Greenland

1000CE

1000 Norse settlement established at L'Anse aux Meadows on North American coast

1014 Danes conquer England
1016–35 King Cnut rules vast kingdom of Denmark, Norway and England

1050CE

1066 The Normans (the Danes that settled in Normandy) conquer England

1100CE

Medieval Europe

Medieval Europe was dominated by two great institutions: the feudal system and the Catholic Church. Feudalism began in France during the 700s CE and eventually spread throughout Europe. Kings granted estates to their leading noblemen in return for military service. Knights fought for these noblemen and received smaller estates of land, farmed by serfs (peasants) in return for military protection. This structure was bound together by oaths of loyalty. The Catholic Church was the sole religious authority in western Europe but also claimed increasing control over secular (non-religious) rulers, leading to constant struggles with powerful emperors and kings.

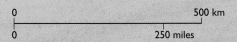

0		500 km
0	250 miles	

The Crusades

In 1095, Pope Urban II (right, above throne) issued a call to European leaders to win back the Holy Land from Muslim control, because the Seljuk Turks were disrupting pilgrimage routes through Asia to the sacred Christian sites. A series of crusades (military expeditions) set out from Europe over the next 200 years, capturing Jerusalem in 1099 and ruling the Holy Land until the crusaders were driven out in 1291.

The Black Death

In the 1330s, bubonic plague broke out in eastern Asia, spreading to the Black Sea in 1346. Rats on ships, infested with parasitic fleas, carried the plague to European ports in 1347 and it soon spread across the continent. By the time the plague died out in 1351, about 24 million people – one-third of Europe's population – had died, causing many social and economic problems. Towns and farms lost their workers, prices fell and wages rose as labour became scarce.

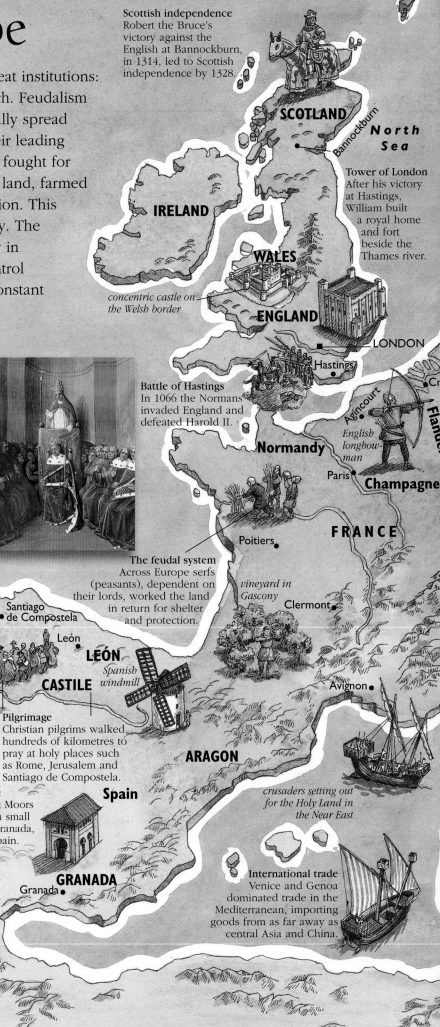

Scottish independence
Robert the Bruce's victory against the English at Bannockburn, in 1314, led to Scottish independence by 1328.

SCOTLAND

North Sea

Bannockburn

Tower of London
After his victory at Hastings, William built a royal home and fort beside the Thames river.

IRELAND

WALES

concentric castle on the Welsh border

ENGLAND

LONDON

Hastings

Battle of Hastings
In 1066 the Normans invaded England and defeated Harold II.

Normandy

Agincourt

English longbow-man

Paris

Champagne

Flanders

FRANCE

Poitiers

The feudal system
Across Europe serfs (peasants), dependent on their lords, worked the land in return for shelter and protection.

vineyard in Gascony

Clermont

Avignon

Santiago de Compostela

León

LEÓN

Spanish windmill

CASTILE

PORTUGAL

Pilgrimage
Christian pilgrims walked hundreds of kilometres to pray at holy places such as Rome, Jerusalem and Santiago de Compostela.

Lisbon

Muslim rule
The Muslim Moors controlled a small region in Granada, southern Spain.

Spain

ARAGON

crusaders setting out for the Holy Land in the Near East

GRANADA

Granada

International trade
Venice and Genoa dominated trade in the Mediterranean, importing goods from as far away as central Asia and China.

SWEDEN

Neva

fir trees

sturdy Hanseatic cog (ship) used to transport goods

Novgorod •

The Hanseatic League
Thirty-seven northern German and Baltic towns formed a league that dominated trade in northern Europe.

Trade settlements
Hanseatic traders set up kontors (foreign depots) where their merchants could live and trade securely.

• Lubeck

Hamburg •

salted fish from the Baltic

European assault
In 1241 the Mongols wiped out vast European armies in Poland and Hungary. They withdrew when their leader Ogedai died, saving Europe from conquest.

HOLY ROMAN EMPIRE

Germany

The Habsburgs
The Habsburg family conquered Austria in 1282. They dominated the Holy Roman Empire from 1274 until its end in 1806.

LITHUANIA

Kiev •

POLAND

Banking
In the 1400s, the Fugger family of Augsburg and the Medicis of Florence ran banks that lent money to local rulers and merchants.

Orthodox Christianity
The peoples of the Balkans and Russia were Orthodox Christians.

Augsburg •

wooden house in Kiev

Austria

C a r p a t h i a n s

HUNGARY

A l p s

The Ottomans
The Ottomans from central Turkey defeated the Serbs at the Battle of Kosovo in 1389. They went on to conquer the rest of the Balkans.

Universities
The first university in Europe was set up at Bologna, Italy, in 1088.

Venice •

B a l k a n s

Genoa •

B l a c k S e a

Bologna •

Florence •

Kosovo

Rome •

Orthodox monastery
Mount Athos in Greece was the most important Orthodox Christian monastery.

Constantinople •

The papacy
The pope was the head of the Catholic Church. He was also an important political figure and owned a lot of land in Italy and France.

NAPLES

Gallipoli •

Mount Athos •

BYZANTINE EMPIRE

SICILY

M e d i t e r r a n e a n S e a

1000CE

1050CE
1054 Final split between Roman Catholic and Orthodox churches
1066 Duke William of Normandy invades England and seizes throne
1073 Pope Gregory VII increases authority of the papacy over secular kings
1095 Pope Urban II calls for First Crusade against Muslim rule in the Holy Land

1100CE

1143 Spanish kingdom of León recognizes Portugal's independence

1150CE
1154 Henry II of England rules vast Angevin empire, which stretches from Scotland down to Spanish kingdoms

1171 English begin to rule Ireland

1200CE
1212 Christian troops win an important battle against Muslim Moors in Spain
1230 Kingdoms of Castile and León unite in Spain
1230 Towns of Lubeck and Hamburg form Hanseatic League
1241 Mongol invasion of Europe called off after Mongol leader dies

1250CE

1274 Rudolph I becomes first Habsburg ruler of Holy Roman Empire

1282 Habsburgs rule Austria
1284 English king Edward I ends Welsh independence

1300CE
1309–77 Papacy moves to Avignon in France; major split in Catholic Church
1314 English defeated by Scots at Bannockburn
1337–1453 Hundred Years' War between England and France — caused by English claims on the French throne
1347–51 Black Death devastates Europe

1350CE
1354 Ottomans seize Gallipoli, their first foothold in Europe

1368 Lithuanians become Christian
1378–1417 Election of rival popes leads to Great Schism (split) in Catholic Church
1380 Hans Fugger sets up bank at Augsburg

1400CE
1414 Medicis of Florence, Italy, become papal bankers
1415 English archers win major battle against the French at Agincourt

1429 Joan of Arc drives English out of France

1450CE

1500CE

Medieval Europe:
Castles and villages

During the medieval period, most people in Europe lived in small villages owned by the lord of the manor. Often, they died in the same village they were born in, and rarely travelled much further than the local market town. Most people were serfs, which means that they were landless peasants who worked the lord of the manor's lands in return for shelter and protection. The great lords of the country – the dukes and earls – lived in vast stone castles, heavily fortified against attack by rival lords or invading armies. The first castles were built in France during the 9th century.

A medieval village
This photograph shows Riquewihr, in France. A medieval village such as this was ruled by the lord of the manor, a knight who had been given the manor (estate) and all its houses and fields by his lord. The lord of the manor sat in judgement at the local manorial court.

Knights in armour
A knight was a mounted warrior granted a fief (estate) by a rich and powerful nobleman in return for loyalty and military service. Knights were trained to ride and fight from an early age, learning their skills in jousts and tournaments. They followed an elaborate code of chivalry, which dictated their behaviour on and off the battlefield.

Siege warfare

Siege warfare became increasingly important as castles became better fortified. A besieging army had two options. The first was to surround the enemy castle and starve the defenders until they gave in. The second option was to try to force a way in, digging under the walls or breaking them down with battering rams, catapults and (from the 14th century) cannons, or climbing over the walls with ladders or movable drawbridges.

Steep river cliff location, above the River Wye, to aid defence

Great tower begun in 1067, one of the first stone castle buildings in Britain

Inner defensive wall

Chepstow castle

The castle at Chepstow in south Wales, UK, was begun in the 11th century. Medieval castles served as a residence for the local nobleman, as well as a military headquarters for his knights and the centre of power in the region. The first castles were built of wood and stood on top of a raised earthwork surrounded by a ditch, but later castles were made of stone and specially designed to withstand a siege.

Fortified gatehouse

Defensive ditch surrounds outer walls to prevent enemy siege equipment getting close

On horseback
Mongol warriors were skilled archers, accurately firing volleys of arrows over 200m while on horseback.

Frozen invasion
In the winter of 1238–39 the Mongols invaded Russia, using its frozen rivers as highways. This was the only successful winter invasion of Russia in history.

• Novgorod

Russian Principalities

Mongol horses could run for up to 95km a day

POLAND

Legnica

European assault
In 1241 the Mongols wiped out vast European armies in Poland and then Hungary.

• Krakow

Kiev •

HUNGARY

• Mohi

The Golden Horde
The Mongol state that ruled southern Russia was known as the Khanate of the Golden Horde, probably after the colour of the first Khan's tent.

Kara-khitai
• Otrar

BYZANTINE EMPIRE

Black Sea

Caspian Sea

Timur
The last great Mongol leader, Timur, was a Turkish-speaking Muslim nomad.

Tashkent •

■ SAMARKAND

• Tiflis

Khwarizm Shahdom

• Kabul

Mongol defeat
In 1260, with nowhere for their horses to graze in the desert, the Mongols were stopped by the Mamlukes of Egypt at 'Ain Jalut.

• Damascus
'Ain Jalut

Siege engines
The Mongols paid foreign engineers to build siege engines capable of destroying city walls – such as at Baghdad in 1258.

Baghdad •

Isfahan •

Abbasid Caliphate

Samarkand
Timur brought skilled workers from across the Middle East to build mosques and public buildings in his capital, Samarkand.

H i m a

SULTANATE OF DELHI

Towers of skulls
In Isfahan, Timur killed 70,000 people so that he could build towers with their skulls.

The Mongols

In 1206CE the young son of a minor Mongol chief united the warring Mongol tribes behind him. These warring people named him Genghis Khan, meaning 'the Great' Khan. By the time of his death in 1227, he had conquered an empire that covered most of central Asia. His successors continued these conquests so that the Mongols soon ruled the biggest empire in world history. Yet the Mongols had no experience of government and could not even read or write. After the death of Ogedai, the second Great Khan, in 1241, the Mongol empire split into smaller 'khanates'. Timur attempted to recreate the empire in the late 1300s, but the Mongols soon disappeared from history – almost as fast as they had arrived.

- - - -
dotted line shows the extent of the Mongol empire at its height in about 1280

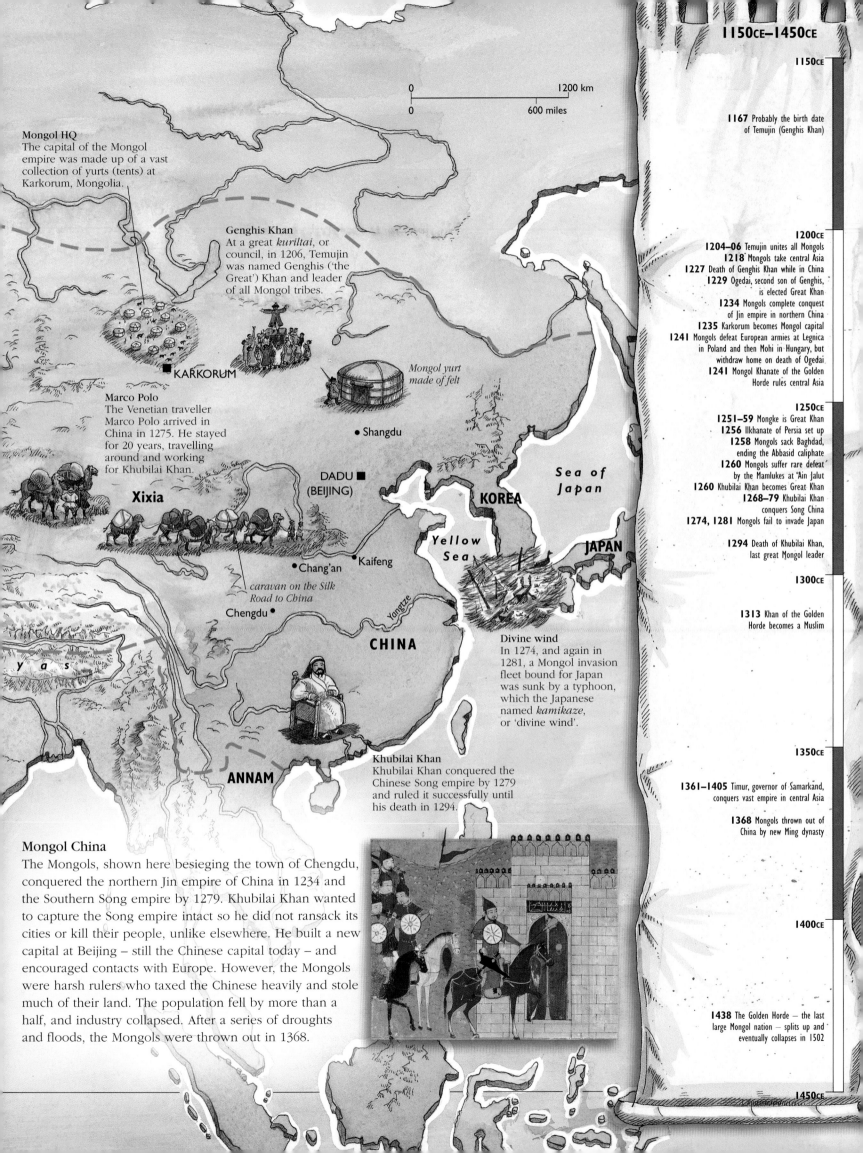

Mongol HQ
The capital of the Mongol empire was made up of a vast collection of yurts (tents) at Karkorum, Mongolia.

Genghis Khan
At a great *kuriltai*, or council, in 1206, Temujin was named Genghis ('the Great') Khan and leader of all Mongol tribes.

KARKORUM

Mongol yurt made of felt

Marco Polo
The Venetian traveller Marco Polo arrived in China in 1275. He stayed for 20 years, travelling around and working for Khubilai Khan.

• Shangdu

DADU
(BEIJING)

Xixia

Sea of Japan

KOREA

caravan on the Silk Road to China

• Chang'an   • Kaifeng

Yellow Sea

JAPAN

Chengdu •

Yangtze

CHINA

Divine wind
In 1274, and again in 1281, a Mongol invasion fleet bound for Japan was sunk by a typhoon, which the Japanese named *kamikaze*, or 'divine wind'.

ANNAM

Khubilai Khan
Khubilai Khan conquered the Chinese Song empire by 1279 and ruled it successfully until his death in 1294.

Mongol China

The Mongols, shown here besieging the town of Chengdu, conquered the northern Jin empire of China in 1234 and the Southern Song empire by 1279. Khubilai Khan wanted to capture the Song empire intact so he did not ransack its cities or kill their people, unlike elsewhere. He built a new capital at Beijing – still the Chinese capital today – and encouraged contacts with Europe. However, the Mongols were harsh rulers who taxed the Chinese heavily and stole much of their land. The population fell by more than a half, and industry collapsed. After a series of droughts and floods, the Mongols were thrown out in 1368.

1150CE

1167 Probably the birth date of Temujin (Genghis Khan)

1200CE
1204–06 Temujin unites all Mongols
1218 Mongols take central Asia
1227 Death of Genghis Khan while in China
1229 Ogedai, second son of Genghis, is elected Great Khan
1234 Mongols complete conquest of Jin empire in northern China
1235 Karkorum becomes Mongol capital
1241 Mongols defeat European armies at Legnica in Poland and then Mohi in Hungary, but withdraw home on death of Ogedai
1241 Mongol Khanate of the Golden Horde rules central Asia

1250CE
1251–59 Mongke is Great Khan
1256 Ilkhanate of Persia set up
1258 Mongols sack Baghdad, ending the Abbasid caliphate
1260 Mongols suffer rare defeat by the Mamlukes at 'Ain Jalut
1260 Khubilai Khan becomes Great Khan
1268–79 Khubilai Khan conquers Song China
1274, 1281 Mongols fail to invade Japan

1294 Death of Khubilai Khan, last great Mongol leader

1300CE

1313 Khan of the Golden Horde becomes a Muslim

1350CE

1361–1405 Timur, governor of Samarkand, conquers vast empire in central Asia

1368 Mongols thrown out of China by new Ming dynasty

1400CE

1438 The Golden Horde – the last large Mongol nation – splits up and eventually collapses in 1502

1450CE

African kingdoms

Trade in gold, ivory, salt, cattle – and also slaves – brought great wealth to the interior (non-coastal parts) of Africa. This led to the creation of a number of wealthy trading nations, such as Ghana, Mali and Great Zimbabwe. The west African states grew rich on trade across the Sahara with the Muslim world and Europe to their north. On the east coast, Muslim merchants set up independent trading cities that prospered by doing business across the Indian Ocean – with the Arabian Peninsula, India and China. Arab merchants introduced Islam to west Africa and coastal east Africa, while Christianity flourished in both Axum and Ethiopia in the east of the continent.

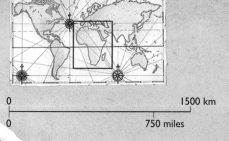

Portuguese exploration
After 1432, Portuguese navigators began to explore the west coast of Africa – in search of trade and wealth.

The Almoravids
In 1056 the nomadic Almoravids began to conquer northwest Africa, building their capital city at Marrakech.

salt mining in the western Sahara

Trading markets
Timbuktu was the main market in west Africa. Gold, ivory and slaves were exchanged for luxuries from the north.

camel caravan on the trans-Saharan trade route

Mansa Musa
Mansa Musa was a wealthy king who ruled Mali from 1312 to 1337. In 1324 he went on the *hajj*, or pilgrimage to Mecca.

PORTUGAL
SPAIN
MOROCCO
MARRAKECH
Sahara
MALI
• Timbuktu
GHANA
Jenne •
Hausa States
KANEM-BORNU
BENIN
• Ife
Igbo-Ukwu
• Benin

mosque at trading city of Jenne

farming

Islam in west Africa
Arab merchants from the north brought Islam into west Africa after 750, making it the main religion in the area by 1000.

Gold mining
Gold was mined throughout the coastal forests of west Africa. It was made into royal jewellery or traded north in return for other precious goods.

Ife people
The Yoruba people of Ife in west Africa made beautiful terracotta sculptures of their rulers and other heroes.

Atlantic Ocean

0 — 1500 km
0 — 750 miles

Congo
CONGO

African trade

East African trade was dominated by a series of independent coastal cities, from Mogadishu in the north down to Sofala. These cities were largely ruled by the Swahilis. The Swahilis were descendants of Arab, Omani, Yemeni and Persian traders who had settled on the coast after 1000, bringing Islam with them. The rulers of these cities acted as middlemen between traders from the African interior and the Arab and Persian merchants who traded across the Indian Ocean. The vast range of these trading contacts can be seen by the presence of this giraffe in Beijing in 1414, a gift from the Swahili ruler of Malindi to the Ming emperor of China.

Cape of Good Hope

Mediterranean Sea

Baghdad

Persia

EGYPT

Mecca

Arabia

Oman

Arabian Sea

Red Sea

Yemen

Islam in North Africa
The Arabs conquered Egypt by 642 and the rest of North Africa by 711, replacing Christianity and native religions with Islam.

NUBIA

MAKKURA

Rock churches
Lalibela, Christian king of Ethiopia, built 11 churches out of solid rock, all in the shape of a cross.

AXUM • Axum

SUDAN • Lalibela

African elephant

ETHIOPIA

ADAL

Arab merchants
Arab and Persian merchants traded gold, ivory and slaves from the east coast across to the Middle East, India and China. They brought back luxuries such as cotton, silk and spices.

simple canoe

Mogadishu

Slavery
Black Africans were captured and taken to the coastal trading towns, where they were sold into slavery.

Manda
Malindi

Mombasa

Zanzibar

Indian Ocean

Kilwa

Trading cities
Muslim merchants from the Arabian Peninsula and Persia settled on the east coast after 1000, building rich and powerful trading cities.

Cattle
Owning cattle brought great wealth to Great Zimbabwe and other inland states, although disputes about grazing rights often led to war.

Iron-working
By about 1000, the Bantus had introduced iron-working to almost all of southern Africa.

Great Zimbabwe • Sofala

Great Zimbabwe
At the centre of Great Zimbabwe was a large stone-walled enclosure housing the royal family and their advisors.

Gold and ivory trade
Gold, copper and ivory from Great Zimbabwe and surrounding states were traded down to Sofala, in return for cotton cloth, beads and manufactured goods.

Khoisan hunter-gatherer

700CE–1500CE

700CE
700 Kingdom of Ghana founded
702 Arabs overcome Berbers of northwest Africa
711 Arabs complete conquest of North Africa
738 Arabs first raid west Africa for slaves
750 Trade across Sahara begins to flourish
750 Abbasid dynasty rules Muslim North Africa from Baghdad in what is now Iraq
789 Rival dynasties break up unity of Muslim North Africa

800CE
800 First trading towns, including Kilwa, founded on east African coast

900CE

975 Christian kingdom of Axum in northern Ethiopia destroyed by pagan invaders

1000CE
1000s Islam becomes major religion in west Africa; Arab merchants bring Islam to east Africa
1000s Bantus introduce iron-working to southern Africa
1056–94 Yahya ibn Masa founds Berber Almoravid emirate, ruling northwest Africa and Spain
1070 Almoravids build new capital at Marrakech
1076 Almoravids invade Ghana

1100CE

1147 Almoravids lose control to Berber Almohads, who then conquer most of north African coast

1200CE
c. 1200 Great Zimbabwe founded
c. 1200 First east African coins issued at Kilwa
1212 Christian armies defeat Almohads and drive them out of Spain
1220 Persian Shairazi dynasty rules Mogadishu
1230s Sun Diata founds empire of Mali
1250 Kingdom of Benin founded in west Africa
1269 Marinids seize Morocco and go on to control whole of northwest Africa
1270 Solominid dynasty takes power in Ethiopia

1300CE

1317 Muslims conquer Christian kingdom of Makkura in Sudan
1324 King Mansa Musa of Mali makes pilgrimage to Mecca

1400CE
1400s Timbuktu becomes major centre of Islamic culture and trade in west Africa
1415 Portuguese establish first European colony in Africa at Ceuta, northeast of Marrakech
1415 Ethiopians defeat Muslim ruler of Saylac and expand their territory to the Red Sea
1432 Portuguese begin to explore west African coast

1500CE

Polar traders
Inuits and Norsemen from Greenland traded ivory, furs, textiles, tools, food and other items as far north as Ellesmere Island in the Arctic Ocean.

Trapping caribou
Native American hunters set up camp by river crossings. They trapped and killed caribou as they crossed the river for their fur, meat and antlers.

Buffalo traps
Plains Indians killed buffalo by driving them over a cliff edge – a practice that lasted for more than 7,000 years.

whale hunting off the Pacific coast

Pacific Ocean

Chaco Canyon
This D-shaped, four-storey apartment building at Pueblo Bonito in the Chaco Canyon housed up to 1,200 people in 800 rooms.

Medicine Creek •

Pueblo Bonito •
• Chaco Canyon

• Cahokia

Shell carving
People in the southern Mississippi river valley carved shells with religious symbols for use in ceremonies at temple mounds.

Cahokia
Cahokia was founded in around 600CE. A vast earth temple mound, used for religious purposes, dominated the city.

Great Plains

Farming the plains
Small farming villages on the Great Plains grew maize, squash and other products for eating or trade with nomadic hunters.

native farmer in Mexico

searching for seashells

Gulf of Mexico

Chichén Itzá
Chichén Itzá, founded in 850, survived as the Toltec capital of the Yucatán Peninsula until it was attacked in 1221.

Tenochtitlán
The Aztec capital city had a vast temple complex at its centre.

Yucatán Peninsula

Toltec statues
The Toltecs lived in the Valley of Mexico and their capital city was at Tula. They erected huge statues at the top of their large pyramid temple at Tula.

■ **TULA**

TENOCHTITLÁN ■

CHICHÉN ITZÁ ■

Mayan scribe writing on folded bark

• Palenque
Tikal •

jaguar in the Mayan jungle

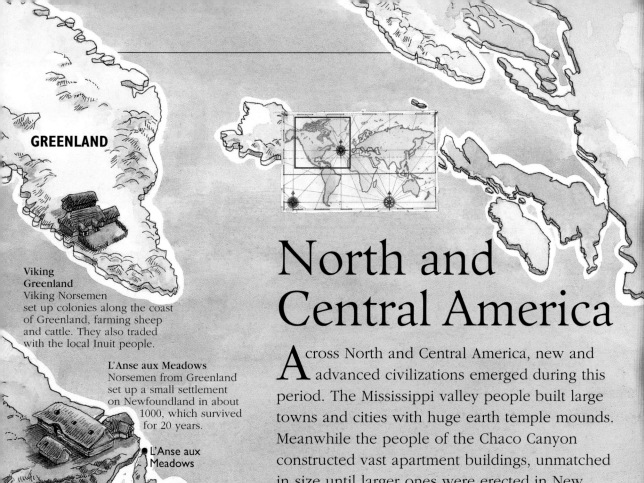

GREENLAND

Viking Greenland
Viking Norsemen set up colonies along the coast of Greenland, farming sheep and cattle. They also traded with the local Inuit people.

L'Anse aux Meadows
Norsemen from Greenland set up a small settlement on Newfoundland in about 1000, which survived for 20 years.

● L'Anse aux Meadows

| 0 | 1000 km |
| 0 | 500 miles |

Atlantic Ocean

North and Central America

Across North and Central America, new and advanced civilizations emerged during this period. The Mississippi valley people built large towns and cities with huge earth temple mounds. Meanwhile the people of the Chaco Canyon constructed vast apartment buildings, unmatched in size until larger ones were erected in New York City during the 19th century. Small farming villages sprang up in the eastern woodlands and on the Great Plains, while the people of the west coast lived settled lives fishing the abundant Pacific Ocean. To their south, the Maya and Toltec civilizations flourished in Central America until the Aztecs emerged to dominate the region during the 1400s.

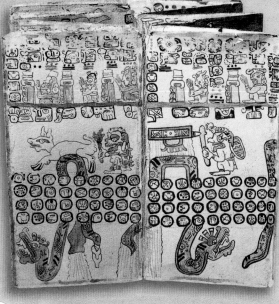

The Maya
The Maya were the only people in the Americas to devise a complete writing system. Their complex script was made up of glyphs (pictures), which represented both entire words and individual sounds. They used these glyphs to record the names and deeds of their families and kings on walls, pillars and other stone monuments in their cities. They also made codices, which were books of bark paper coated with gesso (plaster and glue) and folded like a concertina. Only four of these books now survive, giving us a picture of what life was like in the Maya civilization.

600CE
600 Plains hunters now use bows and arrows to hunt wild game
c. 600 Cahokia founded in northern Mississippi valley

700CE
700 Mississippi valley people begin to build small towns with temple mounds
700 Farming villages flourish in the southwest regions of North America

800CE
800 Hardier strains of maize and beans increase food production in Mississippi valley, allowing population to rise
850 Chichén Itzá, last Mayan state, is founded

900CE
900 Toltecs found state with capital at Tula
900 Network of villages, linked by roads, begun at Chaco Canyon
900 Small farming villages spring up on the Great Plains
900 Hohokam farmers begin to irrigate fields
986 Erik the Red founds Viking settlement in Greenland

1000CE
1000 Permanent farming villages built throughout the eastern woodlands
1000 Viking settlement founded by Leif Erikson at L'Anse aux Meadows in Newfoundland
1000 Toltecs conquer Mayan states in Yucatán Peninsula
1000s Thule Inuits settle in Alaska and gradually move east, forcing out earlier Inuit inhabitants

1100CE
1100 Towns with large ceremonial centres built in Mississippi region
1168 Tula is sacked and the Mexican Toltec state collapses

1200CE
1200 Cahokia at height of its power, with more than 10,000 inhabitants
1200s Aztecs move into Valley of Mexico
1221 Chichén Itzá seized, ending Toltec rule in the Yucatán region

1300CE
1300s Thule Inuits settle in Greenland
1300s Droughts cause decline of Chaco Canyon villages
1325 Aztecs found Tenochtitlán

1400CE
1428–40 Aztecs begin to expand empire under Itzcóatl
1450 Norse settlements in Greenland die out and are occupied by Thule Inuits

1500CE

Central America:
The Aztecs

The Aztecs were the last and most powerful in a long line of peoples who lived in the fertile Valley of Mexico in Central America. They were a warlike tribe who dominated the region after the 1200s, capturing enemy warriors in order to sacrifice them to their own sun god. The Aztecs were spectacular builders, creating vast cities and temple complexes. They kept elaborate records of their achievements painted on sheets of bark that were then folded into books.

The Aztec world
The Aztecs believed that the universe had been created and destroyed four times before the current, 'fifth creation' in which they lived. This vast stone, measuring 4m across, tells this story. The sun god is in the middle, with the four previous creations around him, and then a band showing the 20 days of each Aztec calendar month.

Aztec religion
The main god of the Aztecs was Huitzilopochtli (above), the sun god and god of war. The Aztecs feared that one day the sun god would fail to rise into the sky and their world would come to an end. To keep the sun god alive, the Aztecs made human sacrifices to nourish the god with hearts and blood.

Daily life
Aztec houses were made of adobe (mud brick) and often only had a single room. They were furnished with low tables and reed mats for beds. Aztec women cooked meals of maize tortillas (pancakes) wrapped around meat or vegetables such as beans, peppers, avocados and tomatoes.

The Aztec capital: Tenochtitlán

The name Tenochtitlán means the 'place of the high priest Tenoch'. It was the capital of the Aztec empire and it was built on an island in the middle of a lake, connected to the shore by wide causeways. At the height of its power in the early 1500s, the city housed about 500,000 people and was far larger than most European cities of that time. Tenochtitlán is now buried beneath Mexico City.

Templo Mayor

In the centre of Tenochtitlán was a walled precinct built for ceremonial and religious purposes. It was dominated by the Templo Mayor, a vast pyramid 60m high. At the top were two shrines dedicated to Tlaloc, the god of rain, and Huitzilopochtli, the god of war. Here priests made offerings and human sacrifices to the gods, placing the skulls of the victims on the walls of the two shrines. Each Aztec ruler expanded the Templo Mayor, building a bigger and more impressive temple around and on top of the previous one.

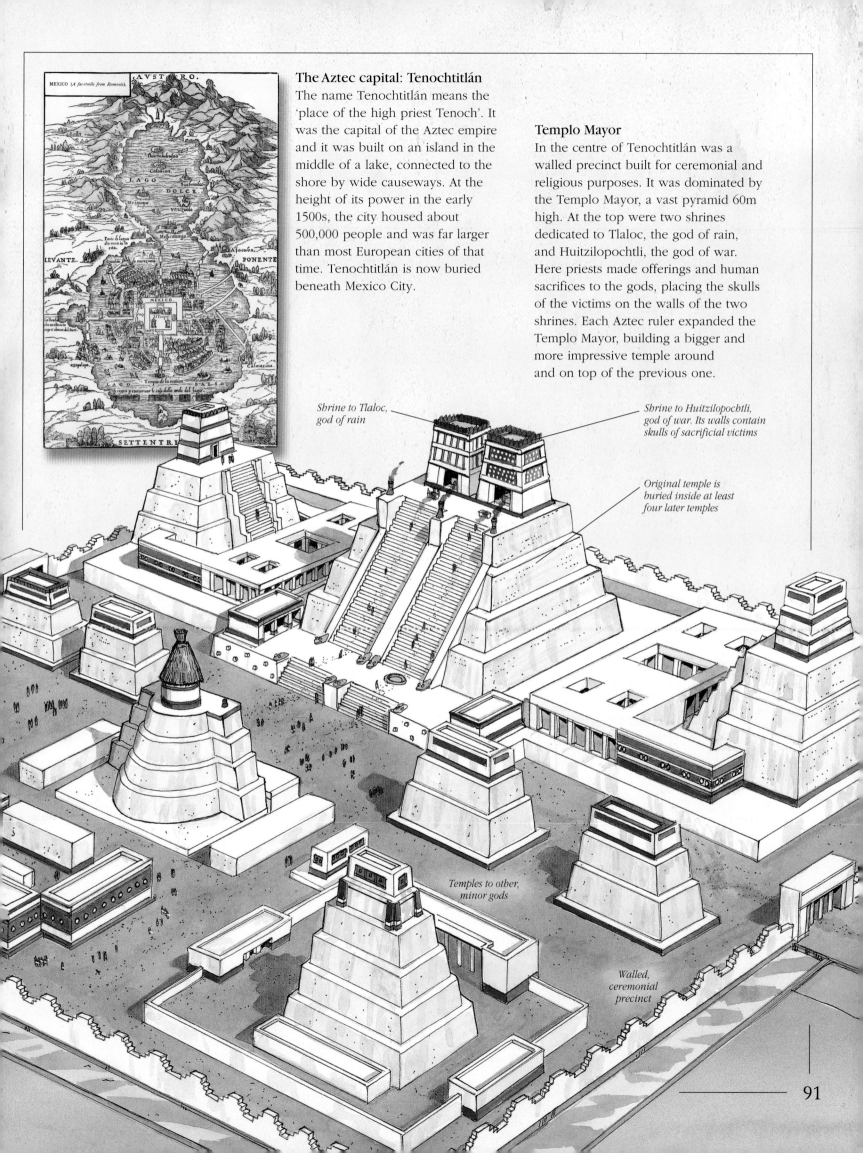

MEXICO (A fac-simile from Ramusio).

Shrine to Tlaloc, god of rain

Shrine to Huitzilopochtli, god of war. Its walls contain skulls of sacrificial victims

Original temple is buried inside at least four later temples

Temples to other, minor gods

Walled, ceremonial precinct

Chimús and Incas

Some time around 1220CE, a semi-legendary figure called Manco Capac founded the Inca state at Cuzco, high in the Andes mountains, in what is now southern Peru. The new state was slow to expand but in the mid-1400s it grew rapidly, conquering the neighbouring Chimú empire to its north and soon controlling 3,500km of Pacific coastline – from modern-day Ecuador in the north to central Chile in the south. The all-powerful Inca emperor governed more than 12 million people, keeping control through a powerful army and a network of fine roads, along which troops could be moved in an emergency. Efficient social services cared for the sick and needy, while everyone was expected to work hard to keep themselves busy and out of trouble at all times.

these lines show the location of the Inca roads

dotted line shows the extent of the Inca empire in 1525

Inca scribes
The Inca scribes who kept the quipus were highly valued, as they were the only people who could 'read' the information recorded in the quipu strings.

Rope bridges
Rope suspension bridges, made from twisted vines and wooden slats, were hung across steep ravines and wide river valleys.

Terraced farming
Potatoes, beans, tomatoes, squash and other root crops and vegetables were grown on irrigated terraces carved out of the steep mountainside.

Alpacas
Alpacas were kept for their fine wool, which was made into clothes, hats and rugs.

Textiles
All the South American peoples were skilled textile weavers, using alpaca and other wools to weave clothes, rugs and wall-hangings.

Chan Chan
Ten walled compounds dominated the centre of Chan Chan, the Chimú capital. Repeated designs were carved onto the walls.

Stone finishing
Inca stonemasons finished off the stone walls of important buildings by polishing them with wet sand.

Sacsahuaman
The vast stone fort of Sacsahuaman protected the Inca capital, Cuzco. It could easily house all the people of the city in times of crisis.

Machu Picchu
The mountain-top city of Machu Picchu was a religious centre and frontier post. After the fall of the Inca empire, it was not discovered again until 1911.

Oracle to the gods
With its temple and oracle, Pachamac was one of the major religious centres and pilgrimage sites in the region.

Quito

Andes

Lambayeque Valley

CHAN CHAN

Moche Valley

harvesting a potato crop

sowing maize seeds

Pachacamac

Nazca

Huari

Machu Picchu

CUZCO

La Paz

Tiahuanaco

Lake Titicaca

Lake Poopó

reed boat on Lake Titicaca

A n d e s

Roadside hostels
Rest houses called tambos, sited one day's journey apart, were built along the main roads to house messengers and weary travellers.

Food supplies
Food and clothes stored in the tambos were given out to the elderly, sick and disabled during times of need.

Imperial messengers
Runners stationed at rest houses along the main roads carried messages to and from the emperor in Cuzco. A team of runners could cover 240km a day.

Pack animals
Llamas, the main pack animals of the Incas, were used to carry heavy loads at high altitudes.

The Inca emperor
The emperor was worshipped as the son of the Sun – a living god. He was carried through his empire in style.

Inca walls
Stonemasons built walls using huge stones. The stones were so carefully shaped and fitted that a blade could not be placed between them.

Fishing
Fresh fish caught offshore were carried by relays of runners to the emperor in Cuzco.

• Santiago

Pacific Ocean

1000 km

500 miles

0

0

Inca roads

The Incas were master builders, constructing a strategic network of roads connecting the furthest reaches of their lengthy empire to the imperial capital, Cuzco. The roads had rest houses called tambos, similar to the reconstruction shown here (left). The entire road system measured more than 20,000km long. These roads enabled the emperor to move his army quickly in times of trouble, as well as keep in touch with his regional governors through the imperial messenger system.

Strings of information

The Incas never developed a system of writing, but they worked out a way of recording facts and figures using a system of knotted string known as the quipu. Various coloured cords with single, double or triple knots tied into them hung from a main cord. The colour, position and number of each hanging cord and knot recorded information such as the size of the food harvest, the amount of tax money collected and the size of the population. This was very useful in times of war or emergency.

800CE

850 Chimú capital Chan Chan founded in the coastal Moche Valley

900CE

900 Sicán state founded in Lambayeque Valley in northern Peru

1000CE

1000 The highland empires of Tiahuanaco and Huari collapse

1100CE

1200CE

1200 Chimú empire begins to expand along the coast

c. 1220 Manco Capac founds Inca state at Cuzco in the Peruvian Andes

1300CE

1370 Chimús conquer Sicán state

1400CE

1400 Yahua Huyacac expands Inca empire into neighbouring Andes valleys

1438–71 Emperor Pachacutec rapidly expands Inca empire northwest to the Pacific coast

1470 Incas conquer Chimú empire

1471–93 Tupac Yupanqui, son of Pachacutec, expands Inca empire southwards

1494–1525 Under Huayna Capac, Inca empire reaches its greatest extent

1500CE

EXPLORATION & EMPIRE

Illustrated by Mark Bergin

CONTENTS

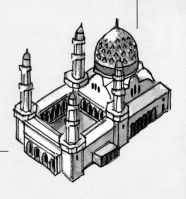

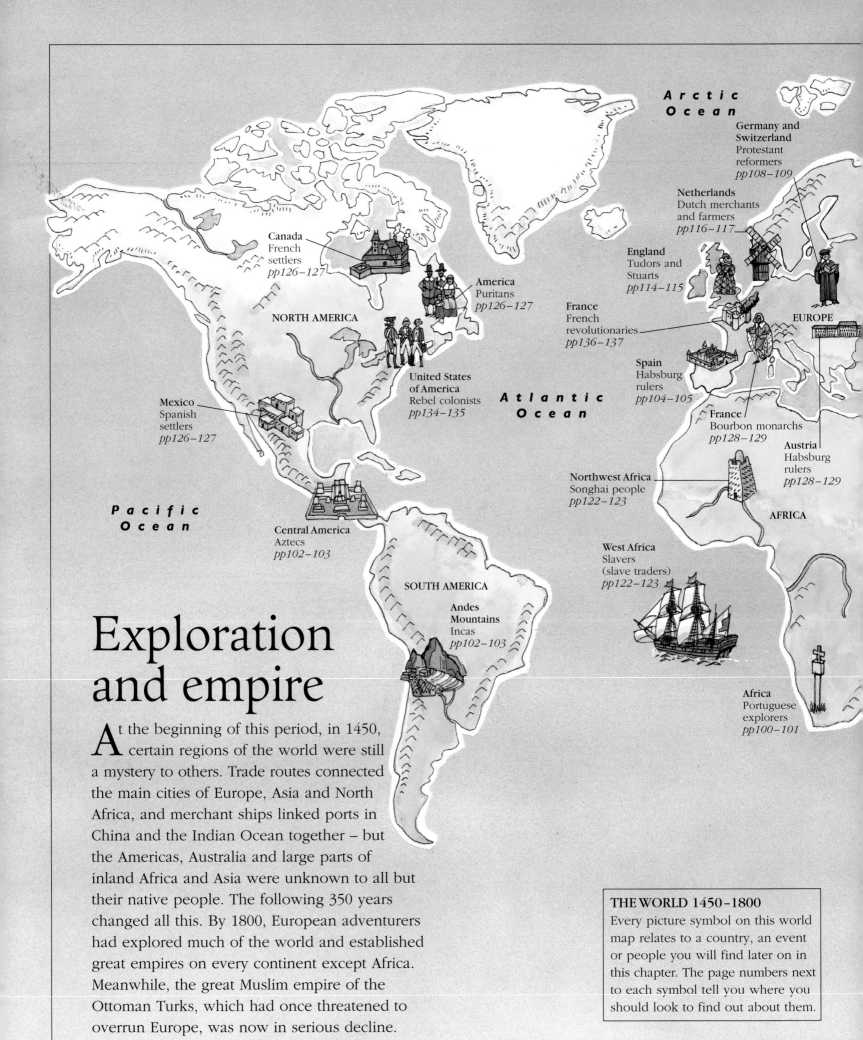

Canada
French
settlers
pp126–127

America
Puritans
pp126–127

NORTH AMERICA

United States
of America
Rebel colonists
pp134–135

Mexico
Spanish
settlers
pp126–127

Central America
Aztecs
pp102–103

SOUTH AMERICA

Andes
Mountains
Incas
pp102–103

Arctic Ocean

Germany and
Switzerland
Protestant
reformers
pp108–109

Netherlands
Dutch merchants
and farmers
pp116–117

England
Tudors and
Stuarts
pp114–115

France
French
revolutionaries
pp136–137

EUROPE

Spain
Habsburg
rulers
pp104–105

France
Bourbon monarchs
pp128–129

Austria
Habsburg
rulers
pp128–129

Northwest Africa
Songhai people
pp122–123

AFRICA

West Africa
Slavers
(slave traders)
pp122–123

Africa
Portuguese
explorers
pp100–101

Atlantic Ocean

Pacific Ocean

Exploration and empire

At the beginning of this period, in 1450, certain regions of the world were still a mystery to others. Trade routes connected the main cities of Europe, Asia and North Africa, and merchant ships linked ports in China and the Indian Ocean together – but the Americas, Australia and large parts of inland Africa and Asia were unknown to all but their native people. The following 350 years changed all this. By 1800, European adventurers had explored much of the world and established great empires on every continent except Africa. Meanwhile, the great Muslim empire of the Ottoman Turks, which had once threatened to overrun Europe, was now in serious decline.

THE WORLD 1450–1800
Every picture symbol on this world map relates to a country, an event or people you will find later on in this chapter. The page numbers next to each symbol tell you where you should look to find out about them.

Russia
Russians
pp118–119

ASIA

Siberia
Russian merchants
pp120–121

Middle East
The Ottomans
pp110–111

China
Manchus
pp120–121

Japan
Shoguns
pp120–121

India
The Mughals
pp112–113

Pacific Ocean
Spanish explorers
pp100–101

Pacific Ocean

East Africa
Portuguese
traders
pp122–123

Indian Ocean

East Indies
European
traders
pp132–133

AUSTRALIA

Australia
British convicts
pp132–133

LOCATOR MAP
You will find a world map like this along with every map in the chapter. This allows you to see exactly which part of the world the main map is showing you.

KEY TO MAPS IN THIS CHAPTER	
JAPAN	Main region or country
Deccan	Other region or province
■ PARIS	Capital city
● Yorktown	City, town or village
Zambezi	River, lake or island
Andes	Ocean, sea, desert or mountain range
— ∙ — ∙ —	National boundary
- - - - - - -	Empire boundary

1450–1800

1400

1450 Renaissance cultural movement flourishes in western Europe
1453 Ottomans capture Constantinople, bringing the ancient Byzantine empire to an end

1479 Ferdinand of Aragon and Isabella of Castile join their thrones through marriage to unite Spain
1480 Muscovy becomes an independent state
1485 Tudor dynasty begins to rule England
1492 Christopher Columbus first lands in the New World
1498 Vasco da Gama becomes the first European to sail around Africa to Asia

1500

1510 Portuguese found Goa, first European colony in Asia
1517 Martin Luther begins the Protestant Reformation in Europe
1517 Regular shipment of African slaves to the Americas begins
1519 Charles V of Spain is Holy Roman Emperor; Habsburgs dominate Europe
1519–22 Magellan and crew complete the first circumnavigation of the world
1519–33 Spanish capture Aztec and Inca empires
1526 Mughals invade India
1534 Jacques Cartier explores Canada
1543 Copernicus proposes that the Sun is at the centre of the solar system
1545 Catholic Counter-Reformation begins
1556 Charles V divides vast Habsburg empire between Spain and Austria
1558–1603 Elizabeth I rules England
1568 Dutch rebel against Spanish rule

1600

1603 England and Scottish crowns united under King James I
1603 Tokugawa shoguns rule Japan
1607 English establish their first permanent colony in North America
1608 French begin to colonize Canada
1618–48 Thirty Years' War engulfs Europe

1643–1715 Louis XIV rules France
1644 Ming dynasty begins in China
1648 Dutch win official independence from Spain
1649–60 Britain becomes a republic after civil war leads to the execution of its king
1667 Dutch control the Spice Islands
1682–1725 Peter the Great modernizes Russia
1683 Ottomans fail to capture Vienna as their empire begins to decline
1698 Portuguese expelled from the east African coast

1700

1700 Enlightenment cultural movement flourishes in Europe
1707 Mughal empire at its height

1740 Maria Theresa builds the powerful Austrian empire
1740–86 Frederick the Great builds up Prussian military power

1763 British drive the French out of North America
1770 Captain Cook lands in Australia
1775–81 American revolutionary war
1776 Thirteen British colonies in America declare their independence
1789 George Washington becomes first US president
1789 Revolution breaks out in France
1799 Napoleon Bonaparte takes power in France

1800

The world 1450–1800:
What we know about the past

The world changed rapidly after 1450. Inventions long known to the Chinese, such as printing and gunpowder, transformed the world when Europeans discovered them for themselves and then exported them to other continents. New ship designs and navigational aids helped European adventurers to explore and then conquer much of the globe. In some countries, systems of government based on the rule of an emperor or king were gradually replaced with 'democratic' rule by the people, although democracy of this kind would not be widespread until the late 19th century. Not everyone was affected at the same time or same speed by these changes, but the world of 1800 was very different to the world of 1450.

Printing
In a German town called Mainz, in 1448, Johann Gutenberg developed a printing press that used movable type. This led to a revolution in learning, as more and more people were able to obtain and read printed books and pamphlets on a wide range of subjects. It also allowed new or revolutionary ideas to circulate freely as never before. Gutenberg's first printed book was the Bible (above).

Democracy
The intellectual revolution of the 18th century – known as the Enlightenment – led many people to question how they were governed, and to seek to govern themselves through a democracy. By 1800, democratically elected parliaments ruled some western European nations, as well as the United States of America. The picture above shows America's Declaration of Independence from British rule, which took place in 1776.

Powerful monarchs
After 1640, a series of powerful kings ruled in Europe. They were known as 'absolute monarchs' because they believed that they held total power and were answerable to nobody else on Earth. One of the most powerful of these kings was Frederick the Great of Prussia (ruled 1740–86), who ordered the construction of the Neue Palais (below) at Potsdam, outside Berlin in Germany.

The Neue Palais was built in 1763–69 to celebrate Prussia's successes in the Seven Years' War (1756–63) against Austria, France and Russia.

Palace contains more than 200 rooms, including four state reception rooms

New forms of warfare

Gunpowder was known to the Chinese and possibly the Arabs by the 10th century, but its use in Europe from the 14th century onwards revolutionized warfare. European armies used gunpowder to fire lead bullets from rifles and muskets. Armed with these weapons, they easily overwhelmed their opponents, helping them to conquer large parts of the globe by 1800.

Early 17th-century European wheel-lock pistol

Exploration

European navigators began to explore the rest of the world after 1450, discovering the American continent and a new sea route to Asia around the south of Africa. These voyages allowed Europeans to dominate world trade and to set up colonies in every continent. In this picture, Dutch merchants are trading with native Americans in what is now New York.

More than 400 sandstone statues, mass-produced by a team of sculptors

Southern wing contains Frederick's apartments and a small theatre used for operas

Statues of the Three Graces (Beauty, Mirth and Good Cheer) support the Prussian royal crown

Voyages of discovery

In the mid-1400s, European sailors explored the oceans in search of trade, wealth and conquest. The Portuguese led the way, exploring the coast of Africa and discovering a sea route to India and Asia. The Spanish sponsored (financially supported) Columbus to find a westerly sea route to Asia. Instead he found America. The English and French then looked for a northwest route to Asia around the north of North America, while the Dutch looked for a northeast route around Siberia. By 1600, Europeans ruled the seas.

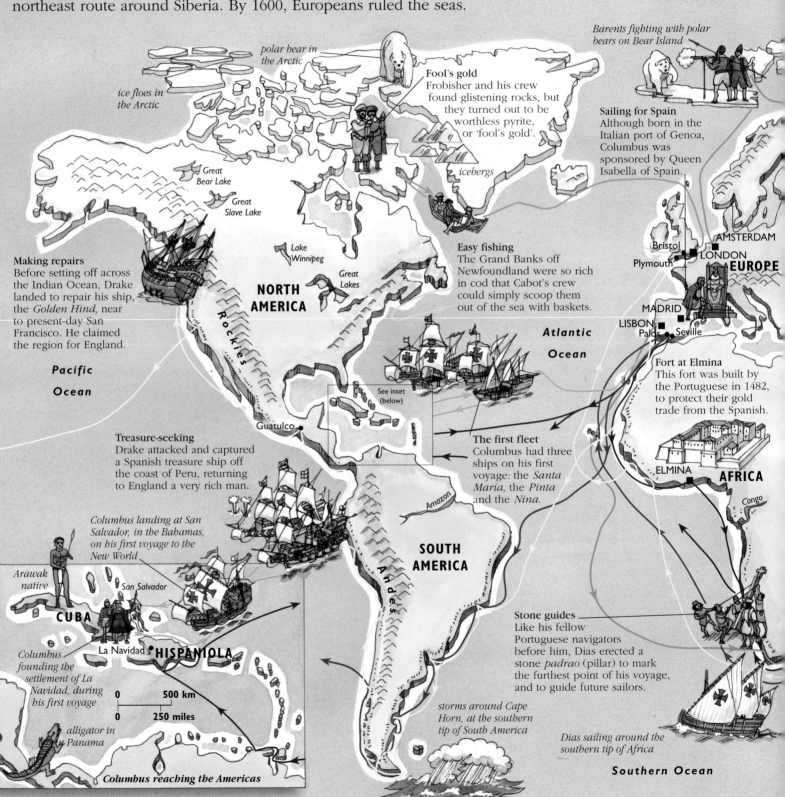

Arctic Ocean

polar bear in the Arctic

ice floes in the Arctic

Barents fighting with polar bears on Bear Island

Fool's gold
Frobisher and his crew found glistening rocks, but they turned out to be worthless pyrite, or 'fool's gold'.

icebergs

Sailing for Spain
Although born in the Italian port of Genoa, Columbus was sponsored by Queen Isabella of Spain.

Making repairs
Before setting off across the Indian Ocean, Drake landed to repair his ship, the *Golden Hind*, near to present-day San Francisco. He claimed the region for England.

Great Bear Lake

Great Slave Lake

Lake Winnipeg

Great Lakes

NORTH AMERICA

Rockies

Pacific Ocean

Easy fishing
The Grand Banks off Newfoundland were so rich in cod that Cabot's crew could simply scoop them out of the sea with baskets.

AMSTERDAM
Bristol
LONDON
Plymouth
EUROPE

MADRID
LISBON
Palos • Seville

Atlantic Ocean

Fort at Elmina
This fort was built by the Portuguese in 1482, to protect their gold trade from the Spanish.

ELMINA
AFRICA

Congo

Treasure-seeking
Drake attacked and captured a Spanish treasure ship off the coast of Peru, returning to England a very rich man.

Guatulco

The first fleet
Columbus had three ships on his first voyage: the *Santa Maria*, the *Pinta* and the *Nina*.

See inset (below)

Amazon

Columbus landing at San Salvador, in the Bahamas, on his first voyage to the New World

SOUTH AMERICA

Andes

Stone guides
Like his fellow Portuguese navigators before him, Dias erected a stone *padrao* (pillar) to mark the furthest point of his voyage, and to guide future sailors.

storms around Cape Horn, at the southern tip of South America

Dias sailing around the southern tip of Africa

Southern Ocean

Columbus reaching the Americas

Arawak native

Columbus founding the settlement of La Navidad, during his first voyage

CUBA

San Salvador

La Navidad • **HISPANIOLA**

| 0 | | 500 km |
| 0 | | 250 miles |

alligator in Panama

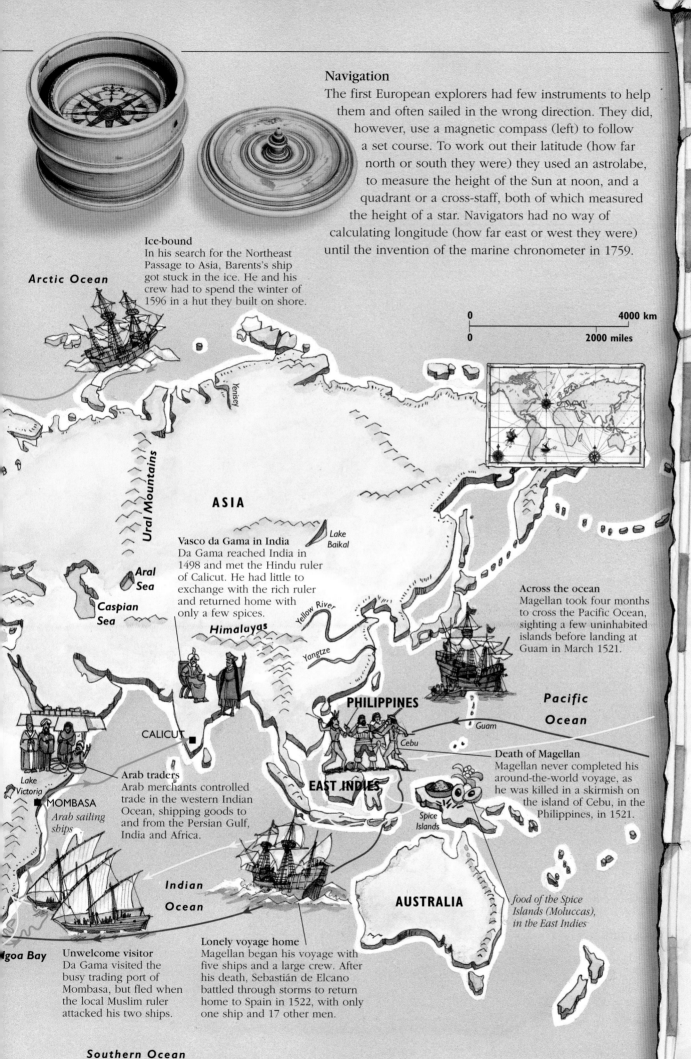

Navigation
The first European explorers had few instruments to help them and often sailed in the wrong direction. They did, however, use a magnetic compass (left) to follow a set course. To work out their latitude (how far north or south they were) they used an astrolabe, to measure the height of the Sun at noon, and a quadrant or a cross-staff, both of which measured the height of a star. Navigators had no way of calculating longitude (how far east or west they were) until the invention of the marine chronometer in 1759.

Ice-bound
In his search for the Northeast Passage to Asia, Barents's ship got stuck in the ice. He and his crew had to spend the winter of 1596 in a hut they built on shore.

Arctic Ocean

0   4000 km
0   2000 miles

Yenisey

Ural Mountains

ASIA

Lake Baikal

Vasco da Gama in India
Da Gama reached India in 1498 and met the Hindu ruler of Calicut. He had little to exchange with the rich ruler and returned home with only a few spices.

Aral Sea

Caspian Sea

Himalayas

Yellow River

Yangtze

Across the ocean
Magellan took four months to cross the Pacific Ocean, sighting a few uninhabited islands before landing at Guam in March 1521.

PHILIPPINES

Pacific Ocean

Guam

Cebu

CALICUT

Arab traders
Arab merchants controlled trade in the western Indian Ocean, shipping goods to and from the Persian Gulf, India and Africa.

Death of Magellan
Magellan never completed his around-the-world voyage, as he was killed in a skirmish on the island of Cebu, in the Philippines, in 1521.

EAST INDIES

Lake Victoria

MOMBASA
Arab sailing ships

Spice Islands

food of the Spice Islands (Moluccas), in the East Indies

Indian Ocean

AUSTRALIA

goa Bay

Unwelcome visitor
Da Gama visited the busy trading port of Mombasa, but fled when the local Muslim ruler attacked his two ships.

Lonely voyage home
Magellan began his voyage with five ships and a large crew. After his death, Sebastián de Elcano battled through storms to return home to Spain in 1522, with only one ship and 17 other men.

Southern Ocean

1450–1600

1450

1460 Death of Prince Henry 'the Navigator', the first Portuguese sponsor (financial supporter) of voyages of discovery

1485–86 Diogo Cao sails down the length of the west African coast for Portugal

1487–88 Dias becomes first European to sail around the southern tip of Africa into the Indian Ocean

1492–93 Columbus becomes first European to sail to the Americas

1493–96 Columbus's second voyage, to the West Indies

1494 Treaty of Tordesillas divides the undiscovered world between Portugal and Spain

1497 Italian John Cabot sails to Newfoundland for the English king

1497–98 Vasco da Gama opens up a new trade route from Europe across the Indian Ocean to India

1498–1500 Columbus's third voyage: he becomes the first European to land in South America

1500

1502–04 Columbus's fourth voyage: he lands in Central America

1519–21 Magellan becomes the first European to sail across the Pacific

1521–22 Sebastián de Elcano completes Magellan's voyage as the first person to sail around the world

1527–28 Pánfilo de Narváez explores the Gulf of Mexico for Spain

1534 Jacques Cartier searches for a Northwest Passage to Asia for the French king, but he discovers Canada instead

1550

1567–69 Álvaro de Mendaña explores the southern Pacific Ocean for Spain

1576 Martin Frobisher explores the Northwest Passage for England

1577–80 Francis Drake sails around the world

1596–98 Dutch navigator Willem Barents explores the Northeast Passage

1600

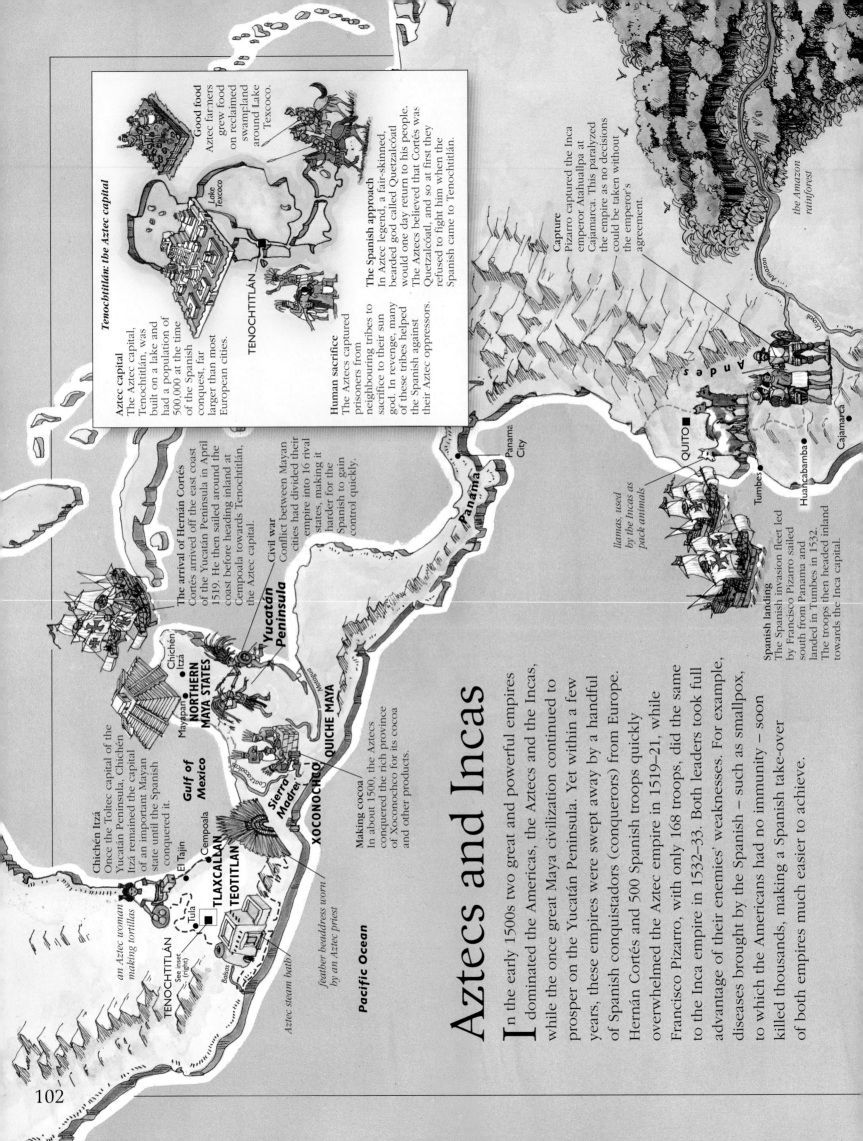

Aztecs and Incas

In the early 1500s two great and powerful empires dominated the Americas, the Aztecs and the Incas, while the once great Maya civilization continued to prosper on the Yucatán Peninsula. Yet within a few years, these empires were swept away by a handful of Spanish conquistadors (conquerors) from Europe. Hernán Cortés and 500 Spanish troops quickly overwhelmed the Aztec empire in 1519–21, while Francisco Pizarro, with only 168 troops, did the same to the Inca empire in 1532–33. Both leaders took full advantage of their enemies' weaknesses. For example, diseases brought by the Spanish – such as smallpox, to which the Americans had no immunity – soon killed thousands, making a Spanish take-over of both empires much easier to achieve.

Tenochtitlán: the Aztec capital

Aztec capital
The Aztec capital, Tenochtitlán, was built on a lake and had a population of 500,000 at the time of the Spanish conquest, far larger than most European cities.

Good food
Aztec farmers grew food on reclaimed swampland around Lake Texcoco.

Lake Texcoco

TENOCHTITLÁN

Human sacrifice
The Aztecs captured prisoners from neighbouring tribes to sacrifice to their sun god. In revenge, many of these tribes helped the Spanish against their Aztec oppressors.

The Spanish approach
In Aztec legend, a fair-skinned, bearded god called Quetzalcóatl would one day return to his people. The Aztecs believed that Cortés was Quetzalcóatl, and so at first they refused to fight him when the Spanish came to Tenochtitlán.

Chichén Itzá
Once the Toltec capital of the Yucatán Peninsula, Chichén Itzá remained the capital of an important Mayan state until the Spanish conquered it.

The arrival of Hernán Cortés
Cortés arrived off the east coast of the Yucatán Peninsula in April 1519. He then sailed around the coast before heading inland at Cempoala towards Tenochtitlán, the Aztec capital.

Civil war
Conflict between Mayan cities had divided their empire into 16 rival states, making it harder for the Spanish to gain control quickly.

Making cocoa
In about 1500, the Aztecs conquered the rich province of Xoconochco for its cocoa and other products.

an Aztec woman making tortillas

TENOCHTITLÁN
See inset (right)

Tula

TLAXCALAN
TEOTITLÁN

Bolsas

Aztec steam bath

feather headdress worn by an Aztec priest

El Tajín
Cempoala

Gulf of Mexico

Chichén Itzá

Mayapán

NORTHERN MAYA STATES

Yucatán Peninsula

Coatzacoalcos

Sierra Madre

XOCONOCHCO

QUICHE MAYA

Usumacinta

Pacific Ocean

Panama
Panama
Panama City

Spanish landing
The Spanish invasion fleet led by Francisco Pizarro sailed south from Panama and landed in Tumbes in 1532. The troops then headed inland towards the Inca capital.

llamas, used by the Incas as pack animals

QUITO

Tumbes

Huancabamba

Cajamarca

A n d e s

Amazon

Ucayali

the Amazon rainforest

Capture
Pizarro captured the Inca emperor Atahualpa at Cajamarca. This paralyzed the empire as no decisions could be taken without the emperor's agreement.

102

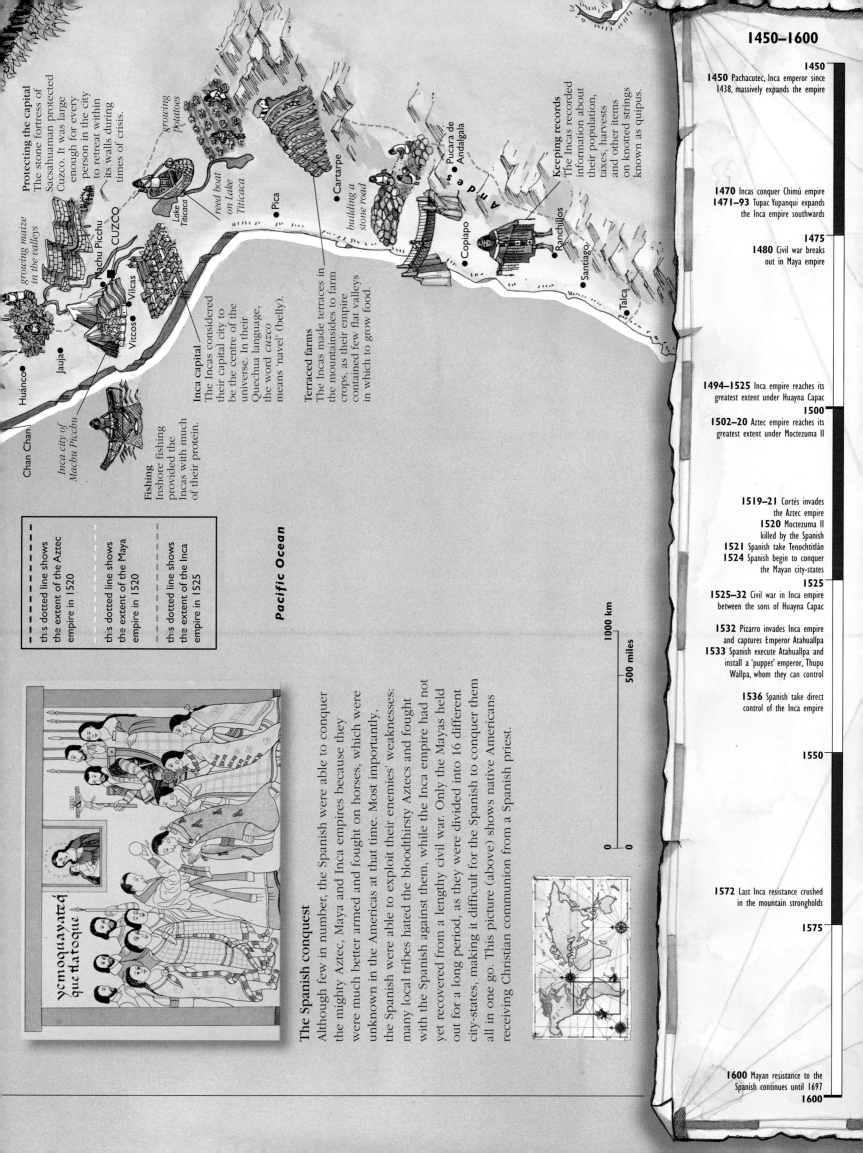

Protecting the capital
The stone fortress of Sacsahuaman protected Cuzco. It was large enough for every person in the city to retreat within its walls during times of crisis.

growing potatoes

Keeping records
The Incas recorded information about their population, taxes, harvests and other items on knotted strings known as quipus.

growing maize in the valleys

Huánco

Chan Chan

Inca city of Machu Picchu

Jauja

Machu Picchu

CUZCO

Vitcos

Vilcas

Lake Titicaca

reed boat on Lake Titicaca

Lake Titicaca

Pica

Cartarpe

building a stone road

Pucara de Andalgala

Copiapo

Ranchillos

Santiago

Talca

A n d e s

Inca capital
The Incas considered their capital city to be the centre of the universe. In their Quechua language, the word *cuzco* means 'navel' (belly).

Terraced farms
The Incas made terraces in the mountainsides to farm crops, as their empire contained few flat valleys in which to grow food.

Fishing
Inshore fishing provided the Incas with much of their protein.

- - - - - this dotted line shows the extent of the Aztec empire in 1520

– – – – – this dotted line shows the extent of the Maya empire in 1520

— — — this dotted line shows the extent of the Inca empire in 1525

Pacific Ocean

1000 km

500 miles

0

0

The Spanish conquest

Although few in number, the Spanish were able to conquer the mighty Aztec, Maya and Inca empires because they were much better armed and fought on horses, which were unknown in the Americas at that time. Most importantly, the Spanish were able to exploit their enemies' weaknesses: many local tribes hated the bloodthirsty Aztecs and fought with the Spanish against them, while the Inca empire had not yet recovered from a lengthy civil war. Only the Mayas held out for a long period, as they were divided into 16 different city-states, making it difficult for the Spanish to conquer them all in one go. This picture (above) shows native Americans receiving Christian communion from a Spanish priest.

ycmoquauayautą que tlatoque

1450

1450 Pachacutec, Inca emperor since 1438, massively expands the empire

1470 Incas conquer Chimú empire
1471–93 Tupac Yupanqui expands the Inca empire southwards

1475

1480 Civil war breaks out in Maya empire

1494–1525 Inca empire reaches its greatest extent under Huayna Capac
1500

1502–20 Aztec empire reaches its greatest extent under Moctezuma II

1519–21 Cortés invades the Aztec empire
1520 Moctezuma II killed by the Spanish
1521 Spanish take Tenochtitlán
1524 Spanish begin to conquer the Mayan city-states
1525

1525–32 Civil war in Inca empire between the sons of Huayna Capac

1532 Pizarro invades Inca empire and captures Emperor Atahuallpa
1533 Spanish execute Atahuallpa and install a 'puppet' emperor, Thupu Wallpa, whom they can control

1536 Spanish take direct control of the Inca empire

1550

1572 Last Inca resistance crushed in the mountain strongholds

1575

1600 Mayan resistance to the Spanish continues until 1697
1600

Charles V and the Habsburg empire
Charles V of Spain was master of Europe. Born in 1500, he inherited the Rhineland and Netherlands from his Habsburg father, plus Spain and its Italian and American empires from his Spanish grandfather and mother. In 1519 he inherited Habsburg Austria from his grandfather and was elected Holy Roman Emperor, in effect the ruler of Germany. He abdicated (resigned) in 1556 and died in 1558.

The Spanish Armada
In 1588 a large fleet left La Coruña to invade England and depose the Protestant queen Elizabeth I. The fleet was defeated by a combination of the English navy and very bad weather.

Don Quixote
The Spanish writer Miguel de Cervantes wrote the classic story of *Don Quixote*. It was published in two parts, in 1605 and 1615.

The Escorial Palace
Philip II ordered a huge palace to be built outside Madrid, from which to govern his vast European and American empire.

cork tree

PORTUGAL

Taking over Portugal
In 1580 Philip II of Spain defeated the Portuguese at Alcantara and seized the Portuguese throne. Spain held on to Portugal's vast empire until 1640.

MADRID ■

SPAIN

Castile

• Toledo

The Morisco revolt
Islamic Moors were converted to Christianity by force in 1492. They rebelled against Spanish rule 70 years later.

Tagus

• Alcantara

Guadiana

Toledo cathedral

Joint monarchs
In 1469 Ferdinand of Aragon married Isabella of Castile. In 1479 they both succeeded to their thrones and ruled their countries jointly, uniting Spain.

School of Navigation
In 1416 Prince Henry the Navigator, son of the king of Portugal, opened a navigation school at Sagres to promote exploration and discovery.

LISBON

Guadalquivir

Córdoba •

Spain and its empire

Sagres

Seville •

End of Moorish rule
Ferdinand and Isabella finally drove the Moors out of Granada in 1492, ending 781 years of Muslim rule in Spain.
Granada

Atlantic Ocean

• Cadiz

In the early 1500s Spain, ruled by the Habsburg family of Austria, emerged as the most powerful nation in Europe. The country and its king, Charles V, had gained a large European empire through marriage and inheritance, and then a second empire in the Americas through conquest. Spain became the major Catholic power in Europe and led the fight against the Protestant Reformation (see pages 108–109). Spanish power attracted many enemies and the empire soon proved too big for one person to rule. In 1556 Charles V split his empire in two, giving Spain and its territories to his son, and other lands to his brother.

Raiding parties
English privateers (pirates sent by the government) led by Francis Drake regularly raided Spanish ports to seize American treasure and disrupt shipping.

• Ceuta

Tangier

Melilla •

Coastal forts
The Spaniards built a series of forts along the north African coast, from which to control the western Mediterranean and fight the Ottomans.

North Africa

Heading south
After 1432, Portuguese navigators began to explore the west coast of Africa, setting up trading posts as they sailed further south.

| 0 | 200 km |
| 0 | 100 miles |

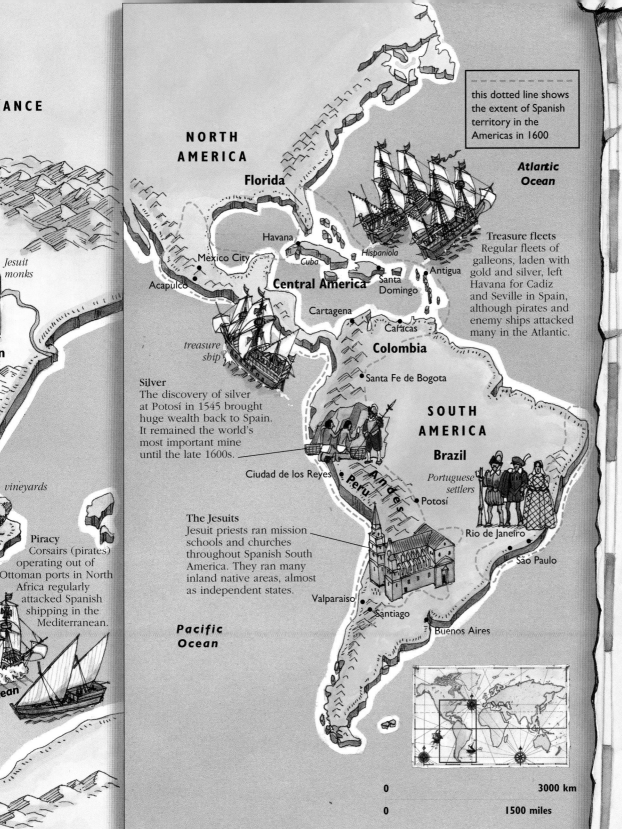

FRANCE

Navarre

Jesuit monks

Aragon

vineyards

Piracy
Corsairs (pirates) operating out of Ottoman ports in North Africa regularly attacked Spanish shipping in the Mediterranean.

Mediterranean Sea

Oran

NORTH AMERICA

Florida

Havana

Mexico City

Acapulco

Cuba

Hispaniola

Central America

Santa Domingo

Antigua

Cartagena

Caracas

Colombia

Santa Fe de Bogota

this dotted line shows the extent of Spanish territory in the Americas in 1600

Atlantic Ocean

Treasure fleets
Regular fleets of galleons, laden with gold and silver, left Havana for Cadiz and Seville in Spain, although pirates and enemy ships attacked many in the Atlantic.

treasure ship

Silver
The discovery of silver at Potosí in 1545 brought huge wealth back to Spain. It remained the world's most important mine until the late 1600s.

Ciudad de los Reyes

The Jesuits
Jesuit priests ran mission schools and churches throughout Spanish South America. They ran many inland native areas, almost as independent states.

Valparaiso

Santiago

SOUTH AMERICA

Brazil

Portuguese settlers

Andes

Peru

Potosí

Rio de Janeiro

São Paulo

Buenos Aires

Pacific Ocean

0	3000 km
0	1500 miles

Spanish wealth

The gold and silver mines of Mexico and Peru brought vast wealth to Spain. Large galleons, accompanied by armed warships, carried the bullion across the Atlantic. Despite these precautions, pirates and enemy ships, particularly from England and Holland, often attacked the fleets. This wealth enabled Spain to dominate Europe, as it could afford to pay for large armies, but it also caused prices to rise at home, eventually ruining the Spanish economy. This picture shows a plan of the silver mines at Potosí, in modern-day Bolivia.

1450–1600

1450

1456 Portuguese colonize Cape Verde islands, off western Africa, and head southwards down west African coast

1469 Ferdinand of Aragon marries Isabella of Castile

1479 Ferdinand and Isabella begin their joint rule of Spain

1487 Portuguese sail around the Cape of Good Hope at the southern tip of Africa

1492 Spain reconquers Granada and converts the Moors to Christianity; Jews are expelled from Spain
1492 Columbus makes first voyage to the New World
1496 Philip of Burgundy, France, marries Joanna, heiress to the Spanish throne, linking his Habsburg family with Spain
1497 Spain builds a fort at Melilla on the north African coast
1498 Portuguese reach India

1500

1500 Birth of Charles, son of Philip and Joanna
1504 Death of Isabella; Ferdinand rules Spain with Joanna and Philip
1506 Philip dies, leaving the Rhineland and the Netherlands to Charles
1509 Spain seizes Oran in North Africa
1512 Spain conquers the kingdom of Navarre in the north of Spain
1516 Death of Ferdinand, leaving Spain to his grandson, who becomes Charles I
1517 Martin Luther's ideas for reform challenge the Catholic Church and Habsburg power in Europe
1519 Death of Maximilian, Habsburg ruler of Austria and Holy Roman Emperor; Charles I succeeds him as Emperor Charles V
1519–21 Spanish capture Aztec empire
1524 Spanish begin to take over Maya empire
1530 Portuguese begin to colonize Brazil in South America
1532–33 Spanish capture Inca empire
1538 Spanish colonize Colombia in South America
1545 Silver discovered at Potosí in Peru, South America
1548 Silver found in Mexico

1550

1556 Charles V abdicates; Philip II succeeds him in Spain; Charles's brother Ferdinand becomes Holy Roman Emperor

1563–84 Escorial Palace is built by order of Philip II
1565 Spanish colonize Florida, in North America, and build a fort there to protect their gold bullion fleets
1566 Dutch begin a revolt against Spanish rule
1569–71 Moriscos revolt in southern Spain
1571 Spanish begin to colonize the Philippines; Manila founded
1574 Spanish lose the important port of Tunis to the Ottomans

1580–1640 Spain rules Portugal and its empire
1581 Spain makes peace with the Ottomans

1588 Spanish Armada fails to invade England

1598 Philip II dies; Philip III succeeds him

1600

The Renaissance:
A world of new learning

The Renaissance – a French word meaning 'rebirth' – was an artistic, cultural and intellectual movement that influenced all the arts and sciences. Renaissance artists and scholars looked back to the art and learning of classical Rome and Greece for their inspiration, reviving the past in order to develop and explore new ideas and methods. This new approach became known as 'humanism', because it encouraged people to achieve things for themselves rather than simply accept what they were taught to be true. The Renaissance began in Italy during the 14th century and reached its height during the 15th and 16th centuries, spreading across all of western and northern Europe.

Scientific invention
A 'Renaissance man' or 'universal man' was someone who could do many things. One such person was Leonardo da Vinci (1452–1519), who, as well as being an artist and a sculptor, drew plans for a helicopter (above), flying machine, and tank. He also dissected human bodies to find out more about how we move and function.

Renaissance art
Renaissance artists depicted people and landscapes in a highly natural way, studying anatomy and perspective to make their paintings more realistic. Michelangelo (1475–1564) was perhaps the greatest Renaissance artist, creating life-like sculptures, such as his *David* (left), and vast paintings such as the ceiling of the Sistine Chapel in Rome, Italy.

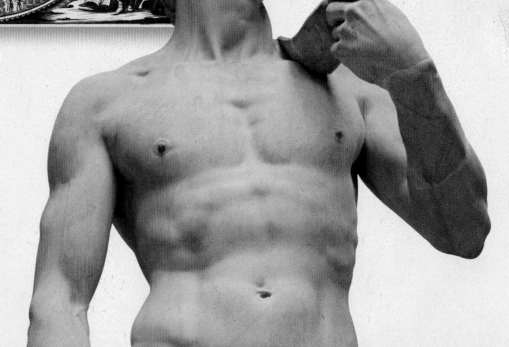

Astronomy
The Renaissance encouraged scientists to explore new ideas and to challenge existing beliefs. In 1543 the Polish astronomer Nicolaus Copernicus (1473–1543) proposed that the Sun is at the centre of the solar system and all the planets revolve around it. This shocked many people, because their religious teachings had always insisted that the Earth was at the centre of the universe. The chart above shows the arrangement suggested by Copernicus.

Patronage

The dukes and church leaders of Italy competed with each other to 'patronize' (financially support) Renaissance artists, in order to glorify their own countries. This painting shows Lorenzo de Medici, duke of Florence from 1469–92, surrounded by artists. He is admiring a sculpture by Michelangelo, who was employed by the Medici family in the 1490s before moving to Rome to work for the Pope.

Architecture

Architects of the Renaissance period looked back to much earlier styles for inspiration. They used classical pillars, rounded arches and domes in their buildings. Work had begun on Florence cathedral (shown in this artwork) in 1296 in the medieval Gothic style, but Filippo Brunelleschi (1377–1446) completed the building by adding a magnificent dome. This set the standard for all future Renaissance churches.

Lantern (top part of dome) lets light into cathedral below

Dome is 42m in diameter and 91m high

Inside of dome painted with The Last Judgement, by Vasari and Zuccari

Method of construction allowed dome to be built without any scaffolding

Rings of brick support both the inner and outer domes

Outer dome covered with red bricks in a 'herringbone' design

Weight of dome supported by 8 external and 16 internal, hidden ribs

Walls covered with marble inlay

Campanile (bell-tower) stands 85m high in four unsupported levels

Marble used in construction comes from three places in Italy – white marble from Carrara, red from Maremma, green from Prato

Campanile was built between 1334 and 1359 and known as 'Giotto's Tower', as it was designed by Renaissance artist Giotto (1266–1337)

The Reformation

For more than 1,000 years, every Christian in western Europe belonged to the Roman Catholic Church, but some began to accuse the Church of abusing its powers. In 1517 a German monk named Martin Luther nailed a list onto his church door. The list contained 95 proposals for reforming the Catholic Church. This was soon printed and distributed, beginning a widespread revolt against Catholicism. The Catholic Church condemned Luther as a heretic (someone whose beliefs go against those of the Church) in 1521, so he set up his own 'Lutheran Church'. Those who followed Luther became known as Protestants, as they 'protested' their new faith against Catholicism. The reformation of the Christian Church led to years of warfare and division in Europe.

John Knox
In 1559 the Calvinist preacher John Knox promoted a reformation of the Church in Scotland, although many Scots remained Catholic.

Mary I
Mary I restored Catholicism to England in 1553, and burned many Protestants at the stake as heretics.

Closing the monasteries
In 1536–39 Henry VIII of England closed all the Catholic monasteries, and other religious houses, and seized all their land and property.

St Batholomew's Day massacre
On 23 August 1572 French Catholics killed more than 3,000 Huguenots (French Protestants) in Paris. Many more were murdered across the country.

The Jesuits
The Society of Jesus was founded in 1534 to convert Muslims to Christianity, but it soon became the leader of the Counter-Reformation (see p109).

John Calvin
In 1536 John Calvin, a Frenchman based in Geneva, set out his ideas for Church reform. Calvinism soon became a major Protestant religion in Europe.

The Spanish Inquisition
In 1478 Pope Sixtus IV set up the Spanish Inquisition to combat heresy in Spain. Their use of torture against Protestants and Islamic Moors made them feared and hated.

The Moriscos
The Islamic Moors of Granada were forced to convert to Christianity after their country was occupied by Spain in 1492. After a revolt in 1569–71, they were sent to live in central Spain.

this dotted line shows the full extent of the Holy Roman Empire in 1550

these dotted lines show other national borders in Europe in 1550

0 — 500 km
0 — 250 miles

SCOTLAND
EDINBURGH
IRELAND
ENGLAND
LONDON
SPANISH NETHERLANDS
PARIS
Nantes
Loire
Seine
FRANCE
Geneva
Rhône
Atlantic Ocean
Pyrenees
PORTUGAL
Tagus
Ebro
MADRID
SPAIN
Granada
Mediterranean Sea

Martin Luther

Martin Luther (1483–1546), pictured here in dark robes, was an Augustinian friar and professor of theology at Wittenberg University in Saxony. He objected to many aspects of Catholic belief and practice, but wanted at first to reform the Church, not divide it. When this proved impossible, he set up his own reformed church.

North Sea

DENMARK–NORWAY

SWEDEN

Baltic Sea

Gutenberg's printing press, developed in the 1440s

German Catholic church in flames

radical preachers

Wittenberg
Elbe

Saxony

Germany

Worms

HOLY ROMAN EMPIRE

Rhine

SWISS CONFEDERATION

Augsburg

Bavaria

Zürich

Danube

Austria

Alps

Trent

VENICE

Po

The 95 Theses
In 1517 Martin Luther nailed 95 proposals for Catholic reform to the door of his church in Wittenberg, Saxony.

Copernicus
In 1531 Copernicus, a Polish astronomer, demonstrated that the planets move around the Sun, and not around the Earth. This went against the teachings of the Catholic Church.

POLAND

Expelling Protestants
In the late 1550s, Protestants were thrown out of Bavaria and Austria as the Catholic Church regained control. Poland, too, became Catholic again.

Council of Trent
Catholic officials met at Trent three times after 1545.

HUNGARY

OTTOMAN EMPIRE

PAPAL STATES

■ ROME

St Peter's Basilica in Rome, Italy

The Pope
As a result of the Reformation, Rome's role as the headquarters of the Christian Church was reduced, but the Pope remained an important figure in Europe for many years.

The Counter-Reformation
From 1545 to 1563, the Roman Catholic Church met at Trent in the Alps to reform the Church and help it fight back against Protestantism. The Counter-Reformation saw great changes in practice, while religious buildings in the new Baroque style of architecture – such as St Peter's Basilica in Rome, Italy (above) – helped to attract people back into the Catholic Church.

1510

1517 Martin Luther nails 95 proposals for Catholic reform onto his church door in Wittenberg, Saxony

1520

1521 Luther presents his ideas for reform to the Holy Roman Emperor at the Diet (council) of Worms

1523 In Zürich, Ulrich Zwingli proposes 67 reforms of the Catholic Church

1524 Religious warfare breaks out in Germany as peasants rise up in revolt

1525 Lutheranism is state religion of Saxony and many other German states

1530

1531 Copernicus suggests the Sun, not Earth, is at the centre of the universe

1534 Society of Jesus (Jesuits) forms

1534 Henry VIII of England breaks away from the Catholic Church when it refuses him a divorce

1536 John Calvin sets out ideas for religious reforms in his book, 'Institutes'

1536–39 Henry VIII closes monasteries

1540

1541 John Calvin begins to organize a strict Protestant church in Geneva

1544 Sweden converts to Lutheranism

1545–63 Roman Catholic Church meets three times at Trent, in the Alps, to launch the Counter-Reformation against Protestant churches

1550

1553–58 England briefly becomes Catholic again under Queen Mary I

1555 After years of war, Holy Roman Emperor agrees the Peace of Augsburg, giving each ruler within the empire the right to choose their own state religion

1558 Elizabeth I comes to the throne and restores Protestantism to England

1560

1560 Scottish parliament declares Scotland to be a Protestant nation

1562–80 French wars of religion divide the country

1566 Dutch Protestants rise in revolt against Spanish Catholic rulers

1570

1572 Thousands of French Huguenots (Protestants) are massacred by Catholics

1580

1589 The Huguenot Henry Navarre becomes king Henry IV of France

1590

1593 Henry IV of France becomes a Catholic

1598 Edict of Nantes grants religious toleration to Huguenots in France

1600

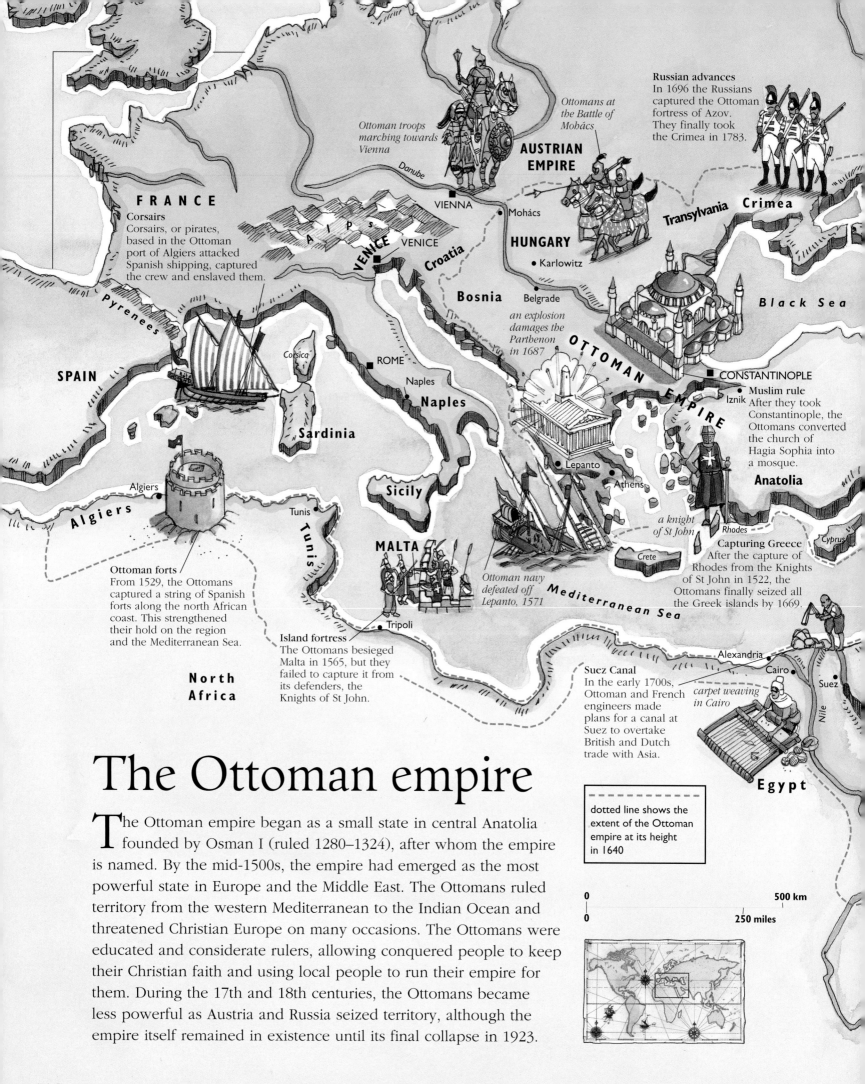

FRANCE

Corsairs
Corsairs, or pirates, based in the Ottoman port of Algiers attacked Spanish shipping, captured the crew and enslaved them.

Pyrenees

SPAIN

Algiers
Algiers

Ottoman forts
From 1529, the Ottomans captured a string of Spanish forts along the north African coast. This strengthened their hold on the region and the Mediterranean Sea.

North Africa

Corsica

Sardinia

Tunis

Tunis

Island fortress
The Ottomans besieged Malta in 1565, but they failed to capture it from its defenders, the Knights of St John.

Ottoman troops marching towards Vienna

Danube

VIENNA

A l p s

VENICE VENICE

Croatia

ROME

Naples

Naples

Sicily

MALTA

Tripoli

Ottomans at the Battle of Mohács

AUSTRIAN EMPIRE

Mohács

HUNGARY

Karlowitz

Bosnia

Belgrade

an explosion damages the Parthenon in 1687

Lepanto

Athens

Ottoman navy defeated off Lepanto, 1571

Mediterranean Sea

Russian advances
In 1696 the Russians captured the Ottoman fortress of Azov. They finally took the Crimea in 1783.

Transylvania

Crimea

Black Sea

O T T O M A N   E M P I R E

CONSTANTINOPLE

Iznik

Muslim rule
After they took Constantinople, the Ottomans converted the church of Hagia Sophia into a mosque.

Anatolia

a knight of St John

Rhodes

Cyprus

Crete

Capturing Greece
After the capture of Rhodes from the Knights of St John in 1522, the Ottomans finally seized all the Greek islands by 1669.

Alexandria

Cairo

Suez

Suez Canal
In the early 1700s, Ottoman and French engineers made plans for a canal at Suez to overtake British and Dutch trade with Asia.

carpet weaving in Cairo

Nile

Egypt

The Ottoman empire

The Ottoman empire began as a small state in central Anatolia founded by Osman I (ruled 1280–1324), after whom the empire is named. By the mid-1500s, the empire had emerged as the most powerful state in Europe and the Middle East. The Ottomans ruled territory from the western Mediterranean to the Indian Ocean and threatened Christian Europe on many occasions. The Ottomans were educated and considerate rulers, allowing conquered people to keep their Christian faith and using local people to run their empire for them. During the 17th and 18th centuries, the Ottomans became less powerful as Austria and Russia seized territory, although the empire itself remained in existence until its final collapse in 1923.

dotted line shows the extent of the Ottoman empire at its height in 1640

0 — 500 km
0 — 250 miles

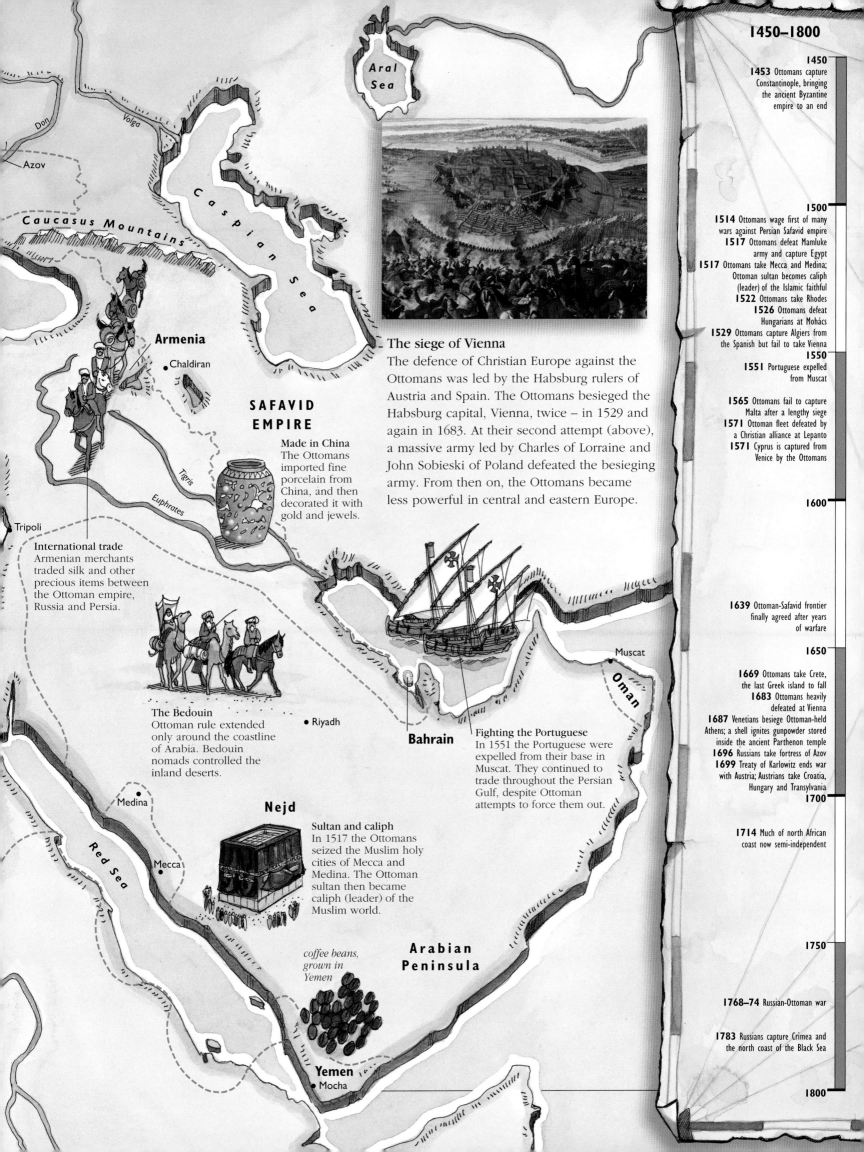

Armenia

• Chaldiran

Caspian Sea

Aral Sea

Don

Volga

Azov

Caucasus Mountains

SAFAVID EMPIRE

Tigris

Euphrates

Tripoli

Made in China
The Ottomans imported fine porcelain from China, and then decorated it with gold and jewels.

International trade
Armenian merchants traded silk and other precious items between the Ottoman empire, Russia and Persia.

The Bedouin
Ottoman rule extended only around the coastline of Arabia. Bedouin nomads controlled the inland deserts.

• Riyadh

Bahrain

Muscat

Oman

The siege of Vienna
The defence of Christian Europe against the Ottomans was led by the Habsburg rulers of Austria and Spain. The Ottomans besieged the Habsburg capital, Vienna, twice – in 1529 and again in 1683. At their second attempt (above), a massive army led by Charles of Lorraine and John Sobieski of Poland defeated the besieging army. From then on, the Ottomans became less powerful in central and eastern Europe.

Fighting the Portuguese
In 1551 the Portuguese were expelled from their base in Muscat. They continued to trade throughout the Persian Gulf, despite Ottoman attempts to force them out.

Nejd

Sultan and caliph
In 1517 the Ottomans seized the Muslim holy cities of Mecca and Medina. The Ottoman sultan then became caliph (leader) of the Muslim world.

Medina •

Red Sea

Mecca •

coffee beans, grown in Yemen

Arabian Peninsula

Yemen
• Mocha

1450–1800

1450

1453 Ottomans capture Constantinople, bringing the ancient Byzantine empire to an end

1500

1514 Ottomans wage first of many wars against Persian Safavid empire
1517 Ottomans defeat Mamluke army and capture Egypt
1517 Ottomans take Mecca and Medina; Ottoman sultan becomes caliph (leader) of the Islamic faithful
1522 Ottomans take Rhodes
1526 Ottomans defeat Hungarians at Mohács
1529 Ottomans capture Algiers from the Spanish but fail to take Vienna

1550

1551 Portuguese expelled from Muscat

1565 Ottomans fail to capture Malta after a lengthy siege
1571 Ottoman fleet defeated by a Christian alliance at Lepanto
1571 Cyprus is captured from Venice by the Ottomans

1600

1639 Ottoman-Safavid frontier finally agreed after years of warfare

1650

1669 Ottomans take Crete, the last Greek island to fall
1683 Ottomans heavily defeated at Vienna
1687 Venetians besiege Ottoman-held Athens; a shell ignites gunpowder stored inside the ancient Parthenon temple
1696 Russians take fortress of Azov
1699 Treaty of Karlowitz ends war with Austria; Austrians take Croatia, Hungary and Transylvania

1700

1714 Much of north African coast now semi-independent

1750

1768–74 Russian-Ottoman war

1783 Russians capture Crimea and the north coast of the Black Sea

1800

The Mughal empire

In the late 1400s, the Mughals, descendants of the famous Mongol leader Timur, were driven out of central Asia by the Mongol Tatars. They moved southwards and began to raid India, mounting a full-scale invasion in 1526. They soon conquered northern India and by 1600 were advancing south into the Deccan. A century later they controlled all but the far south. The Mughals were good administrators and, although Muslims, allowed their Hindu and Sikh subjects to worship freely. In the 1700s the Mughal empire came under attack from the Hindu Marathas of the west coast, while the French and British also gained territory. By 1800 the British had defeated the French and dominated Mughal India.

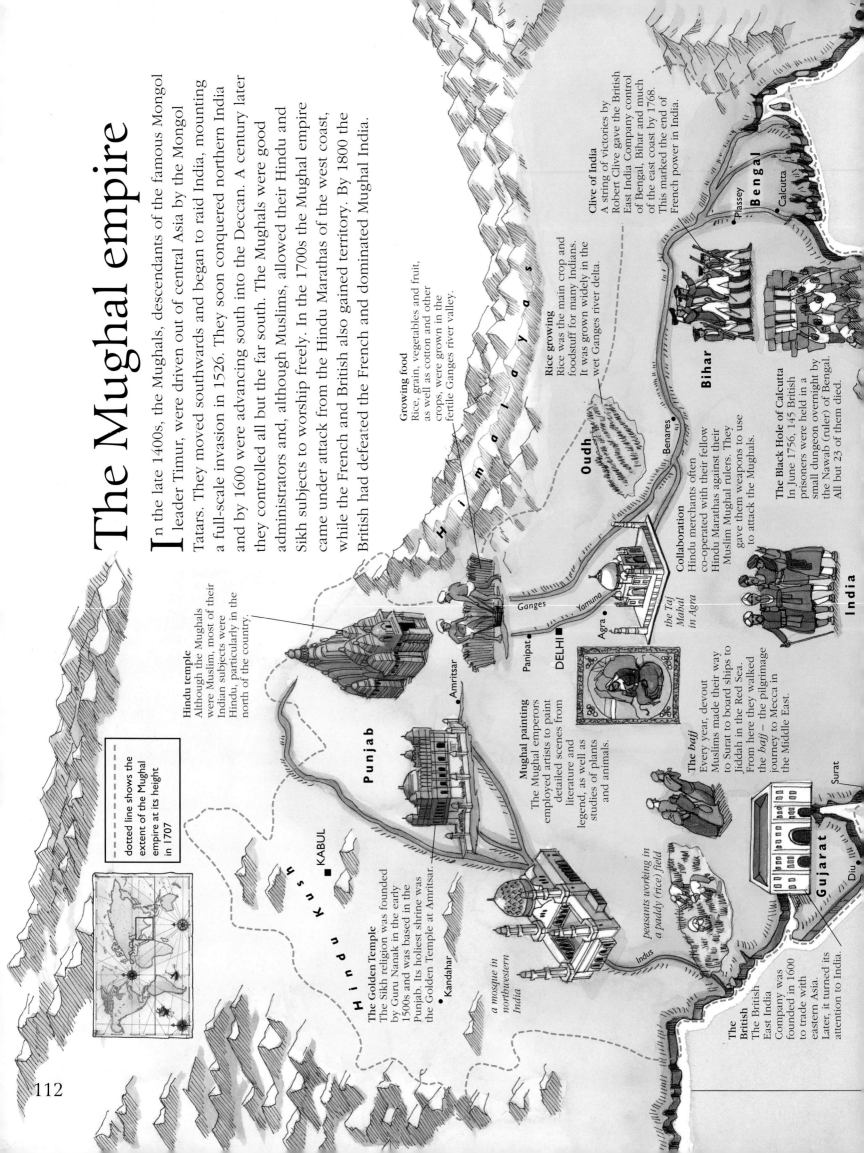

- - - - dotted line shows the extent of the Mughal empire at its height in 1707

Hindu temple
Although the Mughals were Muslim, most of their Indian subjects were Hindu, particularly in the north of the country.

The Golden Temple
The Sikh religion was founded by Guru Nanak in the early 1500s and was based in the Punjab. Its holiest shrine was the Golden Temple at Amritsar.

a mosque in northwestern India

The British
The British East India Company was founded in 1600 to trade with eastern Asia. Later, it turned its attention to India.

peasants working in a paddy (rice) field

The hajj
Every year, devout Muslims made their way to Surat to board ships to Jiddah in the Red Sea. From here they walked the *hajj* – the pilgrimage journey to Mecca in the Middle East.

Mughal painting
The Mughal emperors employed artists to paint detailed scenes from literature and legend, as well as studies of plants and animals.

Collaboration
Hindu merchants often co-operated with their fellow Hindu Marathas against their Muslim Mughal rulers. They gave them weapons to use to attack the Mughals.

the Taj Mahal in Agra

Growing food
Rice, grain, vegetables and fruit, as well as cotton and other crops, were grown in the fertile Ganges river valley.

Rice growing
Rice was the main crop and foodstuff for many Indians. It was grown widely in the wet Ganges river delta.

The Black Hole of Calcutta
In June 1756, 145 British prisoners were held in a small dungeon overnight by the Nawab (ruler) of Bengal. All but 23 of them died.

Clive of India
A string of victories by Robert Clive gave the British East India Company control of Bengal, Bihar and much of the east coast by 1768. This marked the end of French power in India.

Himalayas

Hindu Kush

KABUL

Kandahar

Punjab

Amritsar

Panipat

DELHI

Agra

Yamuna

Ganges

Benares

Oudh

Bihar

Bengal

Calcutta

Plassey

India

Surat

Diu

Gujarat

Indus

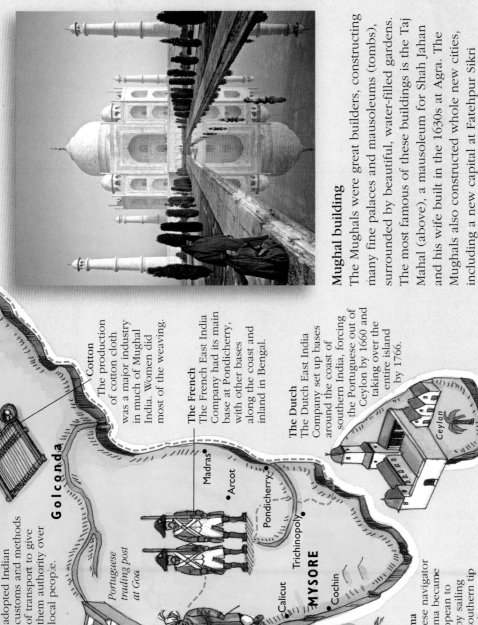

Bay of Bengal

Mughal building

The Mughals were great builders, constructing many fine palaces and mausoleums (tombs), surrounded by beautiful, water-filled gardens. The most famous of these buildings is the Taj Mahal (above), a mausoleum for Shah Jahan and his wife built in the 1630s at Agra. The Mughals also constructed whole new cities, including a new capital at Fatehpur Sikri outside Agra. This city was built by order of the emperor Akbar I between 1571 and 1584, but people lived there for only 14 years because of its poor water supply. A new capital was later built at Delhi.

MUGHAL EMPIRE

Deccan

Golconda

MYSORE

Arabian Sea

Arab traders
Merchants from Arabia and east Africa traded gold, gems, ivory and coffee across the Indian Ocean to India, in return for cotton, silk, spices and dyes.

Going native
European merchants adopted Indian customs and methods of transport to give them authority over local people.

Cotton
The production of cotton cloth was a major industry in much of Mughal India. Women did most of the weaving.

The French
The French East India Company had its main base at Pondicherry, with other bases along the coast and inland in Bengal.

The Dutch
The Dutch East India Company set up bases around the coast of southern India, forcing the Portuguese out of Ceylon by 1660 and taking over the entire island by 1766.

Portuguese trading post at Goa

Goa
In 1510, at Goa, the Portuguese set up Europe's first colony in Asia.

Mysore
The Muslim-run state of Mysore in the south of India was a major power in the region, resisting both Mughal and Maratha rule.

Vasco da Gama
The Portuguese navigator Vasco da Gama became the first European to reach India by sailing around the southern tip of Africa, landing at Cochin in May 1498.

Daman
Bombay
Goa
Calicut
Cochin
Trichinopoly
Pondicherry
Arcot
Madras
Ceylon

500 km
250 miles

The wealth of the empire

The Mughals ran an efficient banking system based on gold and silver coins that provided credit for merchants throughout Asia and east Africa. Trade with Arabs and Europeans across the Indian Ocean brought great wealth to the empire. Mughal agriculture was strong, with greater cereal harvests than in Europe, while their iron industry produced good quality steel. Mughal India also had the world's largest textile industry, exporting cotton goods worldwide.

1500–1800

1500
1501–30 Reign of Babur, first Mughal emperor
1504 Mughals conquer the region around Kabul
1510 Portuguese set up a trading post at Goa, with others at Diu and Daman
1519 Mughals' first raid on India
1526 Full-scale Mughal invasion of India

1539–56 Suri Afghans of Bihar rebel and reclaim a lot of territory from the Mughals
1550

1556–1605 Reign of Akbar I

1572 Mughals conquer Gujarat, giving them access to the sea
1576 Mughals conquer Bengal, India's wealthiest territory

1600
1600 British East India Co founded
1602 Dutch East India Co founded
1605 Mughals advance south into the Deccan
1612 British East India Co defeats a Portuguese fleet at Surat

1628–58 Reign of Shah Jahan, who ordered the building of the Taj Mahal
1639–48 New capital city constructed by order of Shah Jahan at Shahjahanabad (Delhi)
1647–80 Led by Sivaji, Hindu Marathas raid Mughal India
1650

1655–60 Dutch seize bases in Ceylon from Portuguese
1658–1707 Reign of Aurangzeb: Mughal empire at its greatest extent
1661 British East India Co establishes base at Bombay
1664 French East India Co set up

1687 Mughals capture southern state of Golconda

1700

1708 Marathas begin to conquer the Deccan

1739 Persian troops sack Mughal capital of Delhi
1740 War between Marathas and Mughals in southern India draws in the French and the British

1750
1751, 52 British under Robert Clive score decisive victories against the French at Arcot and Trichinopoly
1757 Clive defeats Mughal Nawab (ruler) of Bengal at Plassey
1761 Maratha power ends after massive defeat outside Delhi by an Afghan army that later withdraws from India
1761 British seize Pondicherry, ending French power in India
1775 British control all of Bengal and Bihar
by 1800 Mughal empire survives in name only
1800

The Tudors and Stuarts

Years of warfare in England between rival royal houses ended in 1485 when Henry VII became the first Tudor king. The Tudors were strong rulers who brought peace and prosperity to the country. Under Henry VIII, England broke away from Rome, and the Catholic Church, and became increasingly Protestant. In 1603 the last Tudor monarch, Elizabeth I, died. Elizabeth was succeeded by the Scottish king James VI, of the Stuart family, who united England and Scotland for the first time. But the Stuarts were weak kings. One of them, Charles I, was executed following a civil war, and another, James II (James VII of Scotland), was driven into exile because he was a Catholic. Overseas trade, however, was slowly making Britain one of the wealthiest nations in Europe.

The English Civil War: a war of three kingdoms

Charles I was king of England, Scotland and Ireland. Each country had its own parliament, church and laws. Charles believed he had a "divine right to rule", given to him by God, but his religious policies attracted opposition. Rebellion broke out in Scotland in 1639, then in Ireland in 1641, before king and parliament clashed in England in 1642. Civil war raged in all three kingdoms before Charles was executed by the English parliament, in 1649, for waging war on his people. From 1649 to 1660 Britain was a republic (a nation without a monarch) for the only time in its history.

The Spanish Armada
Defeated in August 1588 (see p115), the Spanish Armada was forced to sail around the rocky north and west coasts of Ireland and Scotland, where many ships were wrecked in storms.

Irish rebellions
Ireland was the only part of the British Isles to remain Catholic. This led to many rebellions against Ireland's Protestant and English rulers.

Union of the crowns
In 1603 the Stuart king of Scotland, James VI, became King James I of England. This united the two crowns, but both nations remained independent.

Suspicious murder
Lord Darnley, husband of Mary, Queen of Scots, was killed in an explosion in Edinburgh in 1567. Mary was accused of being involved, but nothing was proved.

Flodden Field
The English defeat of the Scots at Flodden Field in 1513 weakened Scotland greatly, and put it at the mercy of the English for the rest of the century.

Atlantic Ocean

SCOTLAND

■ EDINBURGH

Tweed

● Flodden

Ulster

● Londonderry

North Sea

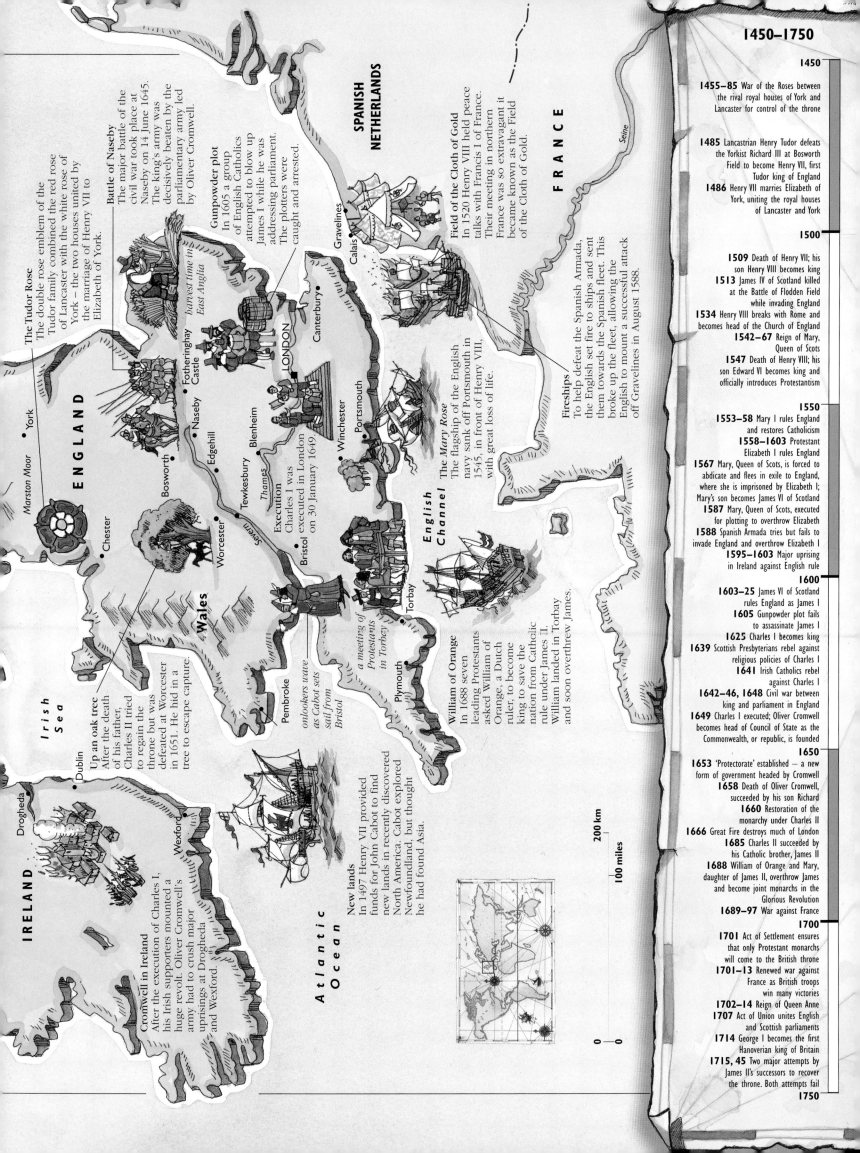

SPANISH NETHERLANDS

FRANCE

Seine

Field of the Cloth of Gold
In 1520 Henry VIII held peace talks with Francis I of France. Their meeting in northern France was so extravagant it became known as the Field of the Cloth of Gold.

The Tudor Rose
The double rose emblem of the Tudor family combined the red rose of Lancaster with the white rose of York – the two houses united by the marriage of Henry VII to Elizabeth of York.

Battle of Naseby
The major battle of the civil war took place at Naseby on 14 June 1645. The king's army was decisively beaten by the parliamentary army led by Oliver Cromwell.

Gunpowder plot
In 1605 a group of English Catholics attempted to blow up James I while he was addressing parliament. The plotters were caught and arrested.

Gravelines

Calais

harvest time in East Anglia

Canterbury

LONDON

Fotheringhay Castle

Naseby

Blenheim

Winchester

Portsmouth

Fireships
To help defeat the Spanish Armada, the English set fire to ships and sent them towards the Spanish fleet. This broke up the fleet, allowing the English to mount a successful attack off Gravelines in August 1588.

The Mary Rose
The flagship of the English navy sank off Portsmouth in 1545, in front of Henry VIII, with great loss of life.

ENGLAND

Marston Moor • York

Bosworth

Edgehill

Tewkesbury

Worcester

Chester

Severn

Thames

Execution
Charles I was executed in London on 30 January 1649.

Bristol

Wales

English Channel

Irish Sea

IRELAND

Drogheda

Dublin

Wexford

Pembroke

Plymouth

Torbay

Up an oak tree
After the death of his father, Charles II tried to regain the throne but was defeated at Worcester in 1651. He hid in a tree to escape capture.

Cromwell in Ireland
After the execution of Charles I, his Irish supporters mounted a huge revolt. Oliver Cromwell's army had to crush major uprisings at Drogheda and Wexford.

a meeting of Protestants in Torbay

onlookers wave as Cabot sets sail from Bristol

William of Orange
In 1688 seven leading Protestants asked William of Orange, a Dutch ruler, to become king to save the nation from Catholic rule under James I. William landed in Torbay and soon overthrew James.

New lands
In 1497 Henry VII provided funds for John Cabot to find new lands in recently discovered North America. Cabot explored Newfoundland, but thought he had found Asia.

Atlantic Ocean

200 km
100 miles

0
0

Divided Europe

After the religious turmoil of the Reformation, a brief period of peace descended on Europe in the 1550s. Differences between Protestants and Catholics continued to divide the continent, however, causing civil war in France and a revolt in the Netherlands against Spanish rule. A major conflict also broke out for control of the Baltic Sea. In 1618, Protestant-Catholic rivalries in Germany led to a war that soon spread across the rest of Europe. By the end of the war, Germany was devastated, Spain lost its leadership of Catholic Europe to France, Sweden dominated northern Europe and the Baltic, and the Dutch were independent and wealthy.

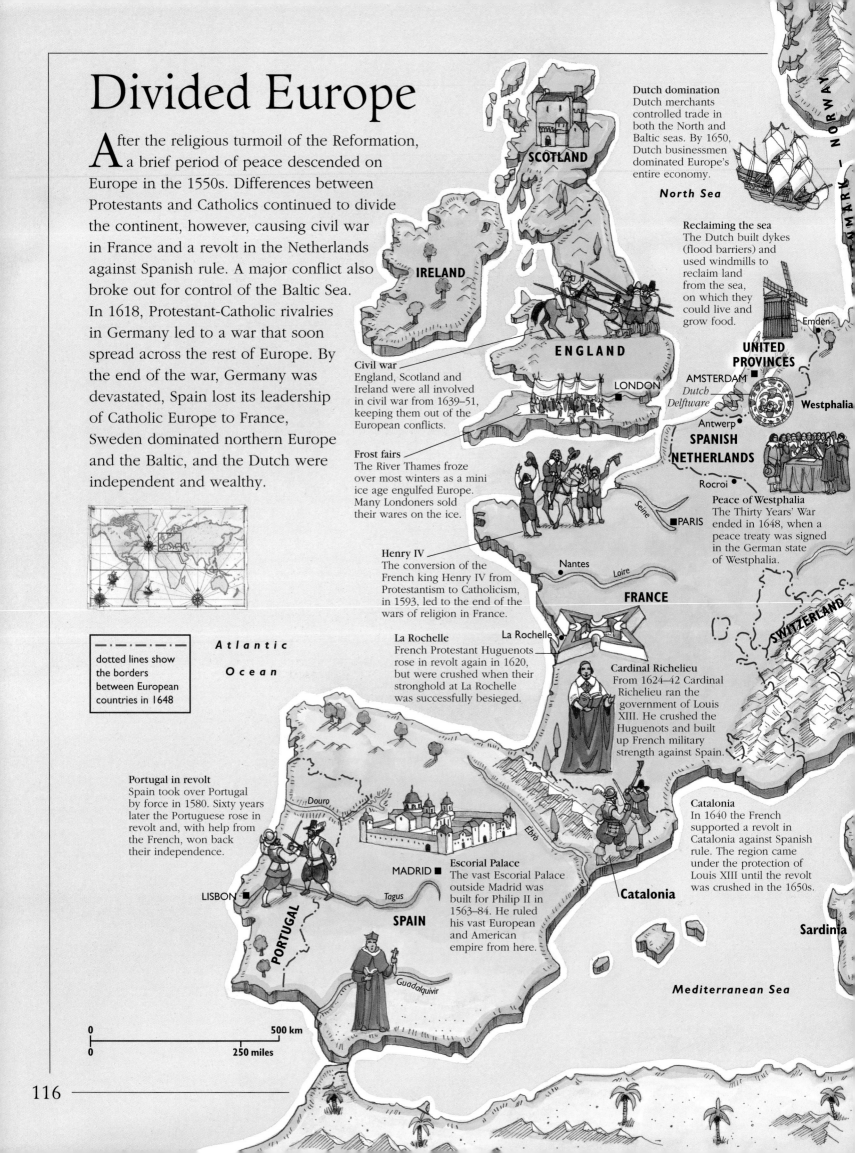

dotted lines show the borders between European countries in 1648

Atlantic Ocean

SCOTLAND

IRELAND

ENGLAND

LONDON

Dutch domination
Dutch merchants controlled trade in both the North and Baltic seas. By 1650, Dutch businessmen dominated Europe's entire economy.

North Sea

Reclaiming the sea
The Dutch built dykes (flood barriers) and used windmills to reclaim land from the sea, on which they could live and grow food.

Emden

UNITED PROVINCES
AMSTERDAM
Dutch Delftware
Antwerp

Westphalia

SPANISH NETHERLANDS
Rocroi

Civil war
England, Scotland and Ireland were all involved in civil war from 1639–51, keeping them out of the European conflicts.

Frost fairs
The River Thames froze over most winters as a mini ice age engulfed Europe. Many Londoners sold their wares on the ice.

Henry IV
The conversion of the French king Henry IV from Protestantism to Catholicism, in 1593, led to the end of the wars of religion in France.

Seine
■PARIS

Nantes
Loire

FRANCE

Peace of Westphalia
The Thirty Years' War ended in 1648, when a peace treaty was signed in the German state of Westphalia.

SWITZERLAND

La Rochelle
French Protestant Huguenots rose in revolt again in 1620, but were crushed when their stronghold at La Rochelle was successfully besieged.

La Rochelle

Cardinal Richelieu
From 1624–42 Cardinal Richelieu ran the government of Louis XIII. He crushed the Huguenots and built up French military strength against Spain.

Portugal in revolt
Spain took over Portugal by force in 1580. Sixty years later the Portuguese rose in revolt and, with help from the French, won back their independence.

Douro

LISBON ■

PORTUGAL

Tagus

MADRID ■

Escorial Palace
The vast Escorial Palace outside Madrid was built for Philip II in 1563–84. He ruled his vast European and American empire from here.

Ebro

Catalonia
In 1640 the French supported a revolt in Catalonia against Spanish rule. The region came under the protection of Louis XIII until the revolt was crushed in the 1650s.

Catalonia

SPAIN

Sardinia

Guadalquivir

Mediterranean Sea

0   500 km
0   250 miles

STOCKHOLM

SWEDEN

Swedish trade
After 1561 Sweden controlled much of the coast with its wealthy trade in timber, amber and other goods.

• Memel

COPENHAGEN

• Königsberg
PRUSSIA

Baltic Sea

• Danzig

Stralsund •
Lübeck •

Magdeburg
The sacking of Magdeburg by Catholic forces in 1631 led to savage acts of retaliation across Germany.

Brandenburg
Magdeburg •
Oder

Germany   **Saxony**   **POLAND**

Breitenfeld •
Lützen •   Elbe

Bohemia

• Prague

HOLY ROMAN EMPIRE

Danube

Austria

• Nordlingen

VIENNA •

Thrown out!
The Thirty Years' War began in 1618, when Bohemian Protestants threw two Austrian imperial officials out of a window at Prague Castle.

Spanish intervention
Spanish troops from Italy regularly fought French and Protestant forces in Germany during the Thirty Years' War.

Dual crown
The Habsburg rulers of Austria also ran the Holy Roman Empire, and were in charge of the imperial forces against France, Sweden and the Protestants.

HUNGARY

OTTOMAN EMPIRE

Adriatic Sea

ROME

NAPLES   **Naples**

Tyrrhenian Sea

The Spanish Mediterranean
Throughout this period, Naples, Sicily and Sardinia were part of Spain, despite French-inspired revolts against Spanish troops in 1647.

Ionian Sea

Sicily

The Dutch revolt

As converts to Calvinism, the Dutch came into conflict with their Spanish Catholic rulers. In 1568 they revolted and declared their independence as the United Provinces in 1581. Supported by the French and English, they fought with Spain until a 12-year truce was declared in 1609. Spain finally recognized their independence in 1648. An example of Dutch prosperity can be seen in this grand area of Amsterdam (above), developed by wealthy Dutch merchants in the 17th century.

The Thirty Years' War

In 1618 Protestants in Bohemia rose up against their Catholic Austrian rulers. Protestant and Catholic states across Germany soon joined in the fighting. After 1625, the war became more about territorial power than religion, as Denmark and then Sweden joined the war on the Protestant side to expand their power in the Baltic. This painting (above) shows the king of Sweden leading a cavalry charge at the Battle of Lützen in 1632.

1550–1650

1550
1555 Peace of Augsburg agreement brings religious stability to Germany
1556 Charles V abdicates, splitting the vast Habsburg empire between Spain and Austria
1556–98 Philip II rules Spain
1557–1629 Russia, Sweden and Poland fight for land around eastern Baltic Sea
1560

1568–1609 Dutch revolt against Spanish rule

1570

1580
1580 Philip II of Spain seizes Portuguese throne
1581 Dutch declare independence from Spain and elect William of Orange as their governor

1590

1593 King Henry IV of France converts to Catholicism

1598 King Henry IV issues the Edict of Nantes, granting religious toleration to French Huguenots (Protestants)
1598 Religious wars end in France
1600

1609–21 Twelve-year truce agreed between Dutch and Spanish

1610

1618–48 Thirty Years' War started by a Protestant revolt in Bohemia

1620
1620 Bohemian revolt ended by Catholic troops
1620–28 Huguenot revolt in France ends with the capture of La Rochelle
1621–25 Spain renews war against Dutch
1624–42 Cardinal Richelieu runs France
1625 Denmark enters Thirty Years' War
1628 France and Spain are at war
1630
1630 Sweden enters Thirty Years' War
1632 Swedish king Gustavus Adolphus dies at the Battle of Lützen
1635 France enters Thirty Years' War

1639–51 Civil war engulfs England, Scotland and Ireland
1640
1640 France supports revolts against Spain in Catalonia and Portugal; Portuguese win back independence
1643 French victory over Spanish at Rocroi
1647 Southern Italy revolts against Spanish rule
1648 Peace of Westphalia agreement ends Thirty Years' War; Dutch gain independence
1650

The expansion of Russia

Over the course of 300 years, the small, poor, landlocked state of Muscovy expanded to become, as Russia, one of the major nations in Europe. To do this, it had to overcome huge problems – a small population, vast distances between towns, a terrible climate, and large areas of empty land in which hostile armies could easily hide. The main driving force behind Russian success was Peter the Great, who modelled Russia on the western countries of Europe and almost single-handedly modernized his backward nation. Victories over Sweden, by 1721, gave Russia access to the Baltic Sea, paving the way for future Russian success and territorial gains during the 1700s.

The Urals
The Ural mountains form the border between Europe and Asia. During the late 1500s, the Russians crossed these mountains and built many new towns in Siberia.

polar bear roaming the Arctic tundra

Metal working
Many new state-owned iron and copper works were built in the Urals to exploit the great mineral wealth of the mountains.

Building St Petersburg
In 1703 work began on a new capital city, which gave access to the Baltic Sea.

Moscow
After the fall of Constantinople to the Muslim Ottomans in 1453, Moscow became the centre of Orthodox Christianity in Europe.

Close shave
To make his country more like those in the west, Peter the Great ordered all his lords and nobles to shave off their beards and dress in western fashions.

Russian navy
Peter the Great studied ship building in England, returning home in 1698 to create a great navy.

International trade
Russian merchants traded silk, tea and gems from China, and textiles from Persia and central Asia. Sugar, tobacco and wine were imported from Europe.

Fur trading
During the 1600s, to develop the local fur trade, a series of fortified trading stations were built along the main trade route to China.

serfs (peasants) working on a farm

Controlling the Caspian
In 1723 Russian troops occupied the west and south coasts of the Caspian Sea, but the Persians forced them to give up these areas in 1732.

SWEDEN

Karelia

Ingria

Estonia

Livonia

ST PETERSBURG

Narva

Novgorod

Pskov

Baltic Sea

Moscow

Smolensk

POLAND

Kiev

Dnieper

Don

Poltava

Azov

KHANATE OF CRIMEA

Sevastopol

Black Sea

Constantinople

Caucasus Mountains

OTTOMAN EMPIRE

Kazan

Ural Mountains

RUSSIA

Siberia

Tobolsk

Tomsk

Yeniseysk

Krasnoyarsk

Irkutsk

Kyakht

Astrakhan

Caspian Sea

SAFAVID EMPIRE

The city of Peter the Great

Peter the Great wanted to give Russia "a window on the west", so that it could trade ideas, goods and technology with western Europe. In 1703, he ordered the construction of a new city – St Petersburg – on marshland next to the Neva river at the eastern end of the Baltic Sea. Many thousands of workers died building the city, which includes the Winter Palace (left) and other grand buildings. St Petersburg became the national capital of Russia in 1712 and one of the leading cultural and diplomatic cities in Europe.

Arctic Ocean

Fur trapping
Siberian tribesmen hunted bears and other animals for their meat and fur. They traded these goods with Russian merchants in return for guns and other items.

tree felling for timber

Bering Strait

Alaska

Amur

Amur

CHINA

Crossing to America
Russian traders crossed the Bering Strait into Alaska, and in 1784 they established the first Russian settlement there. Alaska was sold to the USA in 1867.

Pacific Ocean

dotted line shows the extent of Russian territory in 1783

Fortifying the border
In 1650 Russian troops occupied the Amur region, north of China, and built forts along the Amur river border. The region was returned to China in 1689.

0   500 km
0   250 miles

1450

1478 Led by Ivan III, 'the Great', Muscovy conquers its main rival, Novgorod
1480 Muscovy becomes independent of Mongol Tatar rule

1500

1501 Ivan III expands his territory westwards, towards Poland

1533–84 Reign of Ivan IV, 'the Terrible'

1547 Ivan IV is crowned the first tsar (emperor) of Russia

1550

1552 Russia begins to conquer Tatar khanates north of the Caspian Sea

1581 Russia begins to expand over the Ural mountains and into Siberia
1582 Poland and Sweden prevent Russia from gaining access to the Baltic Sea

1600

1613–45 Reign of Mikhail I, the first tsar of the Romanov family

1637 Russian explorers reach the Pacific coast of Siberia for the first time

1650

1650–89 Russian occupation of the Amur region, north of China

1682–1725 Reign of Peter I, 'the Great'

1696 Russia captures Azov from the Ottomans, giving it access to the Black Sea
1697–98 Peter I travels around western Europe, studying new ideas on how to modernize his country

1700

1700–21 Great Northern War with Sweden brings Russia land around the Baltic Sea
1703 Construction of St Petersburg begins

1712 National capital moved from Moscow to St Petersburg

1750

1762–92 Reign of Catherine II, 'the Great'
1768–74 War against the Ottomans brings gains around the Black Sea
1772 First Partition of Poland: Russia, Austria and Prussia seize Polish territory; Russian frontier extends westwards
1783 Russia captures Crimea
1784 Russians establish first settlement in Alaska

1800

China and Japan

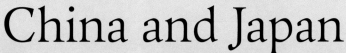

Back in 1368, the Chinese Ming dynasty replaced the foreign-born Mongols as rulers in the region. In 1644, the Ming dynasty was replaced by another foreign dynasty, the Manchus, who came from the northern region of Manchuria. The Manchus quickly adopted Chinese fashions – shaving their heads and wearing pigtails – but most importantly they turned China into a dynamic, efficient state of huge power and wealth. Neighbouring states, such as Korea, came under the control of the Chinese. Japan remained independent, ruled in name by an emperor but in reality by powerful shoguns (military warlords). European contact with China and Japan was very limited.

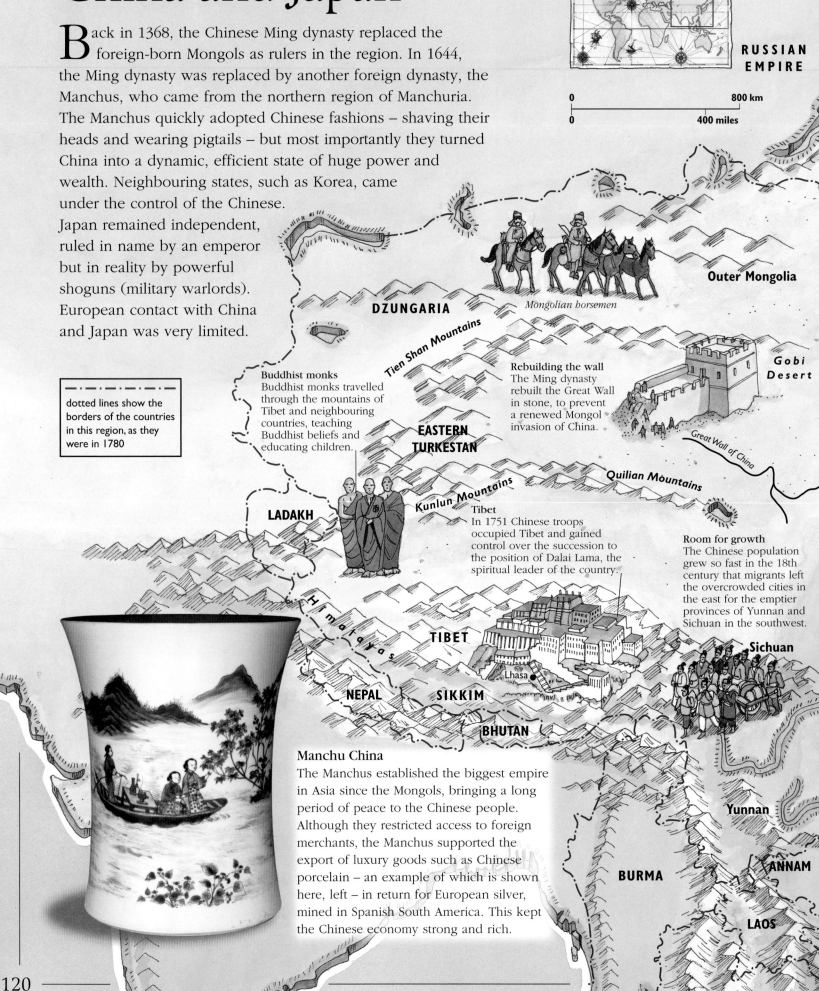

RUSSIAN EMPIRE

0   800 km
0   400 miles

---- · ---- · ----

dotted lines show the borders of the countries in this region, as they were in 1780

Outer Mongolia

Mongolian horsemen

DZUNGARIA

Tien Shan Mountains

Gobi Desert

Buddhist monks
Buddhist monks travelled through the mountains of Tibet and neighbouring countries, teaching Buddhist beliefs and educating children.

EASTERN TURKESTAN

Rebuilding the wall
The Ming dynasty rebuilt the Great Wall in stone, to prevent a renewed Mongol invasion of China.

Great Wall of China

Quilian Mountains

Kunlun Mountains

LADAKH

Tibet
In 1751 Chinese troops occupied Tibet and gained control over the succession to the position of Dalai Lama, the spiritual leader of the country.

Room for growth
The Chinese population grew so fast in the 18th century that migrants left the overcrowded cities in the east for the emptier provinces of Yunnan and Sichuan in the southwest.

Himalayas

TIBET

Lhasa

Sichuan

NEPAL   **SIKKIM**

BHUTAN

Manchu China
The Manchus established the biggest empire in Asia since the Mongols, bringing a long period of peace to the Chinese people. Although they restricted access to foreign merchants, the Manchus supported the export of luxury goods such as Chinese porcelain – an example of which is shown here, left – in return for European silver, mined in Spanish South America. This kept the Chinese economy strong and rich.

Yunnan

BURMA

ANNAM

LAOS

Forts for furs
In 1689 the Russians swapped a fort in Manchuria for better access to Chinese markets, creating a huge demand for Siberian furs in Beijing.

AMUR

Manchu by name
The name 'Manchu' is thought to come from *Manjusri*, a Buddhist *bodhisattva* (holy man) who lived at Mount Wutai, near Beijing.

Noh drama
Local daimyo (lords) were great supporters of Japanese arts, such as noh drama, the tea ceremony, poetry and painting.

Manchuria

Sea of Japan

Growing cotton
Cotton fields planted by the Mongols in northern China supplied a booming textile industry in the Yangtze delta to the south.

The Willow Palisade
The Ming built a continuous wooden wall, with gate towers, to protect Chinese settlements north of the Great Wall.

Inner Mongolia

Great Wall of China

Japanese soldier with a Portuguese-style musket

pirate ships

J A P A N

The Five Highways

Pyongyang

BEIJING

boat on Grand Canal

KOREA
SEOUL

Edo

Azuchi

Kyoto

Horse post
The Ming set up a courier service to carry messages across the empire. It took seven weeks to travel from north to south China.

Grand Canal

Ming porcelain

Invading Korea
A Japanese army of 200,000 troops invaded Korea in 1592, but it was driven out by a vast Chinese army and naval force.

Pusan

HIRADO

Nagasaki

Azuchi castle
The castle of Azuchi, begun in 1576, was designed to dominate the fertile plains. It was an administrative centre as well as a fortress.

C H I N A

Yangtze

Nanjing

textile production

In demand
Raw cotton was shipped in along the Grand Canal and down the Yangtze river to supply the major cotton factories of the delta region.

East China Sea

Nagasaki
In 1570 the local daimyo (lord) Omura developed the small fishing village of Nagasaki as Japan's main port for foreign trade.

The Dutch
Dutch merchants set up a fortified trading base on Taiwan in 1622, so that they could trade with mainland China. The island itself did not become part of China until 1683.

Taiwan

Guangzhou (Canton)

Macao

European trade
The Portuguese set up a permanent trading base at Macao in 1557, the first foreign involvement in the Chinese economy.

South China Sea

Overseas trade
The Chinese traded cotton textiles, silk, tea, porcelain and ironware with countries throughout southeast Asia and the eastern Indian Ocean in return for European silver.

1500–1800

1500

1500 Chinese population at about 90 million people

1520–21 Portuguese make first direct European trade contact with China
1520s Wako pirates from Japan begin to raid the Chinese coastline

1542 Portuguese first arrive in Japan
1542, 50 Mongols invade Ming China

1548–61 Portuguese convert some Japanese to Christianity

1550

1556 Worst-ever Chinese earthquake kills 850,000 people
1557 Portuguese set up a trading base at Macao
1568 Nobunaga, leader of Oda clan, begins to unify central Japan
1570 Nagasaki developed as main Japanese port for foreign trade
1580 Chinese population now 130 million

1580s Ming empire declines
1582 Hideyoshi succeeds Nobunaga and soon controls eastern and northern Japan
1592, 97 Japan invades Korea

1600

1603 New Tokugawa dynasty of shoguns (military commanders) rules Japan
1609 Dutch set up base in Japan
1615 Nurhachi is Manchu leader
1622 Dutch establish trading base on Taiwan
1627 Revolts break out across China

1637 Manchus govern Korea
1638 37,000 Japanese Christians massacred
1641 Portuguese expelled from Japan
1644 Manchus occupy China; beginning of the Qing dynasty

1650

1650 Chinese population drops to 100 million

1662–1722 Kangxi emperor rules China

1683 Chinese conquer Taiwan
1689 Russians leave Amur region in exchange for trade allowances

1700

1715 Japanese limit trade with Dutch

1727 Chinese agree a frontier with Russia

1736–95 Qianlong emperor rules China

1750

1751 Chinese occupy Tibet
1755–60 Chinese conquer Turkestan and Dzungaria in the far west
1760s Widespread peasant uprisings against Tokugawa government in Japan

1800 Chinese population now at 300 million

1800

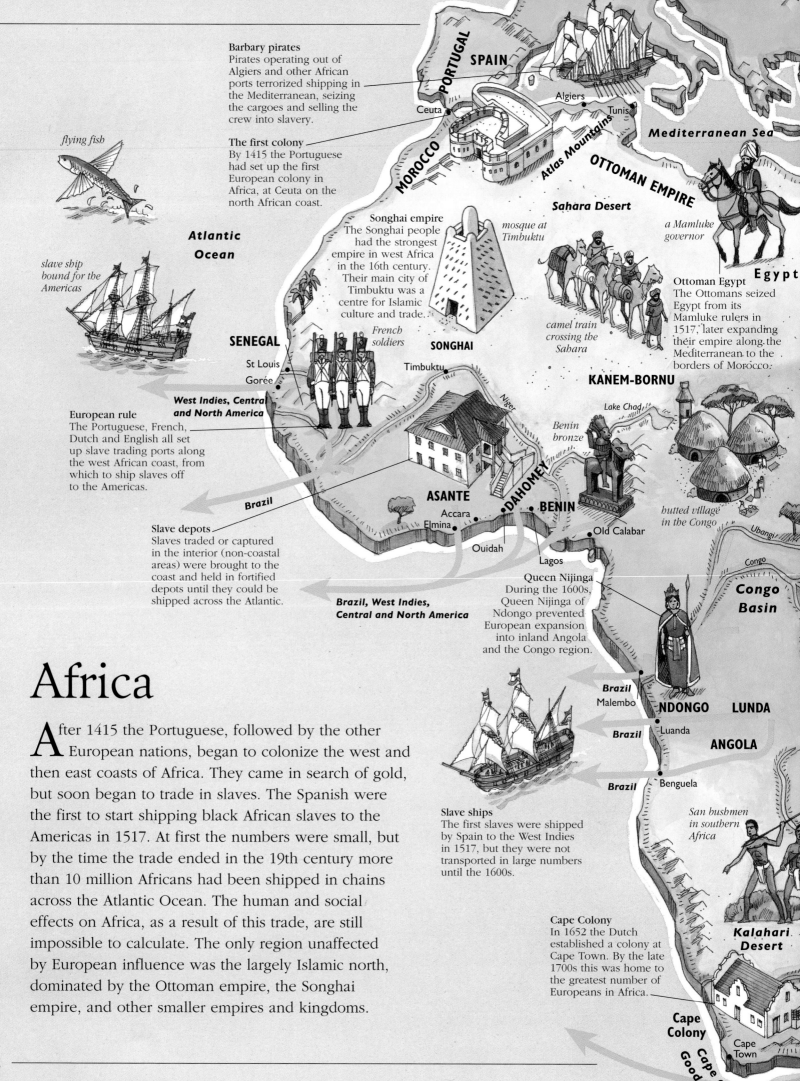

flying fish

slave ship bound for the Americas

Barbary pirates
Pirates operating out of Algiers and other African ports terrorized shipping in the Mediterranean, seizing the cargoes and selling the crew into slavery.

The first colony
By 1415 the Portuguese had set up the first European colony in Africa, at Ceuta on the north African coast.

Songhai empire
The Songhai people had the strongest empire in west Africa in the 16th century. Their main city of Timbuktu was a centre for Islamic culture and trade.

mosque at Timbuktu

a Mamluke governor

Ottoman Egypt
The Ottomans seized Egypt from its Mamluke rulers in 1517, later expanding their empire along the Mediterranean to the borders of Morocco.

camel train crossing the Sahara

French soldiers

European rule
The Portuguese, French, Dutch and English all set up slave trading ports along the west African coast, from which to ship slaves off to the Americas.

Slave depots
Slaves traded or captured in the interior (non-coastal areas) were brought to the coast and held in fortified depots until they could be shipped across the Atlantic.

Benin bronze

hutted village in the Congo

Queen Nijinga
During the 1600s, Queen Nijinga of Ndongo prevented European expansion into inland Angola and the Congo region.

West Indies, Central and North America

Brazil

Brazil, West Indies, Central and North America

Brazil

Brazil

Brazil

Slave ships
The first slaves were shipped by Spain to the West Indies in 1517, but they were not transported in large numbers until the 1600s.

San bushmen in southern Africa

Cape Colony
In 1652 the Dutch established a colony at Cape Town. By the late 1700s this was home to the greatest number of Europeans in Africa.

SPAIN
PORTUGAL
MOROCCO
Ceuta
Algiers
Tunis
Mediterranean Sea
Atlas Mountains
OTTOMAN EMPIRE
Sahara Desert
Egypt
Atlantic Ocean
SENEGAL
St Louis
Gorée
SONGHAI
Timbuktu
Niger
KANEM-BORNU
Lake Chad
BENIN
Ubangi
Congo
Congo Basin
ASANTE
Accara
Elmina
Ouidah
DAHOMEY
Lagos
Old Calabar
NDONGO
LUNDA
Malembo
Luanda
ANGOLA
Benguela
Kalahari Desert
Cape Colony
Cape Town
Cape of Good Hope

Africa

After 1415 the Portuguese, followed by the other European nations, began to colonize the west and then east coasts of Africa. They came in search of gold, but soon began to trade in slaves. The Spanish were the first to start shipping black African slaves to the Americas in 1517. At first the numbers were small, but by the time the trade ended in the 19th century more than 10 million Africans had been shipped in chains across the Atlantic Ocean. The human and social effects on Africa, as a result of this trade, are still impossible to calculate. The only region unaffected by European influence was the largely Islamic north, dominated by the Ottoman empire, the Songhai empire, and other smaller empires and kingdoms.

The Portuguese east coast

In 1498 the Portuguese navigator Vasco da Gama sailed around the Cape of Good Hope on his way to India. This opened up a new trade route between Europe and India across the Indian Ocean. The Portuguese soon set up a string of trading bases up the east coast, such as at Kilwa (left). These bases stretched from Delagoa Bay in the south to the island of Socotra, at the mouth of the Red Sea, in the north.

Jesuit conversions
Jesuit missionaries arrived in Ethiopia in 1557 to convert the Ethiopians from the Coptic Church to the Roman Catholic Church.

Arab traders
Arab dhows (sailing boats) traded goods with India, the Arabian Peninsula and the Persian Gulf, often in competition and conflict with their Portuguese rivals.

Christians united
The Portuguese sent an army to help their fellow Christian Ethiopians defeat an invading Adali army at Waina Dega in 1543.

Portuguese trade
After 1505 the Portuguese set up a string of trading bases along the east African coast. From here they traded gold, ivory and spices across the Indian Ocean.

Gold
The Shona and Makua people mined and panned for gold near Lake Malawi. They traded it for guns, textiles and other goods with Arab and Portuguese merchants on the coast.

these arrows show the direction and destinations of the slave ships that sailed across the Atlantic from African ports

Nile
Cairo
Arabian Peninsula
Arabian Sea
India
Socotra
Waina Dega
ETHIOPIA
ADAL
Lake Turkana
Rift Valley
Mogadishu
SULTANATE OF ZANZIBAR
Lake Victoria
Indian Ocean
Lake Tanganyika
Malindi
Mombasa
Rift
Zanzibar
Kilwa
Great Mosque at Kilwa
Lake Malawi
Valley
Mozambique
Madagascar
MWENEMUTAPA
Zambezi
Limpopo
Delagoa Bay
Brazil

0
2000 km
0
1000 miles

1450–1800

1450

1482 Portuguese establish a fortress at Elmina in west Africa to protect gold trade
1488 Portuguese navigator Bartolomeu Dias becomes first European to sail around Africa into the Indian Ocean
1498 Vasco da Gama opens up a sea route from Europe, around Africa, to India

1500

1505 Portuguese begin to colonize Mozambique and the rest of the east African coast
1517 Spanish begin shipping slaves to the West Indies
1517 Ottomans conquer Egypt
1527–43 Islamic Adal kingdom attacks Ethiopia
1529 Songhai empire is at its greatest extent

1550

1557 Jesuit missionaries arrive in Ethiopia
1570 King Idris III Aloma creates a powerful Islamic state in Kanem-Bornu
1575 Portuguese begin to colonize Angola

1591 Moroccan force overthrows the Songhai empire
1592 British first ship slaves to the Americas
1598 Portuguese colonize Mombasa

1600

1600 East African kingdom of Mwenemutapa is at its greatest extent

1624–43 Queen Nijinga rules Ndongo
1626 French begin to colonize Senegal and Madagascar
1626–32 Roman Catholicism becomes the official religion of Ethiopia
1637 Dutch capture Elmina from the Portuguese

1650

1652 Omanis from the Arabian Peninsula attack Zanzibar, the first major threat to Portuguese trade in east Africa
1652 Dutch establish Cape Town

1698 Omanis set up the Sultanate of Zanzibar and expel the Portuguese from the east coast

1700

1700 Kingdoms of Asante and Dahomey dominate the west African coast
1705–14 North Africa becomes semi-independent from the Ottoman empire
1713 Britain gains 30-year control over the shipping of African slaves to Spanish America
1724 Dahomey provides slaves for European slave-traders

1750

1750s Powerful Lunda empire emerges in central Africa

1758–83 British and French fight for control of Senegal

1800

The slave trade:
The terrible trade in humans

S lavery has existed throughout human history, but in the 16th century a new and terrible chapter in this story began. In 1502 a Portuguese ship transported west African slaves to the Americas. Regular shipments then started up in 1517. At first this trade was slow, but the increasing demand for labour on the new sugar plantations, and in the mines, outgrew the supply of native Americans. So Africans were brought across the Atlantic to fill the gap. The trade flourished during the 17th and 18th centuries, with approximately 10 million Africans enslaved before the trade ended in the 19th century. The human cost of slavery was huge, and while it brought great wealth to European traders and American landowners, it devastated Africa.

Trading in lives

Slaves captured during warfare between rival African kingdoms, or enslaved by their own leaders, were taken to the coast and sold to European slavers. The picture above shows a man buying slaves at Gorée, a French island off Senegal on the west African coast. Here the slaves were branded (marked with hot irons) and imprisoned in slave depots until a ship arrived to take them to the Americas.

On the plantation

Life on the plantations, such as this sugar plantation in Antigua in the West Indies, was harsh. Slaves were the property of the plantation owner and had no rights of their own. They worked long hours, often from sunrise to sunset, and were often whipped to make them work harder. They did not earn any money, but were given enough food to keep them alive.

Male and female slaves hoe the land in a line, making it ready for planting sugar cane

Overseer makes sure slaves work hard for their master

Even young slave children are forced to work on the land

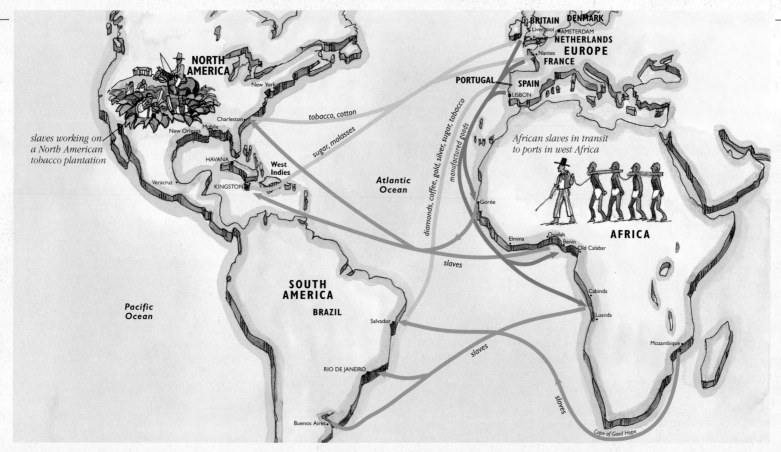

Map labels:
BRITAIN, DENMARK, Liverpool, AMSTERDAM, NETHERLANDS, EUROPE, FRANCE, Nantes, PORTUGAL, SPAIN, LISBON

NORTH AMERICA, New York, Charleston, New Orleans, Mobile, HAVANA, Veracruz, KINGSTON, West Indies

slaves working on a North American tobacco plantation

tobacco, cotton

sugar, molasses

Atlantic Ocean

diamonds, coffee, gold, silver, sugar, tobacco

manufactured goods

African slaves in transit to ports in west Africa

Gorée, Elmina, Ouidah, Benin, Old Calabar, AFRICA, Cabinda, Luanda, Mozambique

Pacific Ocean

SOUTH AMERICA, BRAZIL

slaves

Salvador, RIO DE JANEIRO, Buenos Aires

slaves

slaves

Cape of Good Hope

The slave trade triangle

As shown in this map (above), the path of slave ships formed a triangular pattern across the Atlantic Ocean. Ships carrying manufactured goods such as guns and cotton cloth sailed from western European ports to the west African coast. Here the cargo was traded for slaves, who were then shipped across to Brazil, the West Indies, Central and North America. The slaves were sold to the plantation owners and the ships returned home with a rich cargo of sugar, rum, tobacco, cotton, coffee, and sometimes silver and precious stones.

KEY TO MAP: THE 'TRIANGULAR TRADE'

Ships carry manufactured goods from Europe to Africa

The Middle Passage: slaves are taken across the Atlantic

Ships return home with raw materials from the Americas

Remembering the past

Slavery ended during the 19th century, but its impact is still with us today. The economy and social structure of much of Africa has never recovered from the removal of so many young men and women as slaves, while the free descendants of slaves, particularly in the USA, still face unfair treatment and discrimination. This statue (right) is a memorial to those who were slaves on Barbados, a British island in the West Indies.

The Middle Passage

The voyage across the Atlantic Ocean from Africa to the Americas – known as the Middle Passage – took up to 16 weeks. Conditions on board were appalling. Hundreds of slaves were packed tightly into the hold, as this painting shows (above). They were all chained together to stop them from jumping overboard. As many as four out of every ten slaves died during the journey across.

Colonizing North America

When Europeans first arrived in North America, the land puzzled them. The early explorers thought it was Asia and did not realize it was a continent in its own right, while Spanish conquistadors (conquerors) expected to discover gold-filled cities just as they had found earlier in Mexico and Peru. None of them realized just how big or potentially rich and fertile this continent was. Yet slowly Europeans began to colonize this new world, the French and English trapping and trading furs in the north, while farmers from all nations settled in colonies along the east coast. Once the barrier of the Appalachian mountains was crossed in 1671, the way was clear for pioneer settlers to exploit this fertile land to the full.

Henry Hudson
In 1611 Hudson went in search of the Northwest Passage to the Pacific Ocean, but his crew staged a mutiny. Hudson, his young son and seven loyal sailors were left to die in a small boat.

Lake Winnipeg

Canada

Hudson's Bay Company
After 1670, the English Hudson's Bay Company set up bases around Hudson Bay, to trade furs with the native Cree people. The French captured all the bases in 1686.

The Great Lakes

Lake Superior

Rocky Mountains

buffalo grazing

Hunting buffalo
The Plains Indians hunted herds of buffalo for their meat, skins and bones.

Great Plains

tents of the Plains Indians

Mississippi

New Mexico
The Spaniards set up a permanent base at Santa Fe in 1609, but their settlement in the region was limited by the harsh climate.

The first settlers
The first European settlers, such as those shown in this painting, inhabited the eastern coastline of North America – the Spaniards in the south, the English, Dutch and Swedes in the centre and the French in the north and along the St Lawrence river. Many of the settlers had fled religious or political persecution in Europe and sought to create a new life in a new world. They survived by growing their own crops and raising livestock, and by trading with the local native Americans. They also received some supplies by ship from Europe.

• Santa Fe

In search of gold
From 1539–43 the Spaniard Hernando de Soto led an expedition up the Mississippi in search of gold, inflicting great cruelty on the native Americans he met on his way.

Spanish pueblo village in the southwest

Down river
In 1682 Robert de la Salle became the first person to canoe down the Mississippi river. He was disappointed to find it ended up in the Gulf of Mexico, not the Pacific Ocean.

Louisiana

Spanish explorers
In the 1500s, Spain mounted huge military expeditions from Mexico and the Caribbean into North America in search of gold, and to convert the natives to Christianity. They did not succeed.

Mexico

Hudson Bay

French exploration
The French explored the Great Lakes region between 1613 and 1740, opening up the area for fur trappers to use.

Jacques Cartier
In 1534 Cartier explored the Gulf of St Lawrence for the king of France, returning the following year to sail up the St Lawrence river.

John Cabot
In 1497 Cabot left England in search of the Northwest Passage to Asia. He landed in Newfoundland, thinking it was Asia.

Newfoundland

Gulf of St Lawrence

cod fishing off Newfoundland

General Wolfe
In 1759 the British army, led by Wolfe, seized the French city of Québec, ending French rule in North America. Wolfe died at the battle.

Québec

Montréal

Nova Scotia

De Champlain
In 1608 Samuel de Champlain founded a settlement at modern-day Québec, the first permanent French settlement in North America.

St Lawrence

French Jesuits exploring the Great Lakes

Lake Huron

Lake Ontario

Lake Michigan

Lake Erie

New Hampshire

Massachusetts

Cape Cod

Plymouth

New York

New Amsterdam

Connecticut

The Pilgrim Fathers
In 1620, 101 Puritans (Calvinists from England) sailed across the Atlantic to found a settlement at Plymouth. Modern Americans refer to them as the founding fathers of the USA.

Pennsylvania

New Jersey

Delaware

Maryland

Dutch owned
In 1626 Dutch merchants purchased Manhattan Island from the local Algonquians, establishing New Amsterdam on the site of modern-day New York City.

Atlantic Ocean

A fertile land
Tobacco was the most important crop in Virginia and South Carolina. Rice was grown in South Carolina and Georgia.

Appalachian Mountains

Virginia

Jamestown

Jamestown
The first permanent English settlement in the New World was established in 1607 at Jamestown, named after the English king, James I.

Roanoke Island

North Carolina

South Carolina

rice growing in Georgia

Georgia

Roanoke Island
In 1584 Walter Raleigh set up an English colony at Roanoke Island. The colony was re-settled in 1587, but by 1590 it had been abandoned.

St Augustine

Spanish forts
The Spaniards first landed in Florida in 1513 and explored further inland 30 years later. Their first permanent settlement was set up at St Augustine in 1565.

Slave ships
The first black African slaves in North America arrived with the Spaniards in Florida, in 1526. The direct slave trade from west Africa to North America did not begin until the next century.

Gulf of Mexico

Florida

0 — 1000 km
0 — 500 miles

1450–1800

1450

1492 Columbus lands in the Caribbean
1497 Italian navigator John Cabot makes first European landing in North America on Newfoundland

1500

1513 Ponce de Léon explores the Florida coast for Spain
1524 Giovanni da Verrazano explores Atlantic coast of North America for France
1526 Spanish bring first black slaves in North America into Florida
1534–35 Jacques Cartier explores St Lawrence river in Canada
1539–42 Hernando de Soto explores Florida region for Spain
1540–42 Major Spanish expedition into New Mexico

1550

1565 Spanish establish their first base at St Augustine in Florida, to defend gold bullion ships returning to Spain

1584–87 English establish a colony at Roanoke Island

1600

1607 Jamestown founded
1608 Samuel de Champlain founds Québec
1610–11 Henry Hudson fails to find the Northwest Passage to the Pacific
1613 French begin fur trading around the Great Lakes
1619 Dutch import first 20 African slaves to Virginia
1620 Pilgrim Fathers arrive at Plymouth
1626 Dutch buy Manhattan Island
1630–70 French Jesuits explore the Great Lakes

1650

1664 British acquire New Amsterdam from Dutch and rename it New York
1670 English set up Hudson's Bay Co to trade furs in northern Canada
1671 English explorers Batts and Fallam are first Europeans to cross Appalachian mountains into the Ohio river valley
1681–82 Robert de la Salle canoes down full length of Mississippi river
1681–82 William Penn founds Pennsylvania
1686–90 Spanish explore Texas

1700

1713 Britain gains Nova Scotia and Newfoundland from France

1731 French start fur trade around Lake Winnipeg

1750

1755–63 French and Indian War against the British
1759 General Wolfe seizes Québec
1760 Baron Amherst seizes Montréal, ending French control of Canada
1763 Treaty of Paris gives French Canada to Britain and Louisiana to Spain

1800

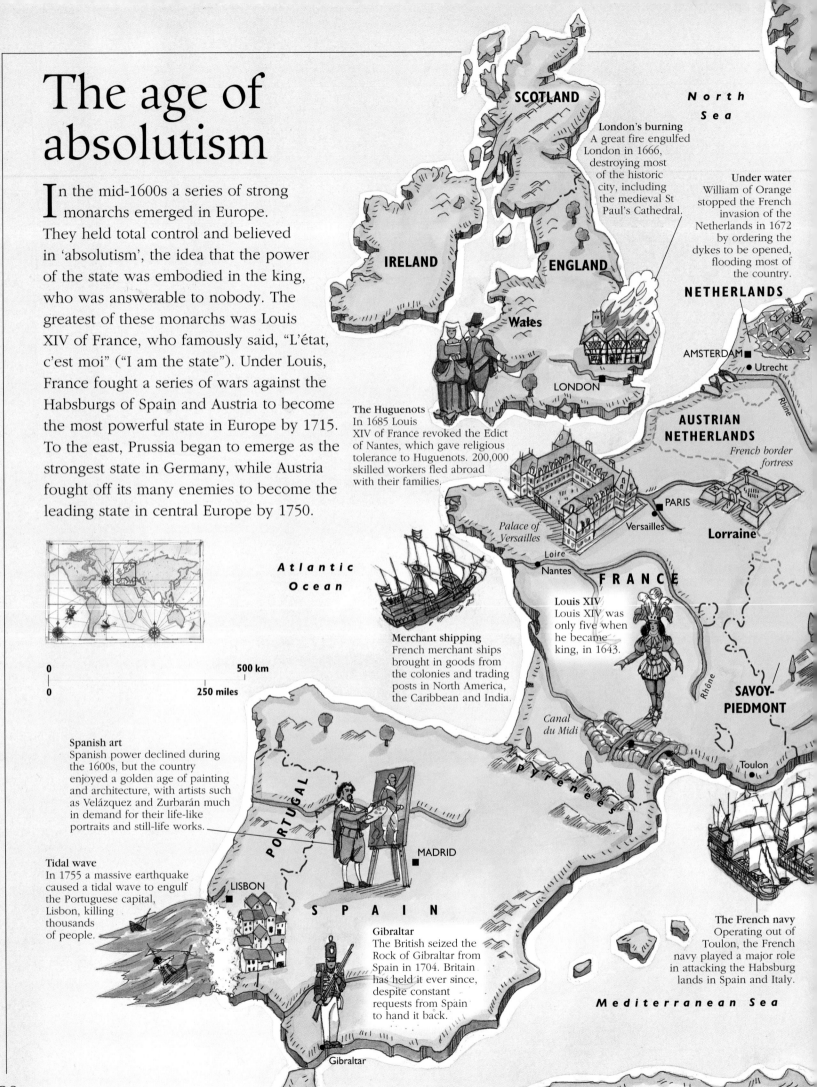

The age of absolutism

In the mid-1600s a series of strong monarchs emerged in Europe. They held total control and believed in 'absolutism', the idea that the power of the state was embodied in the king, who was answerable to nobody. The greatest of these monarchs was Louis XIV of France, who famously said, "L'état, c'est moi" ("I am the state"). Under Louis, France fought a series of wars against the Habsburgs of Spain and Austria to become the most powerful state in Europe by 1715. To the east, Prussia began to emerge as the strongest state in Germany, while Austria fought off its many enemies to become the leading state in central Europe by 1750.

SCOTLAND

IRELAND

ENGLAND

Wales

LONDON

North Sea

London's burning
A great fire engulfed London in 1666, destroying most of the historic city, including the medieval St Paul's Cathedral.

Under water
William of Orange stopped the French invasion of the Netherlands in 1672 by ordering the dykes to be opened, flooding most of the country.

NETHERLANDS

AMSTERDAM
• Utrecht

Rhine

AUSTRIAN NETHERLANDS

French border fortress

The Huguenots
In 1685 Louis XIV of France revoked the Edict of Nantes, which gave religious tolerance to Huguenots. 200,000 skilled workers fled abroad with their families.

Palace of Versailles

PARIS

Versailles

Lorraine

Loire

Nantes

FRANCE

Louis XIV
Louis XIV was only five when he became king, in 1643.

Rhône

Atlantic Ocean

Merchant shipping
French merchant ships brought in goods from the colonies and trading posts in North America, the Caribbean and India.

Canal du Midi

SAVOY-PIEDMONT

Toulon •

0 —————— 500 km
0 —————— 250 miles

Spanish art
Spanish power declined during the 1600s, but the country enjoyed a golden age of painting and architecture, with artists such as Velázquez and Zurbarán much in demand for their life-like portraits and still-life works.

P
O
R
T
U
G
A
L

LISBON

MADRID

S P A I N

P y r e n e e s

The French navy
Operating out of Toulon, the French navy played a major role in attacking the Habsburg lands in Spain and Italy.

Tidal wave
In 1755 a massive earthquake caused a tidal wave to engulf the Portuguese capital, Lisbon, killing thousands of people.

Gibraltar
The British seized the Rock of Gibraltar from Spain in 1704. Britain has held it ever since, despite constant requests from Spain to hand it back.

Gibraltar

Mediterranean Sea

SWEDEN

DENMARK – NORWAY

Baltic Sea

Prussian troops
After 1640, Prussia slowly emerged as the largest state in northern Germany, ruled by a series of brilliant kings and protected by a powerful army.

PRUSSIA

Vistula

POLAND

Hanover

George of Hanover
In 1714 the Duke of Hanover, a minor German state, became king of Great Britain when he succeeded his distant cousin, Queen Anne.

Polish harvests
Constant invasions devastated the grain fields of Poland during the 1750s, leading to a population decline and eventually the collapse of the country itself.

HOLY ROMAN EMPIRE

Elbe

Germany

Duke of Marlborough
Leader of the anti-French armies during the War of the Spanish Succession, the Duke achieved great victories at Blenheim and elsewhere.

Blenheim

Schönbrunn Palace
Maria Theresa saved her bankrupt Austrian empire from collapse during the 1740s. She ruled over a glittering court from her palace outside Vienna.

VIENNA

A L P S

AUSTRIA

Danube

Serfs
In Austria, serfs (peasants) were owned by their landlords and were not legally freed from serfdom until 1781. Many remained tied to this kind of servitude until the 1840s.

this dotted line shows the full extent of the Holy Roman Empire in 1780

these dotted lines show other national borders in Europe in 1780

VENICE

Genoa

GENOA

Corsica

ROME

The Pope
Although still an important ruler in Italy, the Pope's religious and political power in the rest of Europe was minimal at this time.

NAPLES

The Palace of Versailles

In 1662 work began on the construction of a new palace for Louis XIV at Versailles, outside Paris in France. The vast palace took 20 years to build and when complete it became the focus of political, diplomatic and cultural life in France. Louis presided over a glittering court, with playwrights and artists in attendance, as well as his leading nobles. Many other European rulers tried to imitate the grand style and atmosphere of Louis's palace.

1640–1780

1640
1643 Louis XIV becomes king of France, at the age of five. Due to Louis's young age, the government of France is handled by Cardinal Mazarin

1659 France ends 24-year war against Spain
1660
1661 Louis XIV takes over government after death of Cardinal Mazarin
1664–84 Canal du Midi built across France to connect the Atlantic Ocean to the Mediterranean Sea
1667–68 France invades the Spanish Netherlands

1672–78 France invades and occupies most of the Netherlands

1680

1685 Louis XIV cancels the 1598 Edict of Nantes, which granted rights to Huguenots (French Protestants)

1688–97 Nine Years' War begins as Dutch-led alliance tries to prevent France from occupying the Rhineland
1689 William of Orange becomes king of Britain
1700
1701–14 War of the Spanish Succession: Louis tries to place his grandson on the Spanish throne
1704 British seize Gibraltar from Spain
1713 Peace of Utrecht agreement ends Spanish war: Louis's grandson Philip becomes king of Spain
1713–40 Frederick William I builds up Prussian military strength
1714 Hanoverian electors become kings of Great Britain
1715 Death of Louis XIV
1720
1721 Robert Walpole becomes first British prime minister; Britain prospers

1733–35 War of the Polish Succession: Austria and Russia now dominate Poland

1740
1740–48 War of the Austrian Succession: Maria Theresa struggles to keep her throne
1740–86 Frederick II, 'the Great', makes Prussia the strongest state in northern Germany

1756–63 Seven Years' War: France and Austria against Britain and Prussia; Britain gains French colonies in India and North America
1760

1766 France finally gains the eastern province of Lorraine

1769 France buys Corsica from Genoa

1772 First Partition of Poland: Russia, Austria and Prussia all seize Polish territory

1780

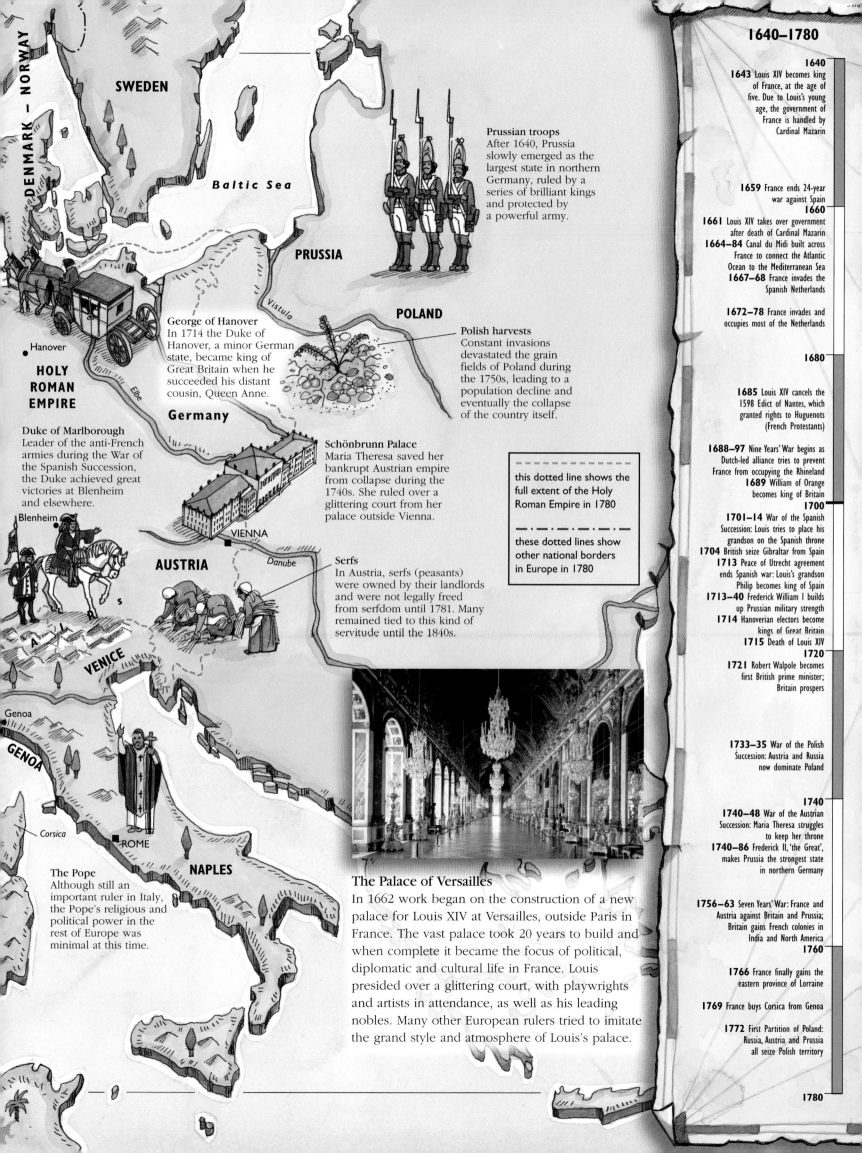

The intellectual revolution:
An enlightened view of the world

During the mid-17th century a new way of looking at the world began to flourish in Europe. This movement is known as the Enlightenment, as it was a time of new ideas based on human logic and reason rather than the old religious beliefs of the Christian Church. The Enlightenment had a huge impact not just on philosophy and politics but also on science and invention. The Enlightenment movement was opposed by the Catholic Church, but some rulers supported these new ideas, setting up universities and scientific societies, and granting religious and political freedoms to their subjects.

Politics

The Enlightenment changed political thinking and influenced the French Revolution of 1789. In 1791–92 the English pamphlet-writer Thomas Paine (1737–1809, right) wrote *The Rights of Man*, in support of the revolution, but was forced to flee to France. There he wrote *The Age of Reason* (1795), attacking Christianity, and was almost executed by guillotine.

Philosophy

The French philosopher René Descartes (1596–1650, left) is often seen as the founder of modern philosophy, putting logic and reason at the heart of his thinking. He summed up his beliefs in the phrase, "I think, therefore I am." A century later, Voltaire (1694–1778) wrote a stream of witty pamphlets, novels and plays that were read by people all across Europe, making the new ideas of the Enlightenment very popular.

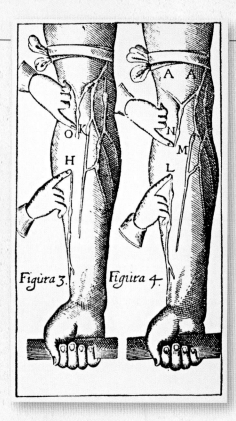

Physics

The English scientist Isaac Newton (1642–1727, right) demonstrated that white light is made up of a spectrum of colours. He did this by 'refracting' it through a glass prism. Most important of all, he defined the three laws of motion and the universal law of gravitation – the invisible force of attraction between objects.

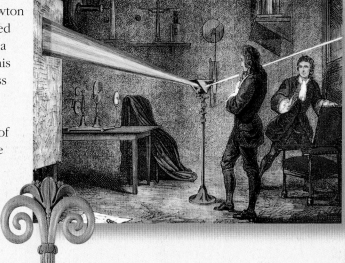

Eyepiece lens turns image right way up

Lenses magnify subject about 21 times, which allowed Galileo to see only one-third of the Moon at one time

Anatomy

In 1628 William Harvey published *De Motu Cordis* – 'On the Motion of the Heart' – in which he suggested that blood is pumped by the heart, and that it is constantly circulating around the body. His explanations overturned medical beliefs that had been followed since the Greeks, 1,400 years before.

Object lens magnifies subject but turns it upside down

Astronomy

Both Galileo Galilei (1564–1642) and Johannes Kepler (1571–1630) developed the basic ideas of Copernicus (see page 106). Galileo invented a telescope for studying the movement of the planets. Kepler discovered that the planets move around the Sun in ellipses (ovals) rather than circles, and move fastest when they are closest to the Sun.

Galileo used this telescope to view the heavens in 1609. The telescope gives a restricted view, as the lenses are small.

Microscopy

Robert Hooke (1635–1703) developed a powerful 'compound' or multi-lens microscope (left) for studying very small organisms. He was the first person to use the word 'cell' to describe the tiny units out of which all living things are made.

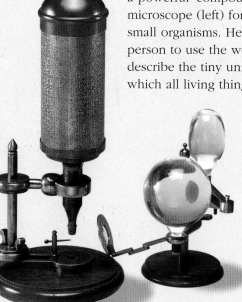

Ornamental stand for the telescope

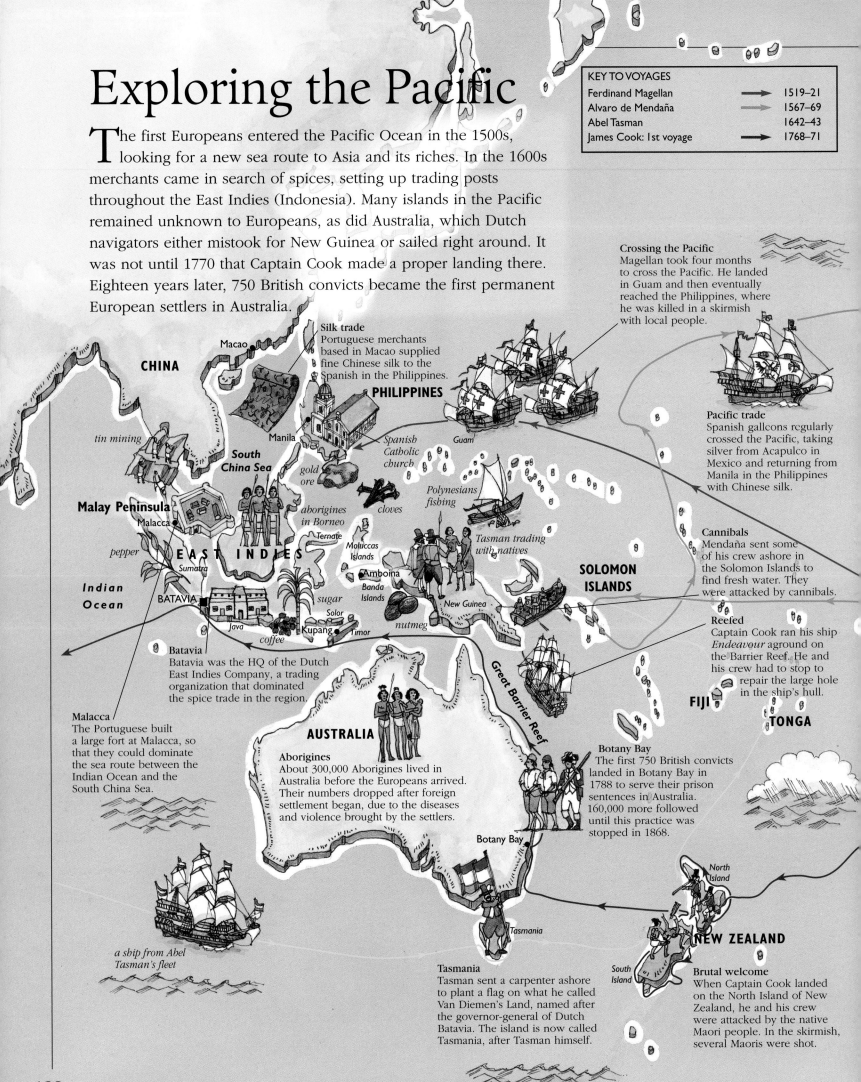

Exploring the Pacific

The first Europeans entered the Pacific Ocean in the 1500s, looking for a new sea route to Asia and its riches. In the 1600s merchants came in search of spices, setting up trading posts throughout the East Indies (Indonesia). Many islands in the Pacific remained unknown to Europeans, as did Australia, which Dutch navigators either mistook for New Guinea or sailed right around. It was not until 1770 that Captain Cook made a proper landing there. Eighteen years later, 750 British convicts became the first permanent European settlers in Australia.

KEY TO VOYAGES

Ferdinand Magellan	⟶	1519–21
Alvaro de Mendaña	⟶	1567–69
Abel Tasman		1642–43
James Cook: 1st voyage	⟶	1768–71

Crossing the Pacific
Magellan took four months to cross the Pacific. He landed in Guam and then eventually reached the Philippines, where he was killed in a skirmish with local people.

Silk trade
Portuguese merchants based in Macao supplied fine Chinese silk to the Spanish in the Philippines.

Pacific trade
Spanish galleons regularly crossed the Pacific, taking silver from Acapulco in Mexico and returning from Manila in the Philippines with Chinese silk.

Cannibals
Mendaña sent some of his crew ashore in the Solomon Islands to find fresh water. They were attacked by cannibals.

Reefed
Captain Cook ran his ship *Endeavour* aground on the Barrier Reef. He and his crew had to stop to repair the large hole in the ship's hull.

Batavia
Batavia was the HQ of the Dutch East Indies Company, a trading organization that dominated the spice trade in the region.

Malacca
The Portuguese built a large fort at Malacca, so that they could dominate the sea route between the Indian Ocean and the South China Sea.

Aborigines
About 300,000 Aborigines lived in Australia before the Europeans arrived. Their numbers dropped after foreign settlement began, due to the diseases and violence brought by the settlers.

Botany Bay
The first 750 British convicts landed in Botany Bay in 1788 to serve their prison sentences in Australia. 160,000 more followed until this practice was stopped in 1868.

Tasmania
Tasman sent a carpenter ashore to plant a flag on what he called Van Diemen's Land, named after the governor-general of Dutch Batavia. The island is now called Tasmania, after Tasman himself.

Brutal welcome
When Captain Cook landed on the North Island of New Zealand, he and his crew were attacked by the native Maori people. In the skirmish, several Maoris were shot.

a ship from Abel Tasman's fleet

CHINA · Macao · tin mining · Malay Peninsula · Malacca · pepper · EAST INDIES · Sumatra · Indian Ocean · BATAVIA · Java · coffee · Batavia · PHILIPPINES · Manila · South China Sea · gold ore · aborigines in Borneo · Ternate · Moluccas Islands · Amboina · Banda Islands · sugar · Solor · Kupang · Timor · nutmeg · New Guinea · Guam · Polynesians fishing · Tasman trading with natives · SOLOMON ISLANDS · Great Barrier Reef · FIJI · TONGA · AUSTRALIA · Botany Bay · Tasmania · North Island · South Island · NEW ZEALAND · Spanish Catholic church · cloves

The spice trade

Spices such as nutmeg, cloves and peppers were much prized in Europe for seasoning food. Until the 1500s, spices reached Europe only via the Arab trading networks of the Indian Ocean and Middle East and were very expensive. In 1519 Magellan set out to reach the Spice Islands (the Moluccas) by sailing west from Spain – but it was the Portuguese and later the Dutch who gained control of this rich trade with Europe. This painting (left) shows the Dutch trading base at Batavia in the East Indies.

Men overboard
Álvaro de Mendaña and his crew suffered from hunger and scurvy, a disease caused by a lack of the Vitamin C found in fresh fruit and vegetables. When crew members died, their bodies were thrown overboard.

Pacific Ocean

Hawaii

Marquesas Islands

Tahiti

Álvaro de Mendaña's ship, San Jeronimo

three ships from Ferdinand Magellan's fleet

Cook's first voyage
In 1768–71 Captain Cook completed his first voyage. He and his crew sailed all the way around New Zealand and then discovered Australia.

Captain Cook's ship, Endeavour

temple at Chichén Itzá

MEXICO

Acapulco

parrot

llama

Amazon rainforest

Callao ■ **LIMA**

Inca city of Machu Picchu

0   **2000 km**

0   **1000 miles**

1500–1800

1500

1511 Portuguese seize Malacca and Malay Peninsula

1520–21 Ferdinand Magellan crosses the Pacific, the first European to do so

1567–69 Álvaro de Mendaña explores the South Pacific and discovers the Solomon Islands
1571 Spanish found Manila as the capital of the Philippines
1579 Francis Drake crosses the Pacific from California, in North America, to the Philippines

1595–96 Álvaro de Mendaña dies in an attempt to set up a Spanish colony in the Solomons
1596 First arrival of the Dutch in Java

1600
1602 Dutch East Indies Co is founded
1605–06 Dutch navigator Willem Jantszoon explores the north coast of Australia but thinks it is part of New Guinea
1606–07 Luis de Torres sails around New Guinea, proving it is an island

1619 Dutch seize Batavia and set up Dutch East Indies Co headquarters there
1623 Dutch drive British out of the Spice Islands (Moluccas)
1629 Dutch drive Portuguese out of the Spice Islands

1641 Dutch seize Malacca from the Portuguese
1642–43 Abel Tasman discovers Van Diemen's Land (Tasmania), New Zealand, Fiji and Tonga

1667 Dutch complete their conquest of the Spice Islands

1684 Dutch seize most of Java and eastern Sumatra

1700
1700 Dutch dominate European trade with the East Indies (Indonesia)

1768–71 Cook's first voyage: he circumnavigates (sails around) New Zealand and discovers Australia
1772–75 Cook's second voyage: he explores Antarctica
1776–79 Cook's third voyage: he sails north, to find an inlet into the Arctic Ocean, and discovers Hawaii, where he dies

1788 First British convicts land in Botany Bay, Australia
1792 First British settlement in New Zealand

1800

The American Revolution

In 1775 13 of the British colonies in North America rose up in revolt. They protested against British attempts to restrict their freedom and to tax them without giving them any representation in parliament. Led by George Washington, and later supported by the French, the colonists declared their independence in 1776 and won a series of military victories before the war ended in 1783. This victory gave birth to a new nation, the United States of America, which at first stretched only as far inland as the Mississippi river. Eventually, it extended right across the continent to the Pacific Ocean in the west.

George Washington
George Washington (1732–99) was a colonial farmer in Virginia who fought for the British against the French in the 1750s. He was the ideal person to command the American forces against the British and led them to victory in 1781. As the first president of the newly independent United States, from 1789–97, he led the nation with great skill and determination.

The Boston Tea Party
Colonists upset by the British government's tax on imported tea dumped a cargo of tea into Boston harbour in 1773.

Loyalists
Americans from New York and South Carolina, loyal to the British crown, fled north to Canada along with Mohawks who had fought for the British. They settled in Ontario and the provinces near to the sea.

Paul Revere
On 18 April 1775, silversmith Paul Revere rode through the night to warn people that British troops were coming to capture military stores at Concord.

Saratoga
A British attempt to isolate the New England colonies from the rest of America was defeated at Saratoga in 1777.

Legend of Betsy Ross
Betsy Ross was asked to make the first American flag using six-pointed stars, but said that five-pointed stars 'would look better'.

Crossing the Delaware
On Christmas Day 1776, George Washington led his recently defeated army across the icy Delaware river, surprising the British and winning a crucial battle at Trenton.

A new capital
In 1791 the decision was taken to build a new national capital on the Potomac river. It was named 'Washington' in honour of the first president, George Washington.

CANADA

Québec

Montréal

Ontario

Lake Superior

Lake Michigan

Lake Huron

Lake Erie

Lake Ontario

Hudson

UNITED STATES OF AMERICA

Mississippi

New Hampshire
Concord
Bunker Hill
Lexington
Boston
Massachusetts
Rhode Island
Connecticut
New York
Saratoga
New York
Princeton
Trenton
Philadelphia
Brandywine
Pennsylvania
New Jersey
Delaware
Baltimore

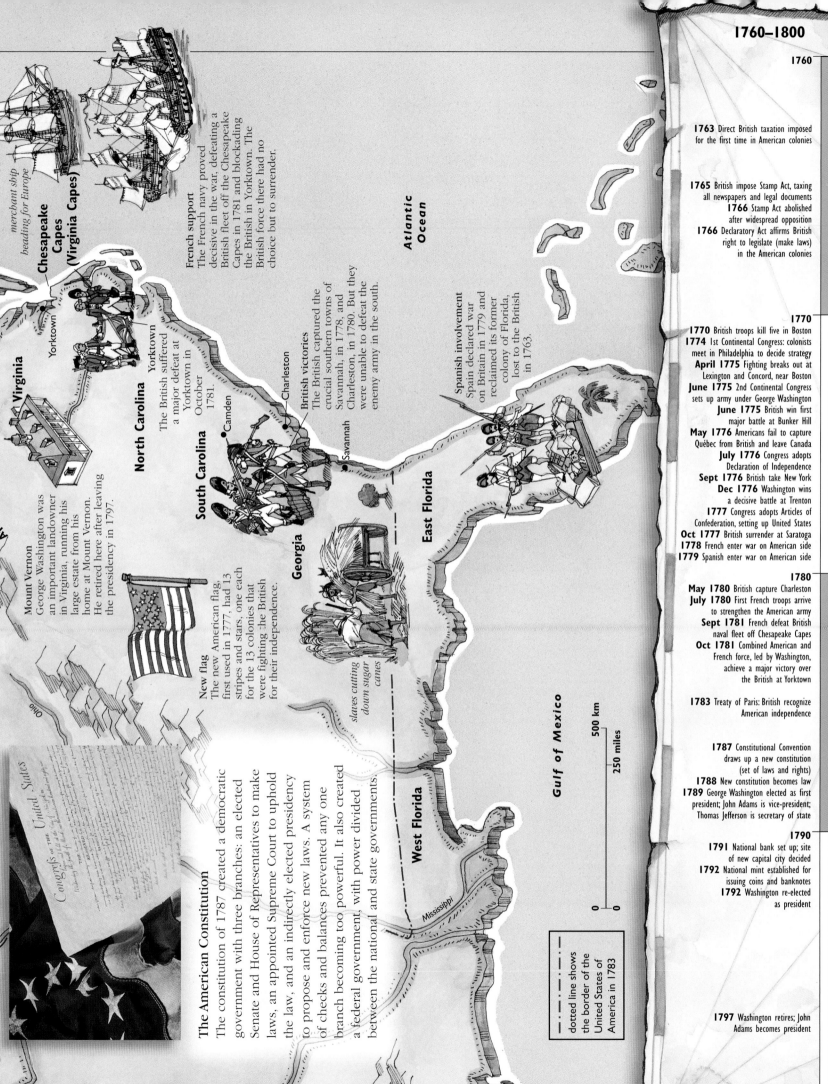

merchant ship
heading for Europe

**Chesapeake
Capes
(Virginia Capes)**

French support
The French navy proved
decisive in the war, defeating a
British fleet off the Chesapeake
Capes in 1781 and blockading
the British in Yorktown. The
British force there had no
choice but to surrender.

*Atlantic
Ocean*

Yorktown

Virginia

Yorktown
The British suffered
a major defeat at
Yorktown in
October
1781.

North Carolina

Camden

Charleston

British victories
The British captured the
crucial southern towns of
Savannah, in 1778, and
Charleston, in 1780. But they
were unable to defeat the
enemy army in the south.

South Carolina

Spanish involvement
Spain declared war
on Britain in 1779 and
reclaimed its former
colony of Florida,
lost to the British
in 1763.

Savannah

Georgia

East Florida

Mount Vernon
George Washington was
an important landowner
in Virginia, running his
large estate from his
home at Mount Vernon.
He retired here after leaving
the presidency in 1797.

App...

New flag
The new American flag,
first used in 1777, had 13
stripes and stars, one each
for the 13 colonies that
were fighting the British
for their independence.

*slaves cutting
down sugar
canes*

Ohio

The American Constitution

The constitution of 1787 created a democratic
government with three branches: an elected
Senate and House of Representatives to make
laws, an appointed Supreme Court to uphold
the law, and an indirectly elected presidency
to propose and enforce new laws. A system
of checks and balances prevented any one
branch becoming too powerful. It also created
a federal government, with power divided
between the national and state governments.

West Florida

Mississippi

Gulf of Mexico

500 km

250 miles

0

0

- - - - - - - - - - - dotted line shows
the border of the
United States of
America in 1783

1760–1800

1760

1763 Direct British taxation imposed
for the first time in American colonies

1765 British impose Stamp Act, taxing
all newspapers and legal documents
1766 Stamp Act abolished
after widespread opposition
1766 Declaratory Act affirms British
right to legislate (make laws)
in the American colonies

1770

1770 British troops kill five in Boston
1774 1st Continental Congress: colonists
meet in Philadelphia to decide strategy
April 1775 Fighting breaks out at
Lexington and Concord, near Boston
June 1775 2nd Continental Congress
sets up army under George Washington
June 1775 British win first
major battle at Bunker Hill
May 1776 Americans fail to capture
Québec from British and leave Canada
July 1776 Congress adopts
Declaration of Independence
Sept 1776 British take New York
Dec 1776 Washington wins
a decisive battle at Trenton
1777 Congress adopts Articles of
Confederation, setting up United States
Oct 1777 British surrender at Saratoga
1778 French enter war on American side
1779 Spanish enter war on American side

1780

May 1780 British capture Charleston
July 1780 First French troops arrive
to strengthen the American army
Sept 1781 French defeat British
naval fleet off Chesapeake Capes
Oct 1781 Combined American and
French force, led by Washington,
achieve a major victory over
the British at Yorktown

1783 Treaty of Paris: British recognize
American independence

1787 Constitutional Convention
draws up a new constitution
(set of laws and rights)
1788 New constitution becomes law
1789 George Washington elected as first
president; John Adams is vice-president;
Thomas Jefferson is secretary of state

1790

1791 National bank set up; site
of new capital city decided
1792 National mint established for
issuing coins and banknotes
1792 Washington re-elected
as president

1797 Washington retires; John
Adams becomes president

1800

The French Revolution

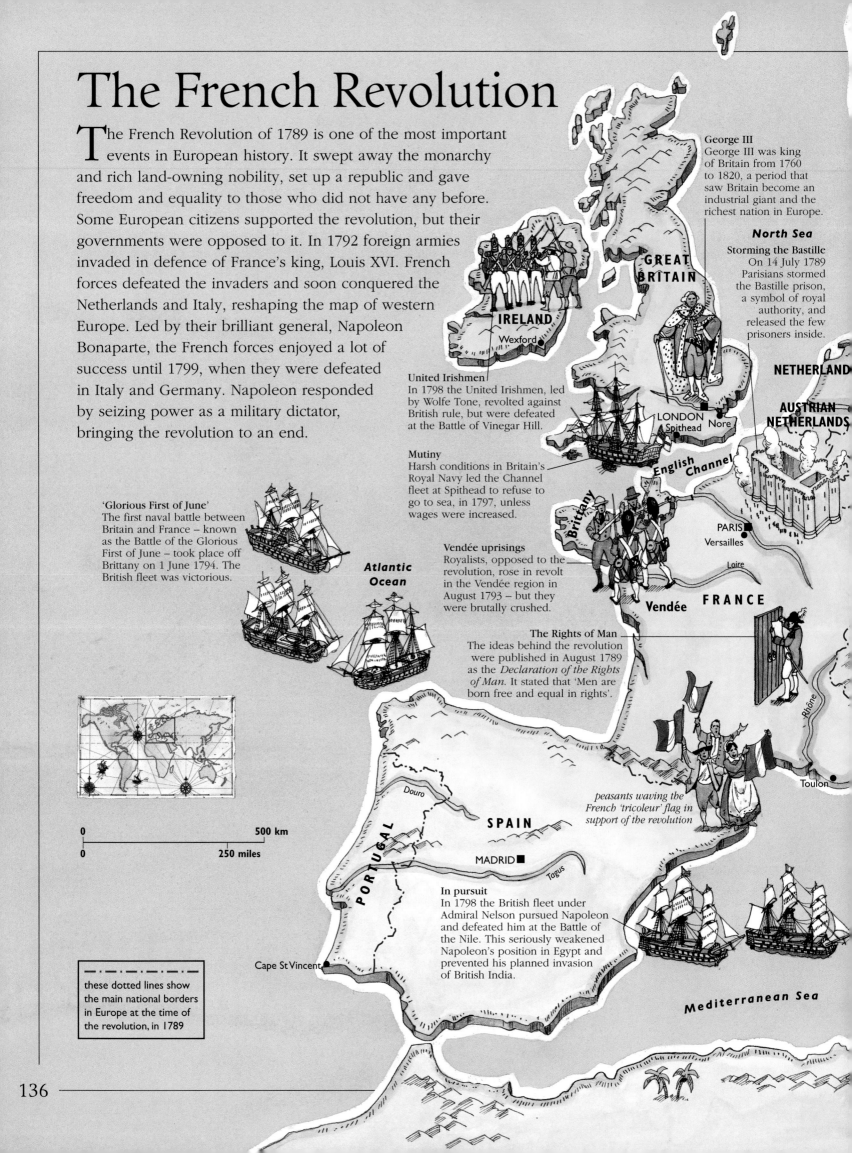

The French Revolution of 1789 is one of the most important events in European history. It swept away the monarchy and rich land-owning nobility, set up a republic and gave freedom and equality to those who did not have any before. Some European citizens supported the revolution, but their governments were opposed to it. In 1792 foreign armies invaded in defence of France's king, Louis XVI. French forces defeated the invaders and soon conquered the Netherlands and Italy, reshaping the map of western Europe. Led by their brilliant general, Napoleon Bonaparte, the French forces enjoyed a lot of success until 1799, when they were defeated in Italy and Germany. Napoleon responded by seizing power as a military dictator, bringing the revolution to an end.

George III
George III was king of Britain from 1760 to 1820, a period that saw Britain become an industrial giant and the richest nation in Europe.

North Sea
Storming the Bastille
On 14 July 1789 Parisians stormed the Bastille prison, a symbol of royal authority, and released the few prisoners inside.

GREAT BRITAIN

IRELAND

Wexford

United Irishmen
In 1798 the United Irishmen, led by Wolfe Tone, revolted against British rule, but were defeated at the Battle of Vinegar Hill.

Mutiny
Harsh conditions in Britain's Royal Navy led the Channel fleet at Spithead to refuse to go to sea, in 1797, unless wages were increased.

LONDON
Spithead   Nore

English Channel

NETHERLAND

AUSTRIAN NETHERLANDS

Brittany

PARIS
Versailles

Loire

'Glorious First of June'
The first naval battle between Britain and France – known as the Battle of the Glorious First of June – took place off Brittany on 1 June 1794. The British fleet was victorious.

Atlantic Ocean

Vendée uprisings
Royalists, opposed to the revolution, rose in revolt in the Vendée region in August 1793 – but they were brutally crushed.

Vendée   **FRANCE**

The Rights of Man
The ideas behind the revolution were published in August 1789 as the *Declaration of the Rights of Man*. It stated that 'Men are born free and equal in rights'.

Rhône

Douro

SPAIN

MADRID

peasants waving the French 'tricoleur' flag in support of the revolution

Toulon

0 ——————— 500 km
0 ——————— 250 miles

Tagus

In pursuit
In 1798 the British fleet under Admiral Nelson pursued Napoleon and defeated him at the Battle of the Nile. This seriously weakened Napoleon's position in Egypt and prevented his planned invasion of British India.

P O R T U G A L

Cape St Vincent

these dotted lines show the main national borders in Europe at the time of the revolution, in 1789

Mediterranean Sea

RUSSIA

Baltic Sea

Prussia
Prussia emerged in the 1700s as the most powerful state in northern Europe. Along with Austria, it declared war on revolutionary France in 1792 to restore the French monarchy.

Partitioning Poland
Three times – in 1772, 1793 and 1795 – Prussia, Russia and Austria divided Poland up between them. The Poles did not regain their independence until 1918.

PRUSSIA

POLAND

Elbe

BERLIN ■

Vistula

Germany

Rhine

Danube

AUSTRIAN EMPIRE

VIENNA ■

Danube

Marie Antoinette
Marie Antoinette, daughter of the Austrian empress, was married to the French king Louis XVI at the age of 14. She was executed for treason in 1793.

Commander-in-chief
Napoleon emerged as the leading French commander, thanks to his brilliant campaigns and victories in Italy in 1796–97.

Sava

VENICE

GENOA

OTTOMAN EMPIRE

Corsica

■ ROME

Island home
Napoleon Bonaparte was born on 15 August 1769 on the French island of Corsica, which until the previous year had been part of the Italian state of Genoa.

Sardinia

Sicily

MALTA

Beheading the king and queen

Due to the monarchy's rising debts, Louis XVI was forced to summon the Estates-General (parliament) in May 1789 to raise taxes. The ministers of the Third Estate (representing the commoners) were angered by this and soon broke away to form a national assembly. Their demands for political reform led to the revolution, which broke out in July 1789 and reached its peak with Louis's execution in January 1793. The queen of France, Marie Antoinette, was also beheaded in October of the same year (above).

1789
May Estates-General meets but soon collapses
June Third Estate of commoners sets up National Assembly
July Parisians storm the Bastille prison
Aug 'Declaration of the Rights of Man' published

1790

1791
June French king Louis XVI and his queen, Marie Antoinette, try to flee Paris

1792
April France declares war on Austria
July France declares war on Prussia
Sept France abolishes monarchy and becomes a republic
Nov French defeat Austrians and seize the Austrian Netherlands

1793
Jan Louis XVI executed on the guillotine
Jan Second Partition of Poland
Feb–Mar France declares war on Britain and the Dutch republic
Feb First Coalition of European powers formed against France
Mar–Oct Royalist uprising in the Vendée

1794
June 1793–July 1794 Robespierre leads a reign of terror against enemies of the revolution

June British defeat French fleet at the Battle of the Glorious First of June

1795
Jan French conquer the Dutch republic
April France and Prussia make peace

Oct Directory takes power in France
Oct Third Partition of Poland: partition of the country between Austria, Prussia and Russia ends Polish independence

1796
Feb British naval victory over Spain (a French ally) off Cape St Vincent
April Bonaparte commands French forces against Austrians in Italy

1797
April, May British Royal Navy twice mutinies over pay and service conditions

Oct British defeat Dutch fleet at Camperdown off the Dutch coast
Oct Austria and France make peace

1798
June United Irishmen fail to win independence from Britain
July Napoleon defeats Egyptians at the Battle of the Pyramids
Aug Nelson defeats Napoleon at the Battle of the Nile

1799
Mar Austria again declares war on France
Mar, April French forces defeated in Germany and Italy
June Britain, Austria and Russia form the Second Coalition
Nov Napoleon overthrows Directory and sets up a three-man Consulate

1800

MODERN WORLD

Illustrated by Kevin Maddison

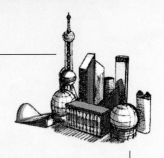

CONTENTS

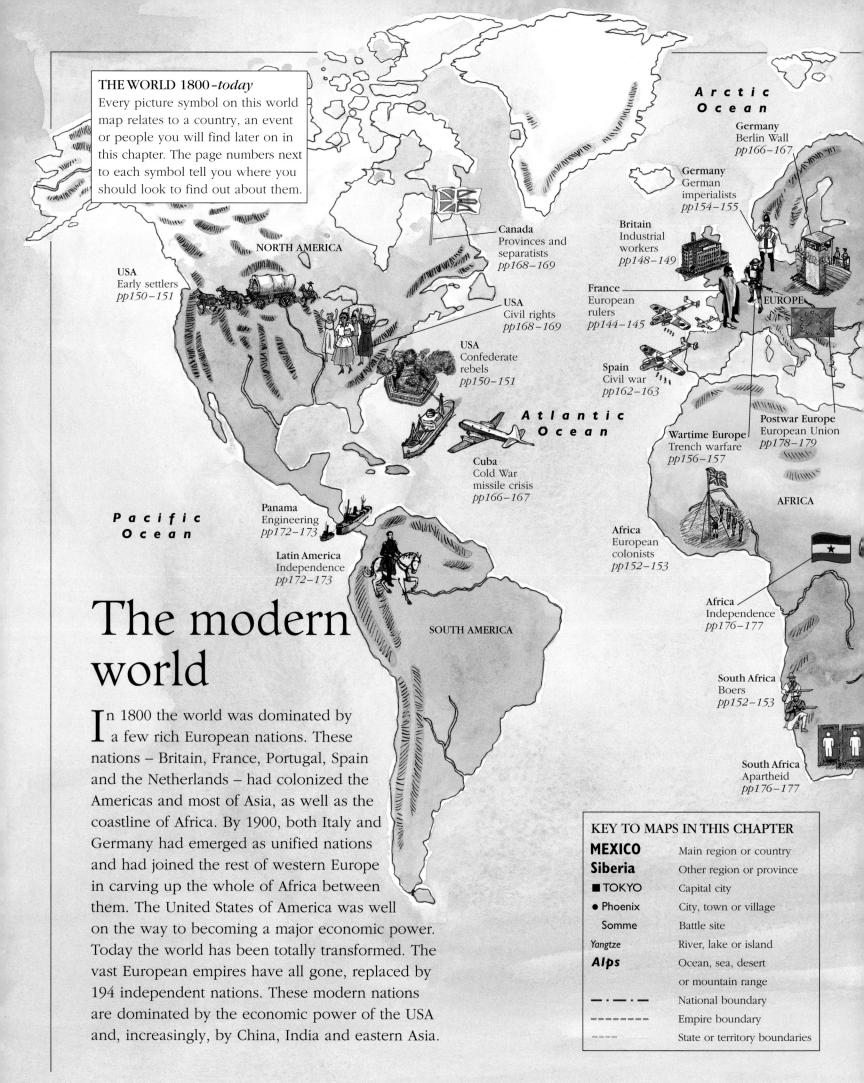

THE WORLD 1800-*today*
Every picture symbol on this world map relates to a country, an event or people you will find later on in this chapter. The page numbers next to each symbol tell you where you should look to find out about them.

Arctic Ocean

Germany
Berlin Wall
pp166–167

Germany
German imperialists
pp154–155

Britain
Industrial workers
pp148–149

Canada
Provinces and separatists
pp168–169

EUROPE

France
European rulers
pp144–145

NORTH AMERICA

USA
Early settlers
pp150–151

USA
Civil rights
pp168–169

USA
Confederate rebels
pp150–151

Spain
Civil war
pp162–163

Atlantic Ocean

Postwar Europe
European Union
pp178–179

Wartime Europe
Trench warfare
pp156–157

Cuba
Cold War missile crisis
pp166–167

AFRICA

Panama
Engineering
pp172–173

Pacific Ocean

Africa
European colonists
pp152–153

Latin America
Independence
pp172–173

Africa
Independence
pp176–177

SOUTH AMERICA

South Africa
Boers
pp152–153

The modern world

In 1800 the world was dominated by a few rich European nations. These nations – Britain, France, Portugal, Spain and the Netherlands – had colonized the Americas and most of Asia, as well as the coastline of Africa. By 1900, both Italy and Germany had emerged as unified nations and had joined the rest of western Europe in carving up the whole of Africa between them. The United States of America was well on the way to becoming a major economic power. Today the world has been totally transformed. The vast European empires have all gone, replaced by 194 independent nations. These modern nations are dominated by the economic power of the USA and, increasingly, by China, India and eastern Asia.

South Africa
Apartheid
pp176–177

KEY TO MAPS IN THIS CHAPTER	
MEXICO	Main region or country
Siberia	Other region or province
■ TOKYO	Capital city
● Phoenix	City, town or village
Somme	Battle site
Yangtze	River, lake or island
Alps	Ocean, sea, desert or mountain range
— · — · —	National boundary
– – – – –	Empire boundary
– – – – –	State or territory boundaries

Russia
Revolutionaries
pp158–159

Russia
Freed serfs
pp154–155

Russia
Space travel
pp158–159

ASIA

Middle East
Oil wealth
pp174–175

China
Communists
pp170–171

Japan
Kamikaze
pilots
pp164–165

India
Independence
pp176–177

Vietnam
Vietnam War
pp176–177

**P a c i f i c
O c e a n**

I n d i a n   O c e a n

AUSTRALIA

Australia
European
settlers
pp148–149

LOCATOR MAP
You will find a world map like this along with every map in the chapter. This allows you to see exactly which part of the world the main map is showing you.

POLITICAL MOVEMENTS
The following definitions may help you when reading this chapter:

CAPITALISM: An economic system based on private ownership, in which there is usually a free market to buy and sell goods.

COMMUNISM: A classless society in which private ownership has been abolished. The means of production and subsistence belong to the community as a whole, although this system is often under the control of the state.

FASCISM: An extreme political movement based on nationalism (loyalty to one's country) and authority, often military, which aims to unite a country's people into a disciplined force under an all-powerful leader or dictator.

FUNDAMENTALISM: A movement that favours a very strict interpretation of any one religion and its scriptures or laws.

MARXISM: A movement based on the ideas of the philosopher Karl Marx (1818–83), often known as the 'father of communism'.

NAZISM: A very extreme form of fascism, often involving highly racist policies.

The world since 1800:
An endlessly changing world

The pace of change over the last 200 years has probably been greater than at any other time in human history. In 1800 the population of the world was about 930 million, and most of these people lived and worked on the land. Today the world is home to about 6.4 billion people, the vast majority of whom live and work in increasingly overcrowded towns and cities. New industrial techniques, mass communications and inventions such as the aeroplane and the computer have transformed the lives of almost everyone today, while few have been able to escape the effects of the wars and conflicts that have raged around the globe during the last century.

Industrial change
The Industrial Revolution began in Britain in the late 1700s, and spread throughout Europe and across to the United States during the 1800s. Millions of people who had previously worked on the land or in small workshops now lived and worked in large industrial towns. They laboured long hours in factories, iron and steel works and shipyards – as in New York (above) – where the working conditions were often difficult and dangerous.

Into space
The first artificial satellite to orbit the Earth, *Sputnik 1*, was launched in 1957. Twelve years later astronauts landed on the Moon, and by the end of the century they lived and worked in space for months at a time in orbiting space stations far above the Earth's surface (below). Unmanned spacecraft have now explored the furthest planets, sending back remarkable photographs of our solar system and beyond.

The impact of war
The 20th century was one of the most brutal periods in all of human history. Two major world wars and many other conflicts killed millions of people, and transformed the lives of many millions more. For example, women worked in jobs previously undertaken only by men, such as in heavy industrial plants (left). In many countries, women also gained the right to vote and to be treated as equals to men for the first time.

The International Space Station (ISS) is made up of separate modules, which have been launched into space individually since 1998.

Space Shuttle astronauts perform spacewalks to join the different modules together.

Communications

The development of the telegraph, postal services, mass printing techniques, the telephone, radio, television and the Internet have transformed communications over the last 200 years. This also means we have a huge volume of historical evidence to tell us about this period – photographs, printed material such as newspapers, and film and sound recordings. Today, information can be spread around the world in seconds via satellite technology, while computers are rapidly transforming the way we work, study, and entertain ourselves.

Television set from the 1960s

Early 20th-century telephone

Modern laptop computer

Newspapers are still an important source of up-to-date information. They are now printed and distributed at great speed, and in huge quantities, thanks to automated printing presses such as this one (above).

Mobile telephone with a digital camera

Napoleonic Europe

In 1804 Napoleon Bonaparte, ruler of France since 1799 and the most successful military leader of his time, crowned himself as Emperor Napoleon I. A series of brilliant victories then brought him control over most of Europe, with only Britain standing out against him. But in 1812 he invaded Russia in a final attempt to end its opposition to his rule. Although he seized the capital, Moscow, he was forced to retreat by the fierce Russian winter. Victories turned to defeats, and in 1815 a joint British and Prussian force finally overcame Napoleon at Waterloo.

After Napoleon
In 1815 the victorious European nations met in Vienna to agree the future shape of Europe. The old order of dictatorial monarchs was re-established, and few changes were made to national borders. Attempts in Spain and elsewhere to introduce limited democratic reforms were quickly crushed. In 1830, however, the people of Paris rose in revolt (above) against the dictatorial Charles X, setting up a new, more liberal monarchy.

Battle of Trafalgar
The British navy under Lord Nelson won a victory against the French at Trafalgar in 1805, ending the threat of an invasion of Britain.

these dotted lines show the borders between European countries in 1815

Industrial revolution
A revolution in the production of coal, iron, cotton and wool textiles turned Britain into the 'workshop of the world' by 1815.

North Sea

Battle of Waterloo
Napoleon was finally defeated, at Waterloo in 1815, by the British and Prussians.

The Great Reform Act
The British parliament was reformed in 1832 to make it fairer and less corrupt.

Self-crowning
Napoleon became emperor of France in 1804, crowning himself at his coronation.

Sent far away
After his defeat at Waterloo, Napoleon was sent into exile on the southern Atlantic island of St Helena, 8,000km away.

Napoleon triumphant
In 1800 Napoleon crossed the Alps, soon to be master of Europe.

rural workers in the fields

Temporary exile
In 1814 Napoleon was sent into exile by Britain and its allies to the island of Elba. He soon escaped back to France.

The Peninsula War
The Spanish rose in revolt against Napoleon in 1808.

Fighting tyranny
In 1820 the Spanish army revolted against the brutal rule of King Ferdinand VII, but was crushed by the French in 1823.

French North Africa
In 1830 the French occupied the city of Algiers, the beginnings of a vast empire in North Africa.

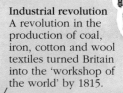

Scotland

Ireland
Dublin

BRITAIN

LONDON

Boulogne

Amiens
PARIS

FRANCE

SWITZERLAND

Waterloo

NETHERLANDS

GERMAN STATES

DENMARK

Rhine

Ulm

ALPS

Elba

Corsica

Sardinia

Vitoria

PORTUGAL

MADRID SPAIN

LISBON

Balearic Islands

Trafalgar

ALGIERS

Atlantic Ocean

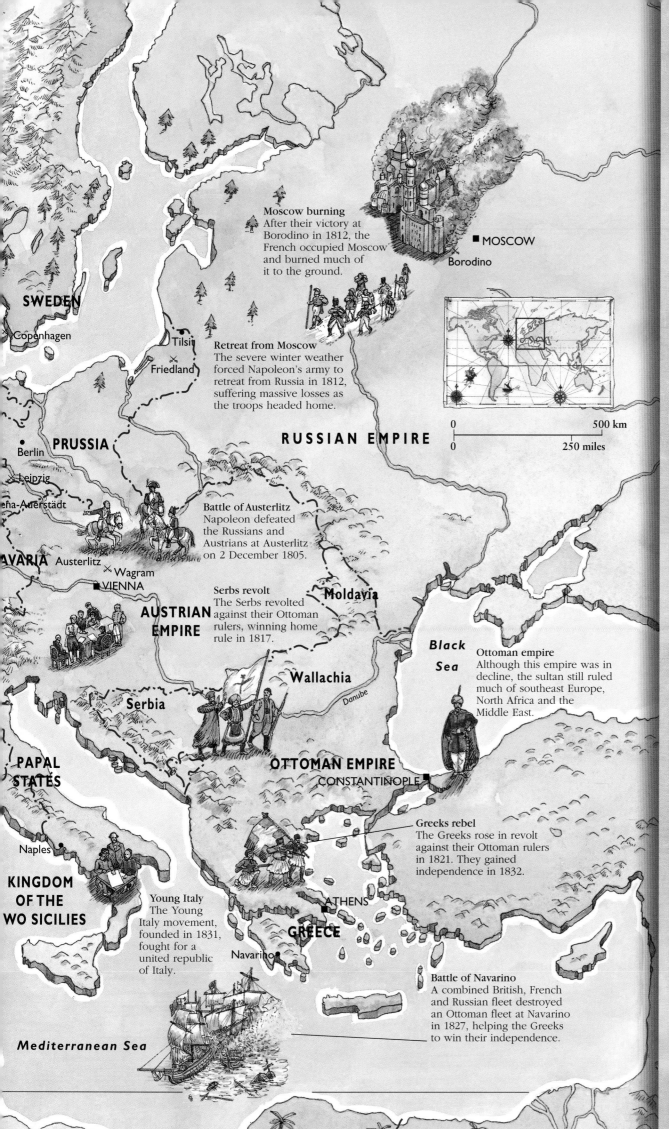

SWEDEN

Copenhagen

Tilsit

Friedland

PRUSSIA

Berlin

Leipzig

ena-Auerstädt

AVARIA Austerlitz

× Wagram

■ VIENNA

AUSTRIAN EMPIRE

PAPAL STATES

Naples

KINGDOM OF THE WO SICILIES

Moscow burning
After their victory at Borodino in 1812, the French occupied Moscow and burned much of it to the ground.

■ MOSCOW

Borodino

Retreat from Moscow
The severe winter weather forced Napoleon's army to retreat from Russia in 1812, suffering massive losses as the troops headed home.

RUSSIAN EMPIRE

Battle of Austerlitz
Napoleon defeated the Russians and Austrians at Austerlitz on 2 December 1805.

Serbs revolt
The Serbs revolted against their Ottoman rulers, winning home rule in 1817.

Moldavia

Wallachia

Serbia

Danube

Black Sea

Ottoman empire
Although this empire was in decline, the sultan still ruled much of southeast Europe, North Africa and the Middle East.

OTTOMAN EMPIRE
CONSTANTINOPLE ■

Greeks rebel
The Greeks rose in revolt against their Ottoman rulers in 1821. They gained independence in 1832.

Young Italy
The Young Italy movement, founded in 1831, fought for a united republic of Italy.

ATHENS

GREECE

Navarino

Battle of Navarino
A combined British, French and Russian fleet destroyed an Ottoman fleet at Navarino in 1827, helping the Greeks to win their independence.

Mediterranean Sea

0 ————— 500 km
0 ————— 250 miles

1800

1802 Britain and France sign the peace treaty of Amiens
1803 Britain and France go to war again; Napoleon prepares to invade Britain
1804 Napoleon becomes emperor of Europe; he applies the 'Code Napoléon' (French civil law) across Europe
1805 Austrians and Russians are beaten at Austerlitz; the British navy defeats the French at Trafalgar, ending the threat of invasion

1807 Russians and Prussians are defeated at Friedland
1808 Peninsula War begins in Spain — a lengthy conflict fought by the Spanish and British against French occupation

1810

1812 Napoleon invades Russia, but the harsh winter forces him to retreat
1813 British under Wellington defeat French at Vitoria, Spain, ending Peninsula War; Napoleon defeated by Russians, Austrians and Prussians at the 'Battle of the Nations', Leipzig
1814 As enemies threaten Paris, Napoleon is forced to abdicate and is exiled to Elba
1815 Napoleon escapes from Elba, but is finally defeated at Waterloo and is sent into exile again
1815 Congress of Vienna redraws the maps of Europe and restores previous kingdoms: Norway is united with Sweden, and Belgium with the Netherlands

1817 Serbia wins home rule from the Ottoman empire

1820

1820 Revolutions crushed in Portugal and Naples
1820–23 Spanish revolt against Ferdinand VII ended by the French
1821 Napoleon dies on St Helena in the southern Atlantic Ocean
1821 Greeks begin war of independence against Ottoman rule

1827 Anglo-French-Russian fleet defeats Ottoman-Egyptian fleet at Navarino

1829 Moldavia and Wallachia win home rule from the Ottoman empire

1830

1830 Revolution in France: King Charles X is overthrown and replaced by Louis-Philippe
1830 French occupy Algiers
1830–31 Revolutions crushed in Italy and Poland
1830–39 Belgian revolt against Dutch rule leads to Belgian independence
1831 Young Italy movement founded
1832 Great Reform Act passed in Britain
1832 Greece becomes an independent monarchy

1840

Industrial Revolution:
Steam, iron and steel

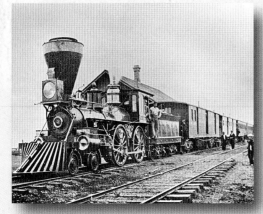

An industrial revolution began in Britain during the 1760s. New machines, driven by steam and water, were used to manufacture textiles and other products in factories manned by hundreds of workers. Steam engines hauled coal and iron out of mines and powered railway engines to transport raw materials and finished goods. New technologies transformed the production of iron, steel and chemicals. The revolution transformed Britain – and later the rest of Europe and the USA – from a mainly rural society into an urban one. New industrial towns, where workers lived, were often squalid. Before long, people began to campaign for social and political reforms to improve living conditions.

The railways

The need to move raw materials to the factories, and to take away their finished products, led to a revolution in transport. A network of canals was built in Britain after the 1760s, but it was the invention of the railways in the early 1800s that led to the biggest changes. The first American steam railroad opened in 1830. Fifty years later there were more railroads in the USA (above) than in the whole of Europe.

Industrial towns

The development of factories led to the rapid growth of many towns, such as Leeds in northern England (shown below). Living conditions in these towns were often dreadful, as new houses for the workers were built back to back and close to the factories, mills and mines where they worked.

Smoke from factory chimneys darkened the sky and polluted the water supply

Nearby farms were quickly swamped by the expanding towns

Workers lived in cramped housing with few amenities

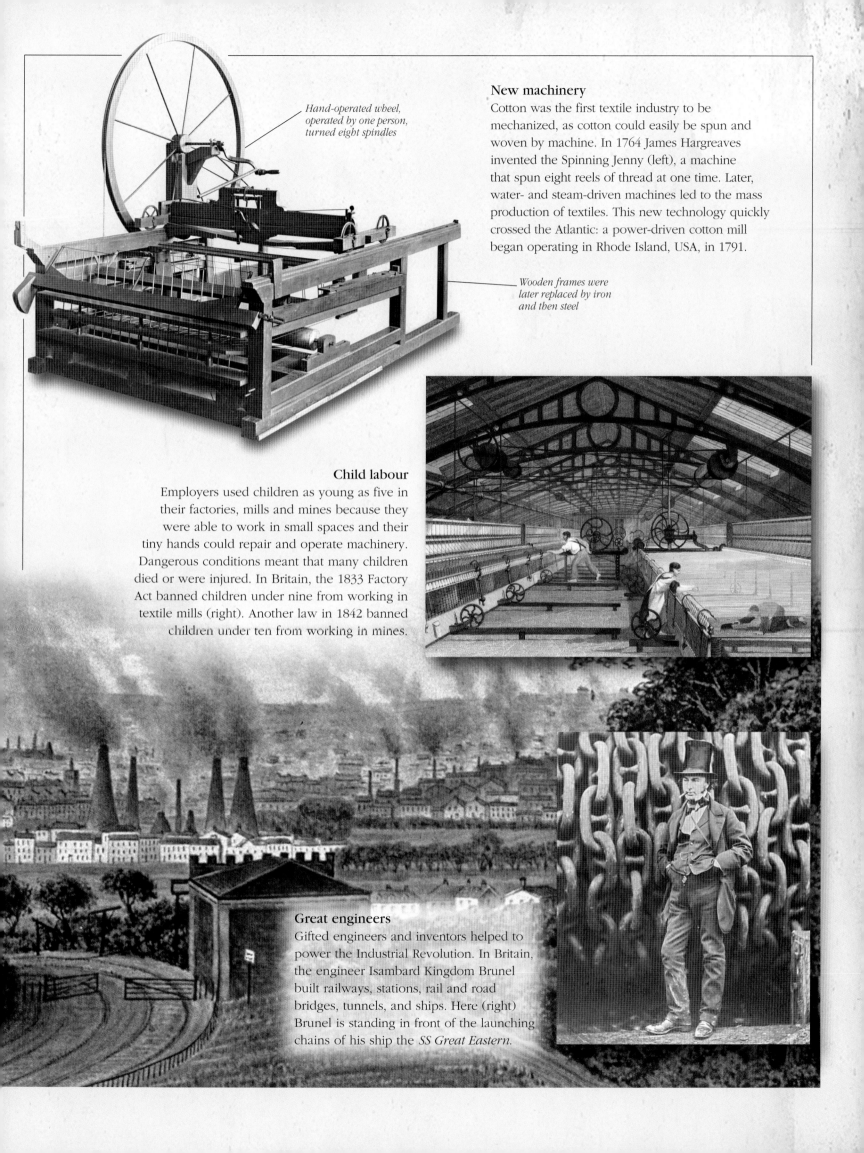

Hand-operated wheel, operated by one person, turned eight spindles

New machinery

Cotton was the first textile industry to be mechanized, as cotton could easily be spun and woven by machine. In 1764 James Hargreaves invented the Spinning Jenny (left), a machine that spun eight reels of thread at one time. Later, water- and steam-driven machines led to the mass production of textiles. This new technology quickly crossed the Atlantic: a power-driven cotton mill began operating in Rhode Island, USA, in 1791.

Wooden frames were later replaced by iron and then steel

Child labour

Employers used children as young as five in their factories, mills and mines because they were able to work in small spaces and their tiny hands could repair and operate machinery. Dangerous conditions meant that many children died or were injured. In Britain, the 1833 Factory Act banned children under nine from working in textile mills (right). Another law in 1842 banned children under ten from working in mines.

Great engineers

Gifted engineers and inventors helped to power the Industrial Revolution. In Britain, the engineer Isambard Kingdom Brunel built railways, stations, rail and road bridges, tunnels, and ships. Here (right) Brunel is standing in front of the launching chains of his ship the *SS Great Eastern*.

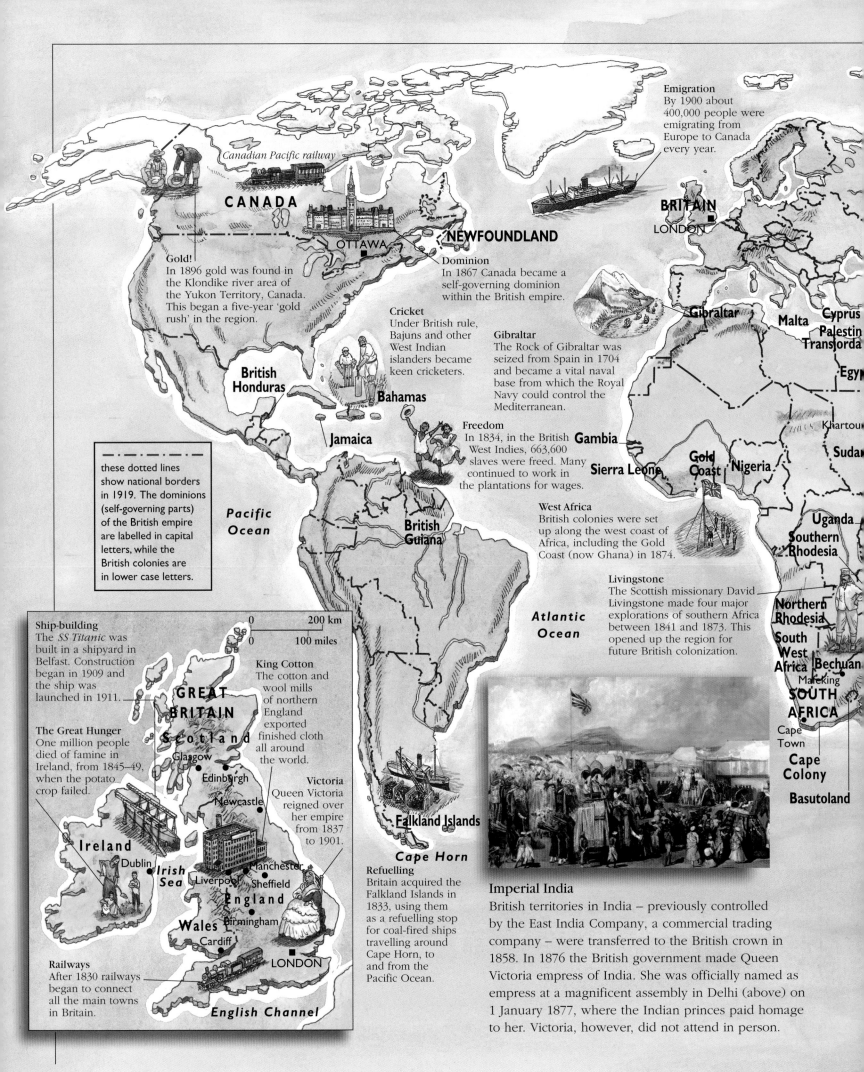

Emigration
By 1900 about 400,000 people were emigrating from Europe to Canada every year.

Canadian Pacific railway

CANADA

OTTAWA

NEWFOUNDLAND

BRITAIN
LONDON

Gold!
In 1896 gold was found in the Klondike river area of the Yukon Territory, Canada. This began a five-year 'gold rush' in the region.

Dominion
In 1867 Canada became a self-governing dominion within the British empire.

Cricket
Under British rule, Bajuns and other West Indian islanders became keen cricketers.

Gibraltar
The Rock of Gibraltar was seized from Spain in 1704 and became a vital naval base from which the Royal Navy could control the Mediterranean.

Gibraltar

Malta **Cyprus** **Palestine** **Transjorda**

British Honduras

Bahamas

Egyp

Jamaica

Freedom
In 1834, in the British West Indies, 663,600 slaves were freed. Many continued to work in the plantations for wages.

Gambia

Khartou

Sierra Leone

Gold Coast

Nigeria

Suda

these dotted lines show national borders in 1919. The dominions (self-governing parts) of the British empire are labelled in capital letters, while the British colonies are in lower case letters.

Pacific Ocean

British Guiana

West Africa
British colonies were set up along the west coast of Africa, including the Gold Coast (now Ghana) in 1874.

Uganda

Southern Rhodesia

Livingstone
The Scottish missionary David Livingstone made four major explorations of southern Africa between 1841 and 1873. This opened up the region for future British colonization.

Atlantic Ocean

Northern Rhodesia

South West Africa

Bechuan

Mafeking

SOUTH AFRICA

Ship-building
The *SS Titanic* was built in a shipyard in Belfast. Construction began in 1909 and the ship was launched in 1911.

0 — 200 km
0 — 100 miles

King Cotton
The cotton and wool mills of northern England exported finished cloth all around the world.

GREAT BRITAIN

Scotland

Glasgow

Edinburgh

Newcastle

The Great Hunger
One million people died of famine in Ireland, from 1845–49, when the potato crop failed.

Victoria
Queen Victoria reigned over her empire from 1837 to 1901.

Ireland

Dublin

Irish Sea

Liverpool

Manchester

Sheffield

England

Birmingham

Wales

Cardiff

LONDON

Railways
After 1830 railways began to connect all the main towns in Britain.

English Channel

Falkland Islands

Cape Horn

Refuelling
Britain acquired the Falkland Islands in 1833, using them as a refuelling stop for coal-fired ships travelling around Cape Horn, to and from the Pacific Ocean.

Cape Town

Cape Colony

Basutoland

Imperial India
British territories in India – previously controlled by the East India Company, a commercial trading company – were transferred to the British crown in 1858. In 1876 the British government made Queen Victoria empress of India. She was officially named as empress at a magnificent assembly in Delhi (above) on 1 January 1877, where the Indian princes paid homage to her. Victoria, however, did not attend in person.

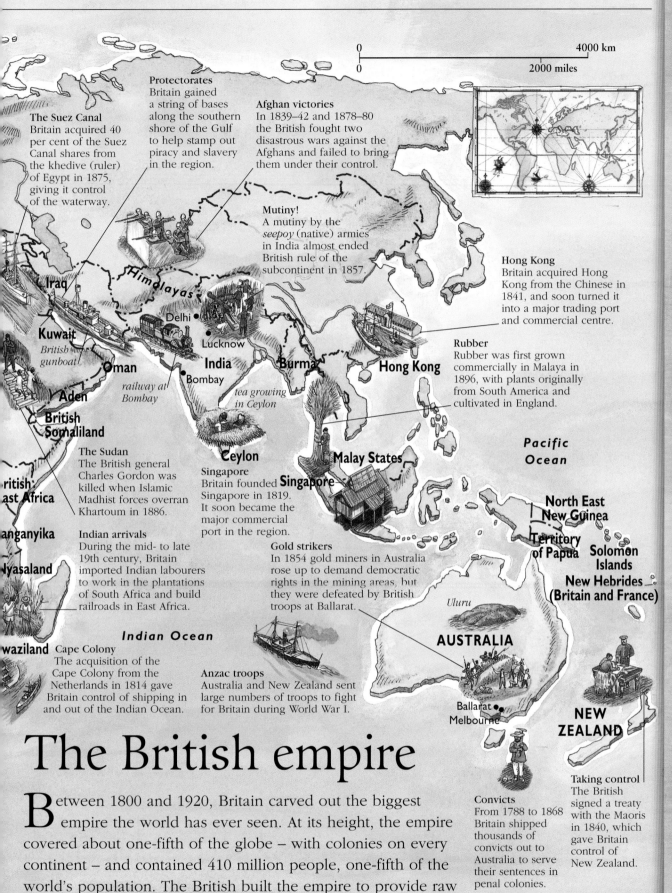

The Suez Canal
Britain acquired 40 per cent of the Suez Canal shares from the khedive (ruler) of Egypt in 1875, giving it control of the waterway.

Protectorates
Britain gained a string of bases along the southern shore of the Gulf to help stamp out piracy and slavery in the region.

Afghan victories
In 1839–42 and 1878–80 the British fought two disastrous wars against the Afghans and failed to bring them under their control.

Mutiny!
A mutiny by the *seepoy* (native) armies in India almost ended British rule of the subcontinent in 1857.

Hong Kong
Britain acquired Hong Kong from the Chinese in 1841, and soon turned it into a major trading port and commercial centre.

Rubber
Rubber was first grown commercially in Malaya in 1896, with plants originally from South America and cultivated in England.

The Sudan
The British general Charles Gordon was killed when Islamic Madhist forces overran Khartoum in 1886.

Singapore
Britain founded Singapore in 1819. It soon became the major commercial port in the region.

Indian arrivals
During the mid- to late 19th century, Britain imported Indian labourers to work in the plantations of South Africa and build railroads in East Africa.

Gold strikers
In 1854 gold miners in Australia rose up to demand democratic rights in the mining areas, but they were defeated by British troops at Ballarat.

Cape Colony
The acquisition of the Cape Colony from the Netherlands in 1814 gave Britain control of shipping in and out of the Indian Ocean.

Anzac troops
Australia and New Zealand sent large numbers of troops to fight for Britain during World War I.

Convicts
From 1788 to 1868 Britain shipped thousands of convicts out to Australia to serve their sentences in penal colonies.

Taking control
The British signed a treaty with the Maoris in 1840, which gave Britain control of New Zealand.

Iraq · *Kuwait* · *British gunboat* · *Oman* · *Aden* · *British Somaliland* · *British East Africa* · *Tanganyika* · *Nyasaland* · *Swaziland* · *Himalayas* · *Delhi* · *Lucknow* · *India* · *Bombay* · *railway at Bombay* · *Burma* · *tea growing in Ceylon* · *Ceylon* · *Malay States* · *Singapore* · *Hong Kong* · *Pacific Ocean* · *North East New Guinea* · *Territory of Papua* · *Solomon Islands* · *New Hebrides (Britain and France)* · *Uluru* · *AUSTRALIA* · *Ballarat* · *Melbourne* · *NEW ZEALAND* · *Indian Ocean*

The British empire

Between 1800 and 1920, Britain carved out the biggest empire the world has ever seen. At its height, the empire covered about one-fifth of the globe – with colonies on every continent – and contained 410 million people, one-fifth of the world's population. The British built the empire to provide raw materials for their industries – such as cotton, silk, sugar, gold and diamonds – and a ready market for finished goods. It also defended vital British shipping and commercial interests around the world. Pride in British values, and a desire to convert local people to Christianity, were also reasons for its creation.

1800
1800 Britain gains Malta

1814 Britain gains Cape Colony from the Dutch

1819 Sir Stamford Raffles founds Singapore
1820

1830 World's first public railway opens between Liverpool and Manchester
1833 Britain gains the Falkland Islands
1834 Slaves freed throughout the British empire
1837 Victoria becomes queen
1839–42 Britain fails to subdue Afghanistan
1840
1840 Treaty of Waitangi between British and Maoris in New Zealand
1841 Britain acquires Hong Kong
1845–49 Great Hunger kills one million people in Ireland
1853–99 Britain establishes protectorates in the Gulf states
1854 Gold miners demand the vote in South Australia
1857–58 Mutiny breaks out in India
1858 East India Company dismantled; India transferred to British crown
1860
1861 Nigerian coast becomes a British colony

1867 Canada becomes a self-governing dominion
1868 Last convicts shipped to Australia

1874 Gold Coast becomes a British colony
1875 Britain gains control of the Suez Canal
1877 Victoria is proclaimed empress of India

1880
1882 Egypt becomes a British protectorate
1884 European nations begin to scramble for African colonies
1888 Britain gains Rhodesia (Zimbabwe)

1893 New Zealand women gain the vote
1894–95 Uganda and Kenya become British colonies
1896 Rubber first cultivated in Malaya

1899–1902 British crush the Boers in South Africa
1900
1901 Victoria dies; Edward VII becomes king
1901 Australian colonies unite to form the Commonwealth of Australia
1907 New Zealand becomes a dominion
1910 Union of South Africa created
1910 George V becomes king

1917–34 Newfoundland is a dominion

1919 Britain, Australia and New Zealand gain German colonies in Africa and Oceania
1920
1920 Britain gains Iraq, Jordan and Palestine – the empire is at its greatest extent
1922 Ireland becomes a Free State within the British empire
1922 Egypt becomes independent
1931 Statute of Westminster makes dominions independent and equal to Britain, and creates the British Commonwealth of Nations
1936 George VI becomes king after his brother, Edward VIII, abdicates
1939 Empire joins Britain in World War II against Germany, Italy and, in 1941, Japan
1940

The USA in the 19th century

In a little over 100 years, the United States of America transformed itself. It grew from a narrow strip of newly independent colonies along the Atlantic coast to a continental power that stretched out across the Pacific Ocean and up towards the Arctic. However, much of this new land was already occupied by native Americans, who fought fiercely to survive and keep their ancient heritage alive. By the end of the 19th century, the native Americans were confined to special reservations, and the USA was on its way to becoming the richest and most powerful nation in the world.

The American Civil War

The southern states of the USA allowed white citizens to keep black slaves to work on their cotton plantations and in their homes. Other states, however, were against slavery. The argument between the two sides erupted in 1861 when 11 southern states left the Union and set up the independent Confederacy. A vicious civil war broke out that lasted four years and killed at least 600,000 people. This picture shows Confederate fortifications near Petersburg, Virginia, in 1865. The Union, led by President Abraham Lincoln, eventually won the war and abolished slavery.

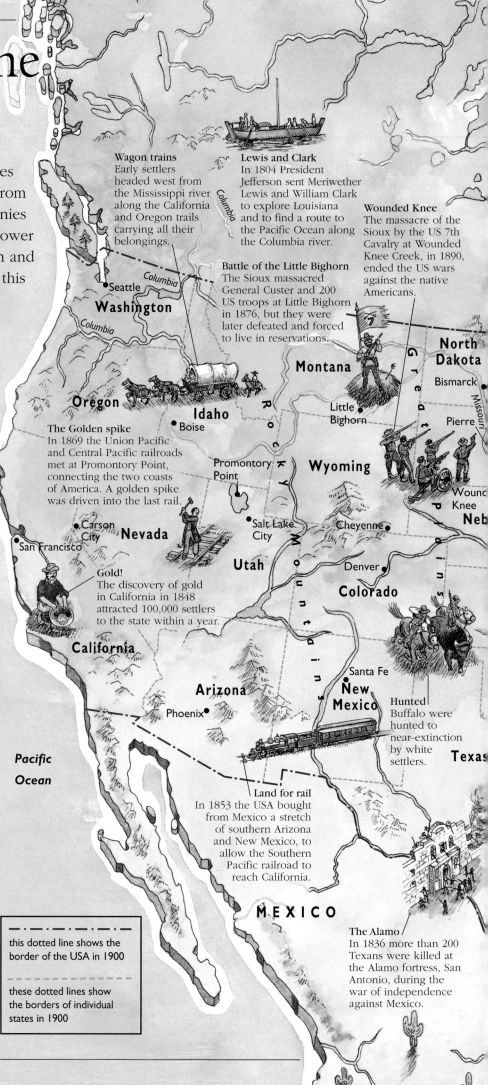

Wagon trains
Early settlers headed west from the Mississippi river along the California and Oregon trails carrying all their belongings.

Lewis and Clark
In 1804 President Jefferson sent Meriwether Lewis and William Clark to explore Louisiana and to find a route to the Pacific Ocean along the Columbia river.

Wounded Knee
The massacre of the Sioux by the US 7th Cavalry at Wounded Knee Creek, in 1890, ended the US wars against the native Americans.

Battle of the Little Bighorn
The Sioux massacred General Custer and 200 US troops at Little Bighorn in 1876, but they were later defeated and forced to live in reservations.

The Golden spike
In 1869 the Union Pacific and Central Pacific railroads met at Promontory Point, connecting the two coasts of America. A golden spike was driven into the last rail.

Gold!
The discovery of gold in California in 1848 attracted 100,000 settlers to the state within a year.

Hunted
Buffalo were hunted to near-extinction by white settlers.

Land for rail
In 1853 the USA bought from Mexico a stretch of southern Arizona and New Mexico, to allow the Southern Pacific railroad to reach California.

The Alamo
In 1836 more than 200 Texans were killed at the Alamo fortress, San Antonio, during the war of independence against Mexico.

this dotted line shows the border of the USA in 1900

these dotted lines show the borders of individual states in 1900

Seattle
Washington
Columbia
Oregon
Idaho
Boise
Carson City
Nevada
San Francisco
California
Arizona
Phoenix
Pacific Ocean
Promontory Point
Wyoming
Utah
Salt Lake City
Montana
Little Bighorn
North Dakota
Bismarck
Pierre
Missouri
Cheyenne
Denver
Colorado
Santa Fe
New Mexico
Wounded Knee
Neb
Texas
MEXICO

0   1000 km
0   500 miles

KEY TO EAST COAST STATES

1	Maine	7	Connecticut
2	Vermont	8	Pennsylvania
3	New Hampshire	9	New Jersey
4	New York	10	Delaware
5	Massachusetts	11	Maryland
6	Rhode Island	12	Virginia

CANADA

Skyscrapers
The Reliance Building, the world's first steel-frame skyscraper, was built in Chicago in 1895.

Model-T Ford
The first Model-T rolled off the Ford production line in 1908. Its low cost made car ownership possible for millions of people for the first time.

Lake Superior

Minnesota

South Dakota

• St Paul

Wisconsin

Lake Huron

Lake Ontario

immigrants arriving in New York in the 1890s

Michigan

Lansing •
Detroit •

Madison •

farming on the plains

Iowa

ska

• Des Moines

• Lincoln

• Chicago

Lake Erie

Illinois

Indiana

Springfield •

Indianapolis •

• Columbus

Ohio

Gettysburg

• New York

9

• Philadelphia

Burning the capital
In 1814 British troops burned down the White House during its war with the USA.

Kansas City •

• Abilene

• Topeka

Missouri

• Jefferson City

slaves in southern plantations

Indian Territory

• Oklahoma City

Kansas

Kentucky

West Virginia

■ WASHINGTON D.C.

10

Id

12

Appomattox

✕ Hampton Roads

Surrender
The Civil War neared its end when Confederate commander Robert E Lee surrendered his army at Appomattox Court House, Virginia, in April 1865.

• Nashville

Tennessee

• Memphis

• Little Rock

Arkansas

Mississippi

Alabama

• Atlanta

North Carolina

South Carolina

Charleston •

Fort Sumter

Atlantic

Ocean

Georgia

Outbreak of war
The American Civil War began when southern Confederate troops bombarded Fort Sumter (a Union fort) in Charleston, South Carolina, in April 1861.

• Jackson

Louisiana

• Baton Rouge

• New Orleans

jazz musicians in New Orleans

FLORIDA

• Austin

• San Antonio

Oil wells
Oil was first discovered at Spindletop in Texas in 1901, giving birth to a massive oil industry.

Cattle driving
Cattle were driven north every year from Texas to Abilene for transport by rail to slaughter-houses in Kansas City and Chicago.

Forced removal
During the 1830s more than 100,000 native Americans were forced to move from the eastern USA to the Indian Territory (now Oklahoma) to make way for white settlers.

Gulf of Mexico

Appalachian Mountains

Mississippi

1800 USA consists of just 16 states
1803 Louisiana purchased from France, doubling the size of the country
1804–06 Lewis and Clark explore Louisiana territory

1812–15 Anglo-American war caused by British attempts to prevent the USA trading with Napoleonic France

1819 Spain gives Florida to the USA

1820

1820 Missouri Compromise allows for equal numbers of slave states and free (anti-slavery) states to join the Union

1830 Indian Removal Act forces native Americans (then called Indians) to move to the Indian Territory

1836 Texas gains independence from Mexico

1840

1845 USA annexes (takes control of) the Republic of Texas
1846 Britain and the USA agree to divide Oregon
1846–48 USA goes to war with Mexico over its border with Texas
1848 USA gains California and other western states from Mexico
1848 Gold discovered in California

1853 USA buys southern New Mexico and Arizona from Mexico

1860

1860 South Carolina leaves the Union, followed by 10 more pro-slavery states
1861–65 Civil War between Union and Confederate states
1865 13th Amendment to the US Constitution formally abolishes slavery
1867 USA buys Alaska from Russia for $7.2 million and acquires Midway Island, its first Pacific island territory
1869 First Transcontinental railroad completed
1870 US population is now at 40 million

1876 Battle of the Little Bighorn

1880

1890 Sioux massacred at Wounded Knee Creek
1892 Ellis Island begins to admit immigrants
1895 First skyscraper built in Chicago

1898 Spain loses Puerto Rico, Guam and the Philippines to the USA
1898 USA gains Hawaiian islands in the Pacific Ocean
1899 USA acquires Samoa in the south Pacific

1900

1901 Oil found in Texas
1905 One million immigrants enter the USA each year

1908 First Model-T Ford car produced in Detroit

1910 US population is now at 92 million

1917 USA enters World War I

1920 USA consists of 48 states

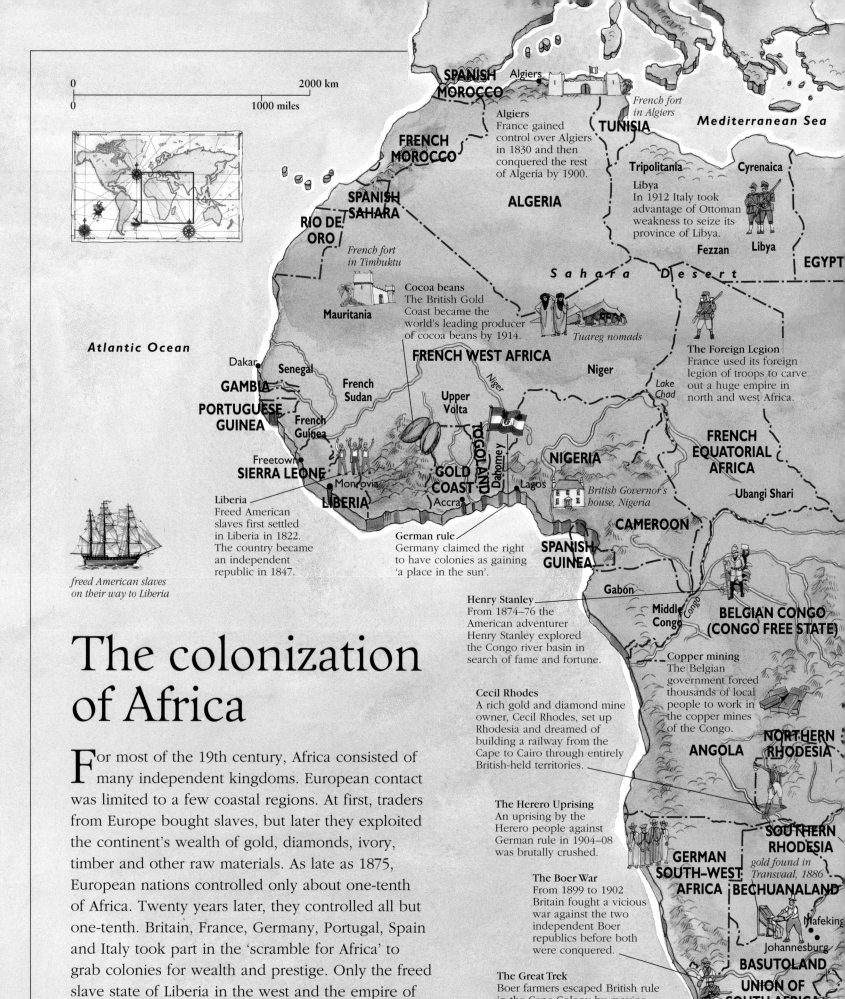

0

2000 km

0

1000 miles

SPANISH MOROCCO

Algiers

French fort in Algiers

TUNISIA

Mediterranean Sea

FRENCH MOROCCO

Algiers
France gained control over Algiers in 1830 and then conquered the rest of Algeria by 1900.

Tripolitania

Cyrenaica

Libya
In 1912 Italy took advantage of Ottoman weakness to seize its province of Libya.

ALGERIA

Fezzan

Libya

EGYPT

RIO DE ORO

SPANISH SAHARA

French fort in Timbuktu

Sahara Desert

Cocoa beans
The British Gold Coast became the world's leading producer of cocoa beans by 1914.

Atlantic Ocean

Mauritania

FRENCH WEST AFRICA

Tuareg nomads

Niger

Lake Chad

The Foreign Legion
France used its foreign legion of troops to carve out a huge empire in north and west Africa.

Dakar

GAMBIA

Senegal

French Sudan

Upper Volta

Niger

PORTUGUESE GUINEA

French Guinea

SIERRA LEONE

Freetown

GOLD COAST

TOGOLAND

Dahomey

NIGERIA

Lagos

FRENCH EQUATORIAL AFRICA

Ubangi Shari

British Governor's house, Nigeria

Monrovia

LIBERIA

Accra

Liberia
Freed American slaves first settled in Liberia in 1822. The country became an independent republic in 1847.

German rule
Germany claimed the right to have colonies as gaining 'a place in the sun'.

CAMEROON

SPANISH GUINEA

Gabon

Middle Congo

Congo

BELGIAN CONGO (CONGO FREE STATE)

freed American slaves on their way to Liberia

Henry Stanley
From 1874–76 the American adventurer Henry Stanley explored the Congo river basin in search of fame and fortune.

Copper mining
The Belgian government forced thousands of local people to work in the copper mines of the Congo.

The colonization of Africa

Cecil Rhodes
A rich gold and diamond mine owner, Cecil Rhodes, set up Rhodesia and dreamed of building a railway from the Cape to Cairo through entirely British-held territories.

ANGOLA

NORTHERN RHODESIA

For most of the 19th century, Africa consisted of many independent kingdoms. European contact was limited to a few coastal regions. At first, traders from Europe bought slaves, but later they exploited the continent's wealth of gold, diamonds, ivory, timber and other raw materials. As late as 1875, European nations controlled only about one-tenth of Africa. Twenty years later, they controlled all but one-tenth. Britain, France, Germany, Portugal, Spain and Italy took part in the 'scramble for Africa' to grab colonies for wealth and prestige. Only the freed slave state of Liberia in the west and the empire of Ethiopia in the east – the only African state to defeat a European nation – remained independent.

The Herero Uprising
An uprising by the Herero people against German rule in 1904–08 was brutally crushed.

The Boer War
From 1899 to 1902 Britain fought a vicious war against the two independent Boer republics before both were conquered.

GERMAN SOUTH-WEST AFRICA

SOUTHERN RHODESIA

gold found in Transvaal, 1886

BECHUANALAND

Mafeking

Johannesburg

BASUTOLAND

The Great Trek
Boer farmers escaped British rule in the Cape Colony by moving north in the Great Trek of 1834–48. They settled in what became the Orange Free State and Transvaal.

UNION OF SOUTH AFRICA

Cape Town

Cape Colony

2

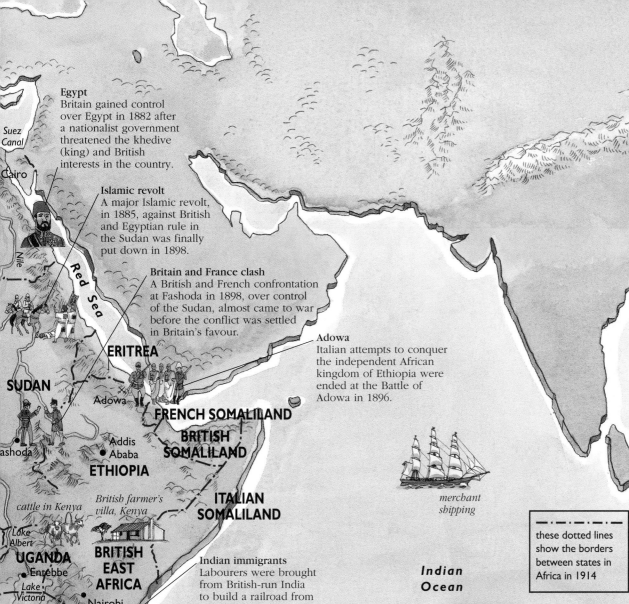

Egypt
Britain gained control over Egypt in 1882 after a nationalist government threatened the khedive (king) and British interests in the country.

Suez Canal

Cairo

Nile

Red Sea

Islamic revolt
A major Islamic revolt, in 1885, against British and Egyptian rule in the Sudan was finally put down in 1898.

Britain and France clash
A British and French confrontation at Fashoda in 1898, over control of the Sudan, almost came to war before the conflict was settled in Britain's favour.

Adowa
Italian attempts to conquer the independent African kingdom of Ethiopia were ended at the Battle of Adowa in 1896.

ERITREA

SUDAN

Adowa

Fashoda

FRENCH SOMALILAND

BRITISH SOMALILAND

Addis Ababa

ETHIOPIA

cattle in Kenya

British farmer's villa, Kenya

ITALIAN SOMALILAND

Lake Albert

UGANDA
Entebbe
Lake Victoria

BRITISH EAST AFRICA

Nairobi

Indian immigrants
Labourers were brought from British-run India to build a railroad from Mombasa on the coast up to Entebbe in Uganda.

merchant shipping

Indian Ocean

these dotted lines show the borders between states in Africa in 1914

Mombasa

Slave trade
The slave market in Zanzibar exported slaves to the Arab world until the British closed it down in 1873.

GERMAN EAST AFRICA

Lake Tanganyika

Lake Malawi

Zanzibar

German Africa
German rule in Africa was ended during World War I, when Britain, France and South Africa occupied all of its colonies.

NYASALAND

Zambezi

Salisbury

MOZAMBIQUE

MADAGASCAR

The Zulu Wars
Conflict between the British and the Zulu kingdom finally ended in Zulu defeat at Ulundi in 1879.

Limpopo

Ulundi

SWAZILAND

Stop-over port
Merchant ships carrying tea and other products from Asia to Europe stopped off for supplies in Cape Town.

The Zulus

Shaka, leader of the Zulus of southern Africa from 1816–28, was an inspired military leader. He replaced the old thrown spear of his warriors with an *assegai*, or short stabbing spear, turning them into the most feared army in the region. The Zulus resisted all attempts by the Boers and British to take over their lands, but were finally defeated by the British at Ulundi in 1879. Unusually, the British allowed them to keep their lands, because of the respect they held for these warrior people.

1800

1807 British end their involvement in the transatlantic slave trade

1814 Britain gains Cape Colony from the Dutch

1822 First freed slaves settle in Liberia

1825
1826 Britain begins to take over the Gold Coast

1830 France invades Algiers
1830–1900 France conquers Algeria

1834–48 Boers move north in the Great Trek

1840–73 David Livingstone explores central Africa

1847 Liberia becomes an independent republic

1850

1852–54 Boers establish the republics of Orange Free State and Transvaal
1854 France takes over Senegal
1855 Emperor Tewedros begins to modernize Ethiopia

1861 Britain begins to colonize Nigeria

1873 British end slave market in Zanzibar
1874–76 Henry Stanley explores the Congo river region
1875
1879 British finally conquer the Zulu kingdom
1882 British take control of Egypt
1884–85 European powers divide up Africa at the Berlin Conference
1885 Leopold II of Belgium makes the Congo his personal possession
1885–98 Islamic revolt by the Mahdi against British rule in Sudan
1886 Gold discovered in the Transvaal
1888 British establish Rhodesia
1889 Italy gains Eritrea and Somaliland
1894 Britain occupies Uganda
1895 Britain occupies Kenya
1896 Italians fail to conquer Ethiopia
1898 Britain retakes Sudan
1899–1902 British defeat the Boers in South Africa
1900
1904 Britain and France settle their colonial disputes in Africa
1904–08 Herero Uprising against German rule in southwest Africa
1906 Morocco is split between France and Spain
1908 Belgium takes control of the Congo
1910 Union of South Africa gains independence from Britain

1914–18 Germany loses its African colonies during World War I

1925

Imperial Europe

In the years after 1848 the map of Europe changed considerably. Germany and Italy emerged as unified nations, and Austro-Hungary became a dual monarchy. France became an empire again and then, after 1871, a republic, while Russia slowly began to reform itself. Britain, the most powerful and richest nation in the world, avoided European entanglements and developed a vast overseas empire. In the Balkans, the Ottoman (Turkish) empire continued to fall apart, losing almost all of its European lands by 1913. The Industrial Revolution that had begun in Britain led to new industries and railways in most nations, creating new industrial towns and a large working class population.

Atlantic Ocean

The unification of Germany

In 1848 Germany consisted of 39 separate states, dominated by Prussia and Austro-Hungary. Otto von Bismarck became prime minister of Prussia in 1862. He defeated Denmark and Austria, set up a North German Confederation, excluding Austria, and took over Hanover and other German states. In 1871 Prussia defeated France and took its two eastern provinces of Alsace and Lorraine. King Wilhelm I of Prussia was then proclaimed emperor of Germany (shown above), uniting the remaining 25 German states under Prussian rule.

Gunboat diplomacy
In 1911 Germany sent a gunboat to protect its interests in Morocco, causing a major diplomatic conflict with France.

MOROCCO

HMS Dreadnought
The battleship *Dreadnought* outclassed every other warship when she was launched in 1906, starting a naval arms race between Britain and Germany.

Queen Victoria
Queen from 1837 to 1901, Victoria was related to almost every European monarch.

North Sea

NORWAY
OSLO ■

Bismarck
With a series of brilliant diplomatic and military victories, Otto von Bismarck unified Germany in 1864–71.

COPENHAGEN
DENMARK

Schleswig-Holstein

coal mine in the Ruhr valley, Germany

GERMAN EMPIRE

BERLIN ■

BRITAIN

NETHERLANDS

free trade in northern Germany

Elbe

Karl Marx
The communist revolutionary Karl Marx fled Germany and took refuge in London in 1848.

LONDON ■

BELGIUM

Rhine

Sedan Frankfurt

Pilsen

Revolution
In 1848 the unpopular King Louis-Philippe was overthrown and France became a republic, a nation not governed by a monarch.

a barricade erected in Paris

PARIS ■

LUXEMBOURG

Alsace-Lorraine

armaments factory in Pilsen

Napoleon III
Nephew of Napoleon Bonaparte, Louis Napoleon became president of France in 1848 before seizing power and becoming emperor in 1851.

SWITZERLAND

ALPS

FRANCE

French farmers

ITALY

PORTUGAL

Pyrenees

Emmanuel II
King of Sardinia since 1849, Victor Emmanuel II became king of a united Italy in 1860.

Corsica

ROME ■

■ MADRID

SPAIN

Sardinia

Balearic Islands

Mediterranean Sea

| 0 | 500 km |
| 0 | 250 miles |

Industrial revolution
In the second half of the 19th century, Russia industrialized very quickly, opening many new coal mines, steel works and factories.

Sadowa
In the Seven Weeks' War of 1866, Prussia defeated Austria at Sadowa and ended the country's influence in Germany.

MOSCOW ■

Trans-continental railway
The Trans-Siberian Railway linking Moscow to Vladivostok, on the Pacific coast, was begun in 1891 but not finished until 1916.

Freedom
Serfs (peasants) in Russia received their freedom from their owners in 1861.

The Dual Monarchy
In 1867 the Austrian empire split into a two-monarch state called 'Austro-Hungary'. United by its Habsburg rulers, it had a common army and currency.

RUSSIAN EMPIRE

WEDEN
■STOCKHOLM

Ukraine
Ukraine was the 'bread basket of Russia', as well as its major industrial area.

Potemkin
Revolution broke out in Russia in 1905 and spread to the armed forces. The crew of the Russian battleship *Potemkin* mutinied and fled to Romania.

wheat being harvested in the Ukraine

Oder

•Sadowa (Koniggratz)

■VIENNA

AUSTRO-HUNGARIAN EMPIRE

Danube

Odessa •

Black Sea

ROMANIA   Ploesti •

BUCHAREST ■

Romanian oil
Before the development of Middle Eastern oil, most European oil came from the oil wells of Ploesti

Bosnia   **SERBIA**

Balkans   **BULGARIA**

MONTENEGRO   ■SOFIA

Constantinople

OTTOMAN EMPIRE

Albania

The Balkan Wars
Two wars in the Balkans in 1912–13 saw the Ottoman Turks almost expelled from Europe, while Serbia emerged as a major Balkan nation.

GREECE

ATHENS ■

• Rhodes

Cyprus

Garibaldi
In 1859–60 the Italian nationalist Giuseppe Garibaldi invaded Sicily and Naples with 1,000 troops, and forced them to unify with the rest of Italy.

Crete

The Royal Navy
The British Royal Navy commanded the Mediterranean, protecting British sea routes to India.

- - - - - -
these dotted lines show the borders between European nations in 1912

Mediterranean Sea

EGYPT

1840

1848 Revolutions in France, Italy, Germany and Austria against conservative rule
1848 Karl Marx flees to London
1849 Attempts to set up a German National Assembly end in failure

1850
1851 Napoleon III seizes power in France and restores the French empire

1859–60 Italian kingdoms united as one nation under Victor Emmanuel II

1860
1861 Russian serfs (peasants) liberated
1862 Bismarck becomes prime minister of Prussia
1863–64 Prussia defeats Denmark to gain two northern duchies
1866 Seven Weeks' War
1866 Italy gains Venice from Austria
1867 Creation of North German Confederation under Prussian rule
1867 Creation of Austro-Hungary

1870
1870 Italy takes over the Papal States to complete its unification
1870–71 Franco-Prussian war ends in French defeat; creation of German empire
1871 Third Republic established in France
1878 Romania gains independence from the Ottoman empire
1878 Britain gains Cyprus from Ottomans
1879–82 Triple Alliance of Germany, Austro-Hungary and Italy

1880

1883 Death of Karl Marx

1888 Wilhelm II becomes emperor of Germany

1890
1890 Bismarck resigns

1894 Franco-Russian military alliance

1900
1901 Death of Queen Victoria

1904 Entente Cordiale ('friendly understanding') agreement between Britain and France
1906 HMS 'Dreadnought' launched; naval arms race begins in Europe
1908 Austro-Hungary takes over Bosnia
1908 Bulgaria becomes independent

1910

1912–13 Two Balkan wars redraw the map of southeast Europe
1913 Albania becomes an independent nation
1914 World War I breaks out in Europe

1920

World War I

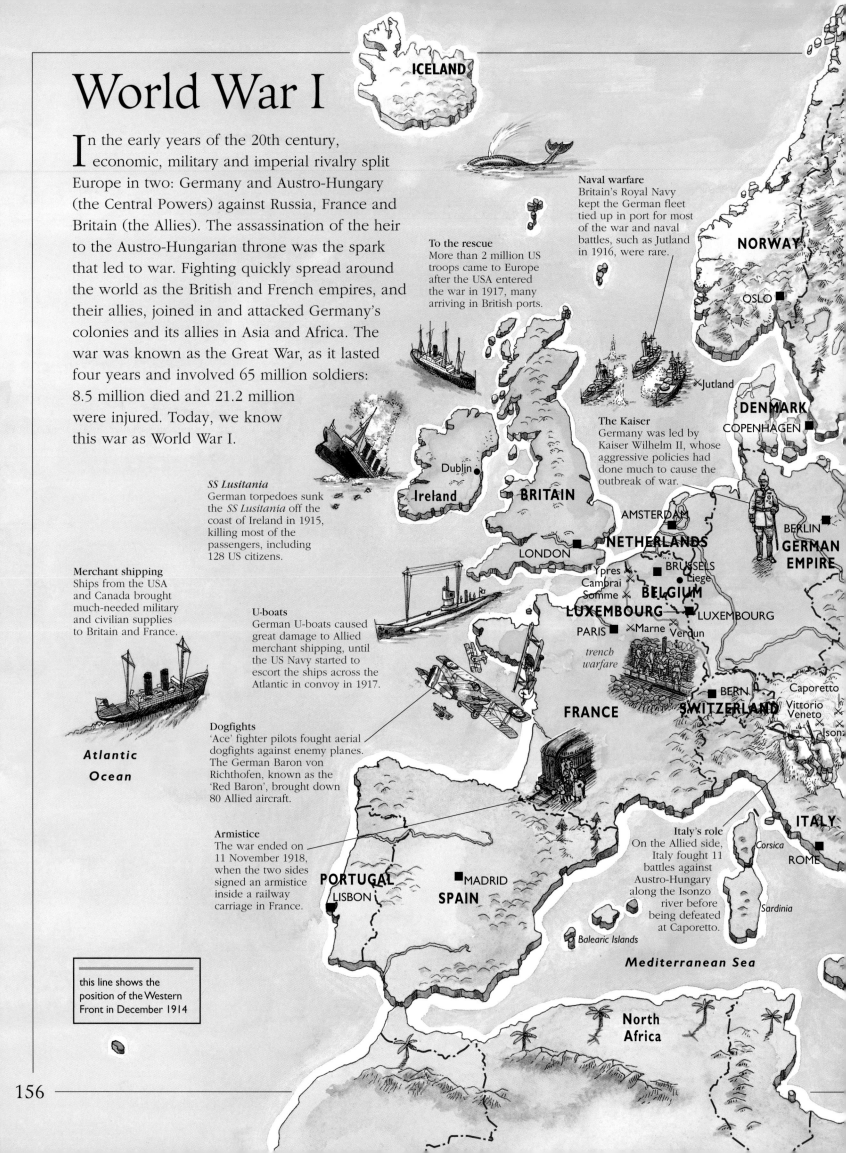

In the early years of the 20th century, economic, military and imperial rivalry split Europe in two: Germany and Austro-Hungary (the Central Powers) against Russia, France and Britain (the Allies). The assassination of the heir to the Austro-Hungarian throne was the spark that led to war. Fighting quickly spread around the world as the British and French empires, and their allies, joined in and attacked Germany's colonies and its allies in Asia and Africa. The war was known as the Great War, as it lasted four years and involved 65 million soldiers: 8.5 million died and 21.2 million were injured. Today, we know this war as World War I.

ICELAND

To the rescue
More than 2 million US troops came to Europe after the USA entered the war in 1917, many arriving in British ports.

Naval warfare
Britain's Royal Navy kept the German fleet tied up in port for most of the war and naval battles, such as Jutland in 1916, were rare.

×Jutland

NORWAY

OSLO

DENMARK
COPENHAGEN

The Kaiser
Germany was led by Kaiser Wilhelm II, whose aggressive policies had done much to cause the outbreak of war.

SS Lusitania
German torpedoes sunk the *SS Lusitania* off the coast of Ireland in 1915, killing most of the passengers, including 128 US citizens.

Dublin

Ireland

BRITAIN

AMSTERDAM

BERLIN

NETHERLANDS

LONDON

BRUSSELS

Liege

GERMAN EMPIRE

Ypres
Cambrai
Somme

BELGIUM

Merchant shipping
Ships from the USA and Canada brought much-needed military and civilian supplies to Britain and France.

U-boats
German U-boats caused great damage to Allied merchant shipping, until the US Navy started to escort the ships across the Atlantic in convoy in 1917.

LUXEMBOURG

LUXEMBOURG

PARIS

×Marne
Verdun

trench warfare

Atlantic Ocean

Dogfights
'Ace' fighter pilots fought aerial dogfights against enemy planes. The German Baron von Richthofen, known as the 'Red Baron', brought down 80 Allied aircraft.

FRANCE

BERN

Caporetto

SWITZERLAND

Vittorio Veneto

Isonzo

Armistice
The war ended on 11 November 1918, when the two sides signed an armistice inside a railway carriage in France.

Italy's role
On the Allied side, Italy fought 11 battles against Austro-Hungary along the Isonzo river before being defeated at Caporetto.

ITALY

Corsica

ROME

PORTUGAL
LISBON

MADRID

SPAIN

Sardinia

Balearic Islands

Mediterranean Sea

this line shows the position of the Western Front in December 1914

North Africa

Tsar
The Russian tsar Nicholas II was a poor military leader who lost the support of his people during the war. He was overthrown in the revolution of 1917.

WEDEN   Finland

HELSINKI

STOCKHOLM

ST PETERSBURG (PETROGRAD)

Moscow •

The Eastern Front
Unlike the stalemate in the west, the war in the east was very mobile, with large-scale battles and troops advancing over hundreds of kilometres.

RUSSIAN EMPIRE

✕ Masurian Lakes

✕ Tannenberg

Russians marching into Austro-Hungary

Brest-Litovsk •

Peace treaty
After two revolutions in 1917, the new Bolshevik (communist) rulers of Russia made peace with Germany at Brest-Litovsk.

War production
Both sides in the war produced vast amounts of shells and other armaments in munitions factories placed well behind the front line.

Trench warfare

The worst fighting took place along the Western Front in western Europe. Each side dug a long line of defensive trenches facing the enemy. They regularly bombarded the opposing side and launched attacks over the top of the trenches, at huge cost to human life. Neither side made any real progress until late in 1918, when fresh American troops and improved artillery bombardment gave the Allies the advantage.

AUSTRO-HUNGARIAN EMPIRE

BUDAPEST ■

ROMANIA

BUCHAREST ■

Black Sea

0 _____ 500 km
0 _____ 250 miles

Genocide
During 1915 the Ottomans deported Armenians from their homeland to stop them helping the Russians. Up to 1.3 million were killed.

Armenia

BELGRADE ■

Sarajevo •   SERBIA   BULGARIA

MONTENEGRO   SOFIA ■

CONSTANTINOPLE ●

Gallipoli ✕

TIRANA ■   OTTOMAN EMPIRE

ALBANIA

Lawrence of Arabia
In 1916 the Arabs rose in revolt against their Ottoman rulers, supported by the British officer T E Lawrence, in the hope of winning their independence.

GREECE

ATHENS ■

Assassination
The assassination of Archduke Franz Ferdinand, heir to the Austrian throne, by Serb nationalist Gavrilo Princip sparked the outbreak of the war.

Gallipoli
Allied landings on the Gallipoli peninsula in the Ottoman empire were a disaster and the troops were forced to withdraw.

cily

Malta   Crete   Cyprus

Mediterranean Sea

1914–1919

1914

June Archduke Ferdinand assassinated in Sarajevo; Austro-Hungary declares war on Serbia
Aug Germany invades neutral Belgium to attack France; Britain, France and Russia now at war with the Central Powers of Germany and Austro-Hungary
Aug Germans defeat invading Russian army at Tannenberg
Aug Allies attack German colonies in Africa, Asia and the Pacific Ocean
Sept Germans advance into France
Oct Ottoman empire enters war on the Central Powers side
Nov Trenches built along the length of the Western Front

1915

Feb Germans begin submarine blockade of Britain
April Germans use poison gas on the Western Front for the first time
April 1915–Jan 1916 Allied troops seize Gallipoli but fail to capture Constantinople
May German torpedoes sink the SS 'Lusitania' off the Irish coast
May Italy enters the war on the Allied side
May Ottoman genocide against Armenians
June 1915–Aug 1917 Italy fights 11 battles against Austro-Hungary
Oct Central Powers invade Serbia

1916

Jan Serbia defeated
Feb–Dec Germans try but fail to break French resolve at the Siege of Verdun
May–June British Royal Navy wins the Battle of Jutland in the North Sea
June Arabs rise in revolt against their Ottoman rulers
July–Nov Massive British losses at the Battle of the Somme

1917

Feb Germans begin submarine warfare in the Atlantic Ocean, hitting US shipping
Mar Russian revolution overthrows Tsar Nicholas II
April USA enters the war on the Allied side
July–Nov Bloody battle at Ypres (Passchendaele)
Nov–Dec British use massed tanks for the first time at Cambrai, France
Nov Bolsheviks seize power in Russia
Dec Austro-Hungarians win the Battle of Caporetto against the Italians

1918

Mar Germany and Russia make peace at Brest-Litovsk
Mar Massive German advance into France
July–Aug Germans halted at the Second Battle of the Marne, near the Marne river in France
Aug Germans pushed back on the Western Front by the Allies
Oct Italy defeats Austro-Hungarians at Vittorio Veneto
Oct Ottoman empire makes peace with the Allies
Nov German fleet mutinies; Kaiser Wilhelm II abdicates and flees into exile
Nov Armistice ends the war

1919

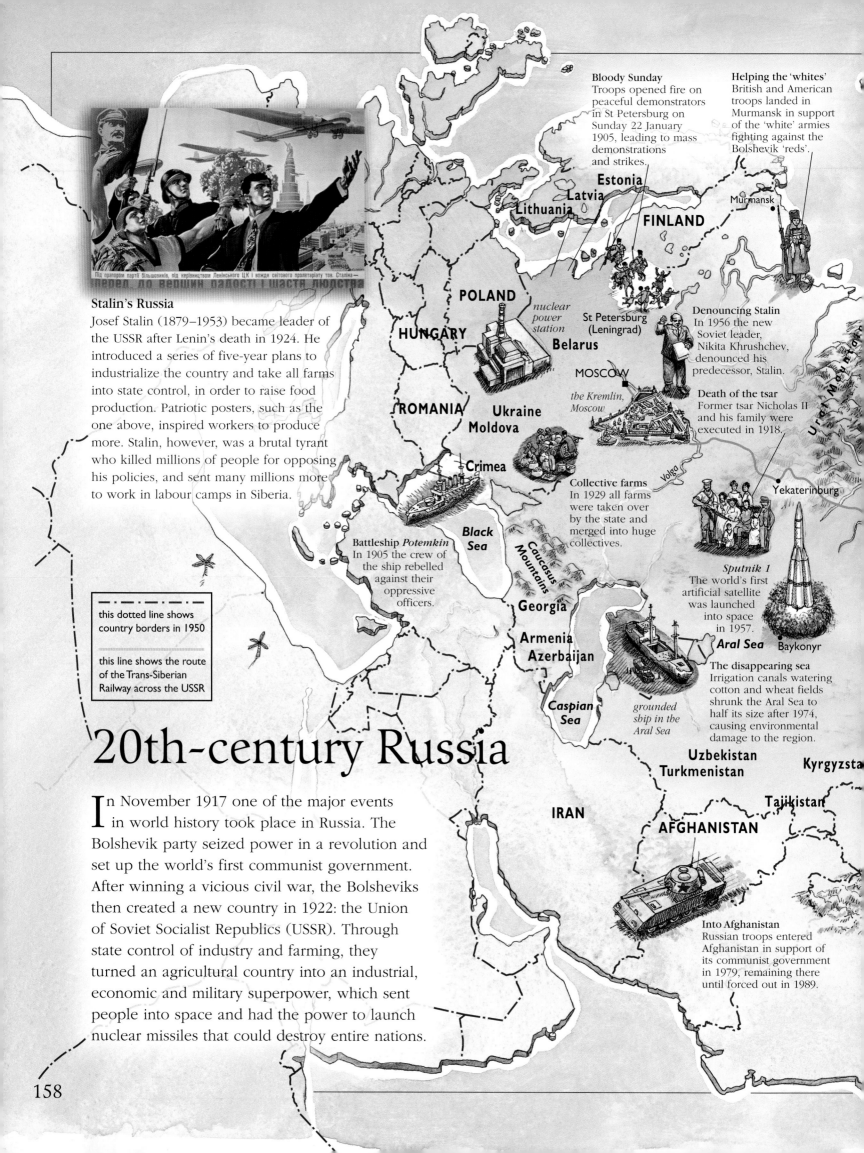

Bloody Sunday
Troops opened fire on peaceful demonstrators in St Petersburg on Sunday 22 January 1905, leading to mass demonstrations and strikes.

Helping the 'whites'
British and American troops landed in Murmansk in support of the 'white' armies fighting against the Bolshevik 'reds'.

Murmansk

Estonia
Latvia
Lithuania

FINLAND

POLAND

HUNGARY

nuclear power station

St Petersburg (Leningrad)

Belarus

MOSCOW

the Kremlin, Moscow

Denouncing Stalin
In 1956 the new Soviet leader, Nikita Khrushchev, denounced his predecessor, Stalin.

Death of the tsar
Former tsar Nicholas II and his family were executed in 1918.

Ural Mountains

ROMANIA

Ukraine
Moldova

Crimea

Yekaterinburg

Collective farms
In 1929 all farms were taken over by the state and merged into huge collectives.

Volga

Stalin's Russia
Josef Stalin (1879–1953) became leader of the USSR after Lenin's death in 1924. He introduced a series of five-year plans to industrialize the country and take all farms into state control, in order to raise food production. Patriotic posters, such as the one above, inspired workers to produce more. Stalin, however, was a brutal tyrant who killed millions of people for opposing his policies, and sent many millions more to work in labour camps in Siberia.

Black Sea

Caucasus Mountains

Battleship *Potemkin*
In 1905 the crew of the ship rebelled against their oppressive officers.

Georgia

Armenia
Azerbaijan

Sputnik 1
The world's first artificial satellite was launched into space in 1957.

Aral Sea   Baykonyr

The disappearing sea
Irrigation canals watering cotton and wheat fields shrunk the Aral Sea to half its size after 1974, causing environmental damage to the region.

Caspian Sea

grounded ship in the Aral Sea

this dotted line shows country borders in 1950

this line shows the route of the Trans-Siberian Railway across the USSR

Uzbekistan
Turkmenistan

Kyrgyzsta[n]

Tajikistan

IRAN

AFGHANISTAN

20th-century Russia

In November 1917 one of the major events in world history took place in Russia. The Bolshevik party seized power in a revolution and set up the world's first communist government. After winning a vicious civil war, the Bolsheviks then created a new country in 1922: the Union of Soviet Socialist Republics (USSR). Through state control of industry and farming, they turned an agricultural country into an industrial, economic and military superpower, which sent people into space and had the power to launch nuclear missiles that could destroy entire nations.

Into Afghanistan
Russian troops entered Afghanistan in support of its communist government in 1979, remaining there until forced out in 1989.

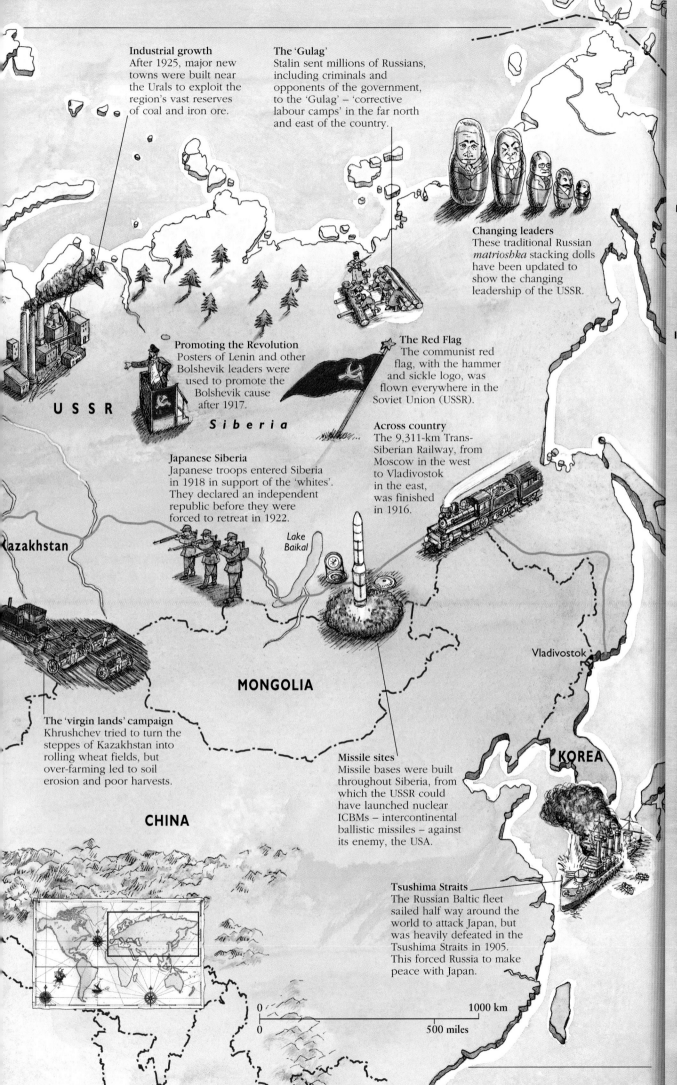

Industrial growth
After 1925, major new towns were built near the Urals to exploit the region's vast reserves of coal and iron ore.

The 'Gulag'
Stalin sent millions of Russians, including criminals and opponents of the government, to the 'Gulag' – 'corrective labour camps' in the far north and east of the country.

Changing leaders
These traditional Russian *matrioshka* stacking dolls have been updated to show the changing leadership of the USSR.

Promoting the Revolution
Posters of Lenin and other Bolshevik leaders were used to promote the Bolshevik cause after 1917.

The Red Flag
The communist red flag, with the hammer and sickle logo, was flown everywhere in the Soviet Union (USSR).

USSR

Siberia

Japanese Siberia
Japanese troops entered Siberia in 1918 in support of the 'whites'. They declared an independent republic before they were forced to retreat in 1922.

Across country
The 9,311-km Trans-Siberian Railway, from Moscow in the west to Vladivostok in the east, was finished in 1916.

Kazakhstan

Lake Baikal

MONGOLIA

Vladivostok

The 'virgin lands' campaign
Khrushchev tried to turn the steppes of Kazakhstan into rolling wheat fields, but over-farming led to soil erosion and poor harvests.

Missile sites
Missile bases were built throughout Siberia, from which the USSR could have launched nuclear ICBMs – intercontinental ballistic missiles – against its enemy, the USA.

CHINA

KOREA

Tsushima Straits
The Russian Baltic fleet sailed half way around the world to attack Japan, but was heavily defeated in the Tsushima Straits in 1905. This forced Russia to make peace with Japan.

0		1000 km
0	500 miles	

1900

1904–05 Russia is heavily defeated by Japan and loses land in the east
1905 Revolution breaks out across Russia

1910

1914 Russia enters World War I against Germany and Austro-Hungary
1917 Tsar Nicholas II abdicates in March
1917 Bolsheviks seize power in November
1918 Treaty of Brest-Litovsk ends war for Russia
1918–21 Civil war between 'reds' and 'whites'; western troops help 'whites'
1918 Bolsheviks murder Nicholas II and family

1920

1920–22 Peasant revolts occur across Russia
1921 'New economic policy' re-introduces free trade to encourage food production
1922 Union of Soviet Socialist Republics (USSR) is set up
1924 Death of Lenin; Stalin takes over as leader
1928 First 'Five Year Plan' introduced to industrialize the country
1929 Collectivization of farms begins

1930

1932–33 Massive famine in Ukraine and central Asia as a result of collectivization
1934 Stalin begins show trials and 'purges' to get rid of opponents

1938 Stalin's purges at their worst
1939 Nazi-Soviet Pact with Hitler

1940

1941 Germany invades the USSR during World War II

1945 Soviet troops enter Berlin at the end of World War II

1949 USSR explodes its first atomic bomb

1950

1953 Death of Stalin; Khrushchev takes over as leader
1954 'Virgin lands' policy launched to grow more crops
1956 Khrushchev denounces (fiercely criticizes) Stalin in a secret speech
1957 USSR launches 'Sputnik I', the world's first man-made satellite, into space

1960

1961 Soviet cosmonaut Yuri Gagarin becomes the first person in space

1964 Khrushchev ousted; Leonid Brezhnev takes over as leader

1970

1972 US president Nixon visits the USSR

1979 Russian troops enter Afghanistan

1980

1982 Death of Brezhnev; Yuri Andropov and then Konstantin Chernenko succeed him

1985 Mikhail Gorbachev becomes leader of the USSR and begins reforms

1990

America and the Great Depression:
Economic boom and bust

The US economic boom of the 1920s ended when the New York Stock Exchange crashed in October 1929. As prices and profits collapsed and banks failed, the USA – and then the world – entered a decade-long economic slump. Millions of people lost their jobs or had their incomes reduced, while world trade was cut by almost two-thirds between 1929 and 1932. In the USA, President Roosevelt's New Deal tried to tackle the problem, but it was the threat of war in Europe and Asia, and the need to make more weapons, that finally produced the jobs that got the unemployed back to work.

The post-war boom
The 1920s were a period of great optimism in America. The economy was booming after World War I, the country was peaceful and prosperous, and women had more freedom than ever before. New forms of entertainment, such as the movies and jazz music, transformed the lives of ordinary people. The picture above shows fashionable women of the 1920s, known as flappers, who summed up the spirit of the decade. Many thought the boom would last for ever.

Hollywood
The invention of a workable sound movie system in 1927 transformed the cinema, killing off silent films by 1930. Millions of people flocked to the cinema during the 1930s to see spectacular films, such as *The Wizard of Oz* (below), and take their minds off the economic gloom of their daily lives.

Worldwide slump
The economic slump began in the USA but had spread around the world by 1931. As millions lost their jobs, social and political unrest grew. In Britain, in 1936, 200 unemployed shipyard workers from Jarrow in northeast England marched south to London to draw attention to the poverty and lack of jobs in their town.

The New Deal

In 1933 Franklin D Roosevelt, pictured here (right), became president, pledging 'a new deal for the American people'. He reformed the banking system, gave financial support to farmers and home owners and, through the Public Works Administration, set millions of people to work building dams, roads, bridges, schools and other public projects.

Extreme poverty

Unemployment in the USA rose from 2 million industrial workers in 1928 to 11.6 million in 1932, and stayed high for the rest of the decade. Millions of people lost their life savings when their banks failed. They were forced to rely on soup kitchens (below) and money from the government to keep them alive. In 1934–38, extreme poverty spread to the farming communities of Oklahoma, Kansas and other mid-western states when high winds stripped a huge area of land of its soil.

Europe between the World Wars

The years after World War I were chaotic across the whole of Europe. Germany tried to recover from its defeat in the war. Meanwhile new countries, which had emerged from the former defeated empires, struggled to establish themselves as independent states. Economic chaos after the slump of 1931 only made matters worse as millions were thrown out of work. Fascist (extreme right-wing and dictatorial) parties came to power in Italy, much of eastern Europe and, in 1933, Germany. This divided the continent between democracies, dictatorships, and the USSR, which was a dictatorship and the world's only communist state.

Atlantic Ocean

The Spanish Civil War

In 1936 the Spanish army, led by the Nationalist General Franco, rose in revolt against the democratic Republican government. The civil war that followed lasted three years and involved many international forces: the USSR sent arms to the Republicans, Germany and Italy sent troops and planes to the Nationalist rebels, volunteers from around the world fought on both sides, while Britain and France remained neutral. The war ended with a Nationalist victory in 1939, starting 36 years of authoritarian government in Spain.

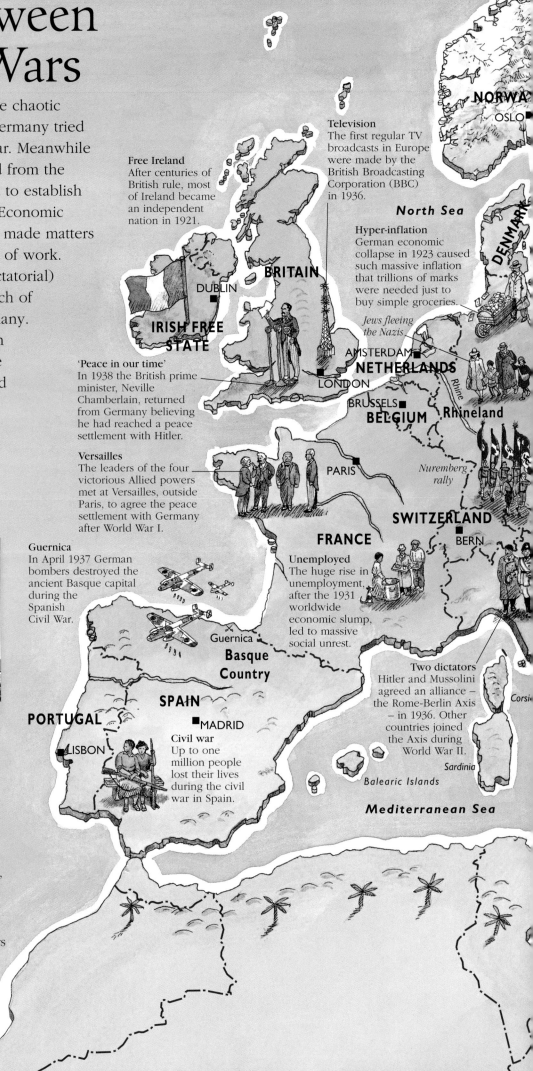

Free Ireland
After centuries of British rule, most of Ireland became an independent nation in 1921.

Television
The first regular TV broadcasts in Europe were made by the British Broadcasting Corporation (BBC) in 1936.

North Sea

Hyper-inflation
German economic collapse in 1923 caused such massive inflation that trillions of marks were needed just to buy simple groceries.

Jews fleeing the Nazis

'Peace in our time'
In 1938 the British prime minister, Neville Chamberlain, returned from Germany believing he had reached a peace settlement with Hitler.

Versailles
The leaders of the four victorious Allied powers met at Versailles, outside Paris, to agree the peace settlement with Germany after World War I.

Guernica
In April 1937 German bombers destroyed the ancient Basque capital during the Spanish Civil War.

Unemployed
The huge rise in unemployment, after the 1931 worldwide economic slump, led to massive social unrest.

Two dictators
Hitler and Mussolini agreed an alliance – the Rome-Berlin Axis – in 1936. Other countries joined the Axis during World War II.

Civil war
Up to one million people lost their lives during the civil war in Spain.

NORWAY
OSLO

DENMARK

AMSTERDAM
NETHERLANDS
LONDON
BRITAIN
DUBLIN
IRISH FREE STATE

BRUSSELS
BELGIUM
Rhine
Rhineland

PARIS
Nuremberg rally

SWITZERLAND
BERN

FRANCE

Guernica
Basque Country

SPAIN
MADRID

PORTUGAL
LISBON

Corsica
Sardinia
Balearic Islands

Mediterranean Sea

SWEDEN

STOCKHOLM

FINLAND

HELSINKI

TALLINN

ESTONIA

RIGA

LATVIA

OPENHAGEN

DANZIG

East
Prussia

LITHUANIA

U S S R

The USSR
As the world's only
communist state, the USSR
under Stalin largely stayed
out of European politics.
It watched the rise of Hitler
with alarm, before allying
with him in 1939.

MOSCOW

BERLIN

GERMANY

WARSAW

The Polish Corridor
The thin strip of land giving
Poland access to the Baltic
Sea contained many Germans
and was a source of tension
between the two countries.

Starvation
Under Josef Stalin,
millions of peasants
starved as their farms
were taken under
state control.

Sudetenland

PRAGUE

POLAND

Communist Hungary
The Communists under
Bela Kun seized power
in Hungary in 1919, but
were quickly forced
out by an invading
Romanian army.

CZECHOSLOVAKIA

VIENNA

ünich

BUDAPEST

HUNGARY

Union
In March 1938
Germany occupied
Austria, causing the
Anschluss – the union
of both countries.

USTRIA

German troops
in Austria

ROMANIA

BUCHAREST

BELGRADE

Danube

Black Sea

YUGOSLAVIA

BULGARIA

SOFIA

Ataturk
Kemal Ataturk, a
World War I hero,
abolished the
Turkish sultanate
in 1922 and set up
an independent
republic in 1923.

TALY

ROME

TIRANA

ALBANIA

TURKEY

Greek immigration
More than 1 million
Greeks were forced
to flee Asia Minor
when Turkey
occupied some
Greek cities in 1922.

GREECE

ATHENS

Sicily

Yugoslavia
Yugoslavia became
one country in
1919, merging the
Serb, Croat and
Slovene peoples
into one state.

Cyprus

Crete

Mediterranean Sea

Mussolini
Mussolini and his
Fascist Party took
power in Italy in
1922 and soon
crushed all
opposition to
their rule.

0   500 km

0   250 miles

1910

1918 World War I ends with the defeat
of Germany and Austro-Hungary
1919–20 Treaty of Versailles, and other
peace treaties, are signed in France to
draw up the post-war borders of Europe

1919 Yugoslavia, Hungary, Czechoslovakia,
Poland, Finland and three Baltic states
(Estonia, Latvia and Lithuania) emerge
from the ruins of the Austro-Hungarian
and Russian empires

1920
1920 Communists try to
take power in Germany
1920–21 Poland wins war against the USSR
1921 Irish Free State established
within the British empire

1922 Mussolini takes power in Italy
1922 Greeks expelled from Asia Minor
1922 Germany and the USSR
sign an economic treaty

1923 Turkish republic set
up under Kemal Ataturk

1926 General Strike in Britain

1928 Kellogg-Briand Pact signed in Paris:
all nations agree to renounce war

1929 Beginning of the Great Depression
1930
1931 Worldwide economic slump
1931 Spain becomes a republic

1933 Adolf Hitler comes
to power in Germany
1934 Greece, Romania, Turkey and
Yugoslavia sign the Balkan Pact
against Germany and the USSR
1935–36 Italy invades Abyssinia (Ethiopia)
1936 British Broadcasting Corporation
(BBC) begins regular TV broadcasts
1936 Germany re-occupies
the demilitarized Rhineland
1936 Germany and Italy agree the
Rome-Berlin Axis alliance
1936–39 Spanish Civil War

1938 Germany takes over Austria
1938 Germany takes Sudetenland
from Czechoslovakia after Britain,
France and Italy agree terms
with Germany in Munich
1939 Germany takes over the
rest of Czechoslovakia
1939 Italy occupies Albania
1939 Nazi-Soviet pact: Germany and Russia
agree to partition (split up) Poland
1939 Germany invades Poland,
beginning World War II

1940

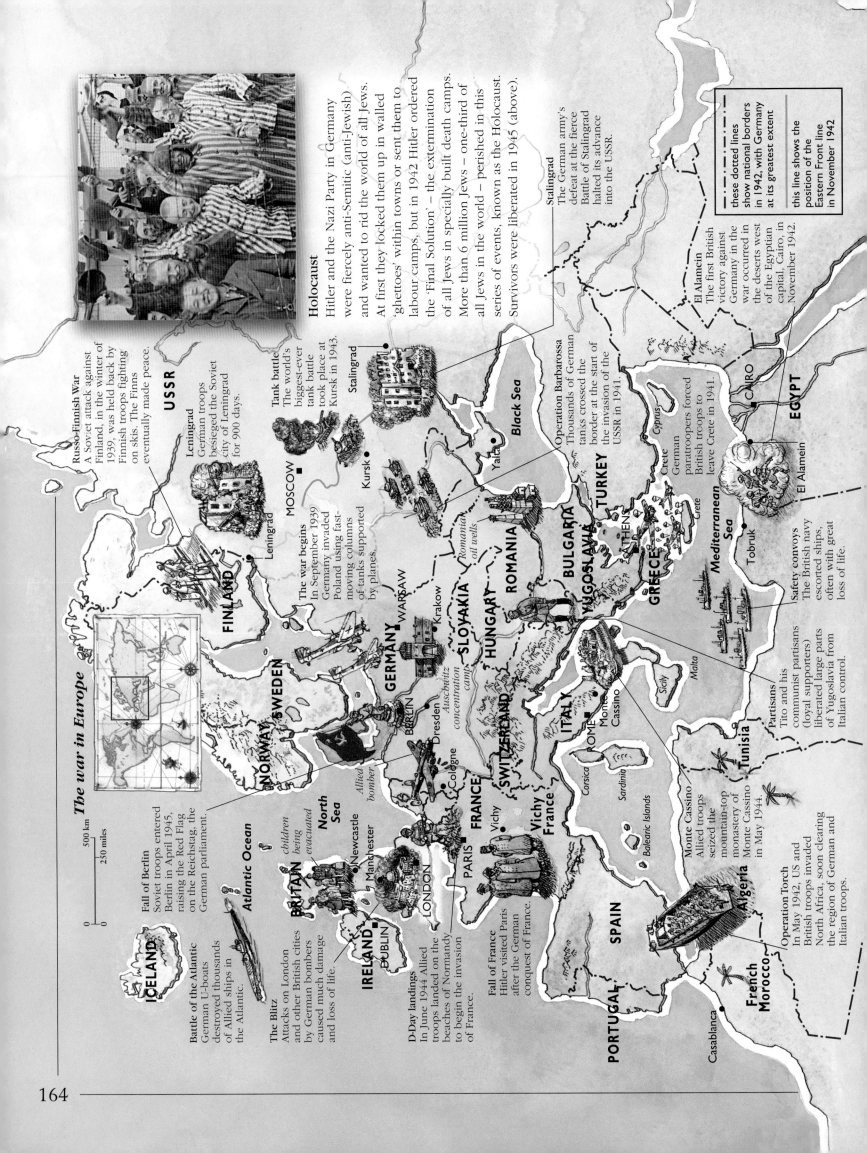

The war in Europe

Holocaust
Hitler and the Nazi Party in Germany were fiercely anti-Semitic (anti-Jewish) and wanted to rid the world of all Jews. At first they locked them up in walled 'ghettoes' within towns or sent them to labour camps, but in 1942 Hitler ordered the 'Final Solution' – the extermination of all Jews in specially built death camps. More than 6 million Jews – one-third of all Jews in the world – perished in this series of events, known as the Holocaust. Survivors were liberated in 1945 (above).

Stalingrad
The German army's defeat at the fierce Battle of Stalingrad halted its advance into the USSR.

these dotted lines show national borders in 1942, with Germany at its greatest extent

this line shows the position of the Eastern Front line in November 1942

El Alamein
The first British victory against Germany in the war occurred in the deserts west of the Egyptian capital, Cairo, in November 1942.

Russo-Finnish War
A Soviet attack against Finland, in the winter of 1939, was held back by Finnish troops fighting on skis. The Finns eventually made peace.

USSR

Leningrad
German troops besieged the Soviet city of Leningrad for 900 days.

Tank battle
The world's biggest-ever tank battle took place at Kursk in 1943.

Stalingrad

MOSCOW

Leningrad

Kursk

Black Sea

Yalta

Operation Barbarossa
Thousands of German tanks crossed the border at the start of the invasion of the USSR in 1941.

CAIRO

EGYPT

El Alamein

Tobruk

Cyprus

Romanian oil wells

TURKEY

BULGARIA

ROMANIA

SLOVAKIA

HUNGARY

YUGOSLAVIA

GREECE

ATHENS

Crete

Crete

German paratroopers forced British troops to leave Crete in 1941.

Mediterranean Sea

Safety convoys
The British navy escorted ships, often with great loss of life.

The war begins
In September 1939 Germany invaded Poland using fast-moving columns of tanks supported by planes.

WARSAW

Krakow

Auschwitz concentration camps

GERMANY

BERLIN

Dresden

Cologne

FINLAND

SWEDEN

NORWAY

North Sea

Partisans
Tito and his communist partisans (loyal supporters) liberated large parts of Yugoslavia from Italian control.

ITALY

ROME

Monte Cassino

Sicily

Malta

Corsica

Sardinia

Balearic Islands

Monte Cassino
Allied troops seized the mountain-top monastery of Monte Cassino in May 1944.

SWITZERLAND

FRANCE

Vichy France

Vichy

PARIS

SPAIN

PORTUGAL

Fall of France
Hitler visited Paris after the German conquest of France.

Tunisia

Algeria

French Morocco

Casablanca

Operation Torch
In May 1942, US and British troops invaded North Africa, soon clearing the region of German and Italian troops.

Fall of Berlin
Soviet troops entered Berlin in April 1945, raising the Red Flag on the Reichstag, the German parliament.

Battle of the Atlantic
German U-boats destroyed thousands of Allied ships in the Atlantic.

The Blitz
Attacks on London and other British cities by German bombers caused much damage and loss of life.

children being evacuated

Allied bomber

D-Day landings
In June 1944 Allied troops landed on the beaches of Normandy, to begin the invasion of France.

BRITAIN

Newcastle

Manchester

LONDON

IRELAND

DUBLIN

ICELAND

Atlantic Ocean

500 km

250 miles

0

0

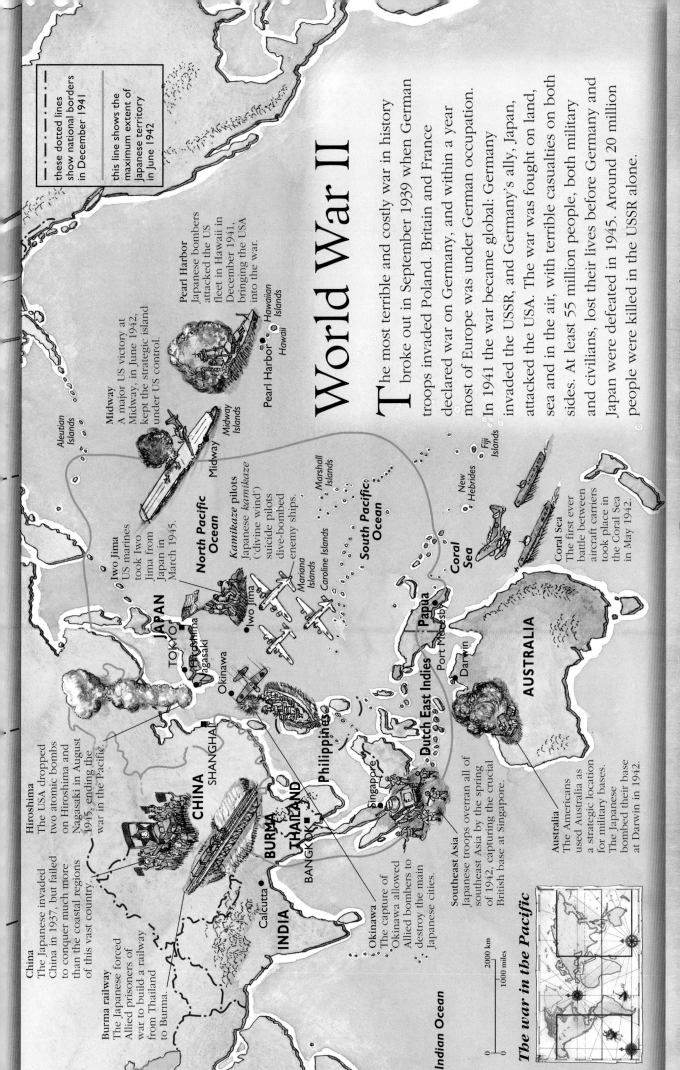

World War II

The most terrible and costly war in history broke out in September 1939 when German troops invaded Poland. Britain and France declared war on Germany, and within a year most of Europe was under German occupation. In 1941 the war became global: Germany invaded the USSR, and Germany's ally, Japan, attacked the USA. The war was fought on land, sea and in the air, with terrible casualties on both sides. At least 55 million people, both military and civilians, lost their lives before Germany and Japan were defeated in 1945. Around 20 million people were killed in the USSR alone.

these dotted lines show national borders in December 1941

this line shows the maximum extent of Japanese territory in June 1942

Pearl Harbor
Japanese bombers attacked the US fleet in Hawaii in December 1941, bringing the USA into the war.

Hawaiian Islands

Pearl Harbor — Hawaii

Midway
A major US victory at Midway, in June 1942, kept the strategic island under US control.

Midway Islands

Midway

Aleutian Islands

North Pacific Ocean

Kamikaze pilots
Japanese *kamikaze* ('divine wind') suicide pilots dive-bombed enemy ships.

Marshall Islands

Fiji Islands

New Hebrides

South Pacific Ocean

Caroline Islands

Mariana Islands

Coral Sea
The first ever battle between aircraft carriers took place in the Coral Sea in May 1942.

Coral Sea

Iwo Jima
US marines took Iwo Jima from Japan in March 1945.

JAPAN

TOKYO

Iwo Jima

Hiroshima
Nagasaki
Okinawa

Papua
Port Moresby

AUSTRALIA

Darwin

Australia
The Americans used Australia as a strategic location for military bases. The Japanese bombed their base at Darwin in 1942.

Hiroshima
The USA dropped two atomic bombs on Hiroshima and Nagasaki in August 1945, ending the war in the Pacific.

China
The Japanese invaded China in 1937, but failed to conquer much more than the coastal regions of this vast country.

Burma railway
The Japanese forced Allied prisoners of war to build a railway from Thailand to Burma.

CHINA

SHANGHAI

BURMA
THAILAND
BANGKOK

Calcutta

INDIA

Philippines

Singapore

Dutch East Indies

Southeast Asia
Japanese troops overran all of southeast Asia by the spring of 1942, capturing the crucial British base at Singapore.

Okinawa
The capture of Okinawa allowed Allied bombers to destroy the main Japanese cities.

Indian Ocean

The war in the Pacific

2000 km
1000 miles

0

1939–1946

1939
Sept Germany invades Poland; Britain and France declare war — start of World War II
Nov USSR invades Finland

1940
April Germany invades Denmark and Norway
May Germany invades the Low Countries and France
June Italy enters the war on Germany's side
July–Oct Battle of Britain: the British air force defeats the German Luftwaffe (air force)
Sept Blitz against British cities begins
Sept Italians invade Egypt
Oct Italians invade Greece
Oct Hungary, Romania and Bulgaria join Germany and Italy

1941
April Germany invades Yugoslavia and Greece
May British are forced out of Crete
June Operation Barbarossa: Germany invades the USSR
Sept Siege of Leningrad begins
Dec Japan attacks Pearl Harbor; the USA enters the war
Dec German advance stopped outside Moscow

1942
Jan Hitler orders the extermination of all Jews
Feb–Mar Japanese bomb Darwin; Japanese take Malaya, Singapore and the Dutch East Indies
April–May Battle of the Coral Sea halts the Japanese advance
May Japanese take the Philippines
May First British area-bombing campaign against Cologne
Oct–Nov British victory at El Alamein, Egypt
Nov Operation Torch: Allied invasion of North Africa
Nov Germans occupy Vichy France

1943
Feb Germans surrender at Stalingrad
April Jewish uprising in Warsaw, Poland
May Battle of the Atlantic ends
May German and Italian troops surrender in Tunisia
June–Aug Soviets defeat German tanks at Kursk
July Allies invade Italy

1944
Jan Siege of Leningrad ends
June D-Day: Allied troops invade France
June Allies begin their bombing of southern Japan from Chinese bases
July Soviet troops enter Poland
Aug Allied troops liberate Paris
Oct British troops liberate Greece
Oct Battle of Leyte Gulf in the Philippines ends Japanese naval power
Nov First Japanese 'kamikaze' attacks on Allied ships

1945
Mar Allied troops cross the River Rhine
Mar US marines take Iwo Jima in the Pacific
April Soviet troops enter Berlin
April Hitler commits suicide
May Italy and Germany surrender: peace in Europe
May US marines take Okinawa and begin to bomb Japan
May Allied firestorm devastates Tokyo
Aug USA drops atomic bombs on Hiroshima and Nagasaki; Soviets attack Japan
Sept Japanese surrender: the war ends

1946

The Cold War

The USA and USSR emerged victorious at the end of World War II, but political differences between them soon erupted into a 'cold' war – one that never reached an all-out military conflict, despite the ever-present threat of war. By 1949 the world was roughly divided between pro-western and pro-communist states. Allies of the two sides fought wars on their behalf, such as in Korea and Vietnam, while both the USSR and USA built up huge arsenals of nuclear and other weapons. Attempts to achieve an understanding between the two sides failed in the 1970s. By the late 1980s, the USA had out-spent the USSR and forced it towards financial ruin. The collapse of communism brought the Cold War to an end in 1991.

CANADA

American firepower
In the 1980s the USA was able to out-spend the USSR on nuclear weaponry, leading to a series of arms reduction agreements in 1988 and 1991.

Fulton

New York

WASHINGTON D.C.

UNITED STATES OF AMERICA

Guatemala
In 1954 the USA backed a counter-revolution in Guatemala to overthrow the socialist government and install a pro-USA, military government.

GUATEMALA

CUBA

NICARAGUA

The Cuban missile crisis
In 1962 the USSR stationed nuclear missiles on Cuba, bringing the world to the brink of nuclear war before they agreed to remove them.

The United Nations
Many of the Cold War diplomatic meetings took place at the UN headquarters in New York City.

Reykjavik

WEST GERMANY
BRITAIN

Greenham Common
LONDON
PARIS
Geneva
FRANCE

SPAIN

Greenham Common
The decision to place US nuclear missiles in Britain, in 1982, led to huge protests at the Greenham Common base. The missiles were removed in 1989.

Atlantic Ocean

Grenada
In 1983 US troops overthrew the left-wing (socialist) government of Grenada, because of its growing ties with communist Cuba.

GRENADA

Pacific Ocean

Nicaragua
In 1978 the radical Sandinista rebels overthrew the military government and introduced many social reforms. This led to a lengthy civil war until peace was declared in 1990.

Chile
In 1973 a US-backed military coup overthrew President Allende, the world's first democratically elected Marxist head of state.

CHILE

these dotted lines show the borders between nations in 1949

0
0

4000 km

2000 miles

SANTIAGO

The end of the Cold War

After 1985 the new leader of the USSR, Mikhail Gorbachev, wanted to reduce military spending and improve the living conditions of Soviet citizens. In 1988 he pulled Soviet troops out of eastern Europe. Without Soviet support, the communist governments there could not survive. One by one, democratically elected governments replaced them. In 1989 a hated symbol of the Cold War, the Berlin Wall (left), was pulled down. One year later, Germany was reunited as one nation. By then the USSR was collapsing, and was replaced by 15 independent nations in 1991.

The Berlin Wall
In 1961 communist authorities in East Berlin erected a wall to prevent its citizens fleeing to freedom in the west.

The USA–USSR arms race
The development of intercontinental ballistic missiles in the 1960s led to an expensive race to build up arms.

Mikhail Gorbachev
In 1985 Gorbachev became leader of the USSR and introduced much-needed social and economic reforms.

Divided Korea
In 1950 communist North Korea invaded capitalist South Korea. A ceasefire was agreed, but the peninsula remains divided.

UNION OF SOVIET SOCIALIST REPUBLICS

■MOSCOW

EAST GERMANY
■WARSAW
PRAGUE
CZECHOSLOVAKIA
■BUDAPEST

The 'Prague Spring'
An attempt to soften the communist rule in Czechoslovakia was crushed by Soviet and other troops in 1968.

Chairman Mao
Mao Zedong led communist China from 1949 until his death in 1976.

HUNGARY

SYRIA
LEBANON
IRAQ
ISRAEL
IRAN

AFGHANISTAN

CHINA

NORTH KOREA

The Vietnam War
In the war of 1954–75, the USA supported South Vietnam. The USSR and China supported communist North Vietnam, the eventual victor.

SOUTH KOREA

Hungary
In 1956 Soviet tanks crushed Hungary's attempt to pull out of the pro-Soviet Warsaw Pact.

EGYPT
JORDAN

INDIA

VIETNAM

Arab–Israeli wars
In these frequent Middle East conflicts, the USA increasingly supported Israel while the USSR supported the Arab states.

Afghanistan
The Soviet invasion of Afghanistan in 1979, to support its communist government, caused a breakdown in relations between the USA and USSR.

CAMBODIA

SOMALIA

Somalia
After Somalia invaded Ethiopia, in 1977, the USSR supported Ethiopia while the USA supported the Somalis.

Nehru of India
Prime Minister Nehru was one of the main leaders of the Non-Aligned Movement, whose members took neither side in the Cold War.

Indian Ocean

MALAYA

ETHIOPIA

Civil war in Angola
After 1975, Cuban- and Soviet-backed forces fought US- and South African-backed forces for control of the country.

Malaya
In 1948 communist forces attacked European settlers in the Malay peninsula. Twelve years of jungle warfare followed, before British troops crushed the communist units in 1960.

Cambodia
In 1970 US planes secretly bombed Cambodia to prevent supplies reaching communists in South Vietnam. This dragged Cambodia into a decade of warfare.

ANGOLA

AUSTRALIA

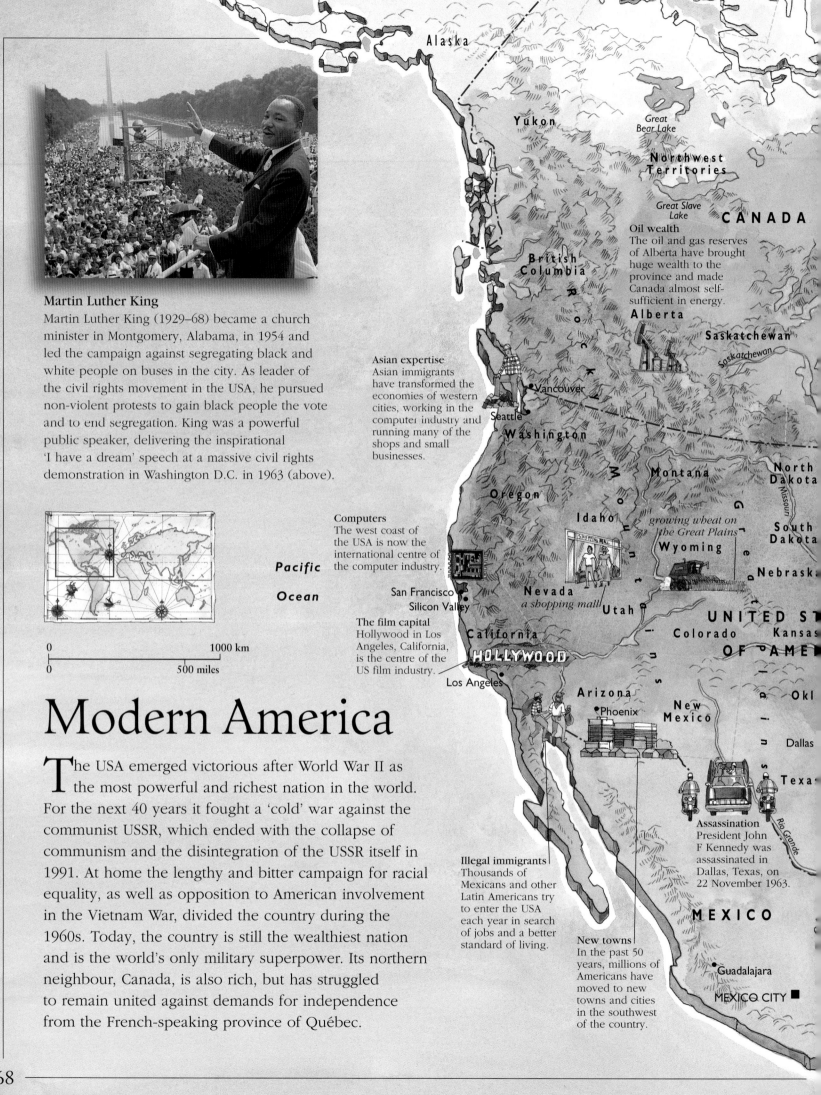

Martin Luther King

Martin Luther King (1929–68) became a church minister in Montgomery, Alabama, in 1954 and led the campaign against segregating black and white people on buses in the city. As leader of the civil rights movement in the USA, he pursued non-violent protests to gain black people the vote and to end segregation. King was a powerful public speaker, delivering the inspirational 'I have a dream' speech at a massive civil rights demonstration in Washington D.C. in 1963 (above).

0 — 1000 km
0 — 500 miles

Computers
The west coast of the USA is now the international centre of the computer industry.

The film capital
Hollywood in Los Angeles, California, is the centre of the US film industry.

Pacific

Ocean

Modern America

The USA emerged victorious after World War II as the most powerful and richest nation in the world. For the next 40 years it fought a 'cold' war against the communist USSR, which ended with the collapse of communism and the disintegration of the USSR itself in 1991. At home the lengthy and bitter campaign for racial equality, as well as opposition to American involvement in the Vietnam War, divided the country during the 1960s. Today, the country is still the wealthiest nation and is the world's only military superpower. Its northern neighbour, Canada, is also rich, but has struggled to remain united against demands for independence from the French-speaking province of Québec.

Asian expertise
Asian immigrants have transformed the economies of western cities, working in the computer industry and running many of the shops and small businesses.

Alaska

Yukon

Great Bear Lake

Northwest Territories

Great Slave Lake

CANADA

Oil wealth
The oil and gas reserves of Alberta have brought huge wealth to the province and made Canada almost self-sufficient in energy.

Alberta

Saskatchewan

Saskatchewan

British Columbia

• Vancouver

Seattle

Washington

Oregon

Montana

North Dakota

Missouri

Idaho

growing wheat on the Great Plains

Wyoming

South Dakota

Nebraska

Nevada
a shopping mall

Utah

San Francisco
Silicon Valley

HOLLYWOOD

California

Los Angeles •

Colorado

Kansas

UNITED STATES

OF AMERICA

Okl

Dallas

Arizona

• Phoenix

New Mexico

Texa

Assassination
President John F Kennedy was assassinated in Dallas, Texas, on 22 November 1963.

Rio Grande

Illegal immigrants
Thousands of Mexicans and other Latin Americans try to enter the USA each year in search of jobs and a better standard of living.

New towns
In the past 50 years, millions of Americans have moved to new towns and cities in the southwest of the country.

MEXICO

• Guadalajara

MEXICO CITY ■

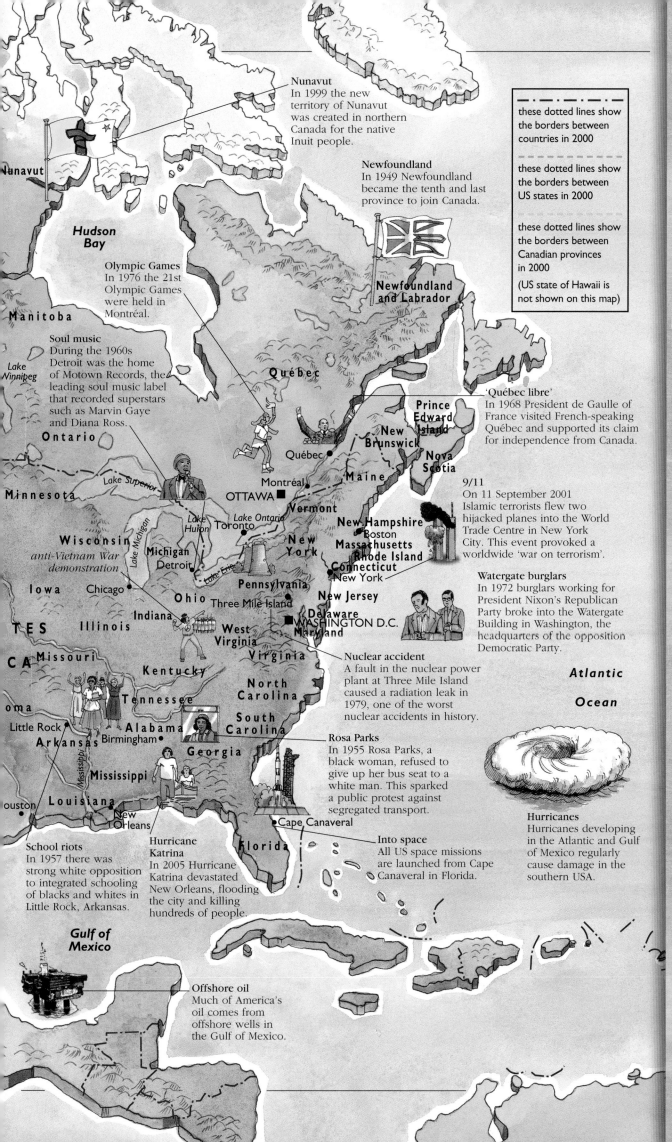

Nunavut
In 1999 the new territory of Nunavut was created in northern Canada for the native Inuit people.

Newfoundland
In 1949 Newfoundland became the tenth and last province to join Canada.

these dotted lines show the borders between countries in 2000

these dotted lines show the borders between US states in 2000

these dotted lines show the borders between Canadian provinces in 2000

(US state of Hawaii is not shown on this map)

Nunavut

Hudson Bay

Olympic Games
In 1976 the 21st Olympic Games were held in Montréal.

Manitoba

Lake Winnipeg

Soul music
During the 1960s Detroit was the home of Motown Records, the leading soul music label that recorded superstars such as Marvin Gaye and Diana Ross.

Ontario

Lake Superior

Minnesota

Québec

Newfoundland and Labrador

Prince Edward Island

New Brunswick

Nova Scotia

Québec

Montréal

Maine

OTTAWA

Vermont

Toronto

Lake Ontario

Lake Huron

Lake Michigan

Wisconsin
anti-Vietnam War demonstration

Michigan
Detroit

Lake Erie

New Hampshire
Boston
Massachusetts
Rhode Island
Connecticut
New York

'Québec libre'
In 1968 President de Gaulle of France visited French-speaking Québec and supported its claim for independence from Canada.

9/11
On 11 September 2001 Islamic terrorists flew two hijacked planes into the World Trade Centre in New York City. This event provoked a worldwide 'war on terrorism'.

Watergate burglars
In 1972 burglars working for President Nixon's Republican Party broke into the Watergate Building in Washington, the headquarters of the opposition Democratic Party.

Iowa
Chicago

Illinois

Indiana

Ohio
Three Mile Island

Pennsylvania

New Jersey

West Virginia
Delaware
Maryland
WASHINGTON D.C.

TES

CA
Missouri

Kentucky

Virginia

North Carolina

Nuclear accident
A fault in the nuclear power plant at Three Mile Island caused a radiation leak in 1979, one of the worst nuclear accidents in history.

Atlantic Ocean

Tennessee

Little Rock

Arkansas
Birmingham
Alabama

South Carolina

Georgia

Rosa Parks
In 1955 Rosa Parks, a black woman, refused to give up her bus seat to a white man. This sparked a public protest against segregated transport.

Mississippi

Mississippi

Louisiana
ouston
New Orleans

Florida

Cape Canaveral

School riots
In 1957 there was strong white opposition to integrated schooling of blacks and whites in Little Rock, Arkansas.

oma

Hurricane Katrina
In 2005 Hurricane Katrina devastated New Orleans, flooding the city and killing hundreds of people.

Into space
All US space missions are launched from Cape Canaveral in Florida.

Hurricanes
Hurricanes developing in the Atlantic and Gulf of Mexico regularly cause damage in the southern USA.

Gulf of Mexico

Offshore oil
Much of America's oil comes from offshore wells in the Gulf of Mexico.

1940–today

1940

1945 President Roosevelt dies in office; Harry Truman takes over the presidency
1945 USA and its allies defeat Japan and Germany in World War II
1946 United Nations (UN) organization meets for the first time in New York City
1948 US armed services end racial segregation
1949 USA sets up North Atlantic Treaty Organization (NATO) to defend western Europe against communist aggression
1949 Newfoundland joins Canada

1950

1950 Senator Joe McCarthy starts an anti-communist witch-hunt
1950–53 US troops fight in Korea
1952 Wartime general Dwight D Eisenhower becomes president of the USA
1954 Supreme Court bans segregated education
1955 Montgomery bus boycott (protest) eventually ends segregated transport
1957 Federal troops help to integrate schools in Arkansas, so that black and white students can be educated together

1960

1960 John F Kennedy is elected as US president
1963 Martin Luther King leads massive civil rights march on Washington D.C.
1963 President Kennedy is assassinated
1964 Civil Rights Act bans racial discrimination
1965 USA sends many troops to Vietnam
1965 Race riots break out in US cities
1968 Martin Luther King is assassinated in Memphis, Tennessee
1968 Richard Nixon is elected as US president
1969 USA lands first astronauts on the Moon

1970

1972 Watergate break-in
1973 USA signs a ceasefire agreement with the North Vietnamese
1974 President Nixon is forced to resign over the Watergate affair

1976 Montrèal hosts the Olympic Games
1976 Jimmy Carter is elected as US president

1979 Serious nuclear accident at Three Mile Island

1980

1980 Ronald Reagan is elected as US president
1980 In a referendum (public vote) Québec narrowly rejects independence from Canada
1981 Reagan survives assassination attempt

1985 USA and USSR begin talks to end the Cold War

1987 First limits on nuclear weapons agreed between the USA and the USSR
1988 George Bush is elected as US president

1990

1991 US troops lead a campaign to end Iraqi occupation of Kuwait in the Middle East
1992 Bill Clinton is elected as US president
1994 North American Free Trade Agreement between Canada, the USA and Mexico
1995 Québec again rejects independence from Canada in a second referendum

1998 Opponents try but fail to remove President Clinton from office
1999 Nunavut territory created in northern Canada

2000

2000 George W Bush is elected as US president
2001 9/11 (11 September) terrorist attacks in New York and Washington D.C.
2001 US-led invasion of Afghanistan, in response to 9/11, marks the start of the USA's 'war on terrorism'

2003 USA and its allies invade Iraq

2005 Hurricane Katrina devastates New Orleans

2010

China in the 20th century

In 1911 the Qing (Manchu) dynasty was overthrown and a republic was established. This led to a lengthy period of civil war and weak government in China. Nationalists, communists and, after 1937, invading Japanese forces all struggled for control of the country. Order was restored when the communists, under Mao Zedong, took power in 1949. They managed to unite the country, although their dictatorial policies caused huge social and economic upheaval. After the death of Mao in 1976, China began to adopt western economic policies, leading to an economic boom that has made the country one of the richest and most powerful nations in the world today.

RUSSIAN FEDERATION

The main food
Rice remains the staple diet for most Chinese people. Here a rice paddy (field) is being prepared for planting.

MONGOLIA

Population control
To restrict rapid population growth, a limit of 'one child per family' was set in 1979. Despite this, the Chinese population today totals 1.32 billion.

Muslim China
The Uyghurs of the Xinjiang province are Turkic-speaking Muslims. They have more in common with their neighbours in central Asia than with the rest of China.

Xinjiang

C H I N A

The 'Great Leap Forward'
In 1958 Mao tried to create a true communist society by setting up huge agricultural communes, in which hundreds of peasant farmers would work. The project was a massive failure.

0 ———— 1000 km

0 ———— 500 miles

Traditional sports
Despite the rapid modernization and industrialization of China, traditional activities such as kite-flying are still very popular.

Tibet

Lhasa●

NEPAL

INDIA

Tibet
Governed by the Dalai Lama from the Potala Palace in Lhasa, Tibet was independent from 1913 until 1950, when Chinese communists occupied the country. A revolt in 1959 failed to regain independence.

INDIA

BANGLADESH

MYANMAR

Communist China
After they took power in 1949, the communists used posters, leaflets, banners and wall paintings to inspire the people to work harder towards achieving a communist society. This poster from 1965 bore the slogan 'Socialism advances in victory everywhere'. However, their methods were brutal and not always successful. The Great Leap Forward of 1958–61 aimed to set up massive farming communes, but it failed and millions died of hunger. The Cultural Revolution of 1966–76 aimed to stamp out old or traditional values, so that people could concentrate on revolution. It caused massive social and political disruption.

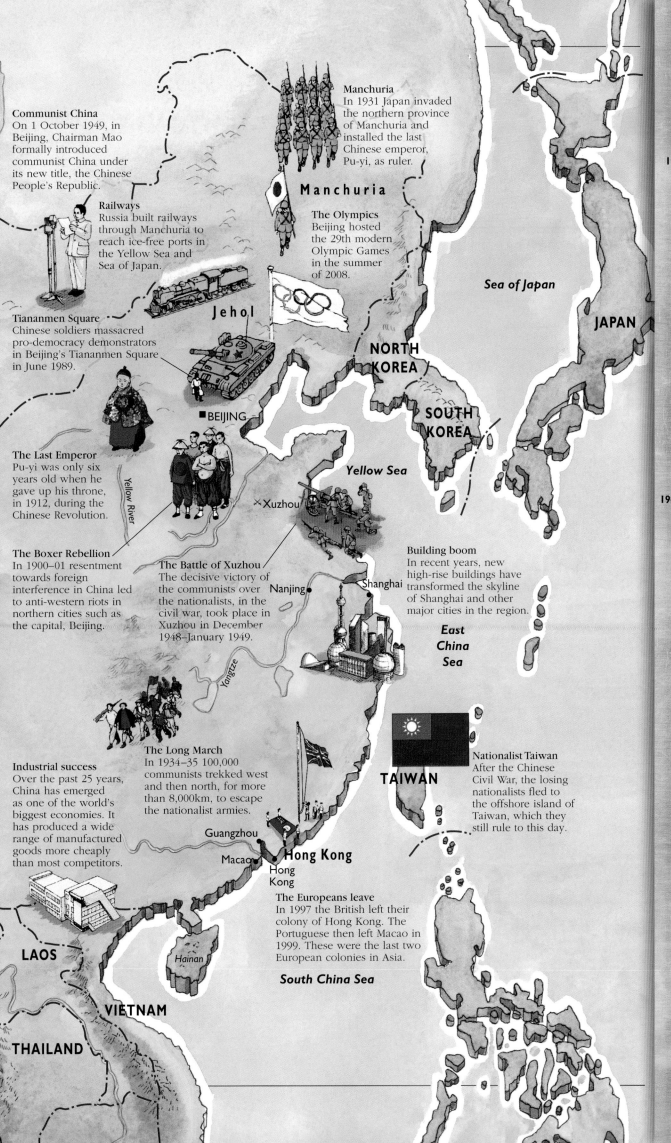

Communist China
On 1 October 1949, in Beijing, Chairman Mao formally introduced communist China under its new title, the Chinese People's Republic.

Railways
Russia built railways through Manchuria to reach ice-free ports in the Yellow Sea and Sea of Japan.

Tiananmen Square
Chinese soldiers massacred pro-democracy demonstrators in Beijing's Tiananmen Square in June 1989.

The Last Emperor
Pu-yi was only six years old when he gave up his throne, in 1912, during the Chinese Revolution.

The Boxer Rebellion
In 1900–01 resentment towards foreign interference in China led to anti-western riots in northern cities such as the capital, Beijing.

The Battle of Xuzhou
The decisive victory of the communists over the nationalists, in the civil war, took place in Xuzhou in December 1948–January 1949.

Industrial success
Over the past 25 years, China has emerged as one of the world's biggest economies. It has produced a wide range of manufactured goods more cheaply than most competitors.

The Long March
In 1934–35 100,000 communists trekked west and then north, for more than 8,000km, to escape the nationalist armies.

The Europeans leave
In 1997 the British left their colony of Hong Kong. The Portuguese then left Macao in 1999. These were the last two European colonies in Asia.

Manchuria
In 1931 Japan invaded the northern province of Manchuria and installed the last Chinese emperor, Pu-yi, as ruler.

Manchuria

The Olympics
Beijing hosted the 29th modern Olympic Games in the summer of 2008.

Jehol

Sea of Japan

JAPAN

■ BEIJING

NORTH KOREA

SOUTH KOREA

Yellow Sea

×Xuzhou

Yellow River

Nanjing ●

Shanghai ●

Building boom
In recent years, new high-rise buildings have transformed the skyline of Shanghai and other major cities in the region.

East China Sea

Yangtze

Guangzhou ●

Macao ●

Hong Kong
Hong Kong

Nationalist Taiwan
After the Chinese Civil War, the losing nationalists fled to the offshore island of Taiwan, which they still rule to this day.

TAIWAN

LAOS

Hainan

South China Sea

VIETNAM

THAILAND

1900–today

1900

1900–01 Anti-western riots across northern China

1908 Pu-yi becomes the last Qing (Manchu) emperor of China, aged two

1910

1911 Nationalists led by Sun Yat-sen overthrow Qing dynasty and establish a republic
1912 Emperor Pu-yi abdicates
1913 Tibet becomes independent

1917 China falls under the power of local warlords

1920

1921 Chinese Communist Party founded

1926 Chiang Kai-shek becomes the nationalist leader

1930

1931 Japanese invade Manchuria
1933 Japanese take province of Jehol
1934–35 The Long March
1937 Japanese launch full-scale invasion of China; more than 250,000 Chinese civilians are killed as Japanese overrun the nationalist capital, Nanjing

1940

1945 After victory over the Japanese, civil war begins in China between the nationalists and the communists

1949 Mao Zedong proclaims the Chinese People's Republic in Beijing; nationalists flee to Taiwan

1950

1950 Chinese occupy Tibet

1958–61 The 'Great Leap Forward' fails to achieve a true communist society
1959 Tibetan rebellions fail to remove the Chinese

1960

1960 China falls out with the USSR
1964 China explodes its first atomic weapon
1965–68 Cultural Revolution: Mao urges the Chinese youth to reject the Soviet style of communism; schools are closed, and the movement turns violent as teachers, intellectuals and others are persecuted

1970

1972 US president Nixon visits China

1976 Chairman Mao (Mao Zedong) dies

1979 'One child per family' policy introduced in China

1980

1980 Deng Xiaoping becomes leader and begins economic reforms
1984 Major reforms introduced to modernize Chinese industry

1989 Pro-democracy movement crushed in Beijing

1990

1992 China begins to introduce a 'socialist market economy'

1997 British return Hong Kong to China

1999 Portuguese return Macao to China

2000

2007 China becomes the world's third richest nation, after the USA and Japan
2008 Beijing hosts the summer Olympic Games

2010

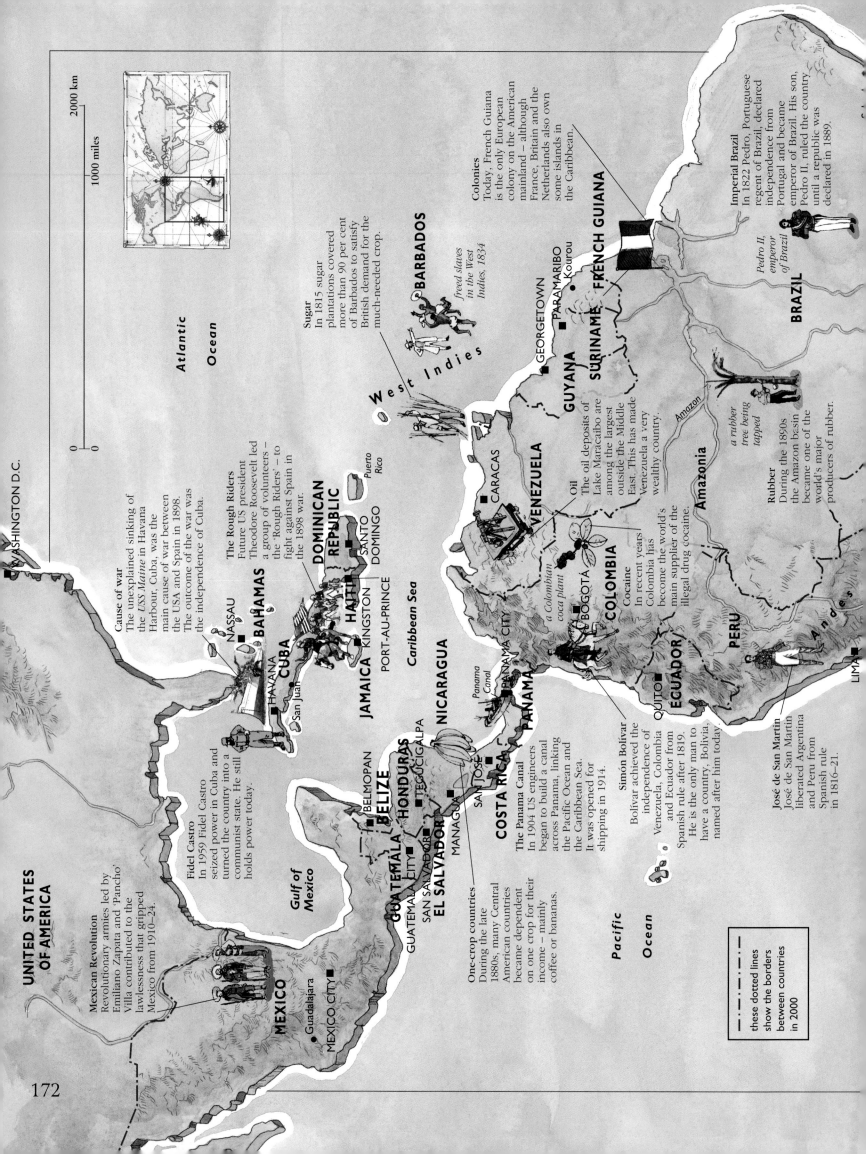

UNITED STATES OF AMERICA

WASHINGTON D.C.

Mexican Revolution
Revolutionary armies led by Emiliano Zapata and 'Pancho' Villa contributed to the lawlessness that gripped Mexico from 1910–24.

MEXICO

Guadalajara

MEXICO CITY

Gulf of Mexico

Cause of war
The unexplained sinking of the *USS Maine* in Havana Harbour, Cuba, was the main cause of war between the USA and Spain in 1898. The outcome of the war was the independence of Cuba.

The Rough Riders
Future US president Theodore Roosevelt led a group of volunteers – the 'Rough Riders' – to fight against Spain in the 1898 war.

Fidel Castro
In 1959 Fidel Castro seized power in Cuba and turned the country into a communist state. He still holds power today.

NASSAU
BAHAMAS

HAVANA
CUBA
San Juan

DOMINICAN REPUBLIC
SANTO DOMINGO
HAITI
KINGSTON
PORT-AU-PRINCE
JAMAICA

Puerto Rico

Caribbean Sea

Atlantic Ocean

Sugar
In 1815 sugar plantations covered more than 90 per cent of Barbados to satisfy British demand for the much-needed crop.

BARBADOS

freed slaves in the West Indies, 1834

West Indies

Colonies
Today, French Guiana is the only European colony on the American mainland – although France, Britain and the Netherlands also own some islands in the Caribbean.

FRENCH GUIANA
Kourou

GEORGETOWN
PARAMARIBO
GUYANA **SURINAME**

Imperial Brazil
In 1822 Pedro, Portuguese regent of Brazil, declared independence from Portugal and became emperor of Brazil. His son, Pedro II, ruled the country until a republic was declared in 1889.

Pedro II, emperor of Brazil

BRAZIL

a rubber tree being tapped

Rubber
During the 1850s the Amazon basin became one of the world's major producers of rubber.

Amazon

Amazonia

CARACAS
VENEZUELA

Oil
The oil deposits of Lake Maracaibo are among the largest outside the Middle East. This has made Venezuela a very wealthy country.

a Colombian coca plant

BOGOTÁ
COLOMBIA

Cocaine
In recent years Colombia has become the world's main supplier of the illegal drug cocaine.

BELMOPAN
BELIZE
GUATEMALA CITY
GUATEMALA
HONDURAS
TEGUCIGALPA
SAN SALVADOR
EL SALVADOR
MANAGUA
NICARAGUA
SAN JOSÉ
COSTA RICA
Panama Canal
PANAMA CITY
PANAMA

The Panama Canal
In 1904 US engineers began to build a canal across Panama, linking the Pacific Ocean and the Caribbean Sea. It was opened for shipping in 1914.

One-crop countries
During the late 1880s, many Central American countries became dependent on one crop for their income – mainly coffee or bananas.

QUITO
ECUADOR

PERU

LIMA

Andes

Simón Bolívar
Bolívar achieved the independence of Venezuela, Colombia and Ecuador from Spanish rule after 1819. He is the only man to have a country, Bolivia, named after him today.

José de San Martín
José de San Martín liberated Argentina and Peru from Spanish rule in 1816–21.

Pacific Ocean

- · - · - · -
these dotted lines show the borders between countries in 2000

Latin America

Charismatic liberators such as Simón Bolívar helped Latin America to win independence from Spain in the early 1800s. The empire of Brazil also gained its independence from Portugal before becoming a republic. All these new nations were politically unstable and were often governed by dictators. During the 20th century, social divisions between rich and poor led to long periods of military rule and revolutionary upheaval. The USA supported the continent's independence from European rule, but often treated Central American nations as its backyard, controlling their economies and intervening when their elected governments threatened US interests.

The end of slavery

The trade in African slaves across the Atlantic, to work in the plantations of Central and South America, was ended by Britain in 1807 and France in 1815 – but a variety of traders continued to supply slaves to Brazil and Cuba until the 1860s. The institution of slavery itself was abolished in all British colonies in 1834, but survived in Brazil until 1888. A lack of alternative work, however, meant that many former slaves were forced to continue working on the plantations as paid labourers.

Che Guevara
The revolutionary leader Che Guevara was killed in Bolivia in 1967 while trying to encourage the tin miners to revolt.

Bernardo O'Higgins
The liberator of Chile was the son of an Irishman who spent his childhood in Europe. He returned to Chile to lead the independence struggle after 1813.

Allende
In 1973 a US-backed military coup overthrew President Salvador Allende of Chile, the world's first democratically elected Marxist head of state.

Brasília
The capital of Brazil was moved from the overcrowded Rio de Janeiro to the new, inland city of Brasília in 1960.

Oil war
The lure of oil in the Gran Chaco region caused war between Bolivia and Paraguay in 1932–35, although no oil was ever found there.

Evita
Juan Péron and his wife Eva (Evita) became hugely popular leaders in Argentina after 1946.

Immigration
From the mid-1850s, more than 4.5 million immigrants from southern Europe arrived in Argentina. This was followed by 115,000 Jews fleeing oppression in Russia after 1881.

Gauchos
Cowboys known as gauchos tended the huge cattle ranches in the pampas regions of northern Argentina and Uruguay.

The Falklands
In March 1982 Argentine forces invaded the British-owned Falkland Islands. Three months later they were defeated by British forces.

BRASÍLIA

Rio de Janeiro

Brasília

São Paulo

BOLIVIA

LA PAZ

Ayacucho

CHILE

Andes

SANTIAGO

PARAGUAY

Gran Chaco

ASUNCIÓN

URUGUAY

MONTEVIDEO

BUENOS AIRES

ARGENTINA

Falkland Islands

Pacific Ocean

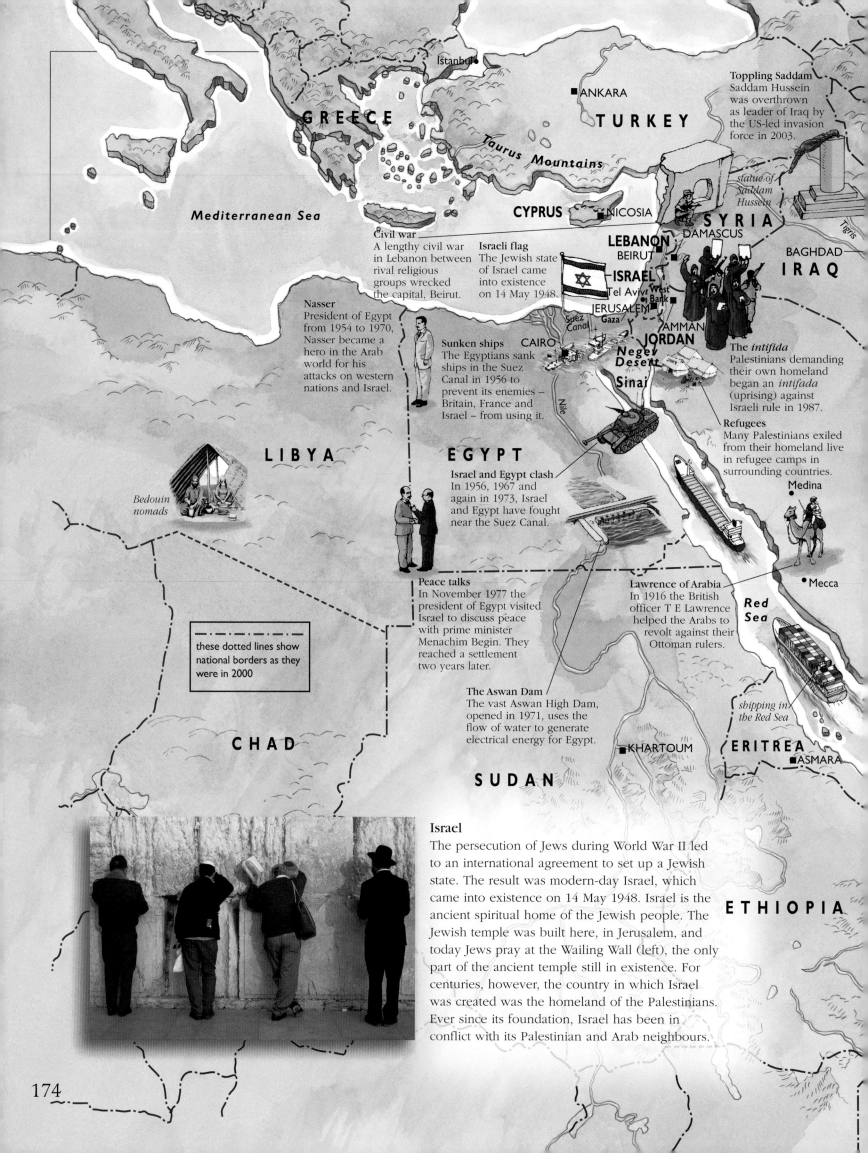

ANKARA

GREECE

TURKEY

Istanbul

Taurus Mountains

Toppling Saddam
Saddam Hussein was overthrown as leader of Iraq by the US-led invasion force in 2003.

statue of Saddam Hussein

Mediterranean Sea

CYPRUS ■NICOSIA

SYRIA

DAMASCUS

Civil war
A lengthy civil war in Lebanon between rival religious groups wrecked the capital, Beirut.

Israeli flag
The Jewish state of Israel came into existence on 14 May 1948.

LEBANON
BEIRUT

ISRAEL
Tel Aviv West Bank
JERUSALEM
Gaza

BAGHDAD

IRAQ

AMMAN

JORDAN

Nasser
President of Egypt from 1954 to 1970, Nasser became a hero in the Arab world for his attacks on western nations and Israel.

Sunken ships
The Egyptians sank ships in the Suez Canal in 1956 to prevent its enemies – Britain, France and Israel – from using it.

CAIRO

Suez Canal

Negev Desert

Sinai

The *intifida*
Palestinians demanding their own homeland began an *intifada* (uprising) against Israeli rule in 1987.

Refugees
Many Palestinians exiled from their homeland live in refugee camps in surrounding countries.

LIBYA

EGYPT

Bedouin nomads

Nile

Israel and Egypt clash
In 1956, 1967 and again in 1973, Israel and Egypt have fought near the Suez Canal.

Medina

Lawrence of Arabia
In 1916 the British officer T E Lawrence helped the Arabs to revolt against their Ottoman rulers.

● Mecca

Red Sea

---

these dotted lines show national borders as they were in 2000

Peace talks
In November 1977 the president of Egypt visited Israel to discuss peace with prime minister Menachim Begin. They reached a settlement two years later.

The Aswan Dam
The vast Aswan High Dam, opened in 1971, uses the flow of water to generate electrical energy for Egypt.

shipping in the Red Sea

CHAD

■KHARTOUM

ERITREA

■ASMARA

SUDAN

Israel

The persecution of Jews during World War II led to an international agreement to set up a Jewish state. The result was modern-day Israel, which came into existence on 14 May 1948. Israel is the ancient spiritual home of the Jewish people. The Jewish temple was built here, in Jerusalem, and today Jews pray at the Wailing Wall (left), the only part of the ancient temple still in existence. For centuries, however, the country in which Israel was created was the homeland of the Palestinians. Ever since its foundation, Israel has been in conflict with its Palestinian and Arab neighbours.

ETHIOPIA

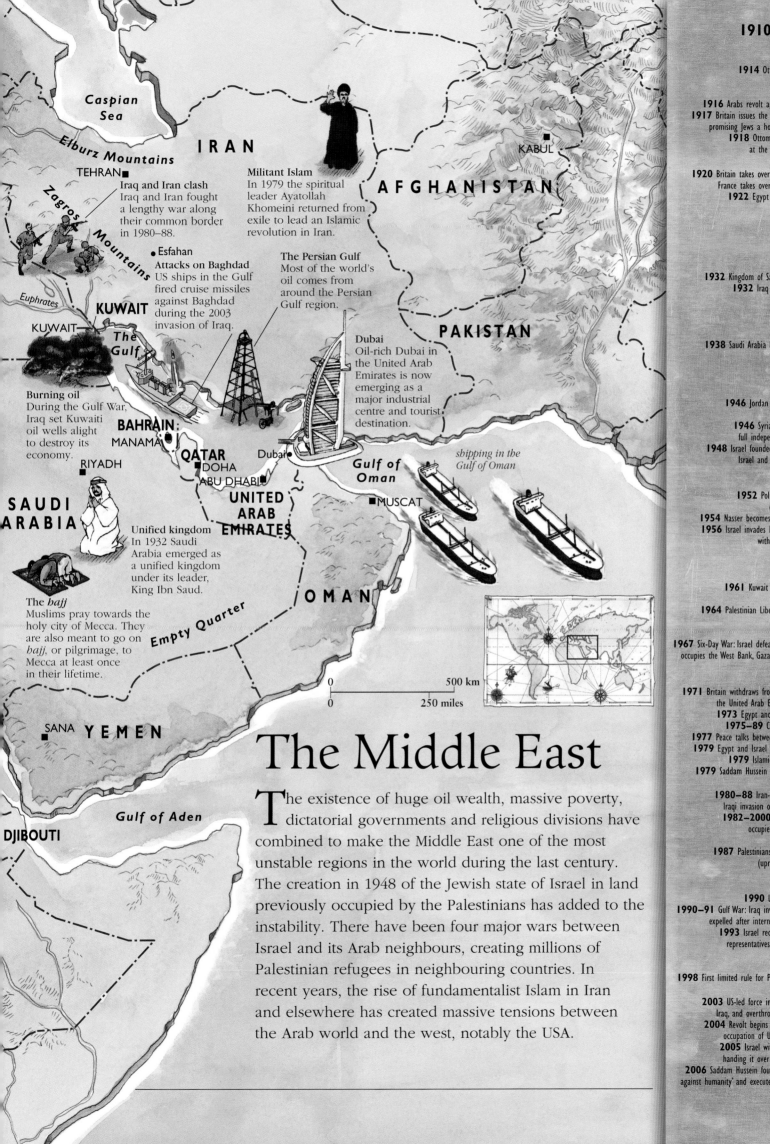

Caspian Sea

Elburz Mountains

IRAN

TEHRAN■

Zagros Mountains

Iraq and Iran clash
Iraq and Iran fought a lengthy war along their common border in 1980–88.

Euphrates

■ Esfahan

KUWAIT

KUWAIT

The Gulf

Militant Islam
In 1979 the spiritual leader Ayatollah Khomeini returned from exile to lead an Islamic revolution in Iran.

KABUL ■

AFGHANISTAN

Attacks on Baghdad
US ships in the Gulf fired cruise missiles against Baghdad during the 2003 invasion of Iraq.

The Persian Gulf
Most of the world's oil comes from around the Persian Gulf region.

PAKISTAN

Dubai
Oil-rich Dubai in the United Arab Emirates is now emerging as a major industrial centre and tourist destination.

Burning oil
During the Gulf War, Iraq set Kuwaiti oil wells alight to destroy its economy.

BAHRAIN
MANAMA ■

RIYADH ■

QATAR
DOHA ■
ABU DHABI ■

Dubai ●

Gulf of Oman

shipping in the Gulf of Oman

SAUDI ARABIA

UNITED ARAB EMIRATES

■ MUSCAT

Unified kingdom
In 1932 Saudi Arabia emerged as a unified kingdom under its leader, King Ibn Saud.

The *hajj*
Muslims pray towards the holy city of Mecca. They are also meant to go on *hajj*, or pilgrimage, to Mecca at least once in their lifetime.

OMAN

Empty Quarter

0 ———— 500 km
0 ———— 250 miles

SANA ■ **YEMEN**

Gulf of Aden

DJIBOUTI

The Middle East

The existence of huge oil wealth, massive poverty, dictatorial governments and religious divisions have combined to make the Middle East one of the most unstable regions in the world during the last century. The creation in 1948 of the Jewish state of Israel in land previously occupied by the Palestinians has added to the instability. There have been four major wars between Israel and its Arab neighbours, creating millions of Palestinian refugees in neighbouring countries. In recent years, the rise of fundamentalist Islam in Iran and elsewhere has created massive tensions between the Arab world and the west, notably the USA.

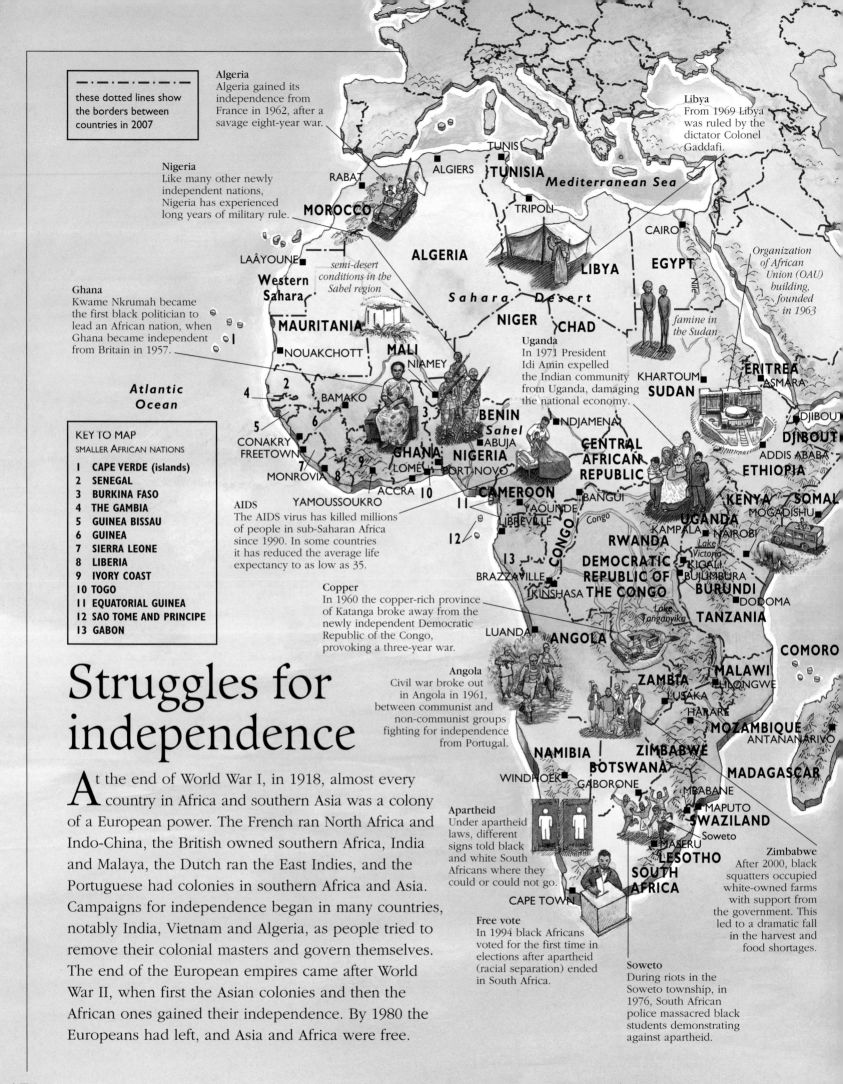

these dotted lines show the borders between countries in 2007

Algeria
Algeria gained its independence from France in 1962, after a savage eight-year war.

Libya
From 1969 Libya was ruled by the dictator Colonel Gaddafi.

Nigeria
Like many other newly independent nations, Nigeria has experienced long years of military rule.

Ghana
Kwame Nkrumah became the first black politician to lead an African nation, when Ghana became independent from Britain in 1957.

Organization of African Union (OAU) building, founded in 1963

Uganda
In 1971 President Idi Amin expelled the Indian community from Uganda, damaging the national economy.

famine in the Sudan

AIDS
The AIDS virus has killed millions of people in sub-Saharan Africa since 1990. In some countries it has reduced the average life expectancy to as low as 35.

Copper
In 1960 the copper-rich province of Katanga broke away from the newly independent Democratic Republic of the Congo, provoking a three-year war.

Angola
Civil war broke out in Angola in 1961, between communist and non-communist groups fighting for independence from Portugal.

Apartheid
Under apartheid laws, different signs told black and white South Africans where they could or could not go.

Free vote
In 1994 black Africans voted for the first time in elections after apartheid (racial separation) ended in South Africa.

Soweto
During riots in the Soweto township, in 1976, South African police massacred black students demonstrating against apartheid.

Zimbabwe
After 2000, black squatters occupied white-owned farms with support from the government. This led to a dramatic fall in the harvest and food shortages.

KEY TO MAP
SMALLER AFRICAN NATIONS

1 CAPE VERDE (islands)
2 SENEGAL
3 BURKINA FASO
4 THE GAMBIA
5 GUINEA BISSAU
6 GUINEA
7 SIERRA LEONE
8 LIBERIA
9 IVORY COAST
10 TOGO
11 EQUATORIAL GUINEA
12 SAO TOME AND PRINCIPE
13 GABON

Atlantic Ocean

Mediterranean Sea

Sahara Desert

semi-desert conditions in the Sahel region

Sahel

Struggles for independence

At the end of World War I, in 1918, almost every country in Africa and southern Asia was a colony of a European power. The French ran North Africa and Indo-China, the British owned southern Africa, India and Malaya, the Dutch ran the East Indies, and the Portuguese had colonies in southern Africa and Asia. Campaigns for independence began in many countries, notably India, Vietnam and Algeria, as people tried to remove their colonial masters and govern themselves. The end of the European empires came after World War II, when first the Asian colonies and then the African ones gained their independence. By 1980 the Europeans had left, and Asia and Africa were free.

Kashmir
Ever since their independence in 1947, Pakistan and India have frequently fought over the state of Kashmir.

Amritsar
The killing of 379 Indians by British troops in 1919 increased support for Indian independence from Britain.

Bangladesh
Bangladesh became independent from the rest of Pakistan in 1971. Its low-lying land is often flooded by the sea.

Cambodia
After 1975, a hard-line communist government murdered more than two million people in Cambodia, before it was expelled in 1979.

Vietnam
Communist soldiers fought first the French and then the Americans before Vietnam was finally united under their rule in 1975.

Partition
When India became independent in 1947, millions of Muslims fled for their lives into neighbouring Pakistan. The Hindus fled in the opposite direction.

Nehru
Pandit Nehru led India to independence and became its first prime minister. He led the country until his death in 1964.

Tamil Tigers
Since 1983 the minority Tamils have fought a vicious civil war for independence from the majority Sinhalese people of Sri Lanka.

Malaysia
Since independence in 1957, Malaysia has become one of the richest countries in the world, with many impressive, high-rise buildings.

Singapore
The island of Singapore became independent from Malaysia in 1965, and has now developed as a major shipping port for the entire region.

East Timor
In 2002 the former Portuguese colony of East Timor finally gained its independence after Indonesia occupied the country in 1975.

the Asian tsunami of 2004

the Petronas Towers in Kuala Lumpur, Malaysia

logging in Indonesia

ISLAMABAD
Kashmir
Quetta
Karachi
PAKISTAN
Delhi
NEPAL
KATHMANDU
THIMPHU
BHUTAN
NEW DELHI
INDIA
Himalayas
Ganges
Indus
Kolkata (Calcutta)
Mumbai (Bombay)
BANGLADESH
DHAKA
MYANMAR (BURMA)
LAOS
HANOI
VIENTIANE
VIETNAM
MANILA
Bay of Bengal
Madras (Chennai)
YANGON (RANGOON)
CAMBODIA
PHNOM PENH
PHILIPPINES
South China Sea
East China Sea
Arabian Sea
SRI LANKA
Kuala Lumpur
MALAYSIA
SINGAPORE
INDONESIA
JAKARTA
SEYCHELLES
Indian Ocean
MAURITIUS
AUSTRALIA

0 — 3000 km
0 — 1500 miles

Indian independence

The struggle for Indian independence from British rule was led by the Congress Party, among whose leaders was Mahatma Gandhi. In 1930 Gandhi led a symbolic march to the sea, where he picked up salt. This broke the British government's control over the production of salt and made British rule look stupid in the process. These and other peaceful protests eventually forced the British to leave India, which was partitioned in 1947 between Muslim Pakistan and the mainly Hindu India.

1910–today

1910

1918 World War I ends
1918 Most of Africa, southern and southeast Asia are under European colonial rule

1920 Britain, France and South Africa take over former German colonies in Africa
1922 Egypt gains independence from Britain

1926 Morocco revolts against French rule

1930

1935 Britain grants home rule to Indian provinces
1935–36 Italy invades Abyssinia (Ethiopia)
1940–41 Japan occupies French Indo-China
1941 Britain occupies Italian east African colonies and frees Abyssinia
1941 Ho Chi Minh forms nationalist Viet Minh guerilla group in Vietnam
1941–42 Japan occupies southeast Asia
1946 Philippines independent of the USA
1946–54 French fight Viet Minh for control of Vietnam
1947 Britain grants independence to India and Pakistan
1948 Britain grants independence to Burma and Ceylon (Sri Lanka)
1949 Dutch grant Indonesia independence

1950

1951 Libya becomes independent
1954 France leaves Indo-China; Laos and Cambodia become independent
1955 Sudan gains independence from joint British-Egyptian rule
1956 France grants independence to Morocco and Tunisia
1957 Britain grants Malaya independence
1957 Ghana becomes the first independent black African nation
1960–62 Most of sub-Saharan Africa gains independence
1962 France grants Algeria independence
1963 Federation of Malaysia created
1964–75 USA supports South Vietnam against communist North Vietnam
1965 Singapore independent of Malaysia

1970

1971 Bangladesh breaks away from Pakistan

1975 Indonesia occupies the Portuguese colony of East Timor
1975 Vietnam is reunited under communist rule
1975 Portuguese colonies in Africa win independence, but civil war continues in Angola
1975–79 Khmer Rouge military regime kills millions in Cambodia
1980 Zimbabwe, Britain's last remaining colony in Africa, wins independence
1983 Tamil Tiger guerillas begin their fight for independence in Sri Lanka

1990

1990 Namibia gains independence from South Africa
1993 Eritrea gains independence from Ethiopia
1994 Apartheid (racial segregation) comes to an end in South Africa; Nelson Mandela elected as president of South Africa
1994 Genocide (mass extermination of native people) in Rwanda by extremist militia groups
2002 East Timor gains independence from Indonesia
2002 Civil war ends in Angola after a ceasefire is arranged
2004 Tsunami devastates coastal regions around the Indian Ocean

2010

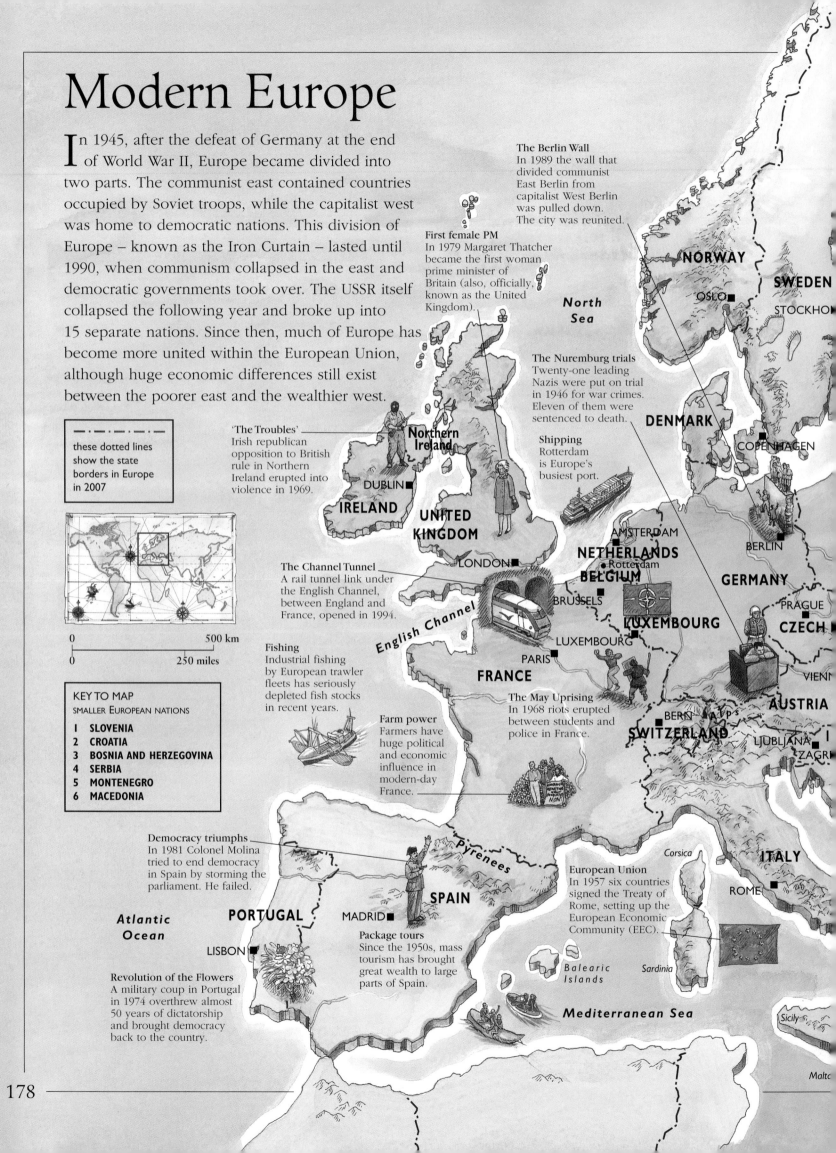

Modern Europe

In 1945, after the defeat of Germany at the end of World War II, Europe became divided into two parts. The communist east contained countries occupied by Soviet troops, while the capitalist west was home to democratic nations. This division of Europe – known as the Iron Curtain – lasted until 1990, when communism collapsed in the east and democratic governments took over. The USSR itself collapsed the following year and broke up into 15 separate nations. Since then, much of Europe has become more united within the European Union, although huge economic differences still exist between the poorer east and the wealthier west.

these dotted lines show the state borders in Europe in 2007

0   500 km
0   250 miles

KEY TO MAP
SMALLER EUROPEAN NATIONS

1 **SLOVENIA**
2 **CROATIA**
3 **BOSNIA AND HERZEGOVINA**
4 **SERBIA**
5 **MONTENEGRO**
6 **MACEDONIA**

The Berlin Wall
In 1989 the wall that divided communist East Berlin from capitalist West Berlin was pulled down. The city was reunited.

First female PM
In 1979 Margaret Thatcher became the first woman prime minister of Britain (also, officially, known as the United Kingdom).

The Nuremburg trials
Twenty-one leading Nazis were put on trial in 1946 for war crimes. Eleven of them were sentenced to death.

Shipping
Rotterdam is Europe's busiest port.

'The Troubles'
Irish republican opposition to British rule in Northern Ireland erupted into violence in 1969.

The Channel Tunnel
A rail tunnel link under the English Channel, between England and France, opened in 1994.

Fishing
Industrial fishing by European trawler fleets has seriously depleted fish stocks in recent years.

Farm power
Farmers have huge political and economic influence in modern-day France.

The May Uprising
In 1968 riots erupted between students and police in France.

Democracy triumphs
In 1981 Colonel Molina tried to end democracy in Spain by storming the parliament. He failed.

European Union
In 1957 six countries signed the Treaty of Rome, setting up the European Economic Community (EEC).

Package tours
Since the 1950s, mass tourism has brought great wealth to large parts of Spain.

Revolution of the Flowers
A military coup in Portugal in 1974 overthrew almost 50 years of dictatorship and brought democracy back to the country.

North Sea

NORWAY

SWEDEN

OSLO

STOCKHO

DENMARK

COPENHAGEN

Northern Ireland

DUBLIN

IRELAND

UNITED KINGDOM

LONDON

AMSTERDAM

NETHERLANDS

Rotterdam

BELGIUM

BRUSSELS

LUXEMBOURG

LUXEMBOURG

PARIS

FRANCE

BERLIN

GERMANY

PRAGUE

CZECH

VIENN

AUSTRIA

BERN

SWITZERLAND

LJUBLJANA

ZAGR

English Channel

ALPS

Pyrenees

Corsica

ITALY

ROME

PORTUGAL

SPAIN

MADRID

LISBON

Atlantic Ocean

Balearic Islands

Sardinia

Mediterranean Sea

Sicily

Malto

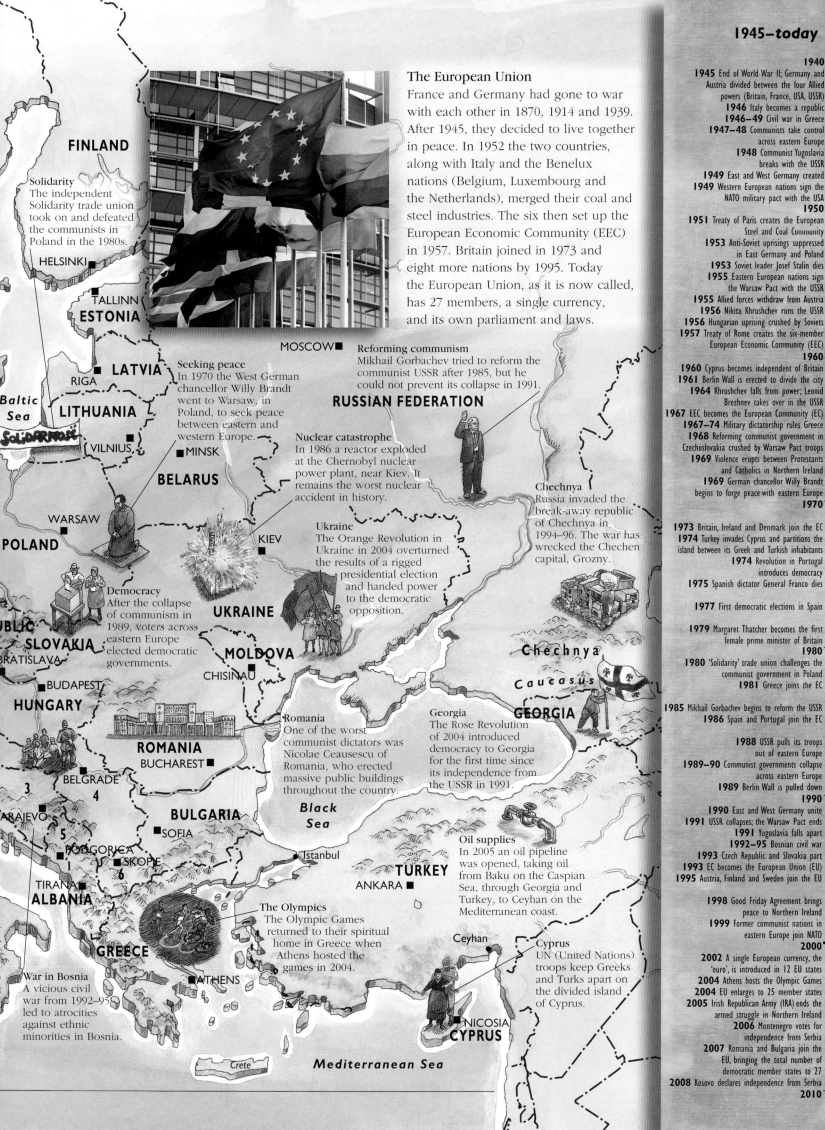

The European Union

France and Germany had gone to war with each other in 1870, 1914 and 1939. After 1945, they decided to live together in peace. In 1952 the two countries, along with Italy and the Benelux nations (Belgium, Luxembourg and the Netherlands), merged their coal and steel industries. The six then set up the European Economic Community (EEC) in 1957. Britain joined in 1973 and eight more nations by 1995. Today the European Union, as it is now called, has 27 members, a single currency, and its own parliament and laws.

FINLAND
HELSINKI
TALLINN
ESTONIA
LATVIA
RIGA
Baltic Sea
LITHUANIA
SOLIDARNOŚĆ
VILNIUS
MINSK
BELARUS
MOSCOW
RUSSIAN FEDERATION
WARSAW
POLAND
KIEV
UKRAINE
SLOVAKIA
BRATISLAVA
MOLDOVA
CHISINAU
BUDAPEST
HUNGARY
ROMANIA
BUCHAREST
BELGRADE
SARAJEVO
PODGORICA
SKOPJE
TIRANA
ALBANIA
BULGARIA
SOFIA
Black Sea
Istanbul
TURKEY
ANKARA
Chechnya
Caucasus
GEORGIA
GREECE
ATHENS
Ceyhan
NICOSIA
CYPRUS
Crete
Mediterranean Sea

Solidarity
The independent Solidarity trade union took on and defeated the communists in Poland in the 1980s.

Seeking peace
In 1970 the West German chancellor Willy Brandt went to Warsaw, in Poland, to seek peace between eastern and western Europe.

Reforming communism
Mikhail Gorbachev tried to reform the communist USSR after 1985, but he could not prevent its collapse in 1991.

Nuclear catastrophe
In 1986 a reactor exploded at the Chernobyl nuclear power plant, near Kiev. It remains the worst nuclear accident in history.

Chechnya
Russia invaded the break-away republic of Chechnya in 1994–96. The war has wrecked the Chechen capital, Grozny.

Ukraine
The Orange Revolution in Ukraine in 2004 overturned the results of a rigged presidential election and handed power to the democratic opposition.

Democracy
After the collapse of communism in 1989, voters across eastern Europe elected democratic governments.

Romania
One of the worst communist dictators was Nicolae Ceausescu of Romania, who erected massive public buildings throughout the country.

Georgia
The Rose Revolution of 2004 introduced democracy to Georgia for the first time since its independence from the USSR in 1991.

Oil supplies
In 2005 an oil pipeline was opened, taking oil from Baku on the Caspian Sea, through Georgia and Turkey, to Ceyhan on the Mediterranean coast.

The Olympics
The Olympic Games returned to their spiritual home in Greece when Athens hosted the games in 2004.

Cyprus
UN (United Nations) troops keep Greeks and Turks apart on the divided island of Cyprus.

War in Bosnia
A vicious civil war from 1992–95 led to atrocities against ethnic minorities in Bosnia.

1945–*today*

1940
1945 End of World War II; Germany and Austria divided between the four Allied powers (Britain, France, USA, USSR)
1946 Italy becomes a republic
1946–49 Civil war in Greece
1947–48 Communists take control across eastern Europe
1948 Communist Yugoslavia breaks with the USSR
1949 East and West Germany created
1949 Western European nations sign the NATO military pact with the USA
1950
1951 Treaty of Paris creates the European Steel and Coal Community
1953 Anti-Soviet uprisings suppressed in East Germany and Poland
1953 Soviet leader Josef Stalin dies
1955 Eastern European nations sign the Warsaw Pact with the USSR
1955 Allied forces withdraw from Austria
1956 Nikita Khrushchev runs the USSR
1956 Hungarian uprising crushed by Soviets
1957 Treaty of Rome creates the six-member European Economic Community (EEC)
1960
1960 Cyprus becomes independent of Britain
1961 Berlin Wall is erected to divide the city
1964 Khrushchev falls from power; Leonid Brezhnev takes over in the USSR
1967 EEC becomes the European Community (EC)
1967–74 Military dictatorship rules Greece
1968 Reforming communist government in Czechoslovakia crushed by Warsaw Pact troops
1969 Violence erupts between Protestants and Catholics in Northern Ireland
1969 German chancellor Willy Brandt begins to forge peace with eastern Europe
1970
1973 Britain, Ireland and Denmark join the EC
1974 Turkey invades Cyprus and partitions the island between its Greek and Turkish inhabitants
1974 Revolution in Portugal introduces democracy
1975 Spanish dictator General Franco dies
1977 First democratic elections in Spain
1979 Margaret Thatcher becomes the first female prime minister of Britain
1980
1980 'Solidarity' trade union challenges the communist government in Poland
1981 Greece joins the EC
1985 Mikhail Gorbachev begins to reform the USSR
1986 Spain and Portugal join the EC
1988 USSR pulls its troops out of eastern Europe
1989–90 Communist governments collapse across eastern Europe
1989 Berlin Wall is pulled down
1990
1990 East and West Germany unite
1991 USSR collapses; the Warsaw Pact ends
1991 Yugoslavia falls apart
1992–95 Bosnian civil war
1993 Czech Republic and Slovakia part
1993 EC becomes the European Union (EU)
1995 Austria, Finland and Sweden join the EU
1998 Good Friday Agreement brings peace to Northern Ireland
1999 Former communist nations in eastern Europe join NATO
2000
2002 A single European currency, the 'euro', is introduced in 12 EU states
2004 Athens hosts the Olympic Games
2004 EU enlarges to 25 member states
2005 Irish Republican Army (IRA) ends the armed struggle in Northern Ireland
2006 Montenegro votes for independence from Serbia
2007 Romania and Bulgaria join the EU, bringing the total number of democratic member states to 27
2008 Kosovo declares independence from Serbia
2010

The world today:
Looking to the future

The world at the start of the new millennium is a remarkably challenging place. Rapid population growth – there are at least 6.4 billion people squashed onto the planet today – and industrial development are straining the world's resources and leading to environmental disasters. Millions of people have left their homes in search of wealth and happiness, creating social and economic problems in both the countries they have left and those where they have settled. Tensions exist between rich and poor, and between people of different religious faiths. But there are also many ways in which human beings are meeting these challenges, and trying to solve the many problems of the modern world.

Multiculturalism
In the past 50 years, large numbers of people left poverty and often oppression in poorer parts of the world and moved to the rich nations of Europe, North America and Australia in search of work and a better life. These migrants took with them their own religions and cultures, turning their host cities into vibrant multi-cultural, multi-ethnic places. While they have benefited economically, many migrants have faced racial hatred and social isolation in their new countries. This picture (above) shows children participating in the Free Time arts festival, held every summer in London, UK. The festival is led by artists from a wide variety of cultures.

A large percentage of the world's population now lives in heavily built-up urban environments. This is the sprawling city of Los Angeles in California, USA.

AIDS awareness

During the 1980s a new disease – AIDS, or Acquired Immune Deficiency Syndrome – spread around the world. There is no known cure for the disease, although an expensive combination of drugs can slow its progress. More than 40 million people now have AIDS, the vast majority of them living in Africa and Asia. Its effect on poorer nations is immense, reducing the overall life expectancy of the population and creating many thousands of orphaned or ill children, such as this baby in Soweto, South Africa (left).

Charity groups working in Africa and Asia have set up projects to help children whose parents have died from AIDS.

Every year, World AIDS Day aims to raise awareness of the disease and raise money for sufferers. Here, Chinese students are taking part in the fund-raising activities.

Sustainable development

The huge increase in the world's population over the past 50 years, and the rapid economic growth of previously poor nations such as India and China (above), have together put a strain on the world's natural resources, such as oil, gas and water. Environmentalists, aid workers and economists are now looking at ways in which economic development can sustain rather than exploit these resources for the benefit of future generations.

Alternative energy sources

It has become clear that humans are having a harmful impact on the world's climate. Pollution from cars, aeroplanes and industry has contributed to a steady rise in temperatures. This may result in the melting of ice caps and glaciers, causing sea levels to rise and flood many low-lying parts of the world. 'Renewable' forms of energy, such as wind power (below), are increasingly being used, because they do not produce any of the 'greenhouse gases' that contribute to global warming.

Vast rows of wind turbines are now a common sight in isolated or mountainous locations such as the Tehachapi Pass in California, USA. Wind farms have been generating electricity in this region since the early 1980s.

Index

This index lists the main peoples, places and topics that you will find in the text in this book. It is not a full index of all the place names and physical features to be found on the maps.

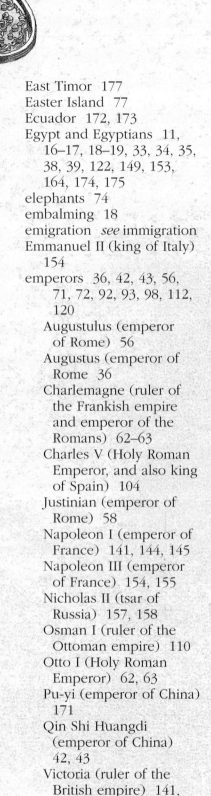

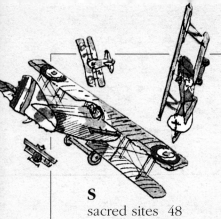

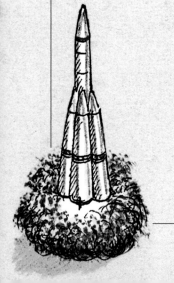

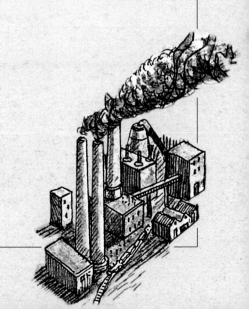

Acknowledgements

The publisher would like to thank the following for permission to reproduce their material. Every care has been taken to trace copyright holders. However, if there have been unintentional omissions or failure to trace copyright holders, we apologize and will, if informed, endeavour to make corrections in any future edition.

Key: *b* = bottom, *c* = centre, *l* = left, *r* = right, *t* = top

Cover NASA (background); *cover* plus pages 1 and 3 (globe and scroll artwork) Mark Bergin.

THE ANCIENT WORLD:
Pages 6 (globe artwork) Katherine Baxter; 10*tr* Alamy/Walter Bibikow/Jon Arnold Images; 10*b* Walter Bibikow/Photolibrary.com; 11*tl* Alamy; 11*tc* The Art Archive/Musée du Louvre, Paris/Dagli Orti; 11*tr* The Art Archive/Archaeological Museum, Tikal, Guatemala/Dagli Orti; 11*bc* Corbis/Alfred Ko; 11*br* Corbis/SABA/Ricki Rosen; 13 Corbis/SABA/David Butow; 15 The Art Archive/British Museum; 17 The Art Archive/Dagli Orti; 18*tr* Corbis/Sandro Vannini; 18*b* The Art Archive/Musée du Louvre Paris/Dagli Orti; 19*t* The Art Archive/Musée du Louvre, Paris/Dagli Orti; 19*b* Corbis; 21 Corbis/Adam Woolfitt; 23 The Art Archive/National Museum, Karachi/Dagli Orti; 25 The Art Archive/Dagli Orti; 27 The Art Archive/Private Collection, Beirut/Dagli Orti; 29 Corbis; 31 Bridgeman British Museum; 32*tr* The Art Archive; 32*b* Corbis/Archivo Iconografico, S.A.; 33*c* Getty/Giulio Andreini; 33*b* The Art Archive/Archaeological Museum, Naples; 35 Corbis/Andrew Brown, Ecoscene; 36*tr* The Art Archive /Archaeological Museum, Naples; 36*l* The Art Archive/Museo della Civilta Romana, Rome; 36–37*b* The Art Archive/Joseph Martin; 37*cl* Corbis/Reuters; 38 Werner Forman Archive; 41 *Sanchi* Alamy/Profimedia; 41 *Ramayana* The Art Archive/British Library; 42 The Art Archive/Musée Guimet, Paris; 45 Corbis/Kevin Fleming; 47 *Chichén Itzá* Corbis/Michele Westmorland; 47 *Nazca pot* The Art Archive/Amano Museum, Lima; 49 Corbis/Michael S. Yamashita.

THE MEDIEVAL WORLD:
50 (globe artwork) Katherine Baxter; 54*t* The Art Archive/Biblioteca Comunale Trento/Dagli Orti; 54*b* Corbis/Jonathan Blair; 55*tl* Alamy/Jeff Morgan; 55*tr* The Art Archive/British Museum, London/Eileen Tweedy; 55*c* The Art Archive/Viking Ship Museum, Oslo/Dagli Orti; 55*b* Corbis/Patrick Ward; 57*t* Corbis/Vanni Archive; 58*c* The Art Archive/Haghia Sophia, Istanbul/Dagli Orti; 60*tl* Corbis/Archivo Iconografico, S.A.; 60*tr* Alamy/National Trust Picture Library/Oliver Benn; 60*br* The Art Archive/Bibliothèque Municipale, Dijon/Dagli Orti; 61*tr* Bridgeman Art Library, London; 62*cr* The Art Archive/Dagli Orti; 62*bl* The Art Archive /Bibliothèque Municipale, Castres/Dagli Orti; 65*bl* The Art Archive/Dagli Orti; 66*tr* Bridgeman Art Library, London/Louvre, Paris, France; 66*cl* The Art Archive/National Museum, Damascus, Syria/Dagli Orti; 66*br* Corbis/Archivo Iconografico, S.A.; 67*tl* Corbis/Patrick Ward; 67*b* (Dome of the Rock) Mark Bergin; 68*bl* Alamy/Neil Grant; 70*cl* The Art Archive/British Library, London; 73*cl* Corbis; 75*t* Corbis/Christophe Loviny; 77*t* Photolibrary; 78*b* The Art Archive/Historiska Muséet, Stockholm/Dagli Orti; 80*c* Bridgeman Art Library, London/Bibliothèque Nationale, Paris, France; 80*bl* The Art Archive/Museo del Prado, Madrid/Dagli Orti; 82*tr* Bridgeman Art Library, London/British Library, London; 82*bl* Corbis/Owen Franken; 83*tl* The Art Archive/British Library, London; 83*b* (Chepstow castle) Mark Bergin; 85*b* The Art Archive/Bibliothèque Nationale, Paris; 86 Los Angeles County Museum, California, USA; 89*bl* The Art Archive/Museo Nacional de Antropologia, Mexico City, Mexico/Dagli Orti; 90*tl* BAL/Museo Nacional de Antropologia, Mexico City, Mexico; 90*c* The Art Archive/Museo Nacional de Antropologia, Mexico City, Mexico/Dagli Orti; 90*bl* The Art Archive; 91*tl* Alamy/North Wind Picture Archives; 91*b* (Templo Mayor); 93*bl* The Art Archive; 93*c* The Art Archive/Archaeological Museum, Lima, Peru/Dagli Orti.

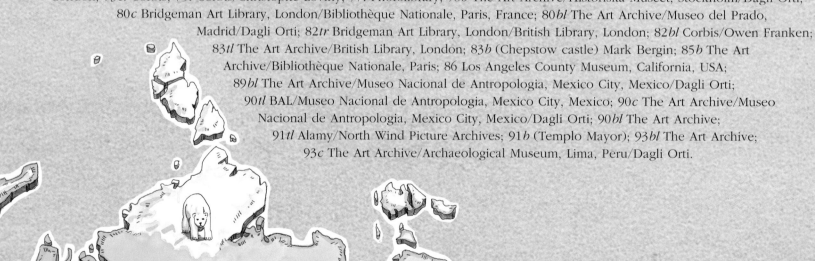

KINGFISHER

First published in 2008 by Kingfisher
an imprint of Macmillan Children's Books
a division of Macmillan Publishers Limited
The Macmillan Building, 4 Crinan Street, London N1 9XW
Basingstoke and Oxford
Associated companies throughout the world
www.panmacmillan.com

Consultants: Professor Jeremy Black, University of Exeter;
Professor Norman Housley, University of Leicester;
Dr Miles Russell, Bournemouth University

Cartography by: Colin and Ian McCarthy
Maidenhead Cartographic Services Limited, Maidenhead, Berkshire

ISBN 978-0-7534-1570-2

1 3 5 7 9 8 6 4 2
1TR/0408/SF/SCHOY/128MA/C

A CIP record for this book is available from the British Library.

Printed in Singapore

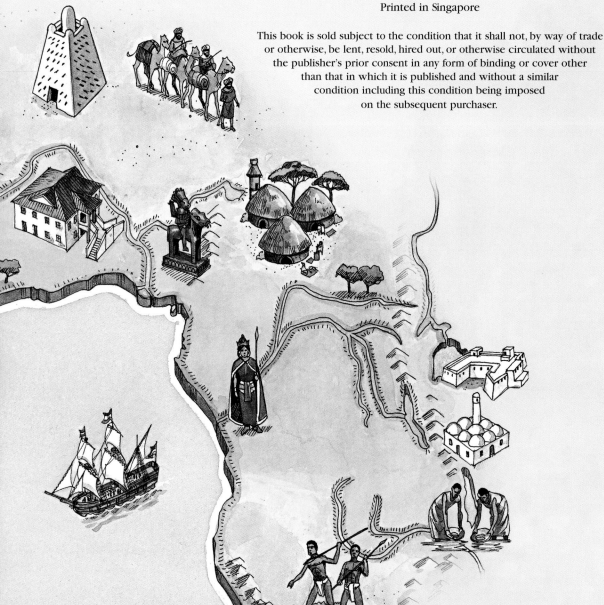